SOCIAL PROBLEMS
AND
SOCIAL POLICY:
The American Experience

This is a volume in the Arno Press Series

SOCIAL PROBLEMS
AND
SOCIAL POLICY:
The American Experience

*See last pages of this volume
for a complete list of titles.*

THE

LIFE

OF

THOMAS EDDY

BY SAMUEL L. KNAPP

ARNO PRESS

A New York Times Company

New York — 1976

Editorial Supervision: SHEILA MEHLMAN

———◆———

Reprint Edition 1976 by Arno Press Inc.

Reprinted from a copy in the University of Illinois Library

SOCIAL PROBLEMS AND SOCIAL POLICY: The American Experience
ISBN for complete set: 0-405-07474-3
See last pages of this volume for titles.

Manufactured in the United States of America

———◆———

Library of Congress Cataloging in Publication Data
Knapp, Samuel Lorenzo, 1783-1838.
    The life of Thomas Eddy.

    (Social problems and social policy--the American
experience)
    Reprint of the 1834 ed. published by Conner & Cooke,
New York.
    1. Eddy, Thomas, 1758-1827. I. Title. II. Series.
HV8978.E3K6 1976   361'.92'4 [B]   75-17229
ISBN 0-405-07499-9

THE

LIFE

OF

THOMAS EDDY;

COMPRISING AN

EXTENSIVE CORRESPONDENCE

WITH MANY OF THE MOST

DISTINGUISHED PHILOSOPHERS AND PHILANTHROPISTS

OF

THIS AND OTHER COUNTRIES.

BY SAMUEL L. KNAPP.

" However statue or monumental trophies may gratify a present feeling of gratitude or honour, it must be admitted, that the noblest memorial to the memory of those who have done good to mankind, is the record of their lives and actions."

——————————" 'Tis still our greatest pride,
To blaze those virtues that the good would hide."

New York:

PUBLISHED BY CONNER & COOKE,

FRANKLIN BUILDINGS.

1834.

EDWARD LIVINGSTON,

LATE SECRETARY OF STATE FOR THE UNITED STATES,

Minister Plenipotentiary and Envoy Extraordinary at the Court of Louis Philippe I., King of the French.

DEAR SIR,

This volume is respectfully dedicated to you, as a philanthropist who has laboured for many years in the science of criminal jurisprudence, who has undertaken, and succeeded in the undertaking, to define crimes with accuracy, to mete out a just punishment for each offence according to its grade, and to make solitary imprisonment conducive to the reformation of individuals and to the safety of society. If your code of penal law, code of procedure, and of state prison discipline, are not wholly adopted by any one state or people at once, (for old habits are hard to be subdued,) its benevolent spirit will shortly pervade the civilized world and at the present time traces of it are to be discovered in the reforms which wisdom and charity are carrying on in this continent and in Europe. No man more highly valued your labours than Thomas Eddy, whose life I have sketched. He rejoiced in every thing which ameliorated the condition of man. I have, therefore, by the license of personal friendship, ventured to unite your names. He has finished his course, and gone to receive his reward; but may your days be long protracted for other useful exertions, and to witness the happy effects of what you have already done for mankind.

Most sincerely,

Your devoted friend,

SAMUEL L. KNAPP.

PREFACE.

In one of my frequent visits to Dr. Hosack, for the purpose of obtaining from him various kinds of information, to aid me in completing a work I was then engaged in editing—the proper acknowledgments for his learned and valuable assistance, I have made in another place—he suggested to me that he had some time since gathered materials for writing the life of a distinguished philanthropist, the late Thomas Eddy; but that numerous circumstances had prevented him from carrying his intentions into effect, and that he could not, at this time, sit down to the work. After some farther conversation, he placed the papers in my hand, and I found them very interesting, much more so than I could have anticipated, from the quiet life of a modest citizen. Among them I discovered a correspondence with some of the first men in Europe and the United States, upon the great objects of reform in prisons, hospitals, penal codes, schools, and almost every other topic, which the best minds of the civilized world are now dis-

1*

cussing. I readily agreed to put those papers in order, connected with a few remarks of my own, to the end that the public might have some idea of Mr. Eddy as a man, and of the great objects of his useful life. To show me the estimation in which Mr. Eddy was held by the wise and good, which had known him well, Dr. Hosack put into my hands the following letters, from men whose sincerity is above all doubt, and whose opinions have a commanding weight in society.

EDITOR.

INTRODUCTION.

INTRODUCTION.

New York, April 9th, 1833.
DEAR SIR,

I have thought it due to the memory of the late Thomas Eddy, whose life has been very much devoted to deeds of benevolence, and the improvement of the numerous public institutions with which he has been connected, to communicate to the public some account of his labours, and the services he has rendered to this city and state.

For this purpose, I have placed the materials which I had collected on this subject, into the hands of our friend, Colonel Knapp, who has kindly undertaken to embody them into a volume, that cannot fail to be gladly received by the community.

Knowing that you were one of the friends of Mr. Eddy, and of his associates, the late General Schuyler, Governors George and Dewitt Clinton, Governor Jay, and others with whom he co-operated in various public measures, I will be obliged by any reminiscenses you may possess, that will give an interest to the contemplated publication of Colonel Knapp.

I am, dear Sir, with great respect and esteem, yours,

DAVID HOSACK.

To the Hon. JAMES KENT.

New York, May 11, 1833.
DEAR SIR,

I was happy to learn, by your letter of the 9th ult., that you had made arrangements for an historical account of the life and services of your late excellent relative, Thomas Eddy, by confiding the materials in your possession, concerning him, to the industry, skill, judgment, and taste of Colonel Knapp. I am satisfied that a biographical sketch of the actions and character of so distinguished a philanthropist, will be interesting to the cause of humanity, and acceptable to the public. It was my good fortune to be numbered among the intimate friends of Mr.

B

Eddy, from the year 1795 down to the period of his death; and I am no stranger to the beneficial influence which he so long and so successfully exerted over the several public institutions with which he was connected. You are pleased to say, that you would " be obliged by any reminiscences I may possess, that will give an interest to the contemplated publication." This request you have recently repeated, and if I was in possession of any facts that were important, and which are not already matter of record, I would most cheerfully communicate them. The quiet and unostentatious private life of Thomas Eddy, afforded, however, very few materials of the kind you allude to, and it is solely from a desire to gratify your wishes, and to show my affection for his memory, that I have ventured (though not without hesitation and reluctance) to submit a few notices respecting my personal knowledge of his character.

When I first became acquainted with Mr. Eddy, about the year 1795, I was struck with the simplicity of his manners, and the reasonableness and benevolence of his views. I soon found that he possessed sound judgment, purity of principle, and an uncommon zeal for the promotion of all kinds of public improvement. His object and unshaken purpose seemed to be, to diffuse, by every possible and reasonable effort on his part, a liberal, enlightened, humane, active, and Christian public spirit. He possessed, far beyond the race of ordinary men, the philanthropy of Howard; and under the influence of so illustrious an example, he appeared to be willing to devote himself " to survey the mansions of sorrow and pain," and to mitigate human misery, in whatever form it might meet the eye or awaken sympathy.

It was among his earliest and most animating objects, to endeavour to work a reformation in our penal code, and disarm it of its enormous abuses and uncompromising severity. His efforts in the year 1794, 1795, and 1796, to arouse public attention to the subject; and to promote the establishment of a state or penitentiary prison, as a substitute for the profligate goals and sanguinary punishments, are matters of fact, which it is not my province to detail ; I would merely observe, that in 1797 I became one of the persons charged *ex officio* with the execution of the penal laws, and this was concurrently in point of time with the melioration of the criminal code to which I have alluded, and it naturally led me to perceive and feel in full force, the inestimable value of the change. My friendly connexion with Mr. Eddy kept gradually increasing, and his ardent and disinterested efforts for the credit and success of the penitentiary system, were constantly passing under my eye and observation. He continued an inspector of the state prison in this city, from its first erection in 1796, to the year 1803, and it is a fact well worthy of notice, that the last year in which he had an agency in the management of the prison, the profits of the labour of the convicts equalled the annual expense of the establishment. The prison for that year, and that year only, maintained itself. But though Eddy had retired from the post, he never ceased to be anxious to improve and recommend the system. So late as the year 1823, he addressed a letter to the may r of this city, suggesting some judicious reforms in the prison discipline; and which have since been essentially adopted. He never placed much reliance on the influence of fear and severity, and he was of opinion that the reformation of the convicts was to be regarded as an indispensable object of the system.

Mr. Eddy was in the habit of recommending to my notice those publications which appeared from time to time, to strike his mind with particular force; and those that he alluded to, or presented to me, uniformly related to charitable, benevolent, or religious objects. I recal the recollection of such acts with much pleasure, because they give us an insight into his real character, and afford incontestable evidence of the goodness of his heart, and of his constant and affectionate solicitude for the happiness of his friends. He appeared to possess a firm Christian faith, without a particle of bigotry or fanaticism, and it was softened or recommended by the spirit of charity. He was the determined enemy of every species of doctrine that was lax in morals, or led to licentiousness in practice; and the anecdote which I am about to relate, is strikingly characteristic of the firm purpose with which he met and resisted the false philosophy and profane speculations that were zealously propagated towards the conclusion of the last century. Having purchased Godwin's "Enquiry concerning Political Justice," which obtained a transient celebrity in the year 1795, his moral sense was so much offended by the abominable doctrines contained in the latter part of the second volume, (and which doctrines Mr. Godwin afterwards exemplified in his own case,) that he took at once a decisive step to clear himself of the folly, or the guilt, of encouraging and circulating the work. He rose one evening at his own fireside, from the perusal of the book, and silently, and with gravity, opened the embers in the fire place, and carefully laid down and buried the two volumes in the fire. His wife, who was sitting by, astonished at the act, and ignorant of the cause, started up and exclaimed, " Thomas, art thou crazy ?"

He was one of the governors of the New York Hospital in 1797, and I believe, had been one for some previous time; and I considered myself as principally indebted to him for my introduction in that year to the same trust. He acted as one of the guardians of the hospital down to the spring of 1827 ; and the value of his services must have been inestimable. The duties which in that place were cast upon him, were congenial with his disposition and character; and that great establishment is deservedly classed among the most comprehensive, practical, and beneficent of all the charitable institutions of this country. I know of none that affords more prompt and effectual relief to the miseries of the poorer and forsaken part of mankind. He was for several years vice president, and at the period of his resignation, president of the board. He came to me in the spring of 1827, (being a few months before his death,) and told me that his declining health would not permit him to continue in the trust, and he earnestly requested my consent to serve, if I should be chosen one of the governors. Moved by his application, I did consent, and faithful to my promise to him, I bore my portion of my burden of the trust, for the three succeeding years ; and while in that place, I could trace the influence and effects of that excellent man, in every branch of the institution. Mr. Eddy was deeply impressed with the account of " *the Retreat*," an asylum near the city of York, in England, erected for insane persons, and which was much indebted for its success to the early and steady efforts of Lindley Murray, a name familiar to the friends of letters and humanity. In 1815, he suggested the propriety of efforts to erect and establish a similar institution on this island; and one that should adopt the same course of moral treatment of the lunatic patients. He presented to me at the time, a description of the

Retreat, written by Samuel Tuke, and he always appeared to be anxious to enlist my humble voice and influence in favour of his plans of public benevolence. Provisions for such an establishment was made by law in 1816, and it was opened in 1820, under very favourable auspices.

In 1819, he read before the governors of the hospital, a *Memoir of John Murray, Jr.*, of this city, and brother to Lindley Murray. This he presented to me, with the grateful remark that it came from my "affectionate friend." He delincates a character of the most distinguished benevolence, and of remarkable purity. He and Eddy were scholars in the same grammar school at Philadelphia, in or about the year 1770, and their subsequent lives were devoted to charitable objects, with a steadiness of purpose, and an ardour of zeal, that were peculiar, and at the same time tempered with reason and discretion. It would appear to me to be very difficult in the annals of mere mortals, to find a higher and brighter example of active and unobtrusive charity, goodness, and piety, than the one afforded by the life of Murray, as sketched by the faithful pencil of his fellow labourer in the cause of humanity.

Mr. Eddy was an official agent in many other public institutions of a charitable kind, and he was engaged for a length of years in some that were more comprehensive in their operation, and related to the great commercial and political interests of the state. He took an early and active part in the cause of internal navigation and improvement. His good sense, striking probity, and public spirit, were known and highly appreciated by General Schuyler, Governor Jay, and other eminent statesmen of their time ; and he became a cherished advocate and assistant in all schemes of a liberal kind, and connected with the public welfare. He was early made a director in the Western Inland Lock Navigation Company, which was established in the year 1792, and he continued a Director and Treasurer of that Company, down to its final termination in 1820. He explored the western country with a view to the introduction of inland navigation in 1796, and his distinguished merits as one of the original authors and promotors of the western canal navigation have been clearly stated and illustrated in your interesting "Memoir of Dewitt Clinton," and I forbear to dwell on the subject. It is well known that he executed the laborious and very responsible duties of one

2

of the canal commissioners with his customary ardour and precision, between the year 1810 and 1817; and he is justly entitled, as you have already shown, to share in the glory attendant on the auspicious results of that magnificent project.

But Mr. Eddy's mind was equally and unremittingly engaged in useful schemes of much more humble pretensions. Whenever there was an institution within the reach of his power and influence, created for any benevolent object, we are almost sure to meet on its records and in its effects, his name and his blessing. I was not associated with him, and I had not therefore any direct personal acquaintance with his services, in many of the public charities in which he was concerned. It ought to be left to his thoroughly informed biographer, to speak of him as a corresponding member of the New York Manumission Society; as one of the founders and trustees of the Free School Society in New York; as one of the founders and directors of the American Bible Society; as one of the first trustees of the Savings Bank in New York; and as one of the first managers of the Society for the Reformation of Juvenile Delinquents. I have endeavoured to confine myself in my remarks to matters of which I had some personal knowledge, or was necessarily led to notice during the course of the transactions.

As the life of Governor Jay, as well as his own, was drawing to a close, Mr. Eddy appeared to be anxious to pay to that great man a parting visit, and he invited me to accompany him. This was in the summer of 1826, and it was one of the most delightful little excursions I ever had. We left New York on the morning of the 26th of July. The day was bright and beautiful, and having landed at Sing Sing, we placed ourselves under the guidance of Captain Lyndes, and visited the new state prison establishment, which was then quite unfinished. We found one hundred and thirty convicts engaged in quarrying and working marble for the building; and they were mostly out under a meridian sun, pouring its fierce blaze upon the white marble blocks around them, with an ardour almost sufficient to blind the eyes. Mr. Eddy seemed to be at home in all the details of the concern. His zeal for the improvement of penitentiary discipline had not diminished in intensity. He was thorough in his inspection, and inquisitive in his examination. We continued our journey that afternoon to the residence of Governor Jay, at Bedford, and we found that illustrious statesman and christian sage, sitting on the piazza under the lengthened shadows of the sun, with a long pipe by his side, in full view of the simple and solid rural improvements of the place; and in the attitude of one at peace with himself, and with all around him. I was painfully struck with the ravages of time upon him, and the change that had taken place in his visage and appearance, since I last had the satisfaction of seeing him some years before. At first, he did not appear to recollect me; and this was the only instance that I perceived of any direct decay of his mental faculties. He conversed that evening and the next morning cheerfully and correctly, and seemed to be much interested in Mr. Eddy's conversation, and to sympathise with him in his feelings and concerns. Those two venerable men (the one then being in his seventy-sixth year, and the other in his eighty-first year) had been intimate friends; with correspondent principles in all matters of personal duty, and of good will to men, from a period which commenced soon after the conclusion of the American war. We returned to town the next day, and Mr. Eddy, in the course of this tour, interested me exceedingly with anecdotes and occurrences connected with his early life, in this city, during the revolutionary war, and down to the period of our first acquaintance. I have only to add, that while upon this last visit, his cheerful, free, varied, and instructive conversation, gave me additional cause to love and admire him.

I am, dear sir, with great respect and esteem,

Your friend and obedient servant,

JAMES KENT.

To DOCTOR HOSACK.

New York, March 10*th*, 1833.

DEAR SIR,

The Life of the late Thomas Eddy is about to be published by Colonel Knapp of this city, into whose hands I have placed the materials I had collected for that purpose. Knowing that upon the subject of prisons, and other objects of benevolence, he was long in correspondence with you as a fellow labourer in the same cause; it occurs to me that you may have some of his communications which are calculated to give interest to the publication in view, and may from your personal knowledge of Mr. Eddy, and of his pursuits, contribute some materials to the volume, that will prove useful and gratifying to the community. If so, I shall feel much obliged by any information you may give me, or by the use of any papers you may possess, relative to this object.

I am, dear sir, respectfully yours,
DAVID HOSACK.

To ROBERT VAUX, ESQ.

Philadelphia, 3mo. 11, 1833.

DEAR DOCTOR,

It gave me much pleasure to learn by thy letter of yesterday, that a memoir of the life of the late Thomas Eddy was about to be published. His long, various, and highly valuable services, entitle him to biographical honour; and the story of his benevolent career will not fail to encourage others, to " *go and do likewise.*" Although much his junior, he kindly presented me with several of his printed essays; occasionally favoured me with a letter, and when we met, freely conversed on topics which were favourite with us both; but on the examination of his correspondence, and recalling to mind our interviews, I do not discover any material, which would be useful to the gentleman who is to prepare the work.

I regret that it is not in my power to do more toward the illustration of the character of our estimable friend, than to bear my humble testimony to his great worth, in all the relations in which it was my privilege to know him.

Accept the assurance of my
respect, and friendship,
ROBERT S. VAUX.

To DAVID HOSACK, M. D. &c. &c.

New York, April, 1833.

MY DEAR SIR,

I some time since determined to prepare a sketch of the life of the late Thomas Eddy, who, like another Howard, has devoted himself to the cause of humanity and benevolence. For this purpose I have collected many valuable materials; these I have placed in the hands of my friend, Colonel Knapp, who will give them to the public. Knowing that you have been many years associated with Mr. Eddy in the various institutions of our city which have been benefitted by your united services, I will feel much obliged by any reminiscences you may possess on this subject.

In the reformation of our penal code, in the establishment of the Lunatic Asylum, in the improvement of the New York Hospital, in the public schools of our city, in the establishment of the House of Refuge, in the Manumission Society, and other benevolent institutions, I know you have long been fellow labourers; you will, therefore, be enabled to furnish me with many interesting memorandums of Mr. Eddy, that cannot fail to prove acceptable to the community. Your early attention to this subject, will greatly oblige me.

Dear sir, your friend and humble servant,

DAVID HOSACK.

To the Hon. CADWALLADER D. COLDEN.

June 23, 1833.

MY DEAR SIR,

It gives me great pleasure to learn that the biography of Thomas Eddy is to be written by so able a hand as Mr. Knapp. I should be very happy to give him any information in my power, which might tend to rescue from oblivion the merits and many virtues of our deceased friend. All I can say might be comprised in these few words :—That I knew him, and was very much associated with him during the last thirty years of his life; and that there is no benevolent or charitable institution founded in that time, of which he was not the zealous promoter, if the project for its establishment did not originate with him. I would be more particular, but my memory does not serve me as to dates, and I have no documents to which I can refer. I will nevertheless attempt to give the general recollections of my associations with Mr. Eddy. If it should be important to ascertain the dates connected with the circumstances I shall mention; it may be done by resorting to the public records, or the records of institutions of which he was a member.

So far as I recollect, my first acquaintance with Mr. Eddy commenced, from our having had the same views as to what has been called the amelioration of our criminal code. I mean the criminal code of the state of New York; and you must understand me throughout as writing as if I were in New York; I was then quite a young man, and I am not certain that my mind did not receive the strong bias it had in favour of the abolition of the punishment of death, from Mr. Eddy; though I, at that time, differed from

C 2*

him as to the extent of this abolition: he desiring that life should not be taken in any case; and I believing that this highest punishment should be reserved for the highest crimes. Afterwards, in the year 1825, I think, when Mr. Allen, Mr. Tibbits, and Mr. Hopkins, were making some investigations relative to the state prison, they circulated a number of queries, and addressed copies of them to Mr. Eddy and myself. We each wrote answers. They came so late, that they are not printed with the report of the commissioners; but Mr. Eddy being unwilling that they should be·lost, obtained from me a copy of my answers to the commissioners, and published his and mine in a small pamphlet at his expense. This is evidence of Mr. Eddy's liberality, not only as to pecuniary consideration, but as to his toleration of principles which differed from his own; for while his letters to the commissioners, zealously maintained that imprisonment was sufficient punishment for any crime; I expressed the opinion that I at that time continued to entertain, that the most atrocious guilt, such as wilful and deliberate murder, should be punished with death. Before I pursue this subject farther, I will mention a circumstance which made a strong impression on my mind, and convinced me, that however adverse the Society of Friends were to the punishment of death, they had rather that it should be inflicted in some cases, than that the guilty should escape with impunity. A female belonging to the Society, or who was at least professedly a Friend, was found a corpse, under circumstances that left no doubt of her having been murdered. I was then assistant attorney general. The first information I had of this crime, was from Mr. Eddy, Robert Bowne, and several others of the same high standing in the Society of Friends, who called on me to institute a prosecution against the person suspected; and through the whole progress of the prosecution they were active and zealous in their efforts to furnish me with the means of developing the truth.

It is well known that the laws for establishing our state prison, owed their origin more to the part taken by the Society of Friends, than to any exertions in their favour by any other class in the community. And among these, Mr. Eddy, as he was in every thing in which he engaged, the most active and the most zealous, in this matter, as in others, in which the public good was concerned, be devoted himself to its success, with all the industry and earnestness, that he could have done if his own interest had been his object; and I am convinced that he would not have felt the same gratification from obtaining any private advantage, that he did, from the adoption of those laws by the legislature, which he had long and ardently advocated, and which he considered as setting an example which would meliorate the condition of mankind. The members of the first board of governors of the state prison were mostly taken from the society of Friends. Mr. Eddy held the principal office, under the title, I think, of superintendent.

The assistant attorney general was, ex-officio, connected with the administration of the prison, and this gave me an opportunity of observing its management and government. The good order, comfort, cleanliness, industry, and devotion which prevailed, as long as the Friends had the management of the institution, were very remarkable. But in 1800, when there was a great revolution in political power, those who had effected the change thought their influence should be felt every where; and though there was no emolument annexed to the office of governor of the prison, there were those of the dominant party, whose ambition was to be gratified by being put in the place of the Friends who were managers of the institution. The difference between the government of those who took the office merely from motives of philanthropy, and who devoted themselves to the discharge of its duties, and those who held it as an honorary distinction, that deserved but little sacrifice of their private business, was soon perceived. The new management was so bad, that it had very nearly occasioned the failure of this great experiment; and nothing was more common than to hear it said, even by many of its original advocates, that it had done so, and that there was no resource but to the former sanguinary penal code. I have often heard Mr. Eddy lament this state of things; but he never abandoned the hope of seeing a system, of which he very justly considered himself as one of the founders, established; and he lost no opportunity of inviting the public attention to means by which he thought the objections to the new code might be obviated. He proposed that county or district prisons or penitentiaries should be erected. That the prison of the state should be reserved for offenders of the highest grade, while those of a lower degree should be punished in the former. I am convinced that among his manuscripts will be found many pieces that he has written on this subject.

It is very possible that my connexion with the Manumission Society, brought me acquainted with him as a member of that institution, previously to my having had intercourse with him as an advocate of the amelioration of our penal code. It is known how much that society is, and always has been, in the hands of members of the society of Friends, and how far the act abolishing slavery, is owing to their exertions. In this, Mr. Eddy took a leading part. I well remember, however, that he was adverse to the colonization society; and he discouraged the first attempts which were made to establish a branch of the society in New York. He thought it was a scheme of the slave holders to perpetuate slavery, rather than intended as a means of emancipation. Their design, in his opinion, was to make the society instrumental in ridding them of their old or worthless slaves, and thereby enable them to perpetuate the bondage of the young and valuable; whereas, if the slave holding states were obliged to bear the burthen of those the society would take off their hands, he thought these states would the sooner be compelled to adopt measures that would give freedom to the blacks. Mr. Eddy's reasoning on this subject, induced me to adopt his sentiments. But if he had lived to have had a better view of the objects of the Society, and to witness their extraordinary success, I cannot doubt but that he would have yielded, as I have done, his prejudices against this valuable institution. I am the more induced to think that this would have been the case, from considering the very active part which Mr. Eddy afterwards took in a project which was set on foot, I think, in the year 1825, and to which, if it had succeeded, there would have been the same objections which there were in his mind to colonization societies. About the time I have mentioned, the President of Hayti sent a Mr. Grandville, a coloured gentleman, as an ambassador to New York. His object was to induce black people to emigrate to that island, at the expense of its government, with an offer of land and means of living when they arrived there. Mr. Eddy was indefatigable in his exertions to promote the views of Mr. Grandville. He formed a society for this purpose. Considerable funds were raised, and the Haytian emissary returned to his government with a cargo of emigrants.

They were accompanied by an agent of the society, who managed to quarrel with the government of the island. The emigrants were disappointed. They alleged that the promises made to them were not fulfilled, and the whole thing ended in a heavy expense to the members of the Society.

There was nothing in which Mr. Eddy took a deeper or more active interest, than in the establishment of our free schools. But I had no particular connexion with that institution. I can therefore only say, that I have often visited them with him, and been witness of the zeal he manifested for their prosperity. Governor Clinton was the great patron of this and other benevolent establishments, in which Mr Eddy was concerned; and I believe we owe the assistance they have derived from Mr. Clinton's great talents and influence, more to Mr. Eddy than to any other man. The history of the New York canals will show how large a share Mr. Eddy had in directing Governor Clinton's attention to these great projects.

I found Mr. Eddy a governor of the New York Hospital, (of which he died president) when I was elected to that office about the year 1812. I believe he had been in that station from a very early date. There, as elsewhere, he was one of the most efficient and useful members of the institution to which he belonged. In the year 1816, I think the legislature made a very liberal grant of an increased revenue to the hospital. This was obtained entirely by the exertions and address of Mr. Eddy, who spent the greater part of a winter at Albany, to obtain the grant. Perhaps the institution is more indebted to the good management of Mr. Eddy, than to the liberality of the legislature. For it has been said, and I believe, not without foundation, that the members of the legislature were not aware of the extent of their endowment. The duration of annuity which is granted, depends on the duration of a previous grant, which, it is said, it was supposed was more limited, than upon examination is found to be the case. But this ample provision induced the governors of the hospital to turn their attention to a separate establishment for the insane, for whom the accommodations afforded by the city buildings were very inconvenient. In making a new provision for this class of patients, Mr. Eddy engaged with his accustomed energy, and from his exertions, and the co-operation of those associated with him, grew the magnificent Lunatic Asylum at Bloomingdale, He was chairman of the committee of Governors of the Hospital under whose superintendence the buildings were erected, and who had the management of the concern till the patients were removed to it; and till long after a system was arranged for the government of the house and the treatment of the subjects. In all this, no one had so large a part as Mr. Eddy, and no one devoted so much time and attention to the establishment.

As any thing I may write, can only serve as memoranda, which will direct the attention of Mr. Eddy's biographer to the history or records of the institutions with which he was connected, I may mention that I was a long time associated with him as a member of the Humane Society. This was an association, which had its origin long before I knew any thing of it. The objects of this association, were to provide food for the destitute, and, particularly, to supply the debtors in prison with some of the necessaries of life. At that time these objects of charity made an irresistible appeal to the attention of the benevolent. For it is strange that the laws which shut a person up within the walls of a prison, because he did not, and in most cases could not, pay his debt, made no provision for supplying him either with fire, food, or raiment. As you well know, the first soup house that was ever opened in New York, was established by this society, and it should not be forgotten, that the fears of the members that their funds were not equal to this enterprise, were overcome by your liberal engagement to defray from out your own purse all that might be required, beyond the means the friends of the society could afford.

The views which were presented to many members of this society, of the condition of the poor in the city of New York, led to the formation, in the year 1816, of a society for the prevention of pauperism ; in the establishment of which, and in its action, Mr. Eddy took a more active part than any other man. This society was merged in the Society for the Reformation of Juvenile Delinquents, or House of Refuge, which was incorporated in the year 1824. This institution, after it had been in operation two years, Mr. Clinton described in his annual message to the legislature of 1826, as " perhaps the best penitentiary institution which has ever been devised by the wit, and established by the beneficence of man." I had a more intimate association with

Mr. Eddy in this charity from its origin to his death, than in any of the others of which we were members. Though there were many who participated with him in this humane enterprise, yet I do not think it is going too far to say that its foundation and success was in a great measure owing to him ; at least it may be questioned whether, without his indefatigable exertions, this important measure for the prevention of crimes, would have been adopted so soon. He devoted so much of his time to this establishment, and occupied himself so much with its concerns for several years, that he seemed to have no business of a public or private nature which he thought so important, or so deserving his attention, It may be worthy of remark, that though there had been penitentiaries or asylums for infant criminals in Europe, previously to the establishment of the House of Refuge, yet there had not been any institution for the reformation of juvenile delinquents. This differed from all others that before existed in this important feature. That the laws subjected to its discipline persons under age, previously to their having committed any crime, when they are without parents, or abandoned by them, and are left without guardian or protection, and are found pursuing vicious courses, they may be committed to the House of Refuge, where they are withdrawn from the power of their parents even, till such provisions is made for them as the law prescribes. The idea of giving this very enlarged power to magistrates and managers of the House of Refuge, I believe, originated with Mr. Eddy. If the society for the reformation of juvenile delinquents was deprived of this power, it would lose the greater part of its usefulness. Another of our most important and benevolent institutions, owes its origin to the members of the society for the prevention of pauperism; I refer to the Savings Bank. To this Mr. Eddy devoted himself with his usual zeal and energy, and remained one of its most efficient and active managers while he lived.

To this list of the numerous benevolent societies of which Mr. Eddy was a member, I must add another establishment, of which he was a founder, and continued a manager, until he thought its successful operation was secured. This was a society to provide fuel for the poor. Those who had not the means of laying up a store, were to deposit their money with the society ; who were to lay it out on wood or coal, at the proper season when these articles are cheapest; and to let the depositor draw to the amount of his deposit when it was most needed, for the cost at which it had been purchased by the society. But Mr. Eddy's other avocations obliged him, after some time, to withdraw from this institution; and for the want of that zeal with which he devoted himself to all affairs of this kind in which he engaged, or from some other cause, this very benevolent attempt to relieve the distress which so often results from cold and poverty, after one or two seasons, was neglected or relinquished. Notwithstanding Mr. Eddy was so successful and useful in the many humane institutions I have enumerated, his active and benevolent mind was engaged in other projects for the advantage or relief of the distressed; among these he had much at heart an asylum for convicts who had expiated their crime, by having suffered the punishment of imprisonment. He saw with all the sympathy of his character, the forlorn condition of those who, without money, without friends, and without character, were turned from the walls of a prison, to provide for themselves means of subsistence, and to whom there seems to be left the only alternative of committing a new crime, or of perishing. He proposed to establish for such objects a House of Refuge, where employment of some profit should be provided for them, until by their good conduct they could retrieve their character, and by their industry provide some means of support, till they could begin the world anew.

I have not referred to Mr. Eddy's connexion with our literary and scientific institutions, of all of which I believe we were members. Of his usefulness as an associate with us in these establishments, you will be much more able to speak of him than I am. And after all, my dear sir, I can not but perceive how little more I have done than if I had given a list of our benevolent and charitable institutions, and said that Mr. Eddy was a zealous and efficient member of each of them. But then I should have lost the opportunity of saying how sincerely I respected his character, and of manifesting the desire that I have, that the memory of his great benevolence, his devotion to the welfare of mankind, and his many virtues, should be preserved; and that he may be pointed out to posterity, as an example of how much good may be done by an individual who will devote his time and talents to its accomplishment. And had I not complied with your request, I should also have lost the pleasure which I have, my dear sir, in assuring you of the sincere respect with which

I am your friend and obedient

CADWALLADER D. COLDEN.

To DAVID HOSACK, LL. D., F. R. S. and E.

New York, April 20, 1833.

DEAR SIR,

Knowing the intimacy which once existed between you and the late Thomas Eddy, whose memoirs I have undertaken to prepare for the public, from papers in my possession, and from such other sources as may be afforded me, I take the liberty to request you to favour me with any passage of his life which may be fresh in your memory, accompanied with such remarks as you may think proper to make. I am aware of the value of your time, to yourself and to others; but I will not offer you any idle apology for taxing you, as I believe you will agree with me in opinion, that if it be a duty, as we are in the habit of thinking it to be, to attend the funereal rites of a departed friend, that it is a higher duty, and of more importance to the living, to assist in giving currency to his virtues.

Most respectfully, your friend and humble servant,

SAMUEL L. KNAPP.

To Professor JOHN W. FRANCIS, M. D.

New York, May 1, 1833.

DEAR SIR,

A personal acquaintance of more than twenty years with the late Mr. Thomas Eddy, might justify me in answering at some length your several interrogatories concerning his life and public services; but I have deemed it most judicious to restrict this communication to a few particulars, inasmuch as you are so amply furnished with authentic materials for your contemplated biography. Mr. Eddy was so intimately and for so long a period associated with the men and measure of most of our humane, benevolent, and literary institutions, that his career is in no small degree connected with the history of those establishments, and demonstrates that a cardinal object of his pursuit, was to meliorate the condition of human society.

D 3

Were I to select the especial objects which, amidst the great variety that demanded his services, more particularly absorbed his attention, and occupied his deepest consideration, I might dwell upon his close devotion to the interests of the African ; the promotion of the leading measures of the Manumission Society; and the enactment of laws for the final abolition of slavery in the state of New York. The education of the blacks, and the establishment of African free schools, were also among the objects of his solicitude. The bettering the condition of the poor, the organization of the Lancasterian free schools, and an improved code of prison discipline, were subjects which engrossed most of his time for many years ; and I think you will find many documents among his papers, which evince his successful efforts to further these benevolent purposes.

The claims of Mr. Eddy to a lasting consideration will, however, I think, rest mainly on the early begun and long continued zeal and abilities which he exhibited on the subject of insanity, and the unfortunate beings afflicted with that calamity. At a comparatively youthful period of his life, he was appointed to the duties of hospital direction ; and he seems at nearly the same period to have turned his attention to the treatment and hospital discipline of those afflicted with mental derangement. Our establishments for the better medical government of lunacy were then very few and imperfect. Pennsylvania had indeed done something—New York nothing. The public spirited governors of the New York Hospital, were induced from urgent representations made them, to erect a separate edifice on the hospital-grounds for the exclusive benefit of lunatics ; and this institution, which opened its doors in 1808, under the professional direction of the late Dr. Bruce, for a while seemed to answer the benevolent intentions of the board of governors. It was, however, ere long, apparent that this city asylum was of too limited a capacity for the accommodation of its numerous applicants ; nor was the receptacle itself of the character demanded for the afflicted and valuable beings of all ranks of society who became the inmates of it. Mr. Eddy had read much, and thought much on the subjects of mental derangement, on prison and penitentiary discipline, on the structure and economy of mad-houses, and on the domestic and sanative treatment of the insane. His correspondence with several distinguished characters abroad, favoured the accuracy and accumulation of his knowledge on these engrossing topics: his intimate and free verbal disquisitions on all these several matters with that excellent man and eminent philanthropist, the late John Murray, jun. strengthened his views: he compared the facts thus derived from these several sources, with his personal experience at the city asylum of the New York Hospital, where he was almost daily engaged: the result was a firmer conviction in him, that much improvement might be made in the government and remedial treatment of mental derangement.

The writings and reports of Howard, of Ferriar, of Haygarth, and of Lind, on prisons, fever hospitals, and houses of recovery, were the principal sources, whence, at that time, information was derived touching these momentous subjects; and few looked further for knowledge on the diseases of the mind than to the pages of Crighton, Haslam, Pinel, and Rush. It was therefore with no ordinary solicitude that the friends of humanity in America heard of the success which crowned the benevolent exertions of the Society of Friends, near York, in England, who had established a Retreat for the Insane, for the express purpose of instituting a milder system of management than had previously been employed. Some account of the Retreat was published by Mr. Tuke in 1813. Mr. Eddy entered into a correspondence with that gentleman, in order to obtain more ample and precise information than Mr. Tuke's work afforded. Shortly subsequent to this date, the important parliamentary investigations on the management of the mad-houses of Great Britain were instituted; and the elaborate reports which soon followed, embodied such a mass of facts, of indubitable authenticity and vital consideration, as left not a doubt in the minds of the most sceptical, that pernicious errors widely prevailed on the nature of insanity; that gross evils and enormous barbarities were inflicted on the unfortunate victims of madness, as salutary and requisite principles of medical treatment; that in several of these institutions, to the miseries inseparable to a loss of reason, were added the horrors and atrocities of brutalized ignorance, refined, if I may so say, by the absurdest therapeutical doctrines which the sophistry of man ever invented. Happily, at the same time, these investigations and inquiries, while they gave multiplied proofs of frightful abuses, demonstrated that in numerous cases mental alienation, like many physical infirmities, strictly so considered, was often remediable; that to pronounce a condemnation of the insane to total incapability of medical relief in all after life, was a decision at variance with the strongest evidence of a contrary character, deduced from the results of the practice, not only at the Retreat at York, but of the Asylums at Nottingham, Glasgow, and other places ; in short, that individuals who had lost health and reason, might be restored to both, by the judicious use of medicine, and a mild moral management.

Fortified with such testimony, Mr. Eddy's zeal was quickened; he united with several eminent citizens among us, of whom I may particularly notice the late Mr. John Murray, jun., the late General Clarkson, and the late Thomas Franklin, in an application to our legislature for efficient means to enable the governors of the New York Hospital, to erect a suitable establishment for the insane, on a scite appropriate to such an object. The result, was the ample grant by the state of New York, and the delightful grounds and improvements connected therewith. The whole is a proud trophy of Mr. Eddy's laudable perseverance ; while the act by which it was secured, will ever remain conspicuous among the many which characterized the administration of Governor De Witt Clinton.

Mr. Eddy, in common with many other benevolent individuals, was at first disposed to place a more entire reliance on the moral management of insanity, to the exclusion of all medical treatment, than, I think, the facts in the case warrant. This belief I know, he for some time cherished; but the enlarged experience and personal observation which for many years he afterwards enjoyed at the noble institution which his own efforts so powerfully contributed to organize, led him to qualify his views on the curative means in lunacy. Having, while in Europe, at the time when the management and treatment of the insane constituted a prominent subject of discussion, visited most of the lunatic institutions of Great Britain, France, and Holland, I became fully convinced that those asylums in which a prompt and judicious medical practice was adopted, afforded the largest favourable results of the tractable nature of many forms of diseased manifestations of mind: that such indeed was the case even at the

Retreat at York, where the number of recoveries was greater when well directed medical discipline was united to moral means of relief; at the asylum at Glasgow, and at La Sal Petrierie, Charanton, France, under the direction of M. Pinel, the first among the moderns for adopting the moral system ; while, on the other hand, in Holland, where through a mistaken belief that the maniac is unsusceptible of mental enjoyment, and that insanity is deemed an intractable disorder, no curative measures were employed, and of consequence, recovery was protracted and indeed rarely took place.*

The evidence deduced from truths of this nature, and the constantly accumulating proofs in behalf of medical treatment which modern experience supplied, doubtless had their influence in causing Mr. Eddy several years before his death, to adopt the opinion that the proper administration of medicinal agents, was favourable to the treatment of insanity ; nay, oftentimes indispensable.

There is another circumstance I can hardly allow to be passed over on this occasion without a remark, and which I think has been a concurring cause of the too hasty and too general adoption of moral management, as of itself alone the essential means of cure of maniacal subjects. The delirium of inebriety, and the more advanced forms of diseased action denominated *delirium tremens*, have inadvertently been confounded with *idiopathic mania;* and inasmuch as the right use of reason is for the most part, in those cases, soon restored by mere abstraction from noxious potation, which is effectually secured by confinement, moral management, without other aid, has been allowed an undue weight in the curative process of genuine mania. I am aware that permanent cerebral disorganization may arise from intem-

---

* Some of the abuses which I witnessed in Holland, in the treatment of the insane, were scarcely inferior in their enormity, to those of the metropolitan Bethlehem Hospital, as brought to light by parliamentary investigation. I hardly know whether the memorable case of William Norris surpassed in cruelty an example which presented itself to me of an aged male adult, who had been manacled and confined for some twelve years, under circumstances of sufferings, privations, and tortures, a parallel to which Mr. Haslam alone could probably supply. Other cases of a like character I might detail as specimens of the practice of that country. Doubtless, the treatment of insanity has been more humanely regarded in Holland, as well as elsewhere, within the past fifteen or sixteen years.

3*

perance in drink, as dissection has repeatedly shown; but the
neglect of a distinct pathognomonic difference between the
ravings of inebriety, or delirium tremens, and mental derangement, strictly so considered, have led to gross miscalculations in
our prognosis. As alcoholic insanity is engendered in every
country where drunkenness prevails, it is perhaps more frequently seen in our *mixed* population, than in that of Europe.
Hence we have sometimes been led to pronounce hastily and
erroneously that our success in the management of lunacy is
greater than that of other nations. We, however, must be supplied with more extensive and more accurate tabular views of the
comparative results of practice, in different institutions abroad and
at home, before we can come to a satisfactory conclusion on this
contested head. It is cheering to the feelings of the philanthropist to know, that by remedial measures, much more is accomplished at the present day, than was at a former time imagined
practicable; and Mr. Eddy's convictions in after life, that the
treatment of derangements of the mind, like that of disorders of
the body, would ere long bear signal triumphs of professional skill
in the healing art, seem likely to be experienced at no very remote
period.

Mr. Eddy's name is associated with those of Fulton, Colden,
Morris, Van Rensselaer, Hawley, and others, in projecting the
canal system of New York. Years before the commencement
of the Erie and Hudson Canal, he entertained enlarged views,
founded on extensive personal knowledge of the country, of the
expediency and practicability of inland communication by water.
A paper on the subject, written by himself, may be seen in Dr.
Hosack's memoir of De Witt Clinton.

He was a member of the Board appointed by the Legislature,
in 1810, to explore the route of an inland navigation from the
Hudson river to Lake Ontario and Lake Erie; and he accompanied the commissioners on that tour of public duty. A copy
of the first published report on this subject, dated February,
1811, may be seen in the American Medical and Philosophical
Register. In common with Clinton, Morris, Pintard, and other
advocates, for the general organization of the canal policy at
that early stage of this great undertaking, odious imputations
were freely bestowed upon him and his compatriots, and with

them he was assailed with the weapons of ridicule, by an opposition thinly scattered throughout the state, but strongly confederated in this city. It was absurdly proclaimed that New York would be utterly ruined by carrying into effect the projected canal measures. Notwithstanding the provocations were many and strong, he betrayed no evidences of irritability or disquietude, but, like primitive Barclay, sustained himself with an unshaken indifference, feeling assured that ignorance could not long retain its usurped powers, and that rancour, the offspring of party hatred and disappointed ambition, would in due time exhaust itself by the force of its own venom.

Little need be said touching the scholastic acquisitions of Mr. Eddy. All I believe he ever received at school, was embraced in an English elementary education. He, however, deeply studied the human character: as opportunities occurred, he read on general subjects of life and letters. He was versed in profane and ecclesiastical story, and might be deemed an adept in Quaker annals, from the History of Sewall down to Sarah Grub's Journal. Knowledge being higher prized for defence than ornament, he turned his information in these matters to an advantageous dexterity, when he encountered, in his journey, that marvellous impostor of the Shakers, Jemima Wilkinson, the elect lady, during his tour of observation as canal commissioner in 1810. He often spoke of this incident with peculiar pleasure. His researches in polemical disquisitions made him often deprecate the folly and injurious tendency of sectarian controversy on religious matters; and confirmed him in the excellence of the more salutary influence of the unsophisticated or orthodox doctrines, as he termed them, of the Society of Friends. Though these were his views, he felt that the intellectual culture of the Quakers was behind that of many other religious communities; and I am persuaded his desire to promote knowledge, made him often regret, that while the society to which he belonged had every reason to boast of its morality, philanthropy, and benevolence; it neglected too much the important advantages arising from the support of a literary order of men for the better education of its youth. Sound knowledge, he would say, subdues idleness, and prevents vacuity; and a disciplined mind enables the possessor to conduct himself with greater safety in the right way. It will readily be allowed, that the ethics of Quakerism, while they lead to the rejection of speculative principles, tend to the acquisition of practical facts ; and, however prone the mind may be to theorize, it is somewhat hard for theory to usurp an undue influence over a Quaker judgment. Mr. Eddy might be fairly cited as an example, in illustration of what is now advanced. Hence I account for his indifference to works of fancy; poetry and prose were alike perused by him for the solid instruction they imparted; and he read Dr. Mitchill's translation of the piscatory stanzas of Sannazarius, and the lofty strains of Dryden, with similar emotions.

No book of modern times stood so high in his estimation, as the Letters on the Christian Religion, by Dr. Olinthus Gregory, and he exerted his influence in the diffusion of that admirable work. As his efforts in behalf of new plans, or modified projects, generally quadrated with the usefulness to be derived from contemplated measures, he was in the constant habit of urging the economical precepts and moral sayings of Franklin, which he often embodied, as the soundest advice, in his confidential letters to those of his young friends, for whom he cherished a particular regard. The intellectuality of Madame De Stael yielded him less gratification than the expositions of Hannah More; and a higher glow of feeling was enkindled in his breast by Rumford on Cookery and Stoves, than by Burke on the Sublime and Beautiful. It is almost superfluous to add, that you may regard him as a decided *utilitarian.*

Of the various societies with which he was associated, he was fairly considered an operative member. Aware that business might be well debated, and yet badly managed; he rarely spoke in a public body, and when his opinions were demanded, he delivered his remarks with plainness, brevity, and pertinency. In the social circle, his conversation was more animated : as he had mixed largely with different classes of mankind, and abounded in lively anecdotes, it was often highly interesting. On occasions, he evinced a wholesome intrepidity and an enlarged charity ; yet he wished every thing congenerous with the practical, and he saw with little satisfaction the diffusion of philippics against luxurious living among a people subsisting mainly on the precarious tenure of the chase, and tractates on extravagance in dress among those whose chief vesture was a blanket.

I need not enlarge. I think you may safely assent to the con-clusion, that the subject of your biography appropriated the best years of a long life to the best purposes of man; that he may be justly deemed enlightened, among a people whose frugal views occasion perhaps too partial and too low an estimation of intellec-tual acquirements; that he was eminently conspicuous in a society deservedly regarded as excelling all others in works of charity and philanthropy.

I am acquainted with but one striking instance in his whole life in which the integrity of his judgment was seriously impugned : he was unwittingly captivated by the enthusiasm which prevailed concerning the metallic tractors, and was led to confide in the remedial efficacy of Perkinism, by experiments instituted at the New York Hospital, where that practice was countenanced for a short while by certain of the physicians of that charity. But little censure can rest with him on this particular account : he was not educated a physician ; and this extraordinary deception received the support of many eminent professional characters, both in Europe and America, and indeed was not completely exploded as an unwarrantable hypothesis until subjected to the clinical acu-men of Dr. Haygarth.

A word or two on your inquiry relative to his son John Eddy. I refer you to a short memoir of him printed in the American Monthly Magazine ; more might have been said of his know-ledge of the physical branches of science, than is there recorded. He was a good zoologist, an excellent mineralogist, and a minute botanist. His acquisitions in this last named department were very remarkable. He was a member of the botanical class when I attended Columbia College in 1809-10. But it was requisite, on account of his being a deaf-mute, that his studies should be prosecuted privately by the intervention of signs and the manual alphabet. He found a friend willing to give him the necessary direction and aid, in his relative, the professor of Botany, Dr. Hosack. By visible signs, instead of accentible sounds, he mas-tered the Linnean system, and subsequently became a practical botanist. He formed an herbarium of some extent, of our indi-genous plants. The greater acuteness of the surviving senses when one or more are destroyed, was verified in the case of John Eddy. His industry was unintermitting, and his attainments

E

seemed incredible to those who are unaware what intellectual power and activity are occasionally displayed by persons to whom one sense is shut out. The blind Rumphius, of Holland, is still recognized as conspicuous among erudite botanical investigators; and John Eddy, had his life been protracted, and he given an exclusive attention to the same kind of studies, might have secured to himself a permanent place in the catalogue of American botanists.

Make such use of this imperfect letter as you may think fit.

With due consideration, I remain, very respectfully,

JOHN W. FRANCIS.

To Colonel S. L. KNAPP.

LIFE OF THOMAS EDDY.

LIFE

OF

THOMAS EDDY.

" But these were merciful men, whose righteousness hath not been forgotten."
" Their bodies are buried in peace, but their name liveth for evermore."

At no period in the history of nations has the mind
of man been more active in the great business of
ameliorating his condition, than that which has elapsed since the close of the American revolution. Invention, industry, and enterprise, have been abroad, and
multiplied conveniences, comforts, and even elegan-
cies, beyond enumeration. Nor has this been all:
Those charitable institutions, which are, at the same
time, the medicine for natural and moral evils, and the
noble ornaments of civil society, have every where
been built up, but especially in this country ; and it
is not too much to say, that, in many instances, our
institutions have become patterns for other nations,
even those of the old world, from which, in other
things, we have taken so much in organizing societies
amongst ourselves. These institutions although of
the first importance to the public welfare, seem to lie
out of the path of the general historian, who contents
himself with some cursory remarks upon them as
domestic matters, and goes on to battles, treaties, and
political occurrences, as making up all that is worthy

4

the attention of the reader, or proper for his pen ; and, it is singular, that the writers of biography should have so seldom taken up the lives of philanthropists. Almost every grade of society, and every adventurer, has been described, while those who laboured for the good of mankind have been, with some few exceptions, neglected. The reading world have been supplied with countless volumes written upon the deeds of warriors, who have desolated nations, and marked their footsteps with blood. In the opinion of men, they had conquered their fame :

> " They were the mighty of the world,
>   The demi-gods of earth;
> Their breath—the flag of blood unfurled
>   And gave the battle birth.
> They lived—to trample on mankind,
> And in their ravage leave behind
>   The impress of *their* worth.·
> And wizzard rhyme, and hoary song,
> Hallowed their deeds, and hymned their wrong.

The statesmen and orators, as well as warriors, have had their Plinys and their Plutarchs to hand them down to posterity in a blaze of glory; and even the poets who were neglected while living, have had their Cibbers and Johnsons to tell the world how they suffered and how they sung; while the philanthropist, whose deeds have an influence on the moral world, as the dews of heaven have upon the natural, has hardly found a poet or historian. Not even a name has been left on record for the good Samaritan. In a few instances, it is true, genius and feeling have burst out into a sweet strain of honest eulogy of the benevolent, such as will never be forgotten. Pope's tuneful tribute to the Man of Ross, and Burke's eloquent description of Howard, can never be lost. Some, in modern times, have sketched the lives of a few philanthropists, but frequently in so tame a manner, that one would think that there was a canon against showing the slightest enthusiasm in commemorating the good. Some few have broken through their shackles, and dared to assign them a place in the history of man, and to say to these doers of good in a spirit of prophecy,

> " Thine was an empire o'er distress;
>   Thy triumph—of the mind ;
> To burst the bonds of wretchedness,
>   The friend of human kind:
> Thy name—through every future age,
> By bard, philanthropist, and sage,
>   In glory shall be shrined."

But these honest chroniclers have as yet had no chance with the delineators of warriors and statesmen, who had astonished, awed, and charmed mankind. It is believed that a day of better taste is dawning upon us, and that men will take as much pleasure in tracing the rise and progress of an asylum for the children of poverty and disease, as in recounting a battle in which thousands were made miserable, and which created many orphans at a blow.

Promiscuous charity has been practised by the kind-hearted and the wealthy in every age and nation. The benevolent have poured the oil and wine into the wounds of the unfortunate, to assuage their anguish, if they could not heal them ; they have fed the hungry and clothed the naked, and in so doing have received their reward in the blessings of the just. The Saviour of the world declared that, inasmuch as this was done to one of the children of misfortune, it was done unto himself. But notwithstanding this generous current of philanthropy has been flowing in the hearts of the virtuous, in all nations, since the birth of man, yet it was left for a late age to collect facts relative to human misery, and from these to form a system for permanent relief. In former times, charity seemed to pour out her heart like water, but never to consult reason upon the true means of preventing the evils she mourned. In this age she has called in industry, sagacity, perseverance, and the highest order of invention, to assist her in her great undertakings.

Prisons, in every age and nation, have been viewed

with horror by the great mass of the people; their bars and gates and chains have been so intimately associated with crime and infamy, that the blood curdled at the very thought of them, and the shortest confinement was a lasting disgrace; and no wonder, for within the four walls, and frequently in the same room, the murderer, the thief, the insane, and the honest debtor, mingled their wailings, and breathed the same tainted atmosphere. It seemed as if the powerful and the benevolent were paralyzed in contemplating these evils, and thought the slightest remedy was beyond all hope. They could do something to soften the miseries of the individual, but dared not combat the prejudices of the age, nor attempt to form a general system to reach a class of cases.

About the middle of the last century, a philanthropist arose in England, who gave a new direction to the alms of individuals, to the sympathy of communities, and to the charity of nations. This philanthropist was John Howard.* He was a man of strict habits, of daring courage, both natural and moral. He began, as it was then considered, a crusade of charity. He examined the state of all the prisons in England and Wales, and then extended his researches through the continent. He made known his discoveries to the grand inquest of the British nation, the House of Commons. This august body heard the relation with surprise, and set about turning the information they had gained to alleviating miseries, which until then had appeared as among legendary tales or incurable evils. Howard was still indefatigable in his new pathway of glory, and at last fell a martyr to his zeal in the cause, on the banks of the Euxine. His exertions, however, were so bold and novel, as to excite general attention, and to give a new impulse to the charitable dispositions of the human mind. He was indeed born for the universe, and the effects of his exertions are pervading the whole of Christendom.

* See Appendix.

America has been so intimately connected with England in science and letters, that all that has been done in that country, was soon known in this, and has generally been imitated, when found to be good; at first, by small beginnings, which were, from time to time, increased and improved, as information and wealth advanced. The privations and sufferings of a new people, taught them to be kind to one another, and gave them the habits as well as the spirit of benevolence. It might, of course, have been expected by the patriot and philosopher, that Howard would have a school in America. This school has been established.

One of the most distinguished disciples of this university of charity, was Thomas Eddy, a merchant of the city of New York. He was born about the period that Howard began to mark out his course of action. Eddy not only made this great philanthropist his pattern, but he carried his reasonings farther than Howard had an opportunity to do. Seizing the facts and reasonings which Howard had furnished, he added others, truly his own, and set about to influence his fellow citizens to make practical efforts to test the correctness of his views, and the soundness of his principles; and such was his success, that he, by general consent, received the appellation of the "HOWARD OF AMERICA." Some notice of the life, writings, and deeds of such a man, it is believed, will not only be acceptable, but useful to the public, as an incentive to like efforts, and as a satisfactory proof of what can be done among men by one individual of intelligence, virtue, and moral courage.

If, in later life, it is difficult for a man to speak of himself and his deeds, particularly, if he has been called to take a conspicuous part on the stage of action; still, that autobiography of such a man which recounts the deeds and trials of childhood and youth, and so far into manhood as to come up to the time when distinction commences, is always the best, when

F 4*

it can be obtained. Fortunately, a plain, modest, and well written account of the early days of Thomas Eddy, has been left from his own hand. It was only intended for the eye of his family and particular friends, but the narrative is so happy, that it would be over fastidious indeed to hesitate to use it on this occasion. It is almost impossible for a biographer, even with every aid before him, to describe the true growth and development of a mind, from the cradle to maturity. The individual himself can alone approximate to the truth. In childhood and youth, when the imagination wanders at will, none but the person himself can tell all the avenues and directions of thought, nor precisely when passion was commingled with judgment, or by what food and exercise the mind obtained its stature. I shall, as the best thing that can be done for my readers, introduce an extract, in Mr. Eddy's own words, giving an account of himself up to the time he began his effectual efforts as a philanthropist :—

"I can only trace my ancestors as far back as my grandfather, John Edie, (by a letter I have seen from him to my father, he so spelled his name,) who lived in Belfast, in Ireland, but he probably came from Aberdeen, in Scotland. He was much respected and esteemed as a remarkably upright honest man—he was in low circumstances, and only able to give my father a small portion of school learning. My father, James Eddy, was born in Belfast, 1712; he served an apprenticeship to William Sinclair, a respectable merchant in Dublin. My mother's name was Mary Darragh ; she was born in Dublin about 1724; she was of a respectable and good family. My parents were married in Dublin about the year 1742. She had a fortune of about £1000 sterling. I believe soon after their marriage, they removed to Belfast, and there my father pursued mercantile business. They had both been educated Presbyterians, but during their residence in that city, he became acquainted with Robert Bradshaw, a Friend, of consi derable estate, who resided at Newtonards, about seven miles from Belfast, and was highly respected and much beloved. He was not a minister, but a meeting was held at his house, which was occasionally attended by some of his tenants. He lent my father some Friend's books, who in this way became acquainted with their principles, and was received as a member in the society. My mother was warmly attached to the Presbyterians, and much prejudiced against the doctrines and principles of Friends; however, she afterwards became convinced of their rectitude, and was received into membership. She was a pious and valuable woman. About the year 1753, they embarked for America, and landed and settled at Philadelphia. My father pursued mercantile business, mostly in shipping, till about 1766, when he went into the ironmongery business. He died in 9th month. My mother had sixteen children, of whom none are now living, but my sister, Mary Hosack, and myself. She was only a few months old at the time of our father's decease. I was born in Philadelphia, 5th of 9th month, 1758. My mother carried on the hardware business extensively after my father's death, till the year 1796, when she removed to Buckingham, in Bucks county. She was induced to quit the city on account of the bitter spirit of persecution of the Whigs (the advocates of American independence) against the Tories, (so called on account of their attachment to the mother country;) and our family being of the latter description, we suffered considerably from the opposite party. Schools were then badly conducted, and many of them broken up, on account of the teachers being Tories, so that I had but a poor chance of getting an education. All the learning I acquired was reading, writing, and arithmetic, as far as vulgar fractions. As to grammar, I could repeat some of its definitions by rote, but was totally ignorant of its principles. About the year 1771, my mother placed me as an apprentice with John Hoskins, of Burlington, to learn the tanning business, but owing to some misunderstanding about my learning the currying trade, I did not continue with him more than two years. Public affairs were in a very unsettled state, and a great deal of bitterness and ill-will subsisted amongst the people, which produced much division and strife between families and near connexions, who had heretofore lived in perfect peace and harmony. The science of government was little understood, yet every bustling politician was a great man. Many of the most respectable citizens were opposed to a separation from Great Britain, yet all acknowledged that the claims of the British Parliament were severe and unjust. Those opposed to independence conceived that more ought to have been done to obtain redress of grievances in a peaceable way, without having recourse to the shedding of blood. Every one seemed to take a decided and warm part, and was attached, and marked as belonging to one or other of the two parties. It now appears very clearly to my mind, that it would have been more wise and consistent with the principles of Friends, if they had more carefully avoided the intemperate political zeal, then manifested by all parties. The advice of George Fox, was for Friends to keep out of all civil commotions, &c., as they are mostly carried on in a temper very opposite to the meek and quiet spirit of the Gospel. From the age of 16 to 20 years, my most particular and intimate friends were Charles Mifflin and William Savary, with whom I daily associated. The former was well educated and of a fine understanding, with sound principles and a marked integrity. The latter was a most valuable character, and a highly pleasing and entertaining companion. We were all fond of such subjects and pursuits as were most likely to promote mirth and pleasantry, yet the wise and excellent sentiments communicated to us by Charles Mifflin were one means of preserving us from much harm;

and happy would it have been for me, if I had, through life, more imitated his excellent character. He possessed fine literary talents, and as a poet was pleasing and instructive. His family connexions were wealthy, and generally fashionable. He, more particularly, during the latter part of his life, was a truly religious and good man. Of William Savary, it would be difficult for me to say too much. No two persons could entertain a more near and tender regard and affection for each other, than always subsisted between us. He was a man of uncommonly strong mind, and good understanding. When about 25 years of age, he became a minister, and perhaps there never was one more highly esteemed and beloved. He was admired by all classes, and openly opposed to every thing in the least marked with bigotry or superstition. As a preacher, he was in the first rank. His manner of delivery was pleasing and solemn, his mind was cultivated and improved, and he was uncommonly liberal in his sentiments towards those of other societies. I have often thought there never was so nearly perfect a character, within my knowledge, in our society, and none that more extensively inculcated and effectually diffused, true, practical, Christian principles. I could do no less than pay this brief tribute to the memory of these two excellent men, who were the friends of my youth, and who early instilled into my mind, opinions and sentiments, that have been instructive and useful to me through life.

In 1777, the British troops took possession of Philadelphia, and soon after their entering the city, the American army attacked them at Germantown. I rode out with William Savary to that place, before the battle was entirely over, and had a view, a mournful view, of the killed and wounded on the ground. When we arrived, the Americans had retreated, and the British army had advanced as far as Chesnut Hill. About a month previous to the arrival of the

British in Philadelphia, a number of Friends, amongst whom was my elder brother Charles, were arrested by a general warrant, by order of the Executive Council of Pennsylvania, and without being admitted to a hearing, were unjustly banished to Winchester, in Virginia. Of this number, I recollect the names of Israel, John, and James Pemberton, Edward Penington, Thomas, Samuel, and Myers Fisher, Thomas Gilpin, and others. The alleged charge against them was, that they were unfriendly to the independence of America. They were absent several months, and were allowed to return, during the time the British occupied the city. The British army evacuated Philadelphia in 6th month, 1778. Soon after, several persons were arrested, under a charge of aiding the British, and were tried for treason. As is common in all civil wars, the minds of people were extremely irritated against each other, and those who were attached to the British government, were often very bitterly persecuted by the opposite party. Amongst those citizens of Philadelphia charged with treason, were John Roberts and Abraham Carlisle. They were both Friends of good reputation, and very respectable men. The former was a miller, and resided near Merion meeting house, about six miles from Philadelphia. The latter was a board merchant, near Vine street. The charge against Roberts was, that when the British troops were on their march to take possession of Philadelphia, and had advanced near Swedes Ford, on the Schuylkill, 17 miles from the city, he sent word to General Howe, who commanded the British, that the Friends, who, as aforementioned, had been banished to Virginia, were then proceeding on the road to Reading, and suggested to the General that he should send a detachment of the army to fall in with them, in order that they might return to their families. After the British took possession of the city, a line of fortifications was completed from the Schuylkill to the Delaware, and gates were placed at different parts of this line. At one of these gates, Abraham Carlisle was stationed by direction of General Howe, in order to examine all who went out of the city, or came into it, and it was made his duty to stop any suspicious persons. This constituted the charge exhibited against him. They were both tried by Judge McKean, condemned to be hanged, and were accordingly executed. John Robert's funeral was at Merion, on which occasion a meeting was held, which was very large. He was extensively known, and much beloved. Nicholas Waln, and others, preached, and I attended, as did a large number from the city. Abraham Carlisle was interred in Friend's burial ground in Fourth street; his funeral, also, was very large. When the British troops evacuated Philadelphia, my brother Charles removed to New York, and in 4th month, 1779, I also left my native city and came by land to New York. At this period it was very dangerous travelling without a passport. I was put over to Staten Island (possessed by the British troops) at night, and next day reached New York. My brother Charles had, some time before, sailed for England. I had sold my horse at Rahway, and had only ninety-six dollars on my reaching New-York, where I was totally a stranger, and as to a knowledge of any kind of business, entirely ignorant. My school learning, as I have before mentioned, was very limited, so that, of course, I had to encounter many difficulties, and laboured under great disadvantage in my attempts to acquire a sufficiency to defray my expenses. I took board with William Backhouse, in the house now occupied by Daniel McCormick in Wall street, at the rate of eight dollars per week, besides having to pay one dollar weekly for washing; Samuel Elain, late of Newport, deceased, John I. Glover, and two or three other respectable merchants, boarded at the same house; becoming acquainted with them was highly useful to me, as it was the first opportunity I had ever had of acquiring a knowledge of commerce, and the course of mercantile dealing. I knew that it was out of my power to support myself with what I then possessed, and that I must soon come to want, unless I could succeed in business. The first thing to which my attention was turned, was daily to attend auctions at the Coffee House, and being sensible of my own ignorance, I endeavoured by every means in my power to acquire information—carefully inquiring of others the names of articles exposed for public sale, as it often happened that I was not even acquainted with the names of many of them. I then inquired their value, and advised with some persons previous to purchasing; sometimes on noticing an article intended to be sold by auction, I would procure a sample, and call on some dealer in the article, and get them to offer me a fixed price on my furnishing it: in this way, by first ascertaining where I could dispose of the goods, I would purchase, provided the price would afford me a profit. On this plan I have found a purchaser for goods, bought and delivered them, and received the money which enabled me to pay the auctioneer the cost of them, without my advancing one shilling. I was obliged to live by my wits, and this necessity was of great use to me afterwards. Some months after my arrival at New York, my brother Charles arrived from Ireland, and brought with him, on account of merchants there, provisions, linens, &c. shipped from Dublin, Cork, Belfast, and other ports. He returned to Europe in 1780, previous to which we formed a copartnership with Benjamin Sykes, under the firm of Eddy, Sykes, & Co.

"This firm prosecuted business mostly in consignments from England and Ireland, and some shipping business. My partner was a good natured honest Englishman, but not possessed of a very intelligent, active mind; in consequence of this, the management and contrivance of the business fell to my lot, and, though very young, and without experience, I had to write all the letters, and carry on every kind of correspondence, besides mostly making all the purchases and sales. By every packet we had to write twenty or thirty letters to England and Ireland, and to accomplish this, had frequently to sit writing till 12 or 1 o'clock in the morning. I was sedulously and actively employed in business, and in this way acquired considerable knowledge of commercial affairs. Our concerns were extensive, and were prosecuted with tolerable success, respectability, and reputation. My brother George was, at this time, in Philadelphia, about 18 years of age. He possessed a remarkably sensible and comprehensive mind. Although he had no knowledge of business, he was full of enterprise. By him, in Philadelphia, and by Eddy, Sykes & Co. in New York, an arrangement was made, with the consent of General Washington, to supply the British and foreign troops with money, who were taken with Lord Cornwallis at York Town. The money was raised by my brother at Philadelphia, drawing on us at New York, and the monies thus raised were paid to the Paymaster of the British and foreign troops, prisoners at Lancaster, Pennsylvania, for which he received and sent to Eddy, Sykes & Co. that Paymaster's drafts on the Paymaster General at New York. By an agreement made with Sir Henry Clinton, the British commander, we were paid six per cent. commission. The whole amount paid amounted to a very large sum, and proved a profitable contract.

" After being some time in business, I kept house in John street. My most intimate friends, at this time, were Richard and Lawrence Hartshorne. I had formed some acquaintance with Lawrence Hartshorne's sister previous to my coming to New York, and then experienced a tender and warm attachment towards her, and about a year after my coming to New York, I went down to Sandy Hook in company

5

with Lawrence Hartshorne, whose object in attempting this dangerous enterprise was to visit his parents, whilst mine was to obtain an interview with his sister.   In the evening, we immediately ventured on shore, and went to his father's, who resided on his farm at Black Point.   The family were all in bed, and we were thus disappointed in seeing any of them.   Lawrence was advised by his father to return immediately to Sandy Hook, as there was reason to suspect that parties of the militia were then near the premises.   We accordingly went to the river side, and taking a small canoe, pushed off in hopes of getting safe to the Hook ; it was moonlight, and as we kept off some distance from the shore, we did not apprehend danger till we should reach the Gut (as it was called) which separated Sandy Hook from the Highlands.   This was very narrow, so that we were obliged to pass within a little distance of the Jersey shore.   There were stationed about thirty of the Jersey militia, and a number of them fired on us. We laid ourselves on our backs in the bottom of the canoe, and some of the balls went through the sides, immediately over our bodies.   Finding we could not escape, we rowed to the shore, and surrendered ourselves prisoners.   At first, they treated us harshly, searched us, and took from us some articles of small value.   In the morning they marched us to Middletown, and then to Monmouth Court-house, where we were taken before Judge Symmes (the father of Capt. Symmes) and committed to prison.   We were put in a small room, about six or seven feet square, in which we found four or five prisoners, some of whom had been confined there some time.   We were much crowded, and had nothing to lie on but extremely dirty straw, which I believe had not been changed since the other prisoners had occupied the room.   On first entering this miserable dungeon, the stench occasioned by foul and noxious air exceedingly alarmed me, and it was strongly fixed on my mind that it would put an end to my life in less than half an hour. However, in time, it did not feel so very offensive, and becoming habituated to it, I was able to eat my meals with a good appetite.

" Elisha Boudinot (now President of the American Bible Society) was then commissary of prisoners; I consulted with him, and he behaved very friendly towards me. One day, it was reported that a woman had offered to swear that she had seen me, a short time before this, at New Brunswick. This was false, as I had not been out of New York for more than a year. It was said, if she would swear I was there, it would enable them to prove me a spy. This served, of course, to alarm me extremely; however, in a little time, no more was said about it. We remained in this loathsome place about eight or ten days, and were then removed to Springfield, six miles from Elizabethtown. At Springfield, we had the liberty of a mile round the village, and in about a month, were exchanged for, I believe, two soldiers of the militia, and returned safe to our friends in New York. Soon after this, Hannah Hartshorne came to the city on a visit to her brother, which afforded me frequent opportunities of being in her company, and resulted in our forming an affectionate and lasting attachment towards each other. We were married on the twentieth of 3d month, 1782, at the old Meeting House in Liberty street. I continued in business till peace was concluded in 1783, and in the 11th month of that year, the British troops evacuated the city. This was a trying period to myself, and others, who had taken refuge in New York, as all persons of our description had thereby incurred the ill-will of those of the opposite party, and we much feared that we should be exceedingly persecuted by them. Great numbers went to Nova Scotia, and amongst others, my brother in law, Lawrence Hartshorne, and his family. I could not reconcile leaving my mother and near connexions in Philadelphia, and this consideration prevented my removing to Halifax. It may now appear strange, that persons born in America, should have been opposed to American independence. It is, however, not surprising, that among the great body of the people, who were all born and educated *British subjects*, that many deep-rooted prejudices should exist, tending to excite an attachment to that government, and an aversion to republicanism.

" These were sensible of the unjust and tyrannical conduct of Great Britain towards this country, but they conceived redress of grievances might be obtained without a separation.

" This, as events proved, was a vain expectation. In truth, the science of government was not then so well understood as at present, and great numbers, having the knowledge they now possess, would then have adopted very different political sentiments. This would certainly have been the fact as regards myself. Before the Americans entered the city, I removed to New Jersey, and soon after to Philadelphia. My brother Charles was married and in business in London, and I formed a connexion in Philadelphia, under the firm of Thomas and George Eddy. In the first month of 1784, I went to Virginia for the purpose of purchasing and making shipments of tobacco. It was a most remarkably severe winter, and I recollect when riding near Port-Royal on the Rappahanock river, that the snow along the fences (drifted) was six feet deep. The winter in 1st month, 1780, was, however, much more severe. All the bay of New York was then frozen, for some weeks, as far as Sandy Hook. Horses and sleighs passed from the city to Staten Island. I remember seeing a number of large cannon, 42 pounders, taken on the ice from Paulus' Hook or New York to Staten Island. Great numbers of people were daily skating on the bay. I went on skates to Governor's Island, Bedlow's Island, and Paulus' Hook.

" During the revolutionary war, tobacco, in Europe,

sold at a very extravagant price, in consequence of which considerable quantities were shipped within a year after the peace, so that the market was overstocked, and the price so reduced, that much money was lost by the shippers; my brother and myself lost considerable. When peace took place, there were scarce any European goods on hand, which occasioned large importations to be made by our merchants. The ill effects of this began to be severely felt in 1786 to 1788, which ruined many in America and London. Almost the whole of the American trade was then confined to London, and very little commercial intercourse with any other port in England. My brother Charles had shipped considerably on credit to Thomas and George Eddy, and many others, who, owing to the country being inundated with every sort of goods, were unable to remit to England. Thomas and George Eddy, had supplied imprudently an individual residing at Fredericksburg, Virginia, with goods to a large amount. He died, and left his affairs in a very unsettled state. On this account I removed with my family to Fredericksburg, and kept a large retail store in the name of Thomas and George Eddy, my brother George remaining in Philadelphia. This Virginia business turned out badly, and my being much exposed to extravagant and dissipated company was a great injury to me in every respect. In 1788, I returned to Philadelphia, and as my brother in London had failed, it became necessary for Thomas and George Eddy to make a settlement with their creditors.

"We were discharged under a general act of bankruptcy for the State of Pennsylvania. Since then, the debts due from them have been mostly paid. Some were not legal demands, and it was thought not right to pay them.

"I now had an opportunity of learning in the school of adversity some useful lessons, that have been of advantage to me. I have often looked back to this

5*

period, and recollected how much I lamented my misfortune, as it is generally termed, but which, indeed, was a "blessing in disguise," for, not succeeding in business in Virginia, obliged me to remove, whereas, had I succeeded, I probably should have remained there, and, considering my weakness, how apt to unite in company in every respect improper and hurtful to my best interests, moral and religious, there is every reason to suppose that I should have partaken of all the evils produced in such a profligate and irreligious state of society, as did then exist in Virginia. I seldom reflect on the circumstances which forced me to leave that place, without feeling my mind warmed with a sense of gratitude to the All-Wise Disposer of human events, that he was graciously pleased so to extend his providential care over me, as to cause my removal from a state of society that might, by my remaining in it, have proved destructive to my family, and ruinous to myself.

"I omitted to mention, that on the 4th of 6th month, 1785, I embarked for England in the English ship Mildred, bound for London. I remained in England only about three months, and returned the latter part of 11th month, being absent near six months. This voyage was not productive of much advantage to me.

"In the year 1790, I went with my family to Black Point, and in the following year removed to New York. On my return to this city, all I had was fifty pounds, supplied me by my father-in-law, but owing to the kind attention of Robert Bowne, and others, I soon got into some little business. At this period, and for some years afterwards, there were no Insurance offices in New York, and being encouraged by my friends, I commenced the business of an Insurance broker. I pursued this with success for three or four years. About 1792, the public debt of the United States was founded; this afforded an opportunity for people to speculate in the public funds. In this business I made a good deal of money. I declined acting as an Insurance broker, and did considerable business as an underwriter, in which I was successful.

"In 1793, or 1794, I was elected a Director in the Mutual Insurance Company, and soon after a Director in the Western Inland Lock Navigation Company, and in 1797, was appointed Treasurer of that Company From early life, all improvement of a public nature, that tended to benefit the country, or in any shape promote the happiness and welfare of mankind, were considered by me as highly important, and claimed my attention. I have been connected with a number of public institutions, and have providentially been the means of their being established."

Mr. Eddy, at this time, being in easy circumstances, had leisure to turn his attention to some of those charities that are of permanent benefit to mankind. He had read the human mind with great sagacity and attention, and had analyzed the spirit of society in his own country. He found, as every wise man will, that if there are inevitable evils in the world, yet much may be done by way of softening them, or preparing the mind to bear them.

One of the first objects of his exertions was that of establishing a penitentiary in the State of New York, for he believed that many who had been allured to the paths of vice might be recalled, if proper methods were taken to instruct them in trades, to give them industrious habits, and to keep them from the pollution of those hardened in iniquity. He was well acquainted with the general plan and economy of the penitentiary establishment in Philadelphia, which had been got up by the influence of the Society of Friends, but he thought even this system was susceptible of improvement. No other state had then followed the example of Pennsylvania, nor had its fame reached the leading philanthropists of New York. The penal code in most of the States still has the sanguinary spirit and hard features of the English penal code, which, with all their boasted love of liberty, was written in blood. The tears of the sympathetic, and the voice of the benevolent, had made but slow progress against the apathy of the great mass of mankind, and the vindictive spirit of a few, who believe, or profess to believe, that the world should be governed by a rod of iron. The hearts of the people were made callous by the sight of stocks, whipping-posts, pillories, in every shire, town, or considerable village. Flagellation with the cat-o'-nine-tails, burning in the hand, or forehead, with a hot iron, cropping the ears of prisoners in the pillory, were all common sights to the youngest, as well as the oldest, portion of the community. The Friends in Pennsylvania were among the first people in the Union to make an effort to change this barbarity for some milder system, thinking, and thinking justly, that severe punishments produced, rather than diminished crime. To this order of Christians the public are indebted for many good examples; but if this was the only thing they had done for mankind, they would deservedly stand high with the historian. By their efforts, the penal code of Pennsylvania was ameliorated, and this good precedent has been followed by most of the States in the Union.

In 1796, Mr. Eddy was on a journey to Philadelphia, in company with General Philip Schuyler, of the State of New York. Schuyler was then a member of the Senate of that State, and was, justly, very influential. He had been for more than forty years a prominent character in the country, first, as an officer in the war of 1755, and then a magnanimous leader in the revolutionary contest. He had talents, integrity, property, and moral courage, and was the very man for the purpose Eddy had in view, which was to engage him in the change he wished to bring about in the penal code of the State of New York, and for the establishment of a penitentiary system. Eddy conversed freely with Schuyler upon every topic that had a bearing upon the subject, and as soon as they reached the city of Philadelphia, they repaired to the prison and made a thorough examination of the edifice, the convicts, the by-laws, the whole economy of the establishment, which were satisfactory to that practical statesman Mr. Eddy had laboured to engage in the cause, and he was now ready to go heart and hand with him. Mr. Eddy procured a large number of copies of the penal code of Pennsylvania, and distributed them freely. To each of the members of the Legislature he presented a copy, at the next meeting of that body, after his visit to Philadelphia. The General, with the assistance of Mr. Eddy, drew up a bill for establishing a penitentiary system in the State of New York. This bill he did not introduce into the Senate himself, but engaged the services of a distinguished member of that body, Ambrose Spencer,* a gentleman of first rate abilities, and who has since filled the important office of Chief Justice of the State of New York, with high honour. Both Spencer and Schuyler made excellent speeches on the subject, which had a surprising effect upon the members of the Senate, and on the audience. Mr. Eddy was at hand to give all the details that were necessary for a proper understanding of the provisions of the bill. The moment the representatives of the people were convinced of the utility and practicability of the measure, the bill was passed without any great difficulty. The bill directed a state prison to be erected, and appointed Matthew Clarkson, John Watts, Thomas Eddy, Isaac Stoutenburg, and John Murray, jun., commissioners to carry the bill into effect. These commissioners designated Thomas Eddy as a committee for building the prison, who engaged the architect and workmen, and went on in his own way with the whole concern. This duty he set about to perform, but imitated very closely the plan of the establishment at Philadelphia ; the plan of the single rooms was an after thought with Mr. Eddy, but

* See Appendix.

which, in fact, is the great improvement of the age. Such was Mr. Eddy's anxiety to have the penitentiary succeed, that he not only consented to serve as a director, but as an agent. He undertook the latter office, as his reputation was involved in the success of the plan, and probably from an honest conviction that he had made himself better acquainted with the whole subject than any other person in the State. In these two offices, as inspector and agent, he acted for more than four years. He was so assiduous and calculating in his duties, that every anticipation of his friends and of himself was more than realized. The expenses of the establishment had been less than were expected, the health of the prisoners better than that of the free and honest citizens in the ordinary walks of life. Such cleanliness, order, and moral discipline, marked the penitentiary system under the administration of this untired philanthropist, that those formerly dissipated and sickly were made sober and healthy. He watched the results of his plans, and held to a theory no longer than he found it good in practice. His, was truly the inductive system of philanthropy. In 1801, Mr. Eddy published an account of the State Prison of New York. His mottos were taken from Beccaria and Montesquieu; in fact, his whole theory of crimes and punishments is drawn from those great friends of liberty, Beccaria, Montesquieu, Howard, Penn, and other celebrated reformers of this and a former age. He pointed out the state of the penal code in New York before 1796, and showed, that after it was altered, diminishing the number of capital punishments, and substituting imprisonment, the humane change was made without increasing crime. In this work, Mr. Eddy recounted the history of the establishment, described the edifice with its workshops, cells, &c.; and no one can deny but that the plan was admirable, according to the state of information on these subjects at that time. The government of the prison is also treated of, its officers named, and their duties minutely pointed out. This, at present, would seem superfluous, but, at that time, it was a new affair. The writer goes on to give a full account of the prisoners in the State, with the treatment, occupations, dress, and diet of the convicts, as also the means used, and to be used, for their reformation. On the subject of food and dress, he is quite minute; all of which goes to prove that cleanliness is the great promoter and preserver of health, and that no effective labour can be expected of men who are not substantially and well fed. In fact, he approves of the maxim of the stable, that *" to get labour from the animal, he should be kept under the full force of feed—good wholesome feed, however coarse."* Among these excellent statistics of the prison, there is nothing to be compared to his doctrines upon the subject of reformation.

" The end of human punishments is the prevention of crimes. In the endeavour to attain this end, three things are to be considered : the amendment of the offender; the deterring of others by his example; reparation to society and the party injured. Of these objects, the first, without doubt, is of the highest importance. Society cannot be better secured against crimes, than by eradicating the evil passions and corrupt habits which are the sources of guilt. The operation of punishment as a terror to others, is generally considered as momentary and uncertain in its effects; for men are often found so regardless of the future, as to perpetrate crimes at the instant they are witnessing the most dreadful execution of a criminal for a similar offence. The punishment of death precludes the possibility of the amendment of the criminal by any human means. Every hope of reformation is at once cut off without a single effort to accomplish so just and benevolent a purpose. Society and the injured party are, indeed, in the strictest sense, avenged on the head of the guilty offender.

Justice, however, not revenge, is the true foundation of the right of punishment. But, it is not the design of the present work to discuss the principles of a code of criminal law, or to point out the errors which have been perpetuated by the passions or ignorance of legislators.

"If society is effectually secured against future mischief by the imprisonment of the offender, it is that mode of punishment also which affords the only chance of reclaiming him from evil. It is by confinement to hard labour in a penitentiary house, that the primary and legitimate purpose of human punishment is to be effected. The character of men are endlessly diversified, and their motives and actions assume a thousand different hues. In considering convicts, we may, in general, distinguish them into three classes: men grown old in habits of profligacy and violence, unfeeling and desperate offenders, who discover no signs of contrition, and yield little hope of amendment: those who, in early life, have received a moral and religious education, and, though afterwards led by passion and evil example into the commission of crimes, still retain some sense of virtue: those who, have sustained a fair reputation, are arrested for the first public offence, before they have become familiar with vice; who wished, perhaps, to return to the path of virtue, but had not energy enough to retrace their steps.

" In forming an opinion of the depravity of convicts, nothing can be more unjust than to confound these different classes in the same judgment. All were once innocent; but, blinded by passion, allured by present temptation, they have mistaken their true interest, and been gradually led into the depths of vice and criminality. In designating punishments for various offences, the legislator can regard only the tendency of actions to injure society, and distribute those punishments according to the comparative degrees of harm such actions may produce. He cannot foresee those circumstances in the moral condition of the agent which may justly lessen or aggravate his guilt; and, by the wise constitution and jealous policy of our laws, judges are not vested with any discretionary power to apportion the punishment according to a greater or less criminality of intention in the offender. It is in a penitentiary house, that an opportunity is afforded of distinguishing the shades of guilt in different offenders, and of correcting that error and injustice, in some degree inseparable from the best system of laws, by which persons, whose guilt admits of different degrees, are subjected to the same punishment.* It is for those to whom the superintendence of such an institution is intrusted, to effect, as far as possible, the amendment of the delinquent, and thus to fulfil the highest duty of humanity. And, it is with no small pleasure that the inspectors have observed, that a number of those who have been discharged from the prison confided to their care, have continued in habits of industry and sobriety, and bid fair to become good members of society. It would, no doubt, be interesting to the philanthropist, to be informed of the particular incidents in the lives of such men, and the circumstances which have furnished ground to predict the rectitude of their future conduct. But this would, in some degree, lead the writer beyond his immediate object; and motives of prudence and charity ought, perhaps, to induce him, for the present, to forbear such a recital.

"The most efficacious means of reformation are to be found in that system of regular labour and exact temperance by which habits of industry and sobriety are formed. The inspectors have not been unmindful of other means of amendment, less immediately

* This topic may be enlarged upon in the conclusion, when we come to speak of *pardons*. It would greatly assist the Inspectors in the just exercise of their power, if the judges who sentence convicts were required to furnish a statement of all the circumstances that attended the trial, or which may have come to their knowledge, and which may serve to render the guilt of the convict, in their opinion, more or less aggravated.

6

connected with the nature of the punishment to which the convicts are sentenced. By the great attention paid to *cleanliness* in every part of the prison, they have shown their opinion of its importance in aiding reformation. Its benign influence on the physical character, though well understood by many, is not duly estimated by the bulk of mankind. Though its effect on bodily health be more obvious, its less striking but equally certain effect on the mind has been no where more fully experienced than in this prison. It is found to soften the temper, meliorate the disposition, and to produce a regard to temperance, order, and industry; and, by exciting more agreeable and tranquil sensations, to render men susceptible of good impressions, and thereby conduce to their future amendment.*

"In the winter, those of the convicts who have appeared to be most meritorious, are allowed, with the approbation of the keeper, to be taught reading, writing, and arithmetic. Teachers are selected from such of them as are competent, and twenty are permitted to meet together daily with one of the keepers, and to receive instruction for about two hours in the evening. This is considered as a privilege, and conferred on those only, who, by a peaceable, industrious, and regular course of conduct, have shown a disposition towards reformation. It is a further requisite for an admission into this school, that the person should have performed labour above his task to the value of four shillings a week, which is to pay for the implements of writing, light, and fuel.

"Care is taken, as far as possible, to separate the less vicious from the more hardened and daring offenders. About twenty-two of the most obdurate criminals are kept confined and at work in separate

---

* Count RUMFORD, in his Essays, speaking of the good effects produced on the mendicants in the House of Industry at Munich, by cleanliness, says, that " virtue never dwelt long with filth and nastiness; nor do I believe there ever was a person *scrupulously attentive to cleanliness*, who was a consummate villain."

apartments, and are not suffered to come out, or to have communication with other prisoners, but are constantly watched by keepers day and night. Experience will evince, that among any given number of convicts, one tenth part may be fairly considered as desperate and hardened villains, who appear incorrigible; and, it is of importance that such should be carefully selected and separated from the rest, as it is more probable they may, by proper management, be reformed.

"As another means of reformation, attention is paid to their religious and moral instruction.

" A large room in the prison, very neatly finished, is set apart for the purpose of divine worship. This room, and the gallery round it, will accommodate about six hundred persons.

" In this place the prisoners are assembled on the first day of each week, when one of their number reads a sermon and prayers, and the rest join in singing psalms.

"It is expected that the public preachers of the gospel in the city will cheerfully devote a small portion of their time to the service of these unhappy beings, who have so much need of their instruction, and of the counsel of the truly good and benevolent.

" As no distinction of sect exists in this great work of charity and benevolence, it is hoped that religious characters of every Christian denomination will feel it their duty to visit them on the day set apart for divine worship ; since it is obvious that a due attention to this important duty must produce the most salutary effects on the minds and conduct of the prisoners, and most powerfully promote the great plan of reformation.*

" Connected with this scheme of punishment and reformation, is another object, which, though of inferior importance in a moral view, is yet deserving of

---

* " As rational and immortal beings, we owe this to them, nor can any criminality of theirs justify our neglect in this particular." Howard.

attention. This is, indemnity to the community for
the expense of the conviction and maintenance of
the offender. It is highly probable, that with due
management and economy, the profit of the labour of
the convicts may be rendered equal to their support.
Such a result, however, has not been anticipated by
the zealous friends of reform in penal law in Europe.
They have regarded it as the indispensable duty of
legislators, to meliorate the laws, and correct the
abuses of prisons, without counting the cost of their
justice or humanity. In Pennsylvania, we are assured, that the experiment has been attended with
success;—and when the improved system of the
penitentiary house of this state has had time to ope-
fully, there can be no doubt of a result equally rate
favourable. It ought to have fair scope, and not to
be thwarted in its infancy, by distrust, or the selfish
views of individuals or particular classes of men. A
wise legislature will extend its concern to the whole
community, and, regardless of private interests, steadily pursue a plan the best calculated to promote the
general good.

"In the first establishment of the prison, the inspec
tors have had to encounter all the difficulties of a
new experiment, with the disadvantage of imperfect
knowledge in many branches of manufacture. A
system was to be formed, by which above two hundred convicts, many of them hardened, desperate,
and refractory, and many ignorant, or incapacitated
through infirmity or disease, might be brought into a
regular course of productive labour. To find suitable
employment for so many persons, was a matter of
considerable difficulty. In the choice of occupations,
regard must be had to those which require the least
capital, are most productive of profit, and most consistent with the health of the convicts, and the general
security of the prison. Among the different kinds
of manufactures, that of shoes was first introduced,
and has been fouud the most convenient and profita-

ble. The capital required for the purchase of the raw materials is not large, and the manufactured article will always meet with a ready sale; since the consumption of so indispensable a part of dress is great, and continually increasing, beyond the power of the tradesmen of the city to supply.* The manufacture of nails, and other articles, has been carried on for about two years. This required more capital; and it was not until very lately that sufficient experience was gained, in the purchase of stock and the use of machinery, to enable the inspectors to manage this branch of business with advantage. These circumstances, and many others that might be detailed, which necessarily attend an infant establishment, and which diminished the profits of the past years, will, in future, cease to produce expense and embarrassment. It is doubtful, whether the manufacture of nails, and of several other articles, ought to be carried on to a great extent, as they require too large a capital in advance. Experience will furnish, every year, grounds for improvement in the mode of conducting the branches of industry, or in the introduction of more advantageous kinds of labour; and there is every reason to believe, that, with a competent capital, the business may be rendered so productive as to defray the expenses of conviction and maintenance of the prisoners. Calculations, however, founded on the statements of the past year, will not furnish adequate means of judging with certainty of the future profits which may be made to arise from the labour of the convicts.

" That the number of convicts has increased since the erection of the State Prison, is evident. But to infer from that fact, that the new and milder scheme of punishment has been less efficacious in preventing crimes than the old and sanguinary system, would be a most partial and erroneous conclusion. The *true*

---

* Large quantities of shoes have heretofore been brought from New Jersey and the Eastern States, and sold in New York.

6*

causes of this increase of crimes are the rapid growth of our population and wealth ; the consequent luxury and corruption of, manners, particularly in the capital of the state; and the great number of indigent and vicious emigrants from Europe and the West Indies, driven hither by the disordered and distressful condition of their native countries, or to escape the vengeance of the laws.

"More than *three fourths* of the whole number of crimes are committed in the city of New York.   Its population has almost doubled in ten years, and the increase of its trade and wealth is unequalled in the history of commercial states.   It is certain also, that under the present system of punishment, a much less number of offenders escape conviction.   Individuals do not, from a sense of the terrible consequences to the party, refuse to prosecute; nor juries, from motives of compassion, forbear to convict the guilty.   This is a most salutary consequence of the melioration of our penal laws.

" The corruption of morals engenders those crimes which pollute society, and undermine the security of life and property.   It is the duty of government to begin at the source, and to endeavour, by every rational and practicable expedient, to prevent crimes, rather than to apply the painful and uncertain remedy of punishment to evils grown formidable by negligence.   It is in vain, under the best devised plan of punishment, to expect that crimes should be diminished or exterminated, if laws are not framed to check the progress of vice, and to arrest the first steps of guilt.

"It is well known, that the greater number of crimes originate in the irregular and vicious habits produced by intoxication, and by the idle, low, and dissipated practices encouraged in taverns and tippling-houses. There are few criminals whose gradual depravation cannot be traced to this source.   It is well ascertained, that in this city there are more than twelve hundred taverns or shops, where spirituous liquors are retailed in drams or in the form of grog. In eight or ten considerable streets, one fourth part of the whole number of houses are *taverns and groceries*, or, in other words, *dram-shops*. The number of taverns is unlimitited by law. By the city charter, the power of granting licenses is vested in the mayor, who is the sole judge of the propriety of granting them, or of their number. Thirty shillings are paid for each license, four fifths of which sum goes into the city treasury, and the residue to the mayor. While a revenue is derived to the corporation from these licenses, it is not to be expected that there will be much solicitude to lessen their number, or to examine minutely into the merits of the applicants for them. Some regulations ought to be adopted for the reformation of the police in this respect. Grocers ought to be strictly prohibited from retailing liquors in drams. The number of taverns ought to be greatly diminished. Licenses should not be granted but to persons who are recommended by five known and respectable citizens, and under much larger penalties than at present, to enforce their observance of the laws.* At present, the temptation to the indigent and labouring classes of the people to indulge in drink is so powerful, and the gratification so easy, at every turn of the street, that the greater number spend a large portion of their time and earnings in repeated indulgences of this depraved appetite, during the day, and return to their families in a state of partial or complete intoxication. The pernicious consequences of such habits, to the individual and to society, are too striking to need any elaborate description, to enforce the propriety of adopting every suitable means of legislative and municipal regulation, for their prevention.

"A further source of vice and criminality is to be found in the *horse-races* which regularly take place

---

* In the town of Boston there are *fifty* taverns, or persons, licensed to retail liquors in small quantities. Three or four times that number, one would imagine, would be more than sufficient for this city.

in New York and some of the neighbouring counties. These draw together crowds of people, who engage in wagering, all kinds of games of chance, and in debauchery, which produce habits that lead to the ruin of many, and drive numbers to the commission of crimes. Horse-races, billiard-tables, and all games of chance, ought to be strictly prohibited. *Baiting* of animals with dogs, and every species of amusement which may tend to harden the heart, and render the manners of the people ferocious, ought to be prevented by a well regulated police. Laws are made for the preservation of decency and order on the first day of the week; and it remains only to have them more faithfully executed. Perhaps there is no city of equal extent, where fewer crimes escape detection and punishment, or where greater order and tranquillity prevail. Too much praise cannot be bestowed on those to whom the peace and safety of our city is entrusted, for their unwearied attention and vigilance in the discharge of duties, the extent and importance of which are not generally understood, or fully estimated. But, notwithstanding the improved state of our police, and the care of our magistrates, every year furnishes new objects of attention, evils which demand additional remedies, and more powerful reasons for devising and applying them in the best and most effectual manner.

"Another object more immediately connected with the subject of this work, is the present mode of punishment for petty crimes. The only prison in this city for the punishment of those convicted of small thefts and other petty offences, is the *Bridewell*, part of which is also appropriated to the safe keeping of prisoners before their trial or conviction. At present, vagrants, disorderly persons, and convicts for petty offences, are confined in this prison; and are put into rooms together, without any discrimination, or regard to difference of character. No proper or adequate means are used to prevent profanity, intoxication, filth, or idleness. In this condition, corrupting and corrupted, their imprisonment, so far from tending to produce the amendment of the culprits, or to secure society against the effects of their future misconduct, serves, by the contagion of example and the exasperation of bad passions, to render them an hundred fold more vicious and untractable. It is, in truth, a *nursery* of criminals for the state prison. As a remedy for this defect in the penal system, it is suggested, that a building should be erected by the corporation, large enough to contain sixty cells, of the same dimensions as those in the state prison;—that the *police magistrates* should have power to try, in a summary way, and to sentence to solitary confinement in these cells, vagrants, drunkards, riotous and disorderly persons, &c. for a time not exceeding thirty days;—that the quarter sessions of the city should send persons convicted of assaults and batteries, petit larcenies, and such offences as are not aggravated or atrocious, for a time not exceeding sixty or ninety days. The convicts should be kept in these cells in perfect solitude, and on spare diet, in the manner practised in the state prison. Such a punishment, for sixty days, would be more severe and terrible, and tend more to the prevention of crimes, than confinement, for one or two years, to hard labour in the state prison. It would also tend more to the reformation of the offender himself. Detached from vicious companions, from temptation, and from all means of gratifying his depraved appetites, conscience would have time to awaken a sense of guilt and remorse for his past folly and misconduct.

Should a plan of such obvious utility be adopted and carried into execution, it would not then be necessary to send convicts to the state prison for a shorter period than three years. For every person once confined in the solitary cells, who should, after his release, commit a second offence, would deserve to be sentenced to hard labour for at least three years. Indeed, it might, with propriety, be left to the discretion of the court, in certain cases of second offences, to inflict the same punishment as in cases of grand larceny ; since it can hardly be supposed, that any material or lasting effect can be produced on a criminal, by the labour and discipline of a penitentiary house, in a shorter time than four or five years. And if he is incorrigible by means of solitude, temperance, and cleanliness, he will not merit, if he is guilty of a second offence, a punishment less severe than imprisonment for that length of time.

It is not requisite, here, to enter into the details of this plan of a county prison; which, if found, on experiment, to succeed in the city of New York, may be extended to Albany, and one or two other counties, where the increase of population, and the frequency of petty offences, may render it necessary.

Before concluding this *account*, it may be proper to make a few remarks, the result of some observation and experience, on a subject which may have an essential influence on the present scheme of punishments.

It has been observed by BECCARIA, whose opinions have the force of axioms in the science of penal law, that " as punishments become more mild, clemency and PARDON become less necessary ;"—that " clemency belongs to the legislator, and not to the executer of the laws : a virtue which ought to shine in the code, not in private judgments. To show mankind that crimes may be pardoned, or that punishment is not the necessary consequence, is to nourish the flattering hope of impunity."—" Let then the executer of the law be inexorable, but let the legislator be tender, indulgent, and humane."*

These principles, though just in theory, necessarily presuppose a perfect system of penal law, by which each punishment is with such exact justice apportioned to each crime, that no difference of circum-

* Dei Delitti e delle Pene, § 20.—A misura che le pene divengono più dolci, la clemenza ed il perdono diventano meno necessari, &c.

stances can arise in any case, which ought to vary the punishment prescribed for the particular offence. No code so perfect has yet been framed, and until such a one is promulgated, it is necessary that the power of pardoning should reside somewhere, to prevent that injustice in particular cases which the legislator did not foresee, or could not avoid. By our constitution, this power is confided to the governor, the chief executive magistrate.*

"And under the present penal laws, except in those cases where the punishment of death still remains, the power of pardoning may be exercised without violating the principle advanced by the philosopher of Milan. It may be asserted, that, in the deliberate and impartial manner in which justice is administered in our courts, it is scarcely possible that any man can be *presented* by a grand jury, tried and convicted by a petit jury of twelve men, in the presence of the court and the world, without a degree of guilt deserving of some punishment. Imprisonment for a short period, under the mild and humane regulations of the state prison, cannot, in cases the most favourable to the prisoners, be deemed unjust. It may be laid down, then, as a general principle, that no person, convicted of a crime, and sentenced to imprisonment, ought to be pardoned, until he has suffered a punishment proportioned to the degree of his guilt, or at least so much as may satisfy the community he has injured. Under the guidance of this principle, it is believed, that the power of pardoning may be made conducive to a more perfect dispensation of justice, and subservient to the plan of reformation intended by a penitentiary prison. It will not be thought useless to endeavour to fix some general rules for the exercise of a power, which, if arbitrary and capricious, may produce consequences neither

---

* In cases of treason and murder, the governor cannot pardon, but may reprieve the convict until the next meeting of the legislature, who may pardon if they think fit.

foreseen nor intended; but, if exerted with sound discretion, so far from weakening the laws, will strengthen their operation.

"1. Where the punishment is fixed by law to a crime of a general legal description, comprehending a great variety of different acts, which must, from the course of human conduct, be accompanied with evidence of greater or less depravity; there, this attribute of the chief executive magistrate seems necessary, to remedy the imperfection of the general law, and to render the punishment more equitably proportioned to the guilt of the offender; since, from the inevitable want of foresight in the legislature, of the circumstances of each case, it could not be so predetermined .by them. Thus, *forgery* and counterfeiting, as well as passing money, knowing the same to be forged or counterfeit, punished by imprisonment for life, is a crime, the objects of which are endlessly diversified, comprehending acts of different degrees of turpitude.*

"2. Where the law has only defined a limit in the time of imprisonment, leaving it to the discretion of the judge to fix the duration of punishment within that limit, according to the circumstances of each case; there, it may be generally said, that the executive ought not to interpose, unless when the discretion of the court has been manifestly exercised under some misapprehension, or where circumstances, favourable to the convict, come to light after trial, of which he could not avail himself at the time, but had they been known, ought to have prevented or lessened his punishment.

"3. Unequivocal evidence of reformation in a convict, after his imprisonment; to ascertain which, as

* It may be fairly questioned, whether this and some other crimes are not improperly punished by imprisonment for life. If the sentence did not exceed a certain number of years, it would be in the power of the court to apply the punishment in a manner more justly proportioned to the offence: there would then be rarely, if ever, any occasion for the executive to remit the sentence. Most of the governments of Europe, excepting England, have, in circumstances of society and manners far less favourable than those of this country, gone farther in the melioration of their penal laws; and the punishment of death is gradually disappearing from their codes.

well as the propriety and safety of discharging a
convict before the expiration of his term of punishment, the judgment of the inspectors of the prison,
from their situation, may be of essential importance.
Indeed, this precaution has been taken by the late
and present governor of the state, who have applied
for the requisite information to the inspectors, the
majority of whom have joined in a recommendation
for pardon, where they thought it clearly merited by
the convict.   Previous to such recommendation, however, the inspectors think it their duty to inquire,—
whether the prisoner was convicted by clear and
undoubted testimony ; which may be ascertained by
the report of the judge before whom he was tried ;—
whether the circumstances attending the commission
of the crime denote a greater or less degree of depravity ;—whether the prisoner has already suffered a
punishment sufficient to satisfy society, and to afford
a reasonable ground to believe that his release will
not diminish the dread of future punishment in him,
or inspire the hope of impunity in others ;—whether,
while in prison, he has conducted himself with uniform decency, industry, and sobriety, and has never
attempted to violate any of its regulations ;—and,
lastly, whether, from what is known of his temper,
character, and deportment, it is probable, that if restored to society, he will become a peaceable, honest, and
industrious citizen.   These inquiries ought to be
satisfactorily answered in favour of the convict,
before he is recommended for pardon ; for it is not a
common or ordinary course of good conduct and industry, but a pre-eminent and unexceptionable behaviour,
that should entitle a prisoner to this grace.   A convict
radically and incurably depraved, in hope of gaining
favour, may, for a season, so far disguise his genuine
character, as to deceive his keepers and inspectors.
Sufficient time should be allowed to discover his real
disposition, which, on some occasion, at an unguarded
moment, will show itself.   In short, pardon ought
9

never to be granted from the momentary impulse of compassion, the indulgence of which may be gratifying to the individual, but as regulated by no fixed principle, must be injurious to the public; nor ought it be to granted, merely at the instance of friends or relations, or from considerations of family, but from the clear and unbiassed dictates of justice and humanity, and in such a manner that the community may be satisfied that the influence of the law is not impaired, nor its severity relaxed, without sufficient reason.

" No man who enters the prison with vicious habits, can be reasonably expected to be divested of them in less than four or five years; and it would greatly injure the penitentiary system, to pardon any prisoner before the expiration of that time, unless in extraordinary cases, which may possibly, but very rarely, happen. When sentenced to imprisonment for life, no person ought to be released, until after seven years confinement. If, under the circumstances which have been mentioned, and on principles here stated, pardons are sometimes granted, instead of counteracting the force of the law, they may be made to harmonize with, and support the general scheme of punishments so widely adopted. Its success must, in a great measure, depend on the wisdom of the regulations devised for the internal management of the prison, and on the prudence, disinterested attention, and perseverance of those to whom that management is entrusted.

" To exhibit a simple and faithful account of those regulations, and to furnish such useful hints as the writer, from his own experience, and the suggestions of others, could impart, is the purpose of the preceding pages. He is sensible that the plan of interior regulation is far from being perfect; but every year will add to its improvement. For, besides relieving the counties from the great burden of keeping convicts, and diminishing the chances of escape, by bringing them all into one prison, under a more vigilant inspection, the establishment of a state prison presents the best opportunity, by the magnitude and liberality of its plan, for the formation of a well-digested scheme of internal management and economy, and the full execution of the only just and beneficent system yet devised for the punishment and correction of criminals. The New York state prison will furnish a model for others, which the increase of population and growth of luxury may render necessary in the distant parts of this extensive country.* And, whatever may be the future condition of mankind, this institution will reflect lasting honour on the state; become a durable monument of the wisdom, justice, and humanity of its legislators, more glorious than the most splendid achievements of conquerors or kings; and be remembered when the magnificent structures of folly and pride, with their founders, are alike exterminated and forgotten."

This extract concentrates much that has been said by seer or sage on this subject since that date. He goes on to demonstrate what can be done by care and sagacity in the great work of reform and economy, and shows that the labours of the convicts almost supported themselves, and that the State was only charged five thousand dollars, and the salaries of the officers and keepers of the prison.

Dissensions soon arose, not among the superintendents of the prison, but amongst the rulers of the state. The council of appointment changed the whole board, and brought into office those who were wholly ignorant of the least of their duties. The funds they were entrusted with were badly spent, and all the land-marks of economy and system swept away. There were two years of returning reason, in Mr. Eddy's opinion, when Mr. William Torry acted as agent. This good man attempted to bring back the laws and customs of the establishment to

* Similar prisons are now established in New Jersey, Virginia, Massachusetts, Carolina, New Hampshire, Vermont, District of Columbia, &c.
EDITOR.

their pristine course, but he, after two years service, ceased to act in the cause.

Soon after the state prison was built in the city of New-York, Mr. Eddy began to think that if he had not committed an error in his plan, it certainly was susceptible of improvement. He found, from careful observation, that several confined in a cell corrupted each other, for each one told to his companions his career of vice, and all joined by sympathetic villany to keep each other in countenance. This, to the eye of the shrewd philanthropist was not long conceal- ed; and like a man of moral intrepidity, he avowed his error and condemned it. There can be no doubt but this single-cell plan now in use, was conceived and made known to the public by Mr. Eddy, before it was thought of either in this country, or in Europe, by any other person. In March, 1802, he visited Al- bany, solely for the purpose of prevailing upon the Legislature to pass a bill for erecting a prison in the city and county of New-York, and by degrees to ex- tend the plan to other districts in the state, which prison was to contain solitary cells. These prisons were to be used for all those who had committed minor crimes, and no one was to be sent to the state prison for a less term than three years. Into the solitary cells in these, the prisoner was to be confined according to his crime. So situated, he would have time to reflect upon his past conduct, and to begin the work of reformation. A bill was passed for this purpose, but by making it optional with the city and county, instead of being imperative, the plan was not carried into effect, notwithstanding every exertion of Mr. Eddy and his friends, in urging it upon the corporation. One committee after another took it into consideration, and seemed highly pleased with the plan, being convinced that it would be a means of preventing crime, yet they did not comply with the requisition. Mr. Eddy was not to be dis- couraged by the failure. He mentioned his plan in a letter to his friend Patrick Colquhoun, Esq. of London, one of the great moral reformers of the day, who highly approved of it, and handed Mr. Eddy's communication to Lord Sidmouth, then Minister for the Home Department, who, as well as Mr. Colquhoun, gave his decided approbation to the plan, and wished it should be introduced into England; and this was done by the London Society for improving Prison Discipline, and one or two prisons were soon after built upon this plan, one near London, containing six or seven hundred cells. A prison was also built at Pittsburgh, in Pennsylvania, upon this construction, containing from five to six hundred cells. When the Auburn state prison was erected, Mr. Eddy urged them to have the buildings wholly divided into cells, seven by nine feet each, but most of the commissioners were afraid to try the experiment fully, but did it only in part, and this change from the old plan was made from their confidence in the judgment of the adviser.

In 1824, Messrs. Tibbits, Allen, and Hopkins, were appointed by the legislature of New-York, to examine and report on certain questions relating to the state prisons; the result of their labours was a confirmation of the system that Mr. Eddy had recommended twenty-two years before. These commissioners, on entering on their inquiries, issued a circular, which was answered by several gentlemen, and amongst them, by Mr. Eddy. Notwithstanding the fact, that loose habits of doing business, and inattention to the proper methods of reformation, united to the expense of the experiment, the public had, in a good degree, become tired of the penitentiary system, and it was thought by many, that it would be abandoned altogether; yet Mr. Eddy adhered to his previous opinion, and returned the following answer.

7*

To GEORGE TIBBITS, STEPHEN ALLEN, *and* SAMUEL
M. HOPKINS, Esquires, *Commissioners appointed by
the Legislature to examine and report on certain
questions relating to the State Prisons.*

RESPECTED FRIENDS,—

I received your circular letter, containing a number
of queries, to which you request distinct replies.

First—"Is the present system established in the
New-York prison, a real system of punishment? Are
the convicts, in general, less comfortable than they
would be if at liberty?

Answer—I beg leave to state that, in my opinion,
the system established in the New-York State Prison
is not a real system of punishment calculated to prevent crimes.

Undoubtedly convicts are, in general, less comfortable than they would be if at liberty.

Second—"Have you ever known any satisfactory
instances of reformation produced by the present, or
any prison discipline? And, if so, please to state the
cases particularly, so far as may be proper?"

Answer—The general habits of intemperance previous to the confinement of convicts, and their extreme attachment to the use of ardent spirits, has
scarcely, in any instance, been cured even by a long
imprisonment; and their minds, owing to a number
of them being together during the night in one room,
have been so corrupted, that experience has proved,
that reformation has rarely taken place. During
several years that I served as an inspector of our
state prison, I only recollect two cases of complete
reformation. One of these has resided many years
in a neighbouring government, the other, in this
state; both are, at this time, men of considerable property, much respected and well esteemed. It is not
known to their present friends and neighbours, that
they ever were under confinement. Each of them

were four years in our state prison, and, on account of orderly conduct and good behaviour, pardoned.

Third—"Has there been sufficient experience of solitary confinement, to enable you to answer the same question in relation to that mode of punishment? And so far as your experience or observation may extend, please to state the result?"

Answer—There has been no experience in the state prison of New-York, that would serve to ascertain how far *continual* solitary confinement may eventually produce reformation; recourse has only been had to it, as a temporary punishment for bad conduct in the prison—in this way it has produced good effects, and has generally been the means of enforcing cleanliness, preserving order, and good behaviour, even among the most hardened convicts.

When I was a member of the Board of Inspectors, by-laws were enacted, which declared, that all conversation, (except such as might be necessary whilst at work,) want of cleanliness, whistling,'attempting to sing, &c., were offences against the laws of the prison, and should meet with *immediate* punishment, by confinement in a solitary cell on bread and water, from one to three days, or longer, according to the nature of the offence. By a faithful and rigid execution of these laws, the quiet and order of this prison was, with some exceptions, perfectly preserved; and, as regarded neatness and extreme cleanliness, no prison in the world could surpass it.

Fourth—"If you shall be of opinion that the present, or any system of prison discipline, may be made to produce material and permanent reformation in any large proportion of cases, then be pleased to state how, and in what way, in your opinion, it becomes operative towards that end? What are the circumstances in the system which will tend to change the character of the convict, and how do they, or will they, operate? What can be done to make them more effectual?

Answer—The subjoined general remarks, will serve as a reply to this query.

Fifth—"Can you suggest any means by which the compulsory labour of convicts, can be made to cover the expense of supporting and guarding them? or any, by which the labour of the convicts of this prison, can be made more productive than at present?"

Answer—I beg to make the same reference, as a reply to this query.

Sixth—"Can you suggest any means by which the expense may be diminished, and how? Can the guard be dispensed with? Can the rations be lessened with propriety, or made cheaper?"

Answer—If the prison was rightly constructed, no military guard would be wanted; but, I apprehend the expenses of the prison in this city cannot be diminished, unless the plan and construction of it should be completely altered. Not being acquainted with the quality and amount of the rations at present served to the convicts, it is impossible for me to say how far they may, with propriety, be lessened, or made cheaper.

Seventh—"Please to state briefly your views of the most effectual system for the protection of society against crimes; and therein note such alterations, if any, as you would suggest, in the present system of management?"

Answer—My views as to the most effectual means for protecting society against crimes, will appear in the subsequent remarks.

General Remarks.

Many reasons might be offered, why the success of the Penitentiary System in this state has not been equal to the expectations of its early patrons, and of the public at large.

1st. The inspectors have generally been changed with every change of our political rulers; hence, men inadequate to the task, were frequently appointed to fill the important office of inspectors. These frequent changes have produced a very-great increase of expenses, and materially tended to prevent suitable and important improvements in the general system.

2d. The number of pardons that have been granted, has been attended with most serious injury, and very much prevented the good effects that the system might otherwise have produced. Pardon should be granted only on the discovery of facts unknown at the trial, which, if known, would probably have produced an acquittal. In fact, it may be truly said, that under a mild system, pardons materially contribute to the increase of crimes.

3d. In the New-York prison, the rooms lodge each about twenty convicts, and owing to so many being brought together every night, they corrupt each other, and thus prevent complete order in the prison, and all chance of reformation is effectually defeated; the elder criminals serve as teachers to the younger, and prepare them for the commission of greater crimes than those for which they have been convicted. Thus the New-York prison, in place of answering the purpose for which the convicts are confined, viz. their reformation, becomes a nursery and seminary of vice.

4th. The authority given to the inspectors to inflict corporal punishment for violating the laws of the prison, respecting good order, &c. has no doubt had a very injurious effect, for, it is directly opposite to the mild system that ought to prevail in a penitentiary. It must tend to harden the minds of the convicts, and materially lessen the chances of reformation. To adopt such a mode of punishment, is extremely unwise, because the more mild plan of occasional confinement in solitary cells on bread and water, has been proved by experience, effectually to answer the most important purposes of strict and rigid discipline. The reasons above assigned are, in my opinion, sufficient to show why the Penitentiary

L

System has failed to answer, fully, the end and purposes for which it was intended, particularly as it regards reformation.

I now shall respectfully offer for the consideration of the commissioners, my views of the most effectual system for the protection of society against crimes, and the most certain means to promote the reformation of convicts.

First. The great preventive of offences is doubtless an early attention to moral and religious instruction, and thus to fortify the infant mind with good principles. The observation made by John Locke, is remarkably appropriate and excellent:—"I think, I may say, that, of all the men we meet with, nine parts of ten, are what they are, good or evil, useful or not, by their education." That a careful attention to educate the children of parents in low circumstances throughout the State, would go far towards the prevention of crimes, is demonstrated by the fact, that in consequence of a diligent search being made by a committee of the New-York Free School Society, it was ascertained that but one boy of those who had received their education in the schools of that institution, had been convicted of a petty crime, although several hundreds who had not been at the Free Schools, had been tried at the Quarter Sessions, and been committed to the City Penitentiary, for vagrancy and various other offences. We are told by high authority—"Train up a child in the way he should go, and when he is old, he will not depart from it."

The great error of all governments has been, not affording instruction to the lower class of society, and inflicting punishments often very disproportionate to offences. It is evident, that civilization has not effected all the moral changes and improvements that can be produced in the constitution of human society, nor have laws and government been carried to the utmost limits of perfection. It is, therefore, highly incumbent for us to cherish the firm and unshaken conviction, that it is not beyond the bounds of human effort to devise a system, that will combine in its tendency, the *prevention* of crimes, and the reformation of convicts. Let us then ask any sagacious observer of human nature, what should be the incipient step in order to protect society against crime. The answer is plain. To afford them a common school education, and fasten on their minds a knowledge of their duties towards God, and carefully instruct them by means of the Holy Scriptures, in the principles of the Christian religion. Let, then, the present laws for common schools be cherished and improved, in such manner as will oblige parents of the poorer classes in society, to send their children to some one of the common schools, to be instructed in reading, writing, and arithmetic, and in a knowledge of the Scriptures.

By a legislative act, rules should be prescribed for enforcing a strict regard to the perfect cleanliness of the persons of the children, to their moral conduct, to oblige the teacher to read at the opening of the school, daily, a chapter from a work entitled Scripture Lessons, which is, on many accounts, preferable to the Bible for the use of schools, as it contains the most important part of the Scriptures appertaining to virtue and good morals. This book has been translated into most of the languages of Europe, and is extensively used in the common schools in that quarter of the globe, and also in the United States. To make it the duty of all overseers of common schools, to employ such teachers only, as are men of suitable qualifications, sober and exemplary characters. Every inducement should be used to encourage parents (in every place where it is practicable) to send their children to school, as soon as they reach three years of age. This might be done, by making it the duty of overseers of each school, occasionally to visit the parents of the children, as has been done by the trustees of the New-York Free School Society. Although the latter have, at present, under their care, above 4000 children, who receive a gratuitous education at the schools under their charge; yet, notwithstanding their care and diligence in endeavouring to prevail on parents to send their children to school, it is believed that there are 8000 children in the city, who are brought up without the advantage of school learning. An inspector might be appointed, in the manner other officers of the state are appointed, who should be of a respectable character and talents, and be allowed a good salary; his duty should be to visit, once in each year, every common school throughout the state, and inquire into the condition of each school, the number of scholars; whether the laws of the state are duly complied with; the salary, name, general character, and qualifications of the teachers, and an account of all the receipts and expenditures; he should make his report annually, to the superintendent of common schools, who should be directed to present the same to the legislature.

Next to providing for the moral and religious education of children, by means of common schools throughout the state, it would be productive of incalculable advantage, to erect a suitable prison, solely for the confinement of boys under sixteen years of age, considered as vagrants, or guilty of petty thefts, or other minor offences: it is believed that there are but few amongst the most guilty of this description of juvenile delinquents, who may not, by proper discipline, be subdued and reclaimed, by the establishment of a well-regulated prison for criminal youth. In Massachusetts, there is a prison for young convicts in each county. A number of the citizens of New-York, conceiving the great benefit that would be derived, by erecting a suitable building for the reception of such objects as has been described, have associated for the purpose, and have been incorporated by the name of "The Society for the Reformation of Juvenile Offenders in the city of New-York." This establishment is in so great a state of forwardness as to be nearly ready for the reception of suitable objects. It is to be denominated the House of Refuge, and youth, not exceeding sixteen or seventeen years of age, are to be committed there by the criminal courts, instead of being sent to the City Penitentiary, or State Prison, as has heretofore been the practice. At night they are to lodge in separate cells, and during the day, to be employed in some useful labour; they are to be instructed in reading, writing, and arithmetic. The utmost degree of cleanliness is to be strictly observed, throughout every part of the building; and in the persons of the boys, good morals and decent behaviour, are to be rigidly maintained; the careful and frequent reading of the Holy Scriptures is to be enforced. The trustees are empowered to bind them as apprentices, to the sea-service, to a trade, or to farmers. A similar establishment might be formed at Albany, to serve for Troy and other towns on the North River, and the state might be divided into convenient districts, and one establishment of this nature erected in each district.

A distinct and separate building should be erected on the premises attached to the state prison, for the confinement of adults, males and females, such as common drunkards, prostitutes, those who keep houses of ill fame, or gambling-houses, or for those guilty of small petty thefts, or vagrants. This prison should be divided into cells about the size of six feet by four.

A single magistrate should be vested with power to commit persons to this prison from three to thirty days. Each prisoner should be obliged to wash his face and hands every morning. Rigid care should be taken to have each cell well ventilated, and kept perfectly clean ; and this care should be extended, as far as possible, to their clothes and personal appearance. He should be confined in a separate cell, and fed only on bread and water, have no work, and no bed, except a single blanket. The prisoners should be allowed

8

no tobacco, and should be deprived of every kind of amusement; they should be permitted to have no books, except the Bible, and perhaps it might be most beneficial that that only be allowed them, when, in the judgment of the keeper, their minds appeared to be in a disposition to read it with profit. No person should be permitted to converse with any prisoner, except the keeper, or those appointed to have the superintendence of the prison, or a magistrate. If the prisoner be guilty of a second offence, he should be tried for it, and receive such punishment as the court, in their discretion, shall award him, either to be re-committed, or sentenced to the state prison.

The plan of confining the above description of minor offenders in solitude *without employment* from three to thirty days, cannot fail, frequently, of having the most beneficial effect, as the prisoner will be then forced to reflect on his past life. It may also tend to convince the convict that his punishment is just; and, unless this effect be produced on the mind of the prisoner, unless he be led to believe that his own welfare, as well as the public good, is consulted in his punishment, it will be in vain to expect reformation; but, on the contrary, to confine a man in a solitary cell for months, or years, is a punishment which may appear to the criminal unnecessarily harsh and unjust, hardens his temper, and excites those feelings of enmity towards his species, that the thought of doing them an injury by the commission of new crimes is gratifying to him.

If it should be urged that solitary confinement will be expensive, it may be answered, that any expense which it can possibly occasion, should be considered as nothing in comparison to the accomplishment of the great object which it concerns. And, besides, in proportion as crimes are lessened or decreased, or as they are summarily punished, the expenses of the state, in relation to the apprehension, detention, and prosecution of criminals, are diminished.

There is, as it appears to me, a moral and religious view of this subject, which should not be without its influence. We are too apt to forget while we are providing for the protection of persons and property by passing laws for the punishment of crimes, that the human beings who may become obnoxious to these laws, have also their claims upon us. If it be admitted that the infliction of solitude, from three to sixty days, for minor offences, will, while it suppresses criminality in an equal degree with any other mode of punishment, also tend to reform the offender more than any other course would do, we are bound by every feeling of humanity, and by all the precepts of the christian religion, to adopt that course which may raise a fellow-creature from degradation, fit him for usefulness in this life, and prepare him for that which is to come.

State Prisons, or Penitentiaries.—Great inconvenience, and apparent injustice, is frequently produced, in making the distinction of the punishment of those guilty of petty larceny, and those guilty of grand larceny:—a person charged with committing the *former*, is at present liable to be sentenced to the county prisons, at hard labour, for a term not exceeding three years; and if guilty of the *latter*, for a term not less than three years, or not exceeding fourteen years. To steal an article of the value of twenty-five dollars, or less, is deemed petty larceny; and, if the value of the article stolen exceeds twenty-five dollars, it is termed grand larceny. So that the stealing of a watch, valued at twenty-five dollars, is deemed petty larceny, but if a watch, valued at twenty-six dollars, grand larceny. Now, the moral turpitude being the same, it is therefore certainly absurd to make any difference in the punishment.

Although the moral turpitude of committing an offence, in law deemed *petty* larceny, may frequently be the same as that denominated *grand* larceny, I do not mean to contend that there should be no line of distinction to mark the difference between them; but considering that, in order to graduate the punishment as near as possible to the nature of the offence, much must necessarily be left to the discretion of the court, I would respectfully suggest the propriety of an alteration in our penal code, so as that petty larceny, should consist in stealing articles not exceeding the value of one hundred dollars. If this were done, the convict might be sentenced to a longer or shorter confinement, *according to his general character*, and other circumstances, and *not according to the value of the goods stolen*. An *old* offender stealing goods to the value of ten dollars, should certainly, in most cases, be punished with more severity than a *young* offender stealing to the value of *fifty* dollars. Unless there be a careful and due discrimination of character, in fixing duration of punishment, courts may frequently commit extreme and barefaced injustice. It is equally as sound a maxim in jurisprudence as in morals, "that he who punishes another for offending against justice, should himself be just."

The state prison in this city is so badly contrived, that it never can be successfully used as a Penitentiary; it should be sold, and a new one erected a few miles from the city, constructed on the same plan as the state prison at Auburn, to have separate cells, so that the prisoners might lodge separately. Every cell should be properly ventilated by means of a small aperture next the ceiling, of three inches diameter.

The prisoners ought to be kept constantly employed at such work as the overseers of the prison should think most suitable. To purchase raw materials to be worked up in the prison, has frequently been attended with loss, owing to want of skill in purchasing, and bad management in disposing of manufactured articles to the best advantage. The most preferable plan would be, to make contracts for the labour of the convicts, with shoe makers, stone-cutters, &c. &c. the contractors furnishing the raw materials; but no contractor should be allowed to enter the prison, or to have any intercourse whatever with the convicts. The prisoners might safely be employed during the day in the yards, and effectually prevented from all improper intercourse or conversation with each other, provided the prison discipline, before recommended in the answer to the third query, be rigidly enforced. The cells should not be used, except to confine a convict on a low diet, when he violates any by-law of the prison. The by-laws relating to the government of the convicts, such as preserving the greatest degree of cleanliness in the persons, and in the rooms, halls, kitchen, and throughout every part of the prison, &c. should be very minutely detailed, printed and fixed in different parts of the prison, and no offence against those rules should ever escape being punished, under any pretence whatever.

The confinement of criminals in a solitary cell during the whole time of their sentence, say, from one to five years, or more, appears to be unnecessarily severe. Suppose the term of his punishment to be three years, and that he should have some kind of daily employment, yet it appears to me, that the project is cruel and unjust, as it is highly probable the health of the convict would be impaired if not destroyed, and in many cases it would produce insanity. We well know, that cruel and severe punishment has never proved sufficient to deter persons from perpetrating crimes; and to confine a man for years in a solitary cell, will be more likely to harden his mind, and brutalize his disposition, than to produce his reformation. I am very willing to admit, that the observations I have made, may not be correct in every instance, as cases may occur, that will serve to prove, that a man may be confined in solitude for several years without injury to his health, and also that reformation has effected its perfect work; but I am well assured that such instances would very seldom occur.

M   8*

It is acknowledged by all, who have reflected on the best means of establishing a penitentiary system, "most likely to protect society against crimes," that the construction of the building should be such, as to prevent the convicts from improper intercourse with each other; and that it is impossible this important end can be attained, unless each be at night lodged separately in a cell. It is in vain to expect any beneficial effects under the best regulations that can be devised, if the prison admit a number of prisoners to lodge in one room.

During the day they may be employed with safety in the yards, under the charge of keepers, and by a rigid discipline, all improper intercourse prevented; this has been fully demonstrated by my own experience as an inspector, during the first four years after the state prison in this city was erected. It is only necessary to punish any offender the moment he commits an offence, by confinement in a solitary cell on bread and water. No person should be allowed to visit the prison, unless accompanied by a magistrate or one of the inspectors. In the foregoing part of this communication, I have stated my sentiments, on the indispensable necessity of preserving the most perfect degree of cleanliness, in the person of the prisoners, and throughout the prison, as it will produce the best moral effects in the preservation of order, and aid materially in the reformation of the convicts.

No undue severity should be exercised towards prisoners. The best general system of government and management is by mild treatment.

The plan of fixing tasks, or agreeing to make allowance for extra work performed by convicts, ought not to be adopted; it is bad policy, as it tends to lessen too much the principle of punishment. It would be much better to give the convict, when discharged on the expiration of his sentence, a small sum to serve him till he can get into a situation to earn something by his own industry, and if he be inclined to endeavour to go to work, from three to five dollars will be sufficient to give him, and if he has no disposition to seek for employment, to give him even a small sum would most likely prove an injury. If he has not learned any regular trade, he can soon get employment on a farm or in the city as a labourer. In England the state of things is widely different to what it is in this country, and it may there be more necessary, that convicts during their confinement should learn some trade.

A school in the evening should be established, and on the First day of the week they should be assembled for the purpose of Divine Worship, and a chapter in the Bible should be read to them every morning or evening.

In selecting inspectors, care should be taken that they are highly respectable men, capable of performing the duties of their office, and who would act solely from benevolent motives, with a religious view to benefit their fellow creatures. Much would depend on their dispositions and exertions, and on their occasionally giving to the convicts suitable religious and moral advice. "Gradual changes may be effected even in the worst of men, by a steady, firm, and persevering attention to correct their acquired bad habits." Those who assert (and there are many respectable men who make the assertion) that to attempt to reform convicts, by exercising kind and conciliatory means, is chimerical and absurd, certainly do not reflect, that to advise and admonish the most profligate and abandoned, is the usual practice of life, and is solemnly enjoined by the precepts of the Founder of our holy religion. We ought not to refrain from using such means as may be in our power, to produce an amendment and change in the dispositions of convicts, from an apprehension that a *complete* reformation cannot be expected. The employments that would be the most suitable for the prisoners, ought to be left to the discretion of the inspectors, and also the sole power to appoint the keeper, agent, and other officers, and to remove them in case of improper conduct, or want of sufficient qualifications to discharge their respective duties.

I do not approve of dividing the prisoners into different classes, and distinguishing each class by different coloured clothing; and, if the plan I have proposed be adopted, of having separate prisons for the different descriptions of convicts, this plan of classification in any one prison will be useless, except having a separate yard for those committed for second offences.

The different prisons I have proposed, might be built adjoining each other, but to have separate yards. The whole might be under the same board of inspectors.

Recapitulation of my views of the most effectual system for the protection of society against crimes:

1. A careful attention to early education, by amending our laws, so that every poor family in the state should partake of the benefit afforded by our Common Schools.

2. To establish a House of Refuge for Juvenile Delinquents.

3. To erect in each county a prison to contain a number of cells, to receive common drunkards, prostitutes, keepers of houses of ill fame, for gambling, or those guilty of petty thefts, or vagrants, to be committed by a single magistrate, and confined from three to thirty days, and kept on low diet without any employment.

4. Two State Prisons or Penitentiaries, properly constructed, and subject to suitable regulations, for persons convicted of grand larceny, and crimes of a higher grade.

I am, with great respect and esteem,
Your assured friend,
THOMAS EDDY.

New York, 1st month, 7th, 1825.

Mr. Eddy answered these inquiries, and others in different walks of life took up the pen. Among them was Cadwallader D. Colden, Esq., who wrote as a lawyer, and a man of philanthropy and experience, and his work is valuable to all who make the subject a matter of inquiry. That bold and original thinker, Doctor Charles Caldwell, of Transylvania University, also wrote upon state prison discipline, and in a striking manner connected the subject with his favourite science, phrenology. Dr. Caldwell's book should be read to set people a thinking, for his singularity is not more striking than his bold and clear logic. We may differ from him in many things, but we feel indebted to a man who teaches us to reason.

Mr. Eddy lived to see his state prison discipline carried into effect in several States of the Union, which was acknowledged to be the greatest improvement of the age. Since his death, this system has received the approbation of the enlightened philosopher, Dr. Leiber, in the Encyclopædia Americana, under the article Prison Discipline, who says, referring to Allen, Tibbits, and Hopkins, "The result of the wise labours of these excellent men was the perfecting of a scheme of prison discipline, which had been begun partially at Auburn, and which is substantially the model on which the reforms attempted in most of the other States have been conducted. It consists, principally, of the solitary confinement of the convicts during the night, and the time of taking their meals; of labour during the day; and of silence at all times, except for the purposes of communication with their keepers: they are never allowed to address each other, not even by signs or looks. The strictest supervision is, of course, necessary, to secure uninterrupted and industrious labour, and to prevent the evil communications which would otherwise abound. The advantages of this system are, that it affords an opportunity alternately for silent and solitary reflection, for the salutary reflection of the mind upon itself; and for that mental activity upon other objects, and that relaxation from the severer task of thinking, which is at once necessary to preserve the healthy state of the mind and body, and to give efficacy to the meditation which is thus encouraged. But this alternation of labour and reflection is not the only, nor, perhaps, the greatest advantage of the plan. The unaided thoughts of the corrupt and hardened might recur to topics which would be any thing but salutary; but, in the silence and darkness of night, the voice of religious instruction is heard; and, if any circumstances can be imagined, calculated to impress the warnings, the encouragements, the threats, or the hopes of religion upon the mind, it must surely be those of the convict in his cell, where he is unseen and unheard, and where nothing can reach him but the voice which must come to him, as it were, from another world, telling him of things which, perhaps, never before entered into his mind; telling him of God, of eternity, of future reward and future punishment, of suffering far greater than the mere physical endurances of the present life, and of joy infinitely beyond the pleasures he may have experienced. These instructions frequently discover to the guilty tenant of the cell, what seems often not to have occurred to him, the simple fact, that he has a spiritual nature; that he is not the mere animal which his habits and hitherto uncontrolled propensities would indicate; and this is a discovery which alone may, and does effect, a great change in a man's whole character. He feels that he is a being superior to what he had thought himself, and that he is regarded as one having higher powers than he had supposed. The first step in the path of improvement is a prodigious one; a new ambition is created, and the encouragement of it is the principal thing now needed. This encouragement it is part of the system to give. The spiritual guide of this outcast flock must study the character and previous cir-

cumstances of every individual ; he must adapt himself and his instructions to their wants ; he must
teach the ignorant, arouse the careless, touch, if it be
possible, the impenitent, lead the willing, and be "all
things to all men, if by any means he may save
some." To the morning and evening services of devotion, are to be added the more direct and elaborate
instructions of the Sabbath, and the no less important
influences which may be effected in private intercourse with the convict. The Sunday school may
communicate the most valuable information on many
subjects ; and every improper influence may be, and
ought to be, absolutely excluded. It is this system
of addressing the intellectual and moral qualities of
man, of treating the convict as a being of a compound
nature—both physical and spiritual—that constitutes
the peculiar merit of the prison discipline, which is
now about to be introduced. No new discovery has
been made, unless it be considered one that criminals
may sometimes be made susceptible of moral influences. It is only the adaptation of well known principles to a new class of subjects. It is merely carrying to the lowest, the most ignorant, and the most
degraded class, that plan of education which is nearly
universal among us, and which should be entirely so
every where. The exercise of mere force, which has
been so long considered the only means of punishment, is at length yielding to the rapidly strengthening conviction of the superior efficacy of moral
influence."

At the same time Mr. Eddy was labouring to change
the penal code of the state of New York, and establish his penitentiary system, his mind was deeply
engaged upon other charities. An Hospital had been
founded in the city of New York, by the munificence
of individuals, on this and on the other side of the
water, a few years before the commencement of the
revolutionary war ; but that momentous event changed the whole course of things in this country, and

the Hospital suffered with other institutions. On
the return of peace, this charity seemed still warm
with life, but was not reanimated until after the
adoption of the Federal constitution. This act,
which gave strength, vigour and reputation to the
nation, was soon followed by great exertions. In
less than two years after the constitution went into
operation, the hospital was open for the reception
of patients. The legislature had lent a helping hand;
but it was not until Mr. Eddy, in 1793, was elected
one of the governors of this institution, that great and
liberal things were done for it. At this time, the
Board met but once in three months; he proposed
that the Board should meet once a month. This
was agreed to, and new life was given to these
meetings by plans proposed by Mr. Eddy. There was
a field back of the Hospital of seven acres, which
might have been purchased for one hundred pounds
an acre, and he urged the Board to buy it without
delay, but in this he was, unfortunately for the institution, overruled; yet nothing abated his ardour in the
cause of this charity. The annual allowance from
the legislature to the hospital was five thousand dollars, and this was limited to four years. In 1795,
Mr. Eddy, being at Albany, held a communication
with that prince of patriotism and benevolence, Gen.
Schuyler.* He prevailed on him to introduce a bill in
the Senate, which passed into a law, giving the Hospital ten thousand dollars a year for four years.
The next year Mr. Eddy again visited Albany, and
procured the passage of a law adding twenty-five
hundred dollars a year to the former grant. In 1800,
Mr. Eddy repaired to Albany, and procured an extension of the grant for five years. Notwithstanding
this liberality, the governors could not extend their
plans according to their wishes, and they did the
best they could until 1806, when they again sent
their faithful representative with a petition, the

* See Appendix.

prayer of which was for an extension of these grants for fifty years, and it was allowed. The indefatigable philanthropist did not become wearied in his cause, for in 1810 he again succeeded in getting an additional sum of three thousand five hundred dollars for ten years, or during the pleasure of the legislature; at this time, the Hospital was in the receipt of sixteen thousand dollars a year. This last act of the Assembly was repealed in 1817, and the income from the State reduced to twelve thousand five hundred dollars.

Early in the year 1815, Mr. Eddy made a written communication to the Governors of the Hospital, which enforced the propriety of introducing an institution for lunatic patients, more extensive than had heretofore been in existence in this country. The communication is full of good sense without any pretensions; and, although all the sentiments it contains are now familiar to us, they were novel then to most of those who had paid attention to the subject of insanity. This communication is mentioned in the history of the hospital, and the proceedings had thereon.

An appeal was again made to the legislature for assistance, and Mr. Eddy was requested to proceed to Albany and present a memorial, but this he declined for various reasons. It is a painful and laborious task to attend a winter session of a deliberative body, and he thought he had done more than his share of this labour. No one can tell how irksome it is to talk with hundreds of persons, clothed with authority, often captious, sometimes suspecting selfishness, and generally impatient listeners, when caught in the lobbies or out of doors; and then it is natural for every man to feel an aversion to any one who often comes on errands of solicitation. To do much and offend but few, was the peculiar gift of Mr. Eddy. The Governors of the Hospital would not vote to relieve him from this duty, but particular-

N   9

ly evaded the subject by leaving it to Peter A. Jay, Esq. then a member of the legislature, a gentleman of talents and weight of character. Mr. Jay went to Albany, but after a while wrote to Mr. Eddy to come to his assistance. The appeal was made in such strong terms, that he could not resist it, and he set out for Albany, and with the exertions of Mr. Jay, an act was passed, giving ten thousand dollars a year for the support of the insane, and for erecting new buildings. This act was limited by the act " for the better support of the hospital," which granted twelve thousand five hundred dollars for fifty years. Probably many members had forgotten when the act would expire, and those who did remember the fact, did not choose to say any thing about it. Viewed in any light, it was a liberal donation for a noble purpose. Nearly eighty acres of land were purchased at Bloomingdale, and a fine building erected for the accommodation of the insane. The success of his exertions, and those of his coadjutors, gave Mr. Eddy the liveliest pleasure, which he took no pains to disguise. He always felt himself an instructor of those whose minds were sickly, and he believed that, though it was difficult, yet it was not impossible to

> —————— " Minister to a mind diseased ;
> Pluck from the memory a rooted sorrow ;
> Raze out the written troubles of the brain ;
> And, with some sweet oblivious antidote,
> Cleanse the stuff'd bosom of that perilous stuff,
> That weighs upon the heart."

The study of mental derangement is one of deep interest to the philanthropist. To mark insanity in all its various forms, to go back to the cause of its existence, whether moral, physical, or accidental, requires acuteness and constant observation. The wise and the kind feel assured that they carry with them many cures and a thousand anodynes for misery. Those who devote a life to doing good, in curing or soothing the maladies of the mind, improve

their own intellects, and at the same time are learning lessons for the government of their own passions,
and purifying their own affections. They find that
the furious maniac yields to gentle firmness, when
he would rave at severity ; that melancholy may be
banished by the voice of cheerfulness and kindness,
when it would grow deeper if attacked by boiste-
rous harshness; and that even demency may be
quickened into life and mental action by proper
moral sentiments. It is an acknowledged fact, that
those who have the care of the insane are generally
cheerful ; one cause of which may be, that they feel
conscious of being in the way of doing good, and the
effects of their exertions are constantly before them ;
and, perhaps, another is, that the same mind is unceas-
ingly dwelling upon the blessings it enjoys in its
sanity, and draws comparisons between itself, and
those unfortunate beings who are deprived of reason,
as we take a more elastic step when we pass a crip-
ple, who moves on slowly in his deformity and anguish, or as we look at the sun, or some bright object,
and see that the petitioner for street alms is blind.

The Indians within the United States have been
harassed, warred upon, driven from their primitive
abodes, and, at times, hunted down as beasts of the
forest. Sometimes they were sinned against, but
often sinning in the causes which produced this distress. They thought this whole continent their own,
and that they were sole proprietors of it. Their
ideas of national rights and of political economy
were not very extensive, but their patriotism and
courage will never be doubted by those acquainted
with their history. At times, they seemed to wish to
be friends; at other times, were vindictive and blood-
thirsty.

The Eastern Indians were among the fiercest on
the continent. King Philip is a noble instance of
sagacity and love of country ; and the Six Nations, so
well known in the history of New York, were brave,

and most generally faithful to their treaties. But it often happened, that when the philosopher was contemplating them as patriots and warriors, he heard of some of their massacres and conflagrations, and his resentment arose against them at their barbarous disposition. Or, he saw them through the medium of taste, and was disgusted with their filthy habits and wandering course of life. When Mr. Eddy began his career of active philanthropy, the Six Nations had been so far reduced as not to be feared, but rather to be pitied. Their case came within the view of the charities of his religious order, and he made himself acquainted with their situation, their habits, and character. In 1793, Mr. Eddy, with his friend, John Murray, junior, visited the Brothertown, Stockbridge, Oneida, and Onondaga Indians, to get more accurate information in regard to them, and see if some plan could not be devised to ameliorate their condition. At this time, the west was a wild ; Utica, now so considerable a place, then contained but three houses. From Utica they travelled on an Indian path to Cayuga lake, and attended the meeting for making a treaty, held by General Schuyler, and other commissioners, with the Indians, seven hundred of whom were present. Mr. Eddy, and his friend Murray, on their return, made so favourable a report to the "Yearly Meeting Committee for the improvement of the Indians," that for several years—and I never have heard that the Friends had relinquished their exertions in the cause—considerable sums were appropriated to instruct and civilize them. He was not very sanguine, in this charity, of doing much good, notwithstanding the great interest he took in the welfare of the Indians. He saw that their original character was every day changing, and that the whites, sometimes honestly, and by fair contract, but often improperly, were encroaching on their grounds : but there was another side to the question ; a race of industrious men, adorned with all the arts and sciences of civilization, was growing up and occupying a space for a village, where thousands were supported, that would not have furnishcd "room and verge enough" for a dozen aboriginal hunters, according to their notions of life. But, if such men as Mr. Eddy had been in the Council for Indian affairs, the tribes would have faded away, if that is their fate—and who can doubt it?—with less suffering and less repining than is now witnessed. His hospitable mansion was a wigwam to the travelling Indian, where he drank when thirsty and ate when hungry. IIe sometimes had a dozen Indians, men, women, and children, in the house at once. Among his Indian acquaintance, was the famous Red Jacket, of the Seneca tribe. This chief was a warrior and orator of high intellectual powers and commanding mien. His head was the admiration of the phrenologist, and his rifle was as unerring as death. This man exhibited all that was noble in the savage; he was brave, sagacious, and patriotic, but he yielded to the weakness of intemperance, and showed the worst as well as the best qualities of their fallen nature. His tribe once deposed him from power as a chief, for his imprudence; but he had energy of character enough to redeem himself, and regain his power in his tribe—a singular occurrence in savage or civil life. To Mr. Eddy, Red Jacket was a study, and so was Eddy to Red Jacket, for he, too, with all his fierceness, was a philanthropist and a philosopher. Since Mr. Eddy's death, the state of the Indians has excited much feeling in the community, but the time is rapidly approaching, when this subject will only be a bygone tale. In New England, there are a few remnants of several once powerful tribes, but they are mixed with the Africans, and have no importance in the community. Though some of their ancient territories are, in some instances, appropriated to their use, and the States act as guardians, in order that these shall not be taken from them. In New York, the Six Nations, once so powerful, are now

9*

fast declining, and in the Western States of Ohio, Kentucky, and Mississippi, they are nearly annihilated. Beyond the settlements, there are a few who have maintained their independence, but these soon will share the fate of other nations of aborigines on this continent. But, if we must come to these melancholy conclusions, we ought not to forget that there have been philanthropists who have struggled to save them, and to press upon them the arts, and teach them the value of civilization and Christianity. The following letters will show how much has been done.

New Stockbridge, Nov. 19*th,* 1795.

BROTHERS,

Our ears have been open to hear from you these many days, but have not heard a word. And we suppose you also have expected to hear our welfare, and have not heard one word.

Brothers—With pleasure we have retained the good counsels you given us when you were here our place. We have been endeavoured to follow the way you pointed out for us. Now we will also inform you that our nation at large enjoy their health ever since you left us. This, we acknowledge, is merely from the *good Spirit.* We are sorry to hear that many of our white brothers at New York, have been taken away by death. This, also, we believe, is by the will of the same *Spirit.*

Brothers—We believe that you have heard the childish conduct of our brethren, the Oneidas, with regard to their land affairs, therefore, 'tis needless that we should say any thing about it.

As we look upon you to be our true Friends, we write to you as such ; you are sincerely wished that our poor Nations should be build up so as to become civilized people ; we, also, have an earnest wish for the same.

We ever have endeavoured to promote the happiness of our Nation here, but our dependance is wholly on him who is able to do more for us than we can ask. Still, we believe, that in some respects he will not do any thing without our endeavours.

Brothers—By your good counsels, you have given us good encouragement to go on in the good way, and although we have been endeavoured to do what we have told you, but as we are new beginners we find ourselves to be as children who could not walk strait or go alone without little help by some Friend.

And we also find some real obstructions in the way which we can avoid if we can get some help. And as you are our Friends, we will open our minds freely unto you. Here we have upwards than sixty families who are not acquainted how to make cloth of no kind; it has been therefore necessary for each one to go out from the Town, at times, to seek some articles of clothing among the white traders; and the traders generally set up great price on their goods.

In this way of living, among so many families, have spend many many a days in one year. Besides all this, there are some Indians who, while they seeking where to purchase some necessary articles for their poor families, they have been overtaken by the strong Heroe, and robbed by him, and come home almost naked and starved.

Brothers—This is one obstruction on our way; in order to avoid it, we would ask your assistance. If you can find it in your minds so as to do it with ease to trust us few articles of clothing, that we may keep little store in our Town, that our people may not spend much of their time as they have done, and that the white traders may not take all the advantages on this respect as they always did. And the great Heroe (whose name is *Rum*) should not rob our Indians as he has done these many years. This means will fasten our Nation at one place, we the subscribers, engage to pay you at such a time as we may agree. If such thing can take place here, it would also great deal help our brethren, the Oneidas and Tuscaroras.   This, Brothers, is our request—and we leave it to your consideration—and desire to hear your voices as soon as you can find it convenient to send answer.   This is all what we have to say.

From your friends,

> HENDRICK AUPAUMUT,
> JOHN QUINNEY,
> SOLOMON QUANQUANCHMUT.

George Embree. ⎫
Thomas Eddy.   ⎬
John Murray. ⎭

We have not received the stove yet, and wish to hear something about it.

Two or three hundred pounds worth of such articles as these :

Three point blankets ; two and half ditto ; linen, and brown linen, and tow cloth ; broadcloths, such as strouds ; rateen for legings ; some calicoes, thread, needles ; some handkerchiefs, and some broadcloth, which may be used for coating,—such colour as Friends generally have for coats.

New York, 12*th mo.* 10*th*, 1795.

BROTHERS,

A few days ago we received your letter, dated 19th of last month. The account you give us of your welfare affords us much satisfaction, and we rejoice to find that you retained the counsel and advice we gave to you at Stockbridge, and our written communications at Brothertown. We hope you will diligently attend to the voice of the good Spirit, which is placed in all men's hearts, and which is all sufficient to lead out of all bad practices—and as you closely pursue those ways which is consistent with this divine Spirit, you will witness, by experience, that it will be your strength, your good Counsellor, and your true Comforter. Since our return home we have been

very thoughtful about our Indian Brethren, and intended soon to have wrote to you.

Our minds, as well as your other Friends in this
city, have been much employed in thinking in what
way we could best serve you; we are sensible you
want assistance, and we are very desirous of helping
you to become Farmers, and learn some useful trades,
so that you may not find it necessary to go so much
out among the white people, which has been already
of great hurt to your young men, by exposing them
to be overtaken by the great Hero, as you very justly
observe.   But, Brothers, we must tell you in plain
words, that unless you are in earnest, and particularly the peace makers and chiefs among yourselves,
to make by-laws to prevent your Nation from going
so much among the white people, or bringing Rum
into your Nation, we may be discouraged from lend-
ing you assistance.   Now, Brothers, we want you to
be wise, study your own good, and endeavour to
promote your own happiness.   We fully depend on
you to use exertions to make a reform in your Nation,
and that you will, in the first place, strive to leave
off drinking *Rum*, as being the first and great step
to your becoming a sober and industrious, and, in
time, a civilized people; and hoping this happy
change may take place, you may likely again receive
another visit next summer from some of our Society;
and in order to encourage you to go on in well-doing,
we have agreed to comply with your request in
sending you a few goods, in confidence that you will
pay us punctually for them in twelve months.

As we have endeavoured to point out the path
which leads to your happiness in this world and the
next, so we hope you will be favoured with strength
and good resolutions to walk in it ; and, as you now
experience a fresh instance of our regard, in furnishing you with some goods, so we particularly request
of you to be very cautious how you suffer them to
go out of your possession.   Only trust such of your

O

Nation as you know are men of uprightness, who will pay you in good season, whereby you will be enabled to be punctual in paying at the time proposed, which will greatly add to the reputation of your character as a people, and, in an especial manner, secure to you the future favour and friendship of our Society; which, that it may be the case, is the sincere desire of

Your real friends and brethren,

JOHN MURRAY, jun.

THOMAS EDDY.

The stove, and sufficient of length of pipe, was sent some time ago to Albany, to the care of Thomas Spencer, merchant there, with directions to him to send it to the care of Peter Smith, at old Fort Schuyler.

Our Assembly will meet next month, and, perhaps, it would be best for you three to come to this city, and try if you can prevail on them to grant you compensation for your old claim. We will give you our assistance, and we believe, if you come, that we can prevail on the Assembly to grant you an annuity. Inclosed is invoice of the goods, amounting to 129*l.* 15*s.* 10*d.*

To the Chiefs and Warriors of the Six Nations.

BROTHERS,

In all my intercourse and acquaintance, I have endeavoured to give you proofs that I am your friend. Of this truth I trust you are well convinced. If, then, you believe me to be your friend, you will listen to my talk; and if you think I have understanding to discern what is for your best good, you will attend to my advice.

Brothers—I have often shown you what good things the white people enjoy, and explained how you might also enjoy them. You have answered, that what I told you was very good, and that you were willing to adopt the useful ways of the white people by degrees, but that you could not lay aside your old customs all at once. This was a wise answer. It will be necessary for you to continue your hunting while the game is so plenty as to be worth pursuing. But you already know that the game is becoming scarce, and have reason to expect, that in a few years more it will be gone. What then will you do to feed and clothe yourselves, your wives and children? Brothers, this is an important question; think well upon it; the oldest hunters may, perhaps, find some game as long as they live; but before the young men grow old, all the game will be destroyed; the young men, then, and the boys, should learn to get food and clothing without hunting. How are they to do this? By cultivating the ground as the white people do; for with what grows out of the ground they can purchase all other necessaries. If you make fences to enclose many fields, you can then securely raise corn, wheat, and hay in abundance, to feed your families, and as many cattle and hogs as you want, and the cattle and hogs will give you more meat than you could ever obtain by hunting, even when game was plentiest.

Now, Brothers, I have the good pleasure to inform you, that your good friends, the Quakers, have formed a wise plan to show your young men and boys the most useful practices of the white people. They will choose some prudent good men to instruct them. These good men will do this only for the love they bear to you, their fellow men, as children of the Great Spirit, whom they desire to please, and who will be pleased with the good they do to you. The Quakers and the good men they employ, will ask nothing from you, neither land, nor money, nor skins, nor furs, for all the good they will render unto you; they will only request your consent, and the attention of the young men and boys to learn what will be so useful.

Brothers---If this first attempt succeeds, the way will be opened in which your young people may learn other useful practices of the white people, so as to enable them to supply all their own wants, and such as choose it may learn to read and write.

Having thus explained to you the plan of your friends, the Quakers, I conclude with heartily recommending it to your adoption, as better calculated to procure lasting and essential benefits to your Nations than any plan ever before attempted. Wishing it great success, I remain your friend and brother,

TIMOTHY PICKERING.*

Philadelphia, Feb. 15th, 1796.

TO MR. JASPER PARISH.

Philadelphia, February 15th, 1796.

SIR,

The Society of Friends, always manifesting a desire to promote the best interest of the Indians, have now formed a plan to introduce among them the most necessary arts of civil life, and have raised, and will raise, money, and employ agents, to carry it into effect, or at least to make a fair experiment to change their present habits, and to adopt in their places the practice of those most necessary arts. In this attempt, the Friends will need the assistance of all well disposed men, who are capable of deriving pleasure from the happiness of their fellow men, and are therefore willing to promote it. But, of all men, those who understand the language of the Indians, if possessed of capacity and humanity, have it in their power to do them most good ; for this reason, the Friends earnestly desire your aid ; their great object is, not to teach peculiar *doctrines*, but useful *practices ;* to instruct the Indians in husbandry, and the plain mechanical arts and manufactures directly

* Timothy Pickering was, in 1796, Secretary of State for the United States; George Washington, President.

connected with it. This is beginning at the right end, and, if so much can be accomplished, their farther improvements will follow of course.

The agents whom the Friends mean to engage to reside among the Indians, will be men divested of all mercenary views, and devoted for the time solely to the pursuit of the object above explained.

To the request of the Friends I add mine, that you will embrace every occasion which shall offer to explain to the Indians of the Six Nations, and to persuade them to adopt, a plan whose sole object is their happiness. I am, Sir,

Your friend and servant,
TIMOTHY PICKERING.

Captain ISRAEL CHAPIN, *Superintendent of the Six Nations.*

Philadelphia, February 15th, 1796.

DEAR SIR,

The Society of Friends have formed a plan to instruct the Indians of the Six Nations in husbandry and the most necessary arts of civil life. The goodness of the design, and the disinterestedness of the motives, must recommend it to the favour and support of all who wish the happiness of their fellow men. You are of this number, and as the Indians have confidence in you, it will be in your power greatly to promote the success of the plan ; and I am sure you will not need urging to exert it, on all fit occasions. The persons who will be employed by the Friends in this benevolent undertaking, will make themselves known to you, and ask your advice and assistance. You will oblige me by presenting my kind regard to your brother and sister, and I beg you to be assured of my esteem and friendship.

TIMOTHY PICKERING.

10

An Account of the Commissioners of Pennsylvania who
were appointed by Government to explore the Back
Country, &c. in 1796.

On their arrival in the town in which the Corn-
planter usually resides, they communicated to him,
and the men of the town, the errand on which they
came. After receiving a welcome, and an approbation of their business, the Commissioners retired, and
were about to proceed forward, when they were
again called to the Council House, where an elderly
Indian woman, in the presence of the Corn-planter
and his Council, gave in charge to the Commissioners
to inform your Excellency,

That, in the Seneca Nation, the women have as
much to say in Council as the men have, and in all
important business have equal authority; that all
affairs of trade and agriculture are under the sole
direction of the women; that having learned from
their Wise Men that the business they came on was
a search after a better road into their country than
the usual trading path, the women had judged it
proper to express their approbation of that measure,
which they saw was equally advantageous to the
Senecas, by lessening the expense of carriage, as to
the white people; that they were sensible that since
the game was going from among them, their men
had been less successful in hunting than formerly,
yet they hoped their trade was well worth their
attention; that the proposals made last Spring by
the Chiefs of their Nations, for introducing the plough
among them, had been considered and approved by
the women, who had the greatest interest in it, as
the labour fell wholly on them; that they had also
approved of the request for teachers to be sent among
them to instruct their young people; that if these
were done, they hoped that their Nation might become one people with the Americans, and the Senecas
would then enjoy the advantages which they per-

ceived they perceived the white people derived from their superior wisdom.

Thus committed to them, it became their duty to lay it before your Excellency.

To the Brothertown Indians.

New York, 6 *mo.,* 2*d,* 1796.

Friends and Brothers,

We expect you have already been informed of the Governor having appointed General William Floyd, with us, superintendants of the affairs of the Indians at Brothertown. This, we expect, will be handed you by General Floyd, whom we recommend, from our knowledge of him, as your good friend. We are satisfied he has the welfare of your Nation much at heart, and, as we have given you many proofs of our steady friendship, we hope you will now closely attend to such advice as General Floyd may give you. He will kindly inquire into your situation, and you must make known your wants to him; he will advise you what by-laws and regulations may be necessary for you to make among yourselves, and you will inform him of such as you have already made, so that he may give you his sentiments thereon. Having had several conversations with him on the subject of your affairs, we shall leave him to inform you of the supplies that is proposed to be handed you this summer. You need not fresh assurances from us, how desirous we are to promote your welfare every way, as we believe a reformation is really began among you ; we earnestly recommend to those sober men and women who have so nobly stepped forward in so good an undertaking, that they persevere in a steady conduct, and, by setting examples of sobriety and industry, induce others to join them, not only in refraining themselves from the least use of spirituous liquors, but to put your laws in full force against all offenders in this respect. Until this shameful practice is entirely laid aside, you will labour under many great disadvantages, and will prevent us from serving you so fully as we wish to do.

We trust you will closely attend to General Floyd's counsel, which will be for your good, as we well know his humane disposition and regard for you will lead him to bestow much pains with you. On your example of industry and sobriety great expectations are formed, with respect to a similar reformation with the neighbouring Indians; and we earnestly hope General Floyd will have it in his power to give a favourable report of you to the Governor, so as to induce him also to be your friend.

We have not time now to enlarge much, recommending you to the strict observance of the dictates of the Good Spirit placed in each of your hearts.

We are, truly, your real friends,

EDMUND PRIOR,
THOMAS EDDY.

Address of the Oneida and other Indians to the Assembly of New York.

MY FRIEND,

As I always had the welfare of my Nation, and Indians in general, at heart, I ever been use my endeavours to prevent drinking the spirituous liquors intemperately—prevailed upon Oneidas to unite with us to send petitions to the Assembly of New York to stop all liquors. I have inclosed the copy which I drawn for our Nations, to send, that you may see it.

Signed,   HENDRICK AUT.

(*A true Copy.*)

To the Great Sachem and Chiefs of the State of New York, sitting around the Great Council Fire of New York.

BROTHERS,

Before you cover your Council Fire, we beg your attention to the voice of your brethren. The different

tribes living at Oneida country, speaks to you in remembrance of the friendship you have manifested
towards them in all our treaties; we ourselves have
held Councils at different times, to contemplate the
welfare of our nations, because we cannot but groan
to see our situation; it is also melancholic to reflect
on the ways of our forefathers.

Brothers—You, also, sometimes sorry to see the deplorable situation of your Indian Brethren, for which
you have given us many good counsels; though we
feel willing to follow your counsels, but it has made
no effect as yet.

Our situation is still miserable. Our ancestors have
been conquered, immediately after you came on this
Island, by the strong Heroe, who does still reign
among Indian tribes with tyranny, who has robbed
us of every thing that was precious in our eyes.
We need not mention every particular, how this
tyrant has used us, for your eyes have been open to
behold our dismal situation.

By the power of our enemy our eyes have been
blinded; our young men became willing slaves to
this despotic Heroe, so that we have displeased the
good Spirit, and we could not become civilized
people.

In looking back, we see nothing but desolation of
our mighty men; in looking forward, we foresee the
desolation of our tribes. Our Chiefs have used their
endeavours to reform their respective people, but,
having seen no success, they seem discouraged, and
hang down their heads.

Brothers—In remembrance of your kind promises,
we unite our cries to you for help.

Perhaps, you are ready to think what man it must
be that have abused so much of our brethren; never
was such Heroe, or tyrant, heard that ever meddled
with Indians. But, in reality, he is your own begot-
ten son, and his name you call Rum, and the names
of his officers, are Brandy, Wine, and Gin, and we

P   10*

know that you have the power to control him ; and, as we desire to live in peace, and to become civilized nations, we earnestly entreat you to use your power and wisdom to prevent all people, whether white or black, who may cause the Rum, and the other spirituous liquors, to come in the hands of our tribes throughout your State. In compliance with this, our request, we will acknowledge your friendship.

Is from your brethren,

Chiefs and Warriors of Oneida Nation,
John Skonnondogh,
Crisdian Thonighgivensera,
William Tatagivesera,
Shagoghyudaha,
Kawegdot,
Cornelius Konoyoung.

Chiefs of Tuscaroras,
Nicholas Cuseck,
David Tyanrescagwendyroras,
Peter Dyongivet.

Chiefs of Maheconneck, or Stockbridge Tribe,
Hendrick Aupaumut,
Joseph Quinney,
Joseph Shanqueathquot,
John Quinney.

The following letters to General Floyd, who was an Indian agent, and took a lively interest in the civilization of those under his care, we copy from Mr. Eddy's manuscripts, which give a full and fair account of the efforts of the philanthropists of that day, in their endeavours to assist the Indians, in which they were joined by the General and States' Governments.

To General William Floyd, *at Fort Stanwick,*
New York, 7th mo. 11th, 1796.

Respected Friend,
Thy favour of 19th ultimo, to Thomas Eddy, is now before us, with the contents of which we are

much pleased. The delay of the buildings, and laying out the money designed for that, in articles more
immediately necessary for the Indians, we think a
very judicious step, as, while it will tend to convince
them how much we wish to serve them, they will
also receive more immediate benefits. We hope, by
this time, the goods proposed to be sent them when
thou wast here, have reached them. Thou wilt observe several additions to them, that were agreed to
before thou left us, which was in consequence of our
interview with the Governor.

As the articles will, probably, be ready for distribution before thou comest away, thou mayest probably learn whether they are suitably adapted to their
wants, and from thence form a judgment how to
proceed in future. When suitable opportunity can be
had to consult with them, we think there would be
a propriety in doing it. And, therefore, as it is
probable, some supplies of clothing, blankets, &c.,
may be wanted for the winter season, it would be
agreeable to us if thou wouldest endeavour to obtain
such knowledge of the articles most necessary, and
furnish us with the list thereof. We also think there
will be a propriety in making an inquiry of them,
what it is probable they will want next season, as that
will afford us time to procure the articles, both in
quantity and quality, much better adapted to their
use, and, perhaps, a saving. This spring, we found
much difficulty in procuring some things, particularly
the hoes, axes, scythes, &c., some of which are short
of the quantity designed, and, we fear, may also be
deficient in the quality, though we spared no pains
to procure them of the most proper kinds.

If thou shouldest have another opportunity with
the Indians before thy return, we wish to inform
them of our uniting with thee in what thou hast done;
and we also unite in sentiment with thee, on the
absolute necessity of their making " *strait by-laws*" to
prevent the introduction of spirituous liquors among

them, and that, when made, they be careful strictly to enforce them in all delinquencies.

The bills thou mentionest having drawn, will all be duly honoured as they appear.

We are, very respectfully, thy Friends,

EDMUND PRIOR,
THOMAS EDDY.

To General WILLIAM FLOYD, *at Fort Stanwick,*

New York, 8th mo. 15th, 1796.

ESTEEMED FRIEND,

Since our last, we have been without any of thy favours, and although we much approved of what thou didst, as being for the most immediate benefit of the Indians, and have paid the bills thou drewest, yet we have since had cause to regret furnishing them with any supplies, till their school house was built. We now find that the law expressly directs, that the school house shall be first built, and a master provided, and until this is done, the Governor is restrained from handing us any more money than may be thought sufficient for those purposes. Of course, when we called on him, in expectation of receiving the money, we could get none, as he said the house must be first completed, as the law directs.

We have now no way of being paid our advances, but by setting about and completing the school house with all possible expedition ; and, on consulting with the Governor, we have approved of erecting only a school house at present, and, at a future time, erect another house, to serve for to transact their town business in, and as a meeting house. We have, therefore, with his approbation, changed the plan of that we sent thee, and, enclosed, thou wilt find one calculated for a school house only. Near where the old one stands, on *John Tuhis's land*, is thought to be an eligible spot for the new house.

Perhaps, if the Indians are informed that the Governor is restrained by law, from granting any farther support to them, until the house is finished, they will generally turn out, and endeavour by their exertions to complete the building in a short time.

We are of opinion, that logs be collected, and sawed into pieces about four or five inches thick, and as wide as the timber will admit of, to be placed on the top of each other, and pinned and dove-tailed together. The building then to be boarded on the outside, with boards to stand upright, not lengthways. These boards may be planed, so as they can be painted, if thought necessary, at a future day. The roof to be shingled; the lower pieces of the building to be pitch pine or white oak, to prevent decay. The house should stand about eighteen inches above the ground, underpinned with brick or stone, and till this can be done, it may remain, perhaps, till next year, supported on blocks. The floor should be pitch pine plank, or, if not to be had, of white pine, and ceiled above with boards. The floor and ceiling should be grooved, but need not to be planed.

On this plan we wish thee to procure as many men as can work, and to proceed immediately, and erect a house in the most convenient situation that can be obtained; and thou wilt readily see the necessity of sending us an acoount of the cost thereof, as soon as it can be ascertained, which, if some part is done by the job, may be done even before the building is finished. Thou wilt please engage young Wampey, or some other, for a master, at a stipulated salary, until we can procure one that may be better qualified.

The Governor agrees to advance us five hundred dollars towards erecting the proposed house; but thou wilt remember, no more can be got till the building is finished, or the cost thereof known, so as to report it to the Governor. It will be also necessary, that thou sendest us an account of articles purchased for, and supplied to, the Indians.

Thou mayest readily procure money for going on with the building, from any of the store keepers, for bills on us, which we would be glad thou couldest make at thirty days' sight, if in thy power. It is probable thou mayest engage Post, at old Fort Schuyler, or Kirkland the Attorney, to superintend the building, after thou engagest a good carpenter. We wish to hear from thee by next post, and are, with much esteem,

Thy assured Friends

THOMAS EDDY,
EDMUND PRIOR.

Plan of the Building.

24 feet by 30, in the clear.

9 do. high   do.

Door in the middle of the front, and 2 windows each side.

Two windows in the west; none in the north.

Chimney in the east. Windows—12 lights, 7 by 9.

To the Chiefs of the Delawares.*

GRANDFATHER,

Attend to the words of your grand-children.

I am glad that, by the goodness of the great Good Spirit, we are allowed to meet together by the side

---

* N. B. Addressed by the Mohigans, (or Stockbridge nation,) to a remnant of Delawares who lived near Atsion, twenty miles from Philadelphia, till 1797, and then united themselves with the Stockbridge Indians, 150 miles west of Albany. The Mohigans always call the Delawares grand-father.— EDDY.

The Delaware, or Lenni Lenape Indians, were the ancestors of the six nations, and of most of the tribes of New England; their language has been considered as the most copious and perfect, of all spoken by the Indian tribes. It is said to be so formed, as to express almost every shade of meaning by prefixes, affixes, and reduplications. Historians have informed us, that the other tribes had children brought up among the Delawares, in order to give correctness and polish to their own language on their return to their respective tribes. Any one acquainted with the history of the Indian, is well aware that every tribe takes especial care to keep its vernacular as perfect as possible. Those who examined the Cherokees and Winnebagoes when they visited the United States, can bear witness to this care to preserve their language pure, and their pronunciation correct. This appellation of grandsire, used by the Mohigans to the Delawares, is in corroboration of this fact.

S. L. K.

of this fire-place, and smoke the pipe of friendship, while we talk together in commemoration of ancient covenant, which our forefathers establishcd, and esteemed it.

I am glad that the Great Spirit puts it in your minds to visit your grandchildren, and preserve you through the tedious journey, so to arrive here safely.

Grandfather—When I look on you, I see your tears flowing down from your eyes, on account of the dust that flew about on the way, as you were coming from your fire-place hither.

In remembrance of the ancient customs of our ancestors, I now stretch forth my hand, and wipe off your tears, that you may see your grandchildren in real appearance; in like manner, I clean your ears, that you may hear plainly the voice of your grandchildren, and also clean your throat, and loose your tongue, that you may speak freely.

Grandfather—And also I find that your heart is hanging downwards, on account of the many losses in your Nation these many days; and, according to the customs of our forefathers, I now set your heart upright, and lay aside all the sound which the white birds have sounded on your ears, that you may, without prejudice, be enabled to consider what your grandchildren may say to you.

Grandfather—Having done so much, then I see mud all over your legs and feet, for an account of the long muddy path in which you have walked through. I now wash your legs and feet, but still I discover some briars and thorns sticking fast in your feet; now I pull out every one of thcm, and I take *weesquos*, in which our ancestors used to put healing oil, and oint your feet and legs, that you may feel well, and walk around by the fire-place of your grandchildren.

(A string of pure white wampum delivered.)

Grandfather—Again listen.

I am glad to find that you still retain our talk,

which passed between us at Philadelphia, when we saw each other there, (about four years ago,) at which time I took hold on your hand, and directed you to my fire-place, which invitations our Chiefs, with our young men, do now renew.

I spread this *unnukkon*, or mat, wide, on which I put you; likewise those pillows to lay your heads on ; then I stretch forth my hand on your fire-place, and. roll your mat, which you used to sit on, and spread it over on the other mat, which I just made ready for you, that you may feel more easy and comfortable; here you will eat with your grandchildren out of one dish, and use one spoon; by the side of this fire-place you can cook what you please, and at night you can lay down to rest, and dream about the welfare of your men, women, and children. In the morning you can get up, and promote the same.

Grandfather—Lastly, I let you know that I put a broom by the side of this bed, so that, whenever you feel something hard on this bed, then when shall use the broom to sweep off every thing, that nothing may interrupt your rest.

(Nunnchtkchk.   String of wampum delivered.)

Grandfather—once more attend.

We will now let you know the reasons which induce your grandchildren to give you such invitations.

1st. Because I believe that it is the will of the great Good Spirit, that our ancestors did enter into covenant, and established a strong friendship between them, which covenant we ever have maintained bright.

2d. Because, by the goodness of the same Spirit, we obtained this good dish, wherein we may eat peaceably; and, by his kind providence, we were enabled to see your dismal situation; and farther, I believe, that it is the same good Spirit who influenced our hearts to have the compassionate feelings towards your Nation.

3d. Because I believe, that if you can only once

make out to bring the whole of your Nation here, you can have better chance to try to live as a people, because this dish is much better than your old dish.

4th. Because you will have the privilege of hearing the glad tidings of the Gospel preached, and your children will be instructed to read and write.

5th. Because here we can live together as one family, and counsel one another, and comfort and exhort one another daily, so long as we are allowed to live this side of eternity.

From your grandchildren,

Sachems,

JOSEPH SKAUQUEATHQUANT,
HENDRICK AUPAMUT.

Counsellors of Maheconneck Nation,

JOHN QUINNEY,
JOSEPH QUINNEY.

Delivered in full Council.

New Stockbridge, October 9th, 1796.

To the Stockbridge.—Answer.

GRANDCHILDREN—Attend.

I am glad that, by the goodness of the Great Spirit, we were allowed to meet together by the side of this fire-place, to smoke the pipe of friendship, as our ancestors were accustomed to do. Grandchildren, I am glad to find a token of your friendship, which you manifested at your grandfather's arrival at this fire-place ; likewise, ever since, for which we are extremely thankful, and ever shall be gratefully remembered.

Grandchildren—At our arrival, you wiped away the tears from our eyes, which were caused by the filth and dust which blew into them in our long journey, as also, on the account of the many tall trees, which are fallen and lost amongst us. Likewise, you have cleared out my ears and throat, and set my heart upright. Likewise, you have wiped off

Q 11

the mud from my legs and feet, and, finding them full of briars and thorns, you reached thither your hands, and plucked them all out, and applied the healing oil of our deceased ancestors upon them.

Grandchildren—Since your performance of this kindness to your grandfather, I see you clearly ; I see the tears running down on your eyes, on the account of the many losses in your Nation, and the many high trees that are fallen.

Grandchildren—Now, in remembrance of our ancient covenant, I stretch forth my hands, and raise up your head, and obliterate from your eyes and mind all tears and sorrow, and fix your eyes forward, that they may not be obstructed from looking forward on the happy days which are coming, in looking back on the trees which are fallen.

Grandchildren—I also cleanse your ears, that you may hear plainly ; and strengthen your tongues, that you may be enabled to speak the things which are profitable for your Nation, both temporally and spiritually.   Likewise, I set your heart upright, that you may be capable of contemplating the welfare and happiness of your old men, women, and children.

Now, Grandchildren, attend.

By these strings you renew the kind invitation you gave us, when we saw each other in Philadelphia.   I think it needless to repeat the same, but for which we again thank you.   Likewise, Grandchildren, be it known unto you, that we have deeply considered your invitation, and finding it heartily sincere, and your dish a lasting good one, and your paths so good and straight, we accept of your invitation, and lay hold on it with both of our hands, hoping that the great Good Spirit may enable and protect us, in promoting each other's welfare and happiness, and that we may live and die together by the side of your fire-place.

Now, Grandchildren, I must tell you, now that I am about turning my eyes towards my fire-place, hoping that, as you have begun and entered in this good path, you may still continue to persevere therein; and although we shall be absent some time in body, our hearts shall still be present with you.

It is evident, that many true philanthropists were feelingly alive to the state of the Indians. The Secretary of State for the United States, at that time the Honourable Timothy Pickering, was deeply engaged for the welfare of the children of the forest. He was a sagacious politician, of great hardihood of character, and was always governed more by the dictates of his understanding than the feelings of his heart. He, as it will be seen by the foregoing letters, from his own hand, did all in his power to aid and abet the Society of Friends, in their benevolent efforts for the Indians.

Certificate.

The subscriber certifies, that the following communications were written by him, in short hand, as they were delivered, at two conferences held in the city of Baltimore, on the 26th and 27th of 12th month, 1801, between several Indian chiefs, residing on the waters of the Wabash, Lake Erie, and Lake Michigan, and the committee for Indian affairs, appointed by the yearly meeting of the Society of Friends, held in Baltimore, at which were also present many others of the Society of Friends, and people of different religious persuasions; and that it is acknowledged by those who were present, that the communications are taken down with accuracy.

GERARD T. HOPKINS.

I have perused the following speeches, written in short hand by Gerard T. Hopkins, as they were delivered in the city of Baltimore, by the Indian

Chiefs, the Little Turtle and the Five Medals, and do hereby certify that they are taken down with accuracy.   WILLIAM WELLS,

Interpreter and Agent for Indian Affairs.

Proceedings of the First Conference.

A member of the Society of Friends opened the conference by addressing the chiefs as follows:

BROTHERS AND FRIENDS,

I am desirous that, in the early part of this opportunity, you may be informed that the people called Quakers, consider all mankind as their brethren; that they believe the Great Spirit and Father of mankind created all men of one blood; and that it is the will of Him, who also created the sun, the moon, and the stars, and causes them to give us light—that Great Spirit and common Father of all mankind—that we should not do one another hurt, but that we should do one another all the good we can; and it is on this ground and this principle, that we believe it right to take you by the hand.

After sitting a short time in silence, another Friend addressed them as follows:

BROTHERS AND FRIENDS,

We, the people called Quakers, believe that it is required of us, that we should all love one another, however separated we may be in our local settlements in the world, or whatever difference there may be in our colour. And, as we are convinced it is not in our power to perform our religious duties to Him that hath created us, without his assistance, so we conceive it to be our duty, when we are about to enter upon such weighty business as, I apprehend, this is, thus to sit down in stillness, in order to endeavour to feel after the operation of his spirit in our hearts; and we believe that this cannot be attained by our own natural powers, but must be under the influence of the Good Spirit.

We also believe that there is an evil spirit, which is always striving to lead us into wrong things: that spirit which leads us to hate and destroy one another; and in this persuasion of mind, we believe it necessary for us to sit down in stillness and quiet, to wait upon the Great Spirit.

Under these impressions, we are concerned often to assemble ourselves together, that we may individually come under an exercise and concern, to be rightly directed in our religious movements; and once in the year we assemble at certain places, in order to have a general and full conference, to know how things are amongst us as a people.

One of these meetings is held at Philadelphia, and another at Baltimore.

At our yearly meeting at Baltimore, several years past, our minds were brought under a concern on behalf of our brethren, the Indians; and remembering the friendship that had subsisted between our society and the Indians, from the first settlement of our fathers upon this continent, and at the same time recollecting that the country to the westward was fast settling, apprehensions arose in our mind, that, as the game became scarce, they would be brought under sufferings; and, as there had been long wars between some of the white people and the Indians, we had not had, for a long time, an opportunity of taking our brothers, the Indians, by the hand.

Now, brothers, as we are thus led by the concerns that arose in our council, some of us were appointed to go out into the wilderness, and endeavour to get amongst our brethren, the Indians, that we might have some talk with them; and amongst those who were appointed, this, my brother, who sits at my right hand, was one; and I have thought that he, perhaps, can give a more full account, both of the times, and of our first movements at the concern.

11*

The Friend alluded to then proceeded :—

BROTHERS,

About six years ago, we believe, the Good Spirit put into our hearts, at our great council, held in this town, to endeavour to do something for the Indians; and, about four years ago, two others, besides myself, went over the Great Mountains, westward, in order to see your situation, and to know your disposition, whether you would receive any thing from us or not.

We wished to go to Sandusky, expecting to find the greatest number of Indians at that place. We could not get a guide till we got to the forks of Scioto, where we agreed with one to take us to Isaac Zane's. At that place, we were informed that a number of chiefs were at Detroit.

We sent for some Wyandot chiefs, who resided about 25 miles from Isaac Zane's, and had a conference with them. We informed them of the desire our society had, to do something for the Indians that would be useful to them. From thence we went to Upper Sandusky. Isaac Zane piloted us, and there, also, we had a conference with some of the Delaware chiefs. We wanted to know whether they would be willing to be instructed, on their own lands, in a way to procure a sufficiency for them to eat; to have a mill to grind their corn, and have their children instructed to read and write ? They informed us, that they could not give us an answer at that time, but would lay our proposals before their council.

About three years ago, we received a speech and a belt of wampum from a council held at Detroit ; the speech did not contain an answer to the proposals made to them, but an invitation to us to attend their council. (A short pause.)

The Little Turtle, chief of the Miamis, said :—

BROTHER,

It is not usual for us to interrupt any one in

speaking, but I wish to inquire, from whom the speech you mention came ?

(The speech was then produced, and the names to it read)—Little Turtle added—

I see that our brothers, the Quakers, are not so fully acquainted with the situation of the Indians as we wish. After we have taken the great chief of the white people by the hand, I hope he will give you full information with respect to us.

The Friend, who had been interrupted, then proceeded :—

BROTHERS,

Two years, last Spring, seven of us went over the Ohio, and thence to Upper Sandusky, at the time mentioned in the speech that was sent to us—we were invited to be there about the first of June, and, accordingly, got there about that time, but were informed, that the council was not to be held till about two weeks after. Not being accustomed to their mode of living, and finding a considerable number of the Indians, at that place, intoxicated with liquor, we were much discouraged, and concluded we might as well return home again. The Indians, however, notwithstanding their situation, treated us very kindly. We got together several Chiefs of the Wyandots, and communicated to them our business. They informed us, they would lay it before the Chiefs, at the council, and return us answer; but we have not received one.

The Friend, who made the second communication, addressed them again, as follows :—

BROTHERS AND FRIENDS,

We were glad when we heard, that some of our red brethren were come to this city, and felt our minds drawn to take them by the hand, in order that we might have an opportunity of knowing them.

As we had not been acquainted with their situations and circumstances, we have not been able to judge, whether any thing we had to propose to do for them, would be accepted ?—Whether they were under the necessity of applying to some other mode for a livelihood ?—Whether the game in their country was in plenty ?—We have thought, brothers, that if it should not yet be the case, that the game is scarce, it probably will be the case at some time; and, therefore, we thought it would be best for our red brethren, to give some attention to the cultivation of the soil.

This is one of the subjects which has claimed our consideration. And, feeling in our hearts, that we loved the Indians, and wished their welfare, it was our concern that they might be instructed to turn their attention to the cultivation of their lands. And, as we believe, brothers, that we derive very great advantages from reading books, which contain much instruction, and wishing our brethren, the Indians, should also derive the same advantage with us, we have wished that they should candidly let us know, whether they desire these things, that we might do for them whatever is in our power to do.

After a pause, the Little Turtle observed :—

BROTHERS AND FRIENDS,

If there is any more that you have to say, we wish to hear it ; but, if not, I will make a short reply to what we have already heard you say.

He was desired to proceed; when, rising on his feet, he said :—

FRIENDS AND BROTHERS,

My heart returns thanks to the Great Spirit above, that has put it in our power to speak to one another. My brother chiefs, with myself, are glad that our friends and brothers, the Quakers, have such great compassion for their red brethren.

Friends and Brothers—Your red brethren believe,

that one man—one Great Man, made all the men that are on the earth; and that he made the sun, the moon, and the stars, to give light, and to be useful to them.

Friends and Brothers—We now rejoice, that the Great Spirit has made you feel, that we stand in need of the assistance which you have been describing to us, and to wish, if possible, to render your red brethren those services which they now are highly in need of.

Brothers and Friends—It appears to us, your red brethren, that you have been kept in the straight path, by the Great and Good Spirit. We have been led astray by inferior spirits; we now hope, that we may come upon your track, and follow it.

Brothers and Friends—The long and destructive wars that have raged in the country of your red brethren, since your fathers first came among them, have caused their numbers to be greatly diminished. Those that have come amongst us, have very much cheated and imposed upon us. They have found us simple and ignorant, and have taken very great care to keep every thing from our knowledge, in order to profit by our ignorance.

Friends and Brothers—We find that you are now disposed, with open arms, to receive us, and we hope the Great Spirit will assist you, together with the great chief of the white people, whom we are now about to apply to for help.

Brothers and Friends—At the treaty of Grenville, which is now a little past six years ago, we received some presents, by the hands of the great war chief of the Americans, (General Wayne,) said to be sent to us by our brothers, the Quakers. After this treaty, I was invited, by the great chiefs of the Americans, to visit them. It is now four years since I visited them, at Philadelphia, whilst the great council was held at that city. I had there opportunity to see our brothers, the Quakers, and received from their mouths

R

some talks : all these talks I wrapped up in my heart, and, when I returned home to my brothers, I communicated to them, faithfully, all those good things which you had told us you were desirous to do for us.

Friends and Brothers—I am happy to say, that these, my red brothers, now present with me, are chiefs, who, in their own country, are equally great with myself. They were rejoiced to hear your words, delivered to them, through me, four years ago, and they are now equally glad with myself, to hear from the mouths of our brothers, the Quakers, the same good words again.

Brothers and Friends—If we understand you right, you wish to add comfort to our women and children, by teaching us some of your ways of living. I am glad that the Great Spirit has put this into your hearts, and am sorry that your exertions have not yet been successful.

Brothers and Friends—I now assure you, that you hear the voice of the Patawattamy, Miami, Delaware, Shawanese, Weas, Eel River, Pisinkashaw, Kickapoo, and Kaskaskias tribes of Indians, and that, if you wish to do any thing for any of these nations of Indians, they will be ready, at all times, to receive you—and we, also, will be ready, at all times, to render you any assistance in our power.

Brothers and Friends—This is the first time that the Great Spirit has brought us to take our brethren, the Quakers of Baltimore, by the hand, and we rejoice to hear them mention the same things to us, that have heretofore been mentioned to us, by our brothers, the Quakers of Philadelphia.

Brothers—I, some time past, received from our brothers, the Quakers of Philadelphia, some tools, amongst which were two ploughs. I used them, and did all I could to keep them from wearing out. I was pleased with them : they have now become necessary to be repaired. We have nobody amongst us that can mend them, and they are now useless to me.

Brothers and Friends—It is now five days since we took our brothers, the Quakers of Philadelphia, by the hand—we then talked over these things together.   They have promised me, that at their next great council, they will hold a talk about these things, and consider what they can do for us.

Brothers and Friends—If our brothers, the Quakers of Baltimore, desire to do any thing for the Indians, I wish to give them full information of the place where we may be found generally together.   The great council of our tribes of Indians, is held at Fort Wayne, at the time we receive our annuity from the United States.   At that time, any communications our brothers wish to make to their red brethren, will be safely handed to us by your white brother, our interpreter, now with us, who is our agent at that place.   (He then sat down, but, after a short pause arose again.)

Brothers—I must add a few words farther: I find that I have not fully answered all the questions that our brothers have put to us.

Brothers and Friends—It is the real wish of your brothers, the Indians, to engage in the cultivation of our lands.   And although the game is not yet so scarce, but that we can get enough to eat, we know it is becoming scarce, and that we must begin to take hold of such tools as we see are in the hands of the white people.

Brothers and Friends—We are now on our way to see the great chiefs of the Americans at their council. We are glad to find that they remember their red brethren, and rejoice to believe that the Great Spirit has put it into the heart of the great chief of the white people to do us such services as will add to the comfort of his red children.

Brothers and Friends—I will now only add, that I rejoice to believe, that your friendship to your red brethren is a friendship that is pure—a friendship that comes from the heart—you want no compensation from the Indians for your services to them.   You do not want to take away our lands from us—you have always made use of this language to us; and it has always been with pleasure that I have communicated it to our brethren.

Brothers—We are a jealously disposed people—almost every white man that comes amongst us, endeavours all he can to cheat us; this has occasioned jealousy among us. But your talks, brothers, are different; we believe you, when you say you want no compensation from us, for your services to your red brethren.

Five Medals, chief of the Pattawattamies, arose.

FRIENDS AND BROTHERS,

I rejoice to hear that you have so much compassion on your red brethren. As my friend the Little Turtle has observed, it is not the first time that we have received tokens of friendship from you.

It is some years since the treaty of Grenville, where we first experienced the friendship of our brothers, the Quakers. He was there informed of their good wishes, and of the great friendship they had for their red brethren.

He returned home, and informed us of all the great talks he had with our brothers, the Quakers of Philadelphia.

It is truly pleasing to me, brothers, to hear the same talks my friend had informed me of, now repeated, on my arrival at Baltimore, by our friends and brothers the Quakers.

I hope, brothers, that the Great Spirit, who has the disposal of men, will assist you in your laudable undertakings, and enable you to be of service to your red brethren.

Friends and Brothers—The talks that you have now delivered to us, shall be carefully collected, wrapped up, and put in our hearts—we will not forget them. On our return home, we will have them communicated from the head to the mouth of the Wabash—from this to the Mississippi, and up that river till it strikes the lakes, thence round by Michili-mackanack, until they come back again to the same place.

What we say to you, you may be assured does not come from one man, it comes from many—and what you have now said to us, you speak it to but a few, but it shall be communicated to many.

Brothers and Friends—I observed to our friends the Quakers of Philadelphia, five days ago, what I now say to you: That we wish our brothers, the Quakers, to render us those services which they have proposed. We promise that nothing shall be wanting on our part, to give aid to so desirable a thing in our country.

Our situation, at present, will not admit of carrying such a plan so fully into execution as might be desired by our brothers; but that, I hope, will not prevent you from making trial. If we had such tools as you make use of, and which add so much to your comfort—for we have been lost in wonder at what we have seen amongst you---if we had these instruments, we should, I hope, be willing to use them; and in the course of a little time, there would be people amongst us, that would know well how to use them, through the assistance they might obtain from you, and the rest of our white friends.

Brothers and Friends—Whatever goods you may have in store for your red brothers, we cannot but wish that you will show them to us as soon as possible.

That we can yet live upon the game of our country is true; but we know that this will not be the case long. Brothers, from the great things, and the aston-ishing wonders which we have seen among you, and finding they all come out of the earth, it makes me anxious to try if I cannot get some for myself. I hope, brothers, that by the aid of the Great Spirit, and of our friends and brothers, the Quakers, together with the government of the United States, that we shall yet be enabled to get these good things for ourselves—such as will make us, our women, and our children happy.

Brothers—We do not know what our brothers, the Quakers of Philadelphia, may have in contemplation to do for their red brethren, but we hope it will be something that will add to our comfort; we hope it will be something by which we shall profit; something by which we shall be enabled to cultivate our lands, and live by the fruits of the earth. We have been walking in a thorny path; we want to get into your track and follow it; and the sooner this is put into our power, I am convinced the better it will be for our red brethren.

Brothers and Friends—I have not much to say further; what has now been said to you is the voice of the Pattawattamy, Miami, Delaware, Shawanese, Weas, Eel-River, Pisinkashaw, Kickapoo, and Kaskaskias tribes of Indians. I rejoice, brothers, that we now know each other, and hope if you have any thing to communicate to your red brethren, that it will come to us through your good brother, William Wells, our interpreter, who resides in our country. We can place great confidence in him. He is the only white man in our country we will trust; we shall then get it, and do now assure you, that it shall be faithfully sent to all these people, in the manner you wish it to be.

Brothers and Friends—I hope the Great Spirit will assist you in your undertakings to do your red brethren good. Your movements towards the Wyandots, have not met with that success which they deserved. It makes me sorry to find an answer from them of the kind you have mentioned. There is a great deal, brothers, in having a good interpreter, and beginning at the right end of the business.

(*The end of the first Conference.*)

Second Conference.

One of the Society of Friends opened the conference as follows :—

BROTHERS AND FRIENDS,

When the talks, which we had last evening at this place, ended, I believe it was generally understood, that the subject matter which had been spoken upon, was satisfactory; but, on considering further, some of us thought that there were some things of considerable importance, which had not been spoken upon—and thought that it would be right to have another opportunity.

We are, accordingly, again assembled—and, seeing that it has been the will of the Great Spirit, and Father of us all, to permit us thus to come together again, it is my desire that any thing we may feel in our hearts, that may be likely to have a tendency to promote the good of our red brethren, may be freely spoken.

Another Friend next addressed them, as follows :—

I may tell you, I have been made glad, that I have an opportunity of sitting once more with you; and as I have found, that the more I am with you, the more the love I have felt for you has increased, and the stronger has been my desire for your welfare, and that this love has taken away all fear of giving offence; I feel myself authorized, I think, as a bro ther, to use freedom of speech with you, and in the freedom which I feel, under the influence of that love which, I trust, has been impressed upon my heart by the Great and Good Spirit, who, as he has made us all of one blood, so he requires of us, that we should love one another. I may tell you, brothers, that, when I was in the Indian country, I had frequent opportunities of observing the pernicious consequences of the use of spirituous liquors, with which the Indians were furnished by the traders; and as I have reason to believe, that you who are now present are wise men, who have eyes in your heads, and are able to see things as they really are, I have felt a desire in my heart to know your opinions, and what is your judgment concerning this thing—the using spirituous liquors to excess; believing, brothers, that if you have seen things in the same light in which I have seen them, that you would be desirous that a stop might be put to the evils, that arise from the use of so destructive a liquor. I may tell you, brothers, who are now present, as well as the Indians in general, that I have believed that there is not any thing that stands more in your way to improvement than this, the too frequent use of spirituous liquors: and I have thought, that if you are of the same mind with us, who are your friends, and have your good at heart, that it would be right for us to take the subject into our serious consideration, to endeavour to discover, whether there may not be some step taken, that would put a check upon this pernicious thing.

Now, brothers, as a hint of this sort was omitted when we were together last evening, some of us did not find our minds easy: we thought it ought to have come under consideration, hoping that you, who, as I have already said, have eyes in your heads, and can see for yourselves, have had this subject under your consideration. We now hope, brothers, that you will express yourselves freely to us on this subject, and let us know how it has happened to you. After which, perhaps, it will open a way for some further observations from us.

After a short pause, the Little Turtle, on his seat, said, I will now make some reply, if none of my brothers have one to offer.

He was desired to proceed—when, rising on his feet, he said,

My Brothers and Friends,

I am happy to find, that it has pleased the Great Spirit, that we should again, this evening, meet in the same house, in which we held our council yester-day. I am happy to find, that it is the will of the Great and Good Spirit, that we should discover, there was something yesterday not mentioned, that was highly necessary for the welfare of your brethren.

Friends and Brothers---I am glad to find that it has pleased the Great Spirit, to put a wish in your hearts, to know our opinions on the subject you have mentioned ; a subject of the greatest moment to us. What you have said, relative to our being one flesh, and one blood, is true. Your brothers, the Indians, believe, that it is in this light the Great Spirit considers all mankind.

Brothers and Friends—My brother chiefs, that are now present, with myself, are happy to find, that you have a good opinion of us. You say, that you apprehend we have eyes in our heads, and can clearly see for ourselves, those things that are injurious to us. This, my friends and brothers, is the case; we clearly see these things : my brother chiefs, that are now present with me, as well as myself, have long seen them ; we have long lamented these great evils that have raged in our country, and that have done your red brethren so much harm ; we have applied for redress, and endeavoured to have them removed from amongst us.

When our forefathers met first on this Island, your red brethren then were numerous; but since the introduction amongst us of what you call spirituous liquors, and what, we think, may be justly called poison, our numbers are greatly diminished : it has destroyed a great part of our red brethren.

My Brothers and Friends—I am glad to hear you observe, that freedom of speech ought always to be made use of amongst brothers ; this, brothers, really ought to be the case. I will now, therefore, take

S 12*

the liberty to mention, that most of the existing evils amongst your red brethren, have been caught from the white people; not only that liquor that destroys us daily, but many diseases that our forefathers were ignorant of, before they saw you.

My Brothers and Friends—I am glad, with my brother chiefs, that are now present, to find that you are ready to assist us in every thing that will add to our good : we hope that the Great Spirit will aid you in all your good undertakings, with respect to us. We plainly perceive, brothers, that you see that very evil that destroys your red brethren. It is not an evil, brothers, of our own making; we have not placed it amongst ourselves; it is an evil placed amongst us by the white people; we look up to them to remove it out of our country: if they have that friendship for us, which they tell us they have, they certainly will not let it continue amongst us any longer. Our repeated entreaties to those who bring this evil amongst us, we find, has not the. desired effect. We tell them—Brothers, fetch us useful things; bring goods that will clothe us, our women, and our children, and not this evil liquor, that destroys our reason—that destroys our health—that destroys our lives : but all we can say on the subject is of no service, nor gives relief to your red brethren.

My Brothers and Friends—I am glad that you have seen into this business as we do—I rejoice to find that you agree in opinion with us, and express an anxiety to be, if possible, of service to us, to remove this great evil out of our country—an evil that has had so much room in it—that has destroyed so many of our lives, that it causes our young men to say, "we had better be at war with the white people: this liquor that they introduce into our country is more to be feared than the gun and the tomahawk; there are more of us dead since the treaty of Grenville, than we lost by the six years war before; it is all owing to the introduction of this liquor amongst us."

Brothers, how to remove this evil from our country we do not know; if we had known it to be a proper subject to have mentioned to you in our council yesterday, we should surely have done it.   This subject, brothers, composes a part of what we intend to make known to the great council of our white brethren.   On our arrival there we shall endeavour to explain to our great father, the President; a great many evils that have arisen in our country, from the introduction of this liquor by the white traders.

Brothers and Friends—In addition to what I have before observed of this great evil in the country of your red brethren, I will say further, that it has made us poor.   It is this liquor that causes our young men to go without clothes, our women and children to go without any thing to eat; and sorry am I to mention now to you, brothers, that the evil is increasing every day, as the white settlers come nearer to us, and bring those kettles they boil that stuff in they call whiskey, of which our young men are so extremely fond.   Brothers, when our young men have been out hunting, and are returning home loaded with skins and furs, on their way, if it happens that they come along where some of this whiskey is deposited, the white man who sells it, tells them to take a little drink; some of them will say no, I don't want it—they go on till they come to another house, where they find more of this same kind of drink; it is there again offered; they refuse; and again the third time; but finally the fourth or fifth time one accepts of it, and takes a drink, and getting one he wants another, and then a third and a fourth, till his senses have left him.   After his reason comes back again to him, when he gets up and finds where he is, he asks for his peltry: the answer is, you have drank them.   Where is my gun? It is gone.   Where is my blanket? It is gone.   Where is my shirt? You have sold it for whiskey!!   Now, brothers, figure to yourselves what a condition this man must be in; he has a family at home, a wife and children that stand in need of the profits of his hunting: what must their wants be, when he himself is even without a shirt?

This, brothers, I can assure you, is a fact that often happens among us. As I have before observed, we have no means to prevent it. If you, brothers, have it in your power to render us any assistance, we hope the Great Spirit will aid you. We shall lay these evils before our great and good father; we hope he will remove them from amongst us; we shall assure him that if he does not, there will not be many of his red children living long in our country. The Great Spirit, brothers, has made you see as we see; we hope, brothers, and expect, that if you have any influence with the great council of the United States, that you will make use of it in behalf of your red brethren.

My Brothers and Friends—The talks that you delivered to us when we were in council yesterday, were certainly highly pleasing to myself, as well as to my brother chiefs; we rejoiced to hear you speak such words to us; but we all plainly saw, that there was a great difficulty in the way, that ought to be removed, before your good intentions towards us, could be carried into effect: we agree with you, brothers, that this great evil amongst us, spirituous liquors, must first be removed; after this is done, we hope you will find an easy access to us, much easier than you can have at present.

My Brothers and Friends—I hope that if we all try to prevent the introduction of spirituous liquors in the country of your red brethren, that the Great Spirit will aid us in it, and that we shall meet with no difficulty in doing it; after this is done, we hope that the great services you have designed to do for us, the great things mentioned by you in our council yesterday, may take place, and have that success you so much desire.

My Brothers and Friends—You have asked us our opinion, on the subject of the introduction of spirituous liquors into our country. I have now given it to you. If I have given it to you in such a manner that you do not understand me, I would wish you to say so; all that I have said to you, I wish to be made known to every body.

We have our enemies in our own country, as all other persons have in theirs; it is no unusual thing, brothers, to hear some people among us, (you will perceive, brothers, that these are people that are interested in keeping us ignorant,) when they hear talks that have been delivered by our chiefs, to people that are capable of rendering us services, they say to our people, "do you not hear? your chiefs have sold you—your chiefs have sold your lands." They put bad stories in the mouths of our young men. For this reason, brothers, all that I have said I wish to be made public; I wish every body to know it. I only mention this to you, brothers. If it is improper, I have no objection to your keeping it amongst yourselves; but if it could be made public, I would wish it—I have nothing further to say. (Sits down.)

Five Medals then arose on his feet.

My Brothers and Friends,

I have nothing to say on the subject we have now been talking over. My friend, the Little Turtle, has given you a full answer to those things you have mentioned to us; we are but one people, and have but one voice.

Brothers and Friends---We have never had it in our power to hold such talks with you at this place before. We have frequently had talks of this kind with our brothers, the Quakers of Philadelphia; they always appeared very glad to see us, and we find you the same. We hope, brothers, that your friendship and ours will never be broken.

The Friend who delivered the second communication, then again addressed them as follows:

FRIENDS AND BROTHERS,

What you have communicated to us at this time has been clearly understood, and we are glad to find that you see things in the same light that we see them. The several matters you have mentioned, and the difficulties you have stated, claim our sympathy and solid consideration, and we shall, I trust, take the subject up, and if a way should open for us to move forward, in aiding you in your application to the general government, we shall be willing, either on this occasion, or any other, to render every service in our power.

To the Congress of the United States.

The members of the committee appointed for Indian affairs, by the yearly meeting of Friends held in Baltimore,

RESPECTFULLY REPRESENT—

That a concern to introduce among some of the Indian tribes northwest of the river Ohio, the most simple and useful arts of civil life, being several years since laid before our yearly meeting, a committee was appointed by that body to visit them, to examine their situation, and endeavour to ascertain in what manner so desirable a purpose could be effected. A part of that committee, after having obtained the approbation of the President of the United States, proceeded to perform the service assigned them; and the result of their inquiries and observations, as reported to the yearly meeting, was, that the quantity of spirituous liquors, with which those people are supplied by traders and frontier settlers, must counteract the effect of every measure, however wise or salutary, which can be devised to improve their situation.

The truth of this is abundantly confirmed, by a

speech recently made before us by the Miami chief, the Little Turtle, which we herewith offer to your consideration, and believe the evil to be of such magnitude, that unless it can be altogether removed or greatly restrained, no rational hope of success in the proposed undertaking can be entertained; we are induced to solicit the attention of the national legislature to this interesting and important subject, a subject which we believe involves not only their future welfare, but their very existence as a people.

Signed in behalf of the committee by,

EVAN THOMAS,   JOHN McKIM.
ELIAS ELLICOTT.   JOEL WRIGHT.
JOHN BROWN.   GEORGE ELLICOTT.
DAVID BROWN.

Baltimore, 1st month, 1st, 1802.

The following address shows, that the female Friends took a deep interest in the cause of the Indians, and that their efforts were duly appreciated by the women of the Stockbridge tribe. In religion, in civilization, and all the useful arts of life, women have been pioneers, but often their efforts have been passed over in silence by the historian.

To Hannah Eddy, Martha Titus, Elizabeth Seaman, and our other Sisters, of the people called Quakers, of the state of New-York, and elsewhere.

DEAR SISTERS,

We take this opportunity to inform you, that we have been happy to see our worthy friends, Thomas Eddy, Thomas Titus, and Gideon Seaman, who have given us good counsel, which do much good on our minds. We thankfully accept of their good words, for we believe they are the children of light, and the words they spoke flow from love.

Sisters—We will also inform you, that we, and a number of our Sisters of this nation, have, this seve-

ral years past, been endeavouring to follow the good
path which leads to everlasting happiness—and that
we experience, in degree, the love of *Jesus Christ*, who
died for such sinners as we are.

Sisters—We find that these friends, who gave us
many good counsels, are true men—so we believe, that
you are, also, our true *Sisters* in the *Lord*.   Therefore, we think, you would be willing to hear from us,
who, though we are poor people, (commonly called by
many white people, Squaws,) we are rejoiced to find
that the Friends have such love, which makes no
distinction.

Sisters—We have religious meetings twice in
every week, to seek after the ways of the *Good Spirit*,
and have, at times, been comforted by him, who
searcheth all the hearts.

Although we never have seen any of you, yet let
us join hand in hand to serve the Lord Almighty,
who is able to put such weapons on our minds, to
withstand all the temptations of the evil one, and
that we may be able to hold out to the end, where
we shall join, to praise our Saviour to all eternity.
Farewell.

New-Stockbridge, 6 *mo.* 24*th*, 1797.

Signed by   Elizabeth Josy,
                   Lydia Hendrick,
                   Catherine ⋈ Naukowwisquok,
                   Catherine Quinney,
                   Catherine Kawhawsquok,
                   Catherine Quauquachmut,
                   Jenny Andrew,
                   Esther Littleman,
                   Mary Taukonnomeen,
                   Mary Holmes,
                   Margaret Quinney,
                   Hannah Seepnommow.

Directed to Hannah Eddy.

Mr. Eddy made the subject of imprisonment for debt, one of deep reflection. He did not believe that a man could, by any contract, pledge his liberty partially; and it is conceded on all sides, that no man can make himself a slave, liberty being an unalienable right. He saw that the gaols were crowded with poor debtors, sent to those awful places for small sums, in general, where their health and morals were injured, and their spirits broken down. The philanthropist alone, whose feelings are enlisted in the spirit of reform, can come to any just calculation of the number who, in former times, suffered as poor debtors. He knew that more than ten thousand were incarcerated in his own State, every year, for sums that would not average fifteen dollars each; and he had sufficient information from many other States, to discover, that the evil existed among them generally to as great an extent, according to their population. He frequently visited the gaol in the city of New York, and assisted the prisoners from his own purse, and from monies belonging to associations among the Friends. He did not live to see imprisonment for debt abolished in the State of New York; but he foresaw that the time would come, when that blot on the fame of our country would be wiped away, not only in this State, but in others. He preserved in his diary, a letter, which he believed to have been written by the celebrated Indian, Brandt, who was educated at Dartmouth College. It is so full of just remarks, and is, in itself, so great a curiosity, that I thought it worthy of being preserved.

My Dear Sir,

Your letter came safe to hand. To give you entire satisfaction, I must, I perceive, enter into the discussion of a subject, on which I have often thought. My thoughts were my own, and, being so different from the ideas entertained among your people, I

T 13

should certainly have carried them with me to the grave, had I not received your obliging favour.

You ask me, then, whether, in my opinion, civilization is favourable to human happiness? In answer to the question, it may be answered, that there are degrees of civilization, from cannibals to the most polite of European nations. The question is not, then, whether a degree of refinement is not conducive to happiness, but whether you, or the natives of this land, have obtained this happy medium. On this subject we are, at present, I presume, of very different opinions. You will, however, allow me, in some respects, to have had the advantage of you in forming my sentiments. I was, Sir, born of Indian parents, and lived, while a child, among those whom you are pleased to call savages. I was afterwards sent to live among the white people, and educated at one of your schools; since which period, I have been honoured much beyond my deserts, by an acquaintance with a number of principal characters, both in Europe and America. After all this experience, and after every exertion to divest myself of prejudice, I am obliged to give my opinion in favour of my own people. I will now, as much as I am able, collect together, and set before you, some of the reasons that have influenced my judgment on the subject now before us. In the government you call civilized, the happiness of the people is constantly sacrificed to the splendour of empire. Hence your codes of criminal and civil laws have had their origin; from hence your dungeons and prisons. I will not enlarge on an idea, so singular in civilized life, and, perhaps, disagreeable to you; I will only observe, that among us we have *no* prisons. We have no pompous parade of courts; we have no written laws, and yet judges are as highly revered among us as they are among you, and their decisions as much regarded. Property, to say the least, is as well guarded, and crimes are as impartially punished. We have among us, no splendid villains above the control of our laws. Daring wickedness is here never suffered to triumph over helpless innocence ; the estates of widows and orphans are never devoured by enterprising sharpers. In a word, we have no robbery under the colour of law. No person among us desires any other reward for performing a brave and worthy action, but the consciousness of having served his Nation. Our wise men are called Fathers—they truly sustain that character; they are always accessible, I will not say to the meanest of our people, for we have none mean, but such as render themselves so by their vices.

The palaces and prisons among you form a most dreadful contrast. Go to the former places, and you will see, perhaps, *a deformed piece of earth*, assuming airs that become none but the Great Spirit above ; go to one of your prisons ;—here description utterly fails. Kill them, if you please—kill them, too, by torture ; but let the torture last no longer than a day. Those you call savages, relent ; the most furious of our tormentors exhausts his rage in a few hours, and despatches the unhappy victim with a sudden stroke. Perhaps, it is eligible that incorrigible offenders should sometimes be cut off—Let it be done in a way that is not degrading to human nature ; let such unhappy men have an opportunity, by the fortitude of their death, of making an atonement, in some measure, for the crimes they have committed during their lives.

But, for what are many of your prisoners confined ?—For debt.—Astonishing ! And will you ever again call the Indian nation cruel ? Liberty, to a rational creature, as much exceeds property, as the light of the sun does that of the most twinkling star. But you put them on a level, to the everlasting disgrace of civilization ! I knew, while I lived among the white people, many of the most amiable contract debts, and, I dare say, with the best intentions. Both parties, at the time of the contract, expect to find their advantage. The debtor, we will suppose, by a train of unavoidable misfortunes, fails; here is no crime, nor even a fault; and yet, your laws put it in the power of the creditor to throw the debtor into prison, and confine him there for life!—a punishment infinitely worse than death to a brave man; and, I seriously declare, I had rather die by the most severe tortures ever inflicted on this continent, than languish in one of your prisons for a single year. Great Spirit of the universe! And do you call yourselves Christians? does, then, the religion of Him whom you call your Saviour, inspire this spirit, and lead to these practices?—Surely, no. It is recorded of Him, that a bruised reed he never broke. Cease, then, to call yourselves Christians, lest you publish to the world your hypocrisy. Cease, too, to call other nations savage, when you are tenfold more the children of cruelty than they.

———

Mr. Eddy did not confine himself to labours of benevolence alone, but entered deeply into every plan suggested by others, or conceived by himself, that could add to the prosperity of his country. Inland navigation had early engaged his attention; but there must have been many minds at work in planning and carrying into effect the grand canal of the state of New-York. The claims of each individual were urged with pertinacity by their friends. De Witt Clinton, the most prominent person in the great work, has established a rule for the just distribution of the honours flowing from this important undertaking, which ought to be regarded. He says, *" For the good which has been done by individuals, or communities, in relation to the work, let each have a due share of credit."* The difficulty of giving each this share, has been met by Doctor Hosack, in his excellent memoir of De Witt Clinton; and as I have never heard this distribution of honours doubted for its fairness, I have ventured to extract it, as no one had better means than this distinguished writer for forming a correct opinion. He says, " In noticing this great event, this era in the life of Mr. Clinton, and which will ever be identified with his fame, posterity will demand a minute detail of the commencement, the progress, and the completion of an undertaking that ranks among the most important that has been effected in any age, or in any country. Posterity will look back to the authors of the blessings, and the benefits, which this great event has secured to this state and nation.

" The question, then, here naturally presents itself, Who first projected the system of inland navigation from the Lakes to the Hudson, and the Atlantic Ocean? and who were the instruments of its accomplishment? In replying to these important inquiries, I am fully aware of the delicacy of the task before me.

"The claimants to this honour are numerous and respectable, ahd the claims of each to a certain extent founded in justice. While the minute details upon this subject are passed over as out of place on the present occasion, I trust it will not be uninteresting to this intelligent assembly, to advert to a brief sketch of the most interesting facts which this examination has enabled me to develop, some of which, it will be found, have hitherto been totally overlooked in the public communications that have appeared upon this subject. In viewing the origin and progress of this great achievement, our attention is drawn to its numerous friends, who have, in various capacities, contributed to its accomplishment. But, in order that each of the numerous benefactors to this work may have his due share of praise, proportioned to the services he has rendered, it is proposed to divide them into various classes, designating the nature, character, and extent of those services. I am fully sensible that fame has given to some a degree of reputation to which they are not entitled, to the extent in which it is bestowed ; while to others much is due for the assistance they have rendered

13*

in the accomplishment of this important work, and whose contributions are comparatively little known to the world, or have been but imperfectly acknowledged. So far, therefore, as laborious inquiry has enabled me to ascertain the facts now to be related, distributive justice, the 'suum cuique tribuito,' shall be most strictly and impartially observed.

'Amicus Plato—amicus Socrates—sed magis amica veritas.'

" The contributors to canal navigation in the state of New-York, may be considered as consisting of four great classes: in the first, may be enumerated, those foreseeing and predicting from the general face of the country, the union of the lakes, the creeks and rivers of the west, by measures calculated to remove obstructions, improve the natural navigation then existing, and ultimately, by different outlets, to connect the same with the ocean. In this class, the names of Cadwallader Colden, Sir Henry Moore, George Washington, George Clinton, and Gouverneur Morris, are prominent. In the second class, are to be noticed, those who proposed, by artificial navigation or canals, to form a connexion between the waters of the Hudson and Lake Ontario, Lake Erie, or both. Christopher Colles, Jeffrey Smith, Elkanah Watson, Philip Schuyler, Jesse Hawley, and Joshua Foreman, deserve the most honourable mention in this place. Thirdly, those who, in the year 1810, have been chiefly instrumental in effecting a direct internal communication between Lake Erie and the Atlantic. In this class, Thomas Eddy, Jonas Platt, and De Witt Clinton, stand conspicuous. Fourthly, another class of benefactors to this great work, is composed of numerous members of both Houses of the Legislature, who took a prominent station in devising and sustaining the measures necessary to carry the same into effect ; the various canal commissioners, engineers, surveyors, and many private but public spirited citizens, in various parts of the state, who have zealously given their personal attentions and services to this herculean undertaking, and to whom too much praise cannot be ascribed : so great is the number composing this class, that I am compelled, at this time, to forbear from their enumeration. The commissioners of the canal fund, as distinguished from that of Canal Commissioners, and composed of the Lieutenant Governor, the Comptroller, the Attorney General, the Surveyor General, the Secretary and Treasurer, to whose special care are committed the regulations of the tolls, and other circumstances relating to the government of the canal, are entitled to high approbation, for their intelligent and faithful discharge of the duties assigned them. To all these different classes of coadjutors, may be ascribed a high and enviable measure of applause.

" The sagacity of some, in early perceiving the practicability, and utility, of the inland communication ; the diligence and zeal of others, in unremitted exertions to accomplish it ; and the devotion and sacrifices of all to its completion, will be remembered by their successors with everlasting gratitude."

We, fortunately, have been able to get Mr. Eddy's own account of his share in the great work of the Erie Canal.

" I was one (says he) of the first Directors of the Western Inland Lock Navigation Company, and continued as a Director, and Treasurer, until the company disposed of their property to the state, in 1820. I applied myself, with much zeal, in forwarding the views of the company, and in improving the internal navigation of the state. Our funds were not sufficient to extend any improvement, further than a few miles west of Rome. The company had in their service, William Weston, an eminent engineer, from England, and in company with him, and General Schuyler, the President, I made several journies to the westward, in order to explore and examine the country, as far as Seneca Lake, in order to ascertain the practicability of making improvements in the navigation, as far as that place. Being well satisfied, from my own observation, of the practicability of making extensive improvements, by means of canals, &c., through the western parts of the state, and considering the incalculable advantages that would result from the completion of such a magnificent work, my mind was devoted to its accomplishment. As I was active in the prosecution of the improvements made by the Western Inland Lock Navigation Company, the geography and topography of the western parts of this state were very familiar to my mind, and having been very intimate with Mr. Weston, when he was in this country, employed by the company as Canal Engineer, and having accompanied him in exploring the country, from Rome to Cayuga Lake, in 1796, and being repeatedly with him, whilst he was employed on the canals on the Mohawk river, my knowledge of the whole face of the country fixed in my mind an ardent desire to extend a complete canal navigation, from Rome to Seneca river. Occasionally, for many years, I urged the Western Canal Company to extend their improvements further west. A vast sum of money had been expended by them in improving the navigation of the Mohawk, which, for many years, absorbed the tolls, and prevented a dividend being made among the stockholders. Under these circumstances, no importunities of mine could prevail on the company to make advances for further improvements. In March, 1810, I was at Albany, and it occurred to me, that probably the Legislature might be induced to appoint commissioners, to examine and explore the western parts of the state, for the purpose of ascertaining the practicability of extending canal navigation, and to estimate the expense, and report thereon. I was perfectly convinced, that if commissioners should be appointed, they would make a very favourable report. My friend, Jonas Platt, (now one of the Judges of the Supreme Court) was then a member of the Senate, and on the evening of the 12th of March, I called upon him, and suggested to him a plan, on which I had never consulted any person, of proposing to the Legislature, to appoint Commissioners, as before mentioned; and I proposed to him, that he should use his endeavours in the Senate, to farther the plan. He replied, he very highly approved of my proposition, and asked why not make it the duty of these commissioners to explore the country, as far as Lake Erie, with the view to ascertain the practicability of making a complete canal, from thence to the Hudson? We immediately drafted a joint resolution, to be offered to both branches of the Legislature, which it was agreed he should present to the Senate next morning. We also thought it would be proper for us, then to fix on suitable names to offer to the Senate, as Commissioners, and we agreed in the necessity of selecting persons equally from the two great political parties, which then divided the state. This we did, according to the best judgment we could form, and the following gentlemen were named, viz., Gouverneur Morris, De Witt Clinton, Stephen Van Rensselaer, Simeon De Witt, William North, Thomas Eddy, and Peter B. Porter. It was concluded that I should meet Judge Platt, at the Senate Chamber, next morning, when I accordingly attended, and we called out De Witt Clinton, and showed him the resolution. He expressed his hearty concurrence with our plan, and as soon as the Senate was formed, Judge Platt presented the resolution, which we had prepared the previous evening. It was seconded by Clinton, and passed without a dissenting voice. It passed the house in the same manner, within an hour after. In the summer of 1810, I accompanied the other Commissioners, in exploring the country, as far as Lake Erie. In 1811, we made our first report to the Legislature. Several laws were enacted, favourable to the prosecution of

U

the project, notwithstanding which, the measure met with a serious and warm opposition. The war with England seemed to put a stop to all farther proceedings, and many persons entertained serious doubts of the practicability of the undertaking, and if practicable, that the resources of the state were incompetent to secure its completion. Besides these difficulties, the measure was opposed, with great warmth, on party grounds. Thus circumstanced, after the war, the friends of the project appeared to be entirely discouraged, and to have given up all hopes of the Legislature being induced again to take up the subject, or adopt any measure to prosecute the scheme. However, I could not thus resign a favourite project; and, it appeared to me, that one more effort should be made; and Judge Platt, being then (Autumn of 1815) in the city, holding court, I wrote a note, inviting him to breakfast with me the next morning. He came, and I proposed to him; that if it met his approbation, I would undertake to get up a public meeting, to be held at the City Hotel, in order to urge the propriety, and policy, of offering a memorial to the Legislature, pressing them to prosecute the canal from Erie to the Hudson. Judge Platt, readily agreed to my proposition, and consented to open the business to the meeting, if one could be obtained. I then called on De Witt Clinton, who united with me in adopting measures to procure a public meeting. Accordingly, a large and respectable meeting was held at the City Hotel. William Bayard was chairman. Judge Platt made an introductory speech, and was followed by De Witt Clinton, John Swartout, and others. Cadwallader D. Colden, De Witt Clinton, John Swartout, and myself, were appointed a committee, to draft a memorial to the Legislature. This memorial was drawn up by De Witt Clinton, and from the masterly manner in which it was written, it was evident he had a complete knowledge of the subject, and evinced the uncommon talents of the author. It was signed by many thousands in the city, and throughout the state. With the Legislature, it had the desired effect, and was the means of establishing the canal policy on a firm basis, and producing the law of 15th of April, 1817, directing the work to be commenced, which was accordingly done on the 4th of July following.

" From the period of presenting the first report of the commissioners to the legislature, in 1812, to the passing of the act of 1817, (excepting two years of the war with England) I attended the several sessions of the Legislature, for the purpose of interesting the members in the great project of the proposed canal, from Lake Erie to the Hudson River. De Witt Clinton, and myself, were uniformly engaged in using every means in our power, by distributing pamphlets, and endeavouring to explain to the members, the great value and importance of such a canal, and showing them the great advantages the state would derive, as to its agricultural and commercial improvements, and the increase of revenue, from tolls. We were encouraged to pursue further exertions, by procuring an act, in 1813, which authorized the commissioners to obtain a loan of five millions of dollars, to enable the state to prosecute the grand undertaking. This act was afterwards repealed, and nothing further was done during the war, and from the period of the termination, until the meeting held at the City Hotel, in the latter part of the year 1815. The friends of the plan were much discouraged, in consequence of the violent opposition it met with from men not capable of forming a correct judgment as to the practicability of the work.

" From the year 1810, I devoted most of my time, in endeavouring, in connexion with De Witt Clinton, and Robert Fulton, to enlighten the public mind, respecting it, by publishing pamphlets, essays in newspapers, &c. &c."

Ever watching the progress of philanthropy, Mr. Eddy early saw the great utility of Savings Banks. This excellent institution had its origin as late as 1803. From this period, the benevolent were deeply engaged in establishing savings banks in every city, town, or village, where they were required. The first savings bank that was put into operation in this country was established at Philadelphia, but almost simultaneously another at Boston. Mr. Eddy had, for some time, made great exertions to get one up in the city of New York, but he met with many difficulties in the attempt. The objections raised were, one after another, combatted with success, and at length, in 1819, Mr. Eddy, with his friends, John Murray, jun. and Jeremiah Thompson, effected this purpose. This bank has been in full óperation ever since. Mr. Eddy was a Director from its commencement until his death, and for some time Vice President of it. There are now more than fifty of these savings banks in the United States, which have been of an incalculable benefit to the poor. A bank not only saves their money, which might have been foolishly expended, but it gives a poor person no small degree of respectability among all classes of people, when he is provident enough to put his spare earnings into such an institution.

Mr. Eddy was an active and zealous member of the New York Bible Society, and amongst the first to lend his aid to its establishment as early as 1806, and continued his connexion with it until the time of his death. This Society was founded only two years after the parent society in London. The origin of the Society is a singular fact in history. It is said, that a Welsh divine, good as he of the same country described by Swift, whose cassock was out at elbows, travelled to London, and stated to some of the religious societies the want of bibles in his flock, and the great scarcity of them throughout all Wales. This statement set the pious to making inquiries, and a great want of them was discovered in the army and navy, and in fact almost every where. In a short time a society was formed, whose growth has no parallel in the history of nations. In less than thirty years, the branches of this noble society have caused the Scriptures to be translated and printed in more than a hundred different languages, and spread it over the charitable globe. This book is now familiar to the Esquimaux of our northern regions, is spread throughout Asia, and is known in Africa. From five thousand Bible Societies that can be enumerated, issued every year almost an incredible number of volumes, and therefore no one will perish for lack of vision. These bibles have not only spread the christian religion, but have been the means of introducing letters where they have been unknown before. The first talents of Europe have been engaged in translating them into various languages, previously but little known, even to the learned.

With a sagacity that seems to foresee the results of the experience of many years, Mr. Eddy was for having the bible go out without note or commentary, that good sense and faith might have their full influence. This is now, after all the experience had on the subject, thought to be the best course to pursue.

The success of these societies have had salutary influence among those who have been engaged in the cause. Many young men have read the Bible with care and attention, who never would have done it, if the societies of which they were members had not had before them subjects of discussion, requiring something more than a cursory knowledge of the Scriptures. Youth is ambitious, and will not be ignorant of that which it is praiseworthy to obtain, if rightly set before them. Another beneficial effect of the Bible, and other societies, of a charitable and religious kind, is, that they draw young men from gay habits, and give them stability and gravity in early life. In truth, it may be set down as an axiom,

14

that when institutions of learning and benevolence increase, frivolity and dissipation decrease.

The following reflections were found among Mr. Eddy's papers, in his own hand writing, and show how deeply this great cause had sunk into his heart.

"The formation of the American Bible Society, has often disposed my mind, to reflect on the past and present state of society in the world. In the course of such reflections, I am naturally led to admire the goodness and love of the divine author of our existence, in preparing, in his own way, the improvement and melioration of mankind. His wisdom is displayed, in proportioning the degree of light to our weak and feeble state. The splendour of the sun is preceded by the dawn of day—so it is with respect to the many essential and important truths, with which the minds of men have been enlightened at different periods of the world. Thus, formerly, an eye for an eye, a tooth for a tooth, or the life of an offender as an expiation for his crime, were the rude summary laws, which *then* seemed to be the perfection of justice. But the mild principles of the Christian religion, held out an easy and simple lesson for the instruction of men, and taught them—' Whatsoever ye would that men should do to you, do you even so to them'—' love your enemies—do good unto them that despitefully use you.'—It is certain, that even many of those, who were not baptized into the spirit of our holy religion, were considerably influenced by these solemn and self-evident truths.

"It requires but a very slight acquaintance either with the principles of human nature, or the history of civil society, to be convinced, that until the human mind became capable of perceiving the enormity of tolerating slavery, and the cruel injustice of holding a portion of human beings in a state of abject bondage, we should never have been able to discover the necessity of those prudent, humane, and salutary regulations, which have taken the place of sanguinary penal laws.—Thus, also, has christian sympathy been gradually developed, and brought into action that spirit of philanthropy, which desires to promote the welfare of *every* part of the human family.   Hence we have been led into the exercise of those benign affections, which have pointed out to us the reasonableness and propriety of pursuing a course of mild and humane treatment, towards those unfortunate persons who are afflicted with a diminution or aberration of intellect.

" At this auspicious period let us pause—a scene of activity presents itself, fraught with an increase of knowledge, enlargement of mind, and new powers of rational enjoyment.—A new impulse has been given to the Christian family, and its influence extends to every part of the world.

"The present age may be regarded as most remarkably auspicious to the interests of mankind, it is marked by the union of benevolent persons of all religious denominations, for the promotion of useful objects ; an improved system of education has been reared up for youth, which has laid the foundation of the greatest progress in intellectual and moral improvement that the world has hitherto known. First day, or Sunday Schools, are established; and to crown all, the British and Foreign Bible Society has been organized, and in full operation, with wonderful success, and on this day we celebrate the third anniversary of the American Bible Society.—The effects produced by *this* union are equal to the most sanguine expectations of its founders—' But Paul may plant, and Apollos may water, but God alone giveth the increase.'—Relying on a continuance of blessings from on high, the fervent friend of Bible Societies, viewing with gratitude the success of these institutions in disseminating the oracles of divine truth, looks towards the times, when the fruits of this seed shall be universally visible—he anticipates, with joy, what has been in part accomplished—that

Bible Societies throughout the Christian world, have been, in the hands of Providence, the means of effecting a union of Christians, who, once widely separated from each other, by countries, forms, and names, have daily approximated, and coalesced, as it were, into one spiritual body, proclaiming to the world, 'that the true and invisible church, is not to be restricted by the narrow limits of *any* particular sect, or outward form, but comprehends all the genuine worshippers of our God, and his Christ, in every part of the habitable globe.' How cheering, how animating are the happy effects, prospectively, that must result from supplying the poor and destitute with that book, which contains the words, the sayings, and testimonies of God, pointing out a direct, plain, and luminous path to immortality, promising the assistance, and requiring submission to the same spirit that inspired the holy penmen.

"In the present enlightened period, when peace pervades the whole world, is it too much to indulge the hope, that the time is not *very* remote, when the prophecy shall be fulfilled—' Nation shall not lift up sword against nation, neither shall they learn war any more.'—Though the Prince of this world may still have rule among the people, we may in the spirit of meekness pray—*thy* kingdom come.—We may hope, that predisposing causes, in the hand of divine Providence, may effect such a universal change in the minds of men, as will finally extirpate the root of bitterness, and every evil passion that serves to engender wars and fightings; and in room thereof, men may learn to love each other, which is the essential and true mark of a disciple and follower of the Prince of Peace."

From observations made upon the state of society in the city of New-York, Mr. Eddy came to the conclusion, that one great cause of crime was pauperism, which, in most instances in this country, arose from ignorance in the poorer classes of the people; and, that those who would do the best for the community, must strike at the root of this evil, by teaching the children of the poor to read and write, that they might be able to find useful employment, or learn some trade to enable them to earn a competent subsistence. As this subject was deeply impressed on his mind, he frequently corresponded with his friend Patrick Colquhoun, of Westminster, who entertained similar views, and he had, of course, the light of that powerful mind to assist him. Mr. Eddy was thoroughly convinced of the efficacy of the system of general instruction in operation in the Eastern States; but, he thought, that it would be quite impossible to bring the Legislature of New-York to pass a law for such a school system, at that time;—such a one must grow up radically with a people—it cannot easily be done, after the population is numerous, and wealth has greatly increased. The rich man will not consent that he should be taxed, according to his property, to maintain schools, and then see that money distributed in districts, according to the number of children under a certain age, such as usually attend an instructor the whole or a portion of a year.

Mr. Eddy had frequently conversed with his friends, John Murray, jun. and Matthew Franklin, on the subject of schools; and, in February, 1805, they proposed to him, to form an association of Friends, to establish a free school, for the benefit of poor children, not members of their religious society. To this Mr. Eddy objected, as he thought it would be impossible to raise funds sufficient to support a school, except on a small scale, if it was confined to Friends alone. He then proposed to call to his aid a number of respectable citizens, of different religious denominations. The meeting was called; it was generally attended by the most active classes in the city, and a committee was appointed to raise funds by subscription; and, also, to apply to the Legislature

V   14*

for assistance. An act of incorporation, under the name of the Society for establishing a Free School, in the city of New-York, for the education of such poor children as do not belong to, or are not provided for by, any religious society, was obtained. The school was soon opened, and twelve scholars admitted. From this exertion, grew the splendid system of education now in operation in the state of New-York. There had been some legislative provisions previously enacted, but the act had expired, without producing any beneficial effects. At the commencement of the system, the instruction was confined to the poor, who were not otherwise provided for; at length it extended to all classes, and the reluctance that was felt, by those in good circumstances, to sending their children to these common schools, is every day diminishing, and will soon cease altogether. The first men of New England were educated in their common schools.* Professor Johnson has written a fair and pretty full account of education in the state of New-York, which I here insert, as it is the best extant. This system has even exceeded the calculation of Mr. Eddy himself.

* In New England, although every man who pays a tax, has a vote, not only in general elections, but, also, in town offices, and in raising money, and expending it; yet, the wealthy and well-to-do, have to take care of the poor; for, in many instances, they have been opposed to raising money for their common schools. In a town in Massachusetts, of no inconsiderable size, where education is under the best of regulations, a proposition was made, in town-meeting, to establish another school. A poor man, who often admired his own eloquence in these primary assemblies, opposed the measure, on the ground of oppressive taxation, and spoke so strongly, that many began to doubt the expediency of establishing another school at that time. A friend to the proposition for another school followed the orator. He had prepared to meet this influence. He showed, in the first place, that the speaker, who alone opposed the measure, had been the father of ten sons, who were all educated at the common schools in the town, and that these sons had, on an average, been at school seven years each. The gentleman who argued in favour of the additional school, next exhibited the school tax, from the time the opposer first paid a tax, to that year, and showed that his proportion of the whole sum, for the seven years schooling of his boys, had been 39 cents only. They were bright boys, and often obtained prizes of books. Such is prejudice without calculation. EDITOR.

EDUCATION.

Though not the first among the states of the con-
federacy to introduce the system of universal education, New-York may, with some truth, be said to
have surpassed all the other states, in the liberality,
as well as the sound policy, of her provisions for its
maintenance.　She has happily taken the due means
between relying wholly upon taxation on the one
hand, and upon accumulated funds on the other, for
the support of schools throughout her community.
She has avoided the error of applying all her legislation to a single class of institutions ; thus showing
a spirit above the petty jealousy that would annihi-
late the higher, and a sense and patriotism that im-
peratively forbade her to neglect the lower seminaries of learning.　We do not find colleges and uni-
versities multiplied till one actually devours another,
while the mass of the community is without even
the ordinary rudiments of knowledge ; nor do we
perceive, on the contrary, the avenues to classical attainments so hedged about by the expensiveness, the
useless requisitions, and the forbidding ceremonials
which might appal the youth, whose *treasures were
only of the mind*, from attempting to gain the station
in society, for which his natural endowments had
qualified him.

There does not appear any ostentatious display
of extravagance in her expenditures for education,—
nor any of that niggardly parsimony which would
compel the people to buy a cheap commodity of
learning, sure, at the same time, that it must be a
poor one.

She has not hesitated, while prosecuting the most
magnificent schemes for improving the value of her
physical resources, to devise and execute plans far
more magnificent for the development of her intellectual treasures.　It has not been the spirit of her

measures to consign a whole generation *now existing* to brutish ignorance, in order that the *next* might riot in its earnings, and sink in the same manner into oblivion, without having been provided with means of any rational enlargement of the most ennobling faculties. She has not been terrified by the fear that the coming age, which is to be the heir of her noble heritage of knowledge, freedom, and moral power, should be compelled to pay out of its immense resources, a few of the millions by which that heritage was originally obtained. She has perceived it to be sound policy to incur a *debt*, when the transaction is sure to multiply a hundred fold the power of repaying it. The system of internal improvements, instead of absorbing and annihilating those very resources which are wanted to sustain public spirit and intelligence, by means of education, is, in New-York, made to minister directly and effectually to that object, and thus to react in producing again the foresight and discernment which were alone requisite to understand the utility of those improvements, even before they had an existence.

Origin of the System. The foundation of a system of common schools was laid in this state nearly forty years ago. The first act to that effect was passed April 9, 1795, appropriating out of the annual revenues of the state, twenty thousand pounds annually, for five years, for the purpose of encouraging and maintaining schools in the several cities and towns in the state. The several counties were required to raise a sum equal to one half of that appropriated to each by the state. At the expiration of this law, in 1800, the legislature refused to renew it; but, in 1805, impelled, probably, by a sense of the deprivation under which the state laboured, in being again thrown back upon voluntary, individual, or local efforts, the legislature passed an act, providing that the nett proceeds of five hundred thousand acres of vacant and unappropriated public lands should

be applied to form a permanent fund for the support
of common schools. In the same year, three thousand shares of bank stock were ordered to be subscribed by the state, and to belong to the school
fund. No part of this fund was to be applied to its
ultimate object, until the interest should amount to
fifty thousand dollars annually.

In 1811, measures were taken to organize and establish, in active force, a system of schools; such a
system was *reported* in 1812, and the first distribution of money under the provisions of 1805, and in
accordance with this system, were made in the year
1816. Besides the avails of the lands, and of the
bank stock, above mentioned, the legislature enacted,
in 1819, that one half the amount to be received from
quit rents; the *loans* of 1790, and of 1808; the *shares*
of the capital stock of the Merchant's Bank, held by
the state; the nett proceeds of *lands escheating* to
the state, in the military tract; and the nett proceeds
of the *fees* of the clerks of the supreme court, should
all be assigned to this fund. In 1824, a reservation
in certain grants for lotteries, amounting to forty
thousand dollars, was added to the fund. In 1826,
it was enacted, that one hundred thousand dollars
should be annually distributed, by the state, for the
support of common schools; but, as the fund then
produced but eighty-five thousand dollars, the remaining fifteen thousand dollars were paid from the general funds of the state. In 1827, further appropria-
tions, to make up the full amount of one hundred
thousand dollars, were made from the state loans of
1786, and from the bank stock still held by the state.
These two items amounted to one hundred and
thirty-three thousand six hundred and sixteen dollars.

In the same year, the credit of the state was
pledged, in certificates of stock, to a canal company,
(the Hudson and Delaware,) which certificates were
to be sold, and the premiums obtained added to the
school fund; this transaction produced fifty thousand

dollars ; and, finally, a large number of town lots, at
Oswego, amounting to ninety-one thousand three
hundred and forty-nine dollars, were sold in the
same year, and the proceeds, together with all the
sums obtained from the above-mentioned sources,
swelled the productive capital at the beginning of
1828, to one million six hundred and thirty thousand
eight hundred and ninety-five dollars. The *constitution of the state* provides, that the proceeds of all
lands which shall be hereafter sold, or disposed of,
shall belong to the fund for the support of common
schools. In 1830, these lands consisted of eight hundred and sixty-nine thousand one hundred and
seventy-eight acres, estimated at half a million of
dollars, which, added to the productive capital,
makes two millions one hundred and thirty thousand
eight hundred and twenty-five dollars. Besides the
general fund of the state, there are likewise several
local funds arising out of certain reserved lands in
the respective counties. More than eighty towns are
stated to participate in the benefit of these funds,
amounting to the sum of about seventeen thousand
dollars annually.

Progress of the System. The first distribution of
public moneys, out of the fund, was made, as we
have said, in 1816, and not till then, can the system
be said to have gone into actual operation. An estimate may be formed of the influence of this system,
by comparing the state of things before the funds
became available, with that which has existed since.
In sixteen counties in which the state of schools was
reported in 1798, the number of schools was then one
thousand three hundred and fifty-two, and of scholars
fifty-nine thousand six hundred and sixty. In the
same counties, in 1828, the number of school districts
established was two thousand five hundred and
eighty-six, and of scholars attending them, one hundred and forty-two thousand three hundred and
seventy-two. Even this comparison falls far short

of exhibiting the actual increase of schools, and of pupils throughout the state ; for, in 1798, there were in all but twenty-three counties organized, and therefore only seven which did not report. But, in 1828, there were fifty-five counties, divided into seven hundred and forty-two towns and wards, and eight thousand two hundred and ninety-eight school districts, containing four hundred and forty-one thousand eight hundred and fifty-six children. It is true, there are other causes besides the inherent efficacy of the system, which should be regarded in accounting for the rapid increase of schools and pupils. The new counties formed subsequently to 1798, were settled chiefly by emigrants from New-England, who brought with them, as an essential part of their existence, a habit of regarding *universal education in common public schools*, as among the primary objects for which *laws* are to be enacted. And when the system had been once established, it is easy to see that its operation upon the minds of new companies of such emigrants, must be to determine them to select the state which had made this munificent provision for that, which they consider as one of the first wants of their nature, to be their permanent abode, in preference to another, where no such allurement was held out, whatever might otherwise be the physical superiority of the latter. Thus we see, that the system of common schools has reacted, in turn, in favour of population, and consequently in favour of wealth and of power. physical, moral, and political.

A Comparative View of the Returns of Common Schools,
from 1816 *to* 1832, *inclusive.*

The year in which the report was made to the Legislature.	Number of towns from which the returns were made.	Whole number of school districts in the said towns.	Number of school districts from which returns were received.	Amount of public moneys received in said towns.	Number of children taught in the school districts making returns.	* Number of children between 5 and 15 years of age, residing in those districts.	Proportion of the number of children taught to the number of children reported between the age of 5 and 15 years.
1816	338	2755	2631	$55,720 98	140106	176449	4 to 15
1817	355	3713	2873	64,834 88	170385	198440	6 to 7
1818	374	3264	3228	73,235 42	183253	218969	5 to 6
1819	402	4614	3844	93,010 54	210316	235871	8 to 9
1820	515	5763	5118	117,151 07	271877	302703	9 to 10
1821	545	6332	5489	146,418 08	304559	317633	24 to 25
1822	611	6659	5882	157,195 04	332977	339258	42 to 43
1823	649	7051	6255	173,420 60	351173	357029	44 to 45
1824	656	7382	6705	182,820 25	377034	373208	94 to 93
1825	698	7642	6876	182,741 61	402940	383500	101 to 96
1826	700	7773	7117	182,790 09	425586	395586	100 to 93
1827	721	8114	7550	185,720 46	431601	411256	21 to 20
1828	742	8298	7806	222,995 77	441856	419216	96 to 91
1829	757	8609	8164	232,343 21	468205	449113	47 to 45
1830	773	8872	8292	214,840 14	480041	468257	48 to 47
1831	785	9063	8631	238,641 36	499424	497503	50 to 49
1832	793	9339	8841	244,998 85	507105	509967	1 to 1

"The above table exhibits only the amount of
money paid out of the funds, and so much as the
authority of the state imposes on the towns, to be
raised by them, in consideration of their receiving
those funds, which is an *equal sum.* The several
school districts have, besides, the authority to levy a
certain proportional sum, about double, it is believed,
of that derived from the fund.

"But this, which makes in all four times the amount
distributed from the fund, does not show the total

* The returns of the last three years embrace the number of children over
five and under sixteen years of age.

expenditure on this noble object of legislative provision.

" It was estimated at the beginning of the present year (1832), that in the nine thousand and fifty-four districts, where schools are supported, that two hundred dollars each are invested, on an average, in *school-houses*. This gives a total of one million eight hundred and ten thousand eight hundred dollars, which, together with one hundred and seventy thousand dollars invested in the same way in the city of New-York, gives a total of one million nine hundred and eighty thousand dollars, vested in school-houses, which, at an interest of six per cent. per annum, would be $118,848

Annual expense of books for 506,887, at 50 cents each, 253,443

Fuel for 9054 schools, at $10 each, 90,540

Amount of public money for teachers' wages, 244,886

Amount paid for teachers' wages, besides public money, 372,692

_____

1,080,409

showing the present annual expenditure of the citizens of this state, for the support of common schools, to be one million and eighty thousand dollars, and proving that the application of one hundred thousand dollars out of the fund, induces them to raise voluntarily more than nine times the same amount for the same object.

" *Police of the System.* This exists in the hands of one *superintendent* of common schools, who is likewise the secretary of the commonwealth ; fifty-five *clerks of counties ;* the *commissioners* of about seven hundred and ninety towns, and the *trustees* of nine thousand school districts.

" These several agents are in regular subordination to each other, and, in succession, receive and distribute the funds appropriated by the state for the support of schools. The highest officer, the *superinten-*

W 15

dent, is made directly amenable to public opinion, as well as to the law, in being required to present to the legislature annually, in the month of January, a report containing :—

" 1. A statement of the condition of the common schools in the state.

" 2. Estimates and accounts of expenditures of the school moneys.

" 3. Plans for the improvement and management of the common school fund, and for the better organization of the common schools.

" 4. All such matters relating to his office, and to the common schools, as he shall deem expedient to communicate.

" The collection of documents already issued under this requisition, contains a most useful and instructive mass of facts, which ought to be in the hands of every state legislator in the union. It may be observed, that the police of the general system is not applied in the city of New-York; where, instead of commissioners of towns and trustees of the schools, *chosen by the people*, the disbursements of the public money is entrusted to a company, called the " Public School Society." The reason or necessity of this difference of organization has never, to our knowledge, been made evident.

" In 1832, the number of academies had risen to fifty-nine, and the number of pupils was four thousand eight hundred and eighty-eight, or seventy-one to each academy. In addition to the means for supporting common schools, the state has another extensive fund, called the *literature fund*, under the management of the " *Regents of the University*," to which one hundred and fifty thousand dollars was added in 1827, the income of which was required to be distributed to the several incorporated academies and seminaries, in proportion to their numbers of pupils. It is gratifying to observe, that a liberal spirit has been manifested in furnishing to these institutions various means and implements for cultivating the natural sciences, and that some of them have already become useful to science, by their application of these means. We may refer particularly to the numerous sets of meteorological observations occasionally published by the 'Regents,' and which are all made at the academies under their charge. The money appropriated to these institutions, has been thus applied with a view of converting them into nurseries of *teachers* for the common schools.

" As the latter are generally taught but a part of the year, that is, on an average, not more than eight months, and as the teachers will generally be otherwise engaged for a portion of their time, and will not be permanently devoted to the business, it is highly important that the greatest possible number of intelligent men should be found in every precinct, capable of understanding the duties, if not of performing the labours, of teachers. In a community thus fully supplied with intelligent members, and impressed with the value of thorough instruction, dulness and mediocrity will seldom find encouragement to usurp the office and responsibility of guiding the intellectual pursuits of the young ; while the agents entrusted with the execution of the laws on education will hesitate before they ' lay careless hands on sculls that cannot teach, and will not learn.'

Mr. Eddy was also deeply engaged in the erection of a House of Refuge, in the city of New-York. His worthy friend, Professor John Griscom, made the first suggestion of such an institution to Mr. Eddy, Isaac Collins, and others, and in 1823, they succeeded in establishing this truly useful charity. The learned and benevolent professor lives to see his institution flourish, as an auxiliary to all the great purposes of philanthropy to which his friend, Mr. Eddy, was devoted.

With a strong desire to promote the interest of the State of New-York, several intelligent gentlemen of the state formed a society "for the acquisition and diffusion of all useful intelligence connected with the inland trade and navigation of the country." The society was called, the New-York Corresponding Association for the Promotion of Internal Improvement. When the association was organized, De Witt Clinton was chosen President, and Doctor Samuel L. Mitchell, and the Hon. Cadwallader D. Colden, Vice Presidents, and Thomas Eddy, Chairman of the committee of correspondence and publication. The association exerted themselves for several years with great assiduity, and the labours of the chairman were very arduous, but promptly discharged. Who has now the records of that association, I have not been able to discover, but much valuable information must have been collected by such indefatigable and intellectual men as formed that association; and it is well known, that their publications were numerous.

On the great subject of slavery, which is now agitating the world, Mr. Eddy took an early part. He saw millions suffering in bondage, and willed them to be free; but this was not enough; he knew that means must be applied to ends, and that it was in vain to deplore the condition of the Africans without strenuous exertions. He was an active member of the Abolition and Manumission Societies, and corresponded with the philanthropists of Europe on the subject, as well as with the leaders in the cause of freedom in Hayti. He saw, as every wise man does, that the evil was one that increased in magnitude every day, and as time advanced, became more difficult to eradicate. It was the voice of such philanthropists, that assisted the politicians in fixing the boundaries of the slave-trade, which was the first step in the march of this charity ; and which, if judiciously followed up, will, in the end, drive the evil from this country and the West Indies, and perhaps from

the world.   The curse is becoming more intolerable
to the man who is considered the wealthy owner of
slaves, than even the imagination of the opposers of
slavery could have pictured.

The great work of emancipation and colonization
is going on with zeal and success.   Beside the Parent
Colonization Society, fifteen State Colonization Societies have been formed, and more than two hundred
and fifty auxiliaries established.   New associations
are every day forming, to raise the condition of the
coloured free population; and these societies greatly
assist each other.   These associations, formed for the
purpose of enlightening and benefiting the world,
are the great moral engines by which it is now and
hereafter to be moved.

———

In the course of Mr. Eddy's progress in the various
walks of philanthropy, he kept up a correspondence
with several distinguished philanthropists in Europe,
and in this country.   Several of those letters which
passed between Mr. Eddy and his coadjutors, I shall
here insert; for what such men as Colquhoun,
Lushington, Roscoe, Clinton, Livingston, Colden,
Schuyler, Throop, and others of the same high reputation, have committed to paper, should be safely recorded for all future times.   They were among the
pioneers of true reform, and exhibited a rare union
of intellectual light with moral courage.   The letters
are given according to date, as it would not have
been possible to have arranged them in order of subjects, as some of the communications touch on a
number of topics.

New York, 12th month, 7th, 1799.
DEAR FRIEND,
As it may be proper for the Canal Company to
make an application to the legislature this winter, I
think it would be right to be prepared early.   We
15*

are in debt to the State 15,000*l.* Many reasons may be urged to induce the legislature to take so many of the unsubscribed shares, as amount to that sum; they certainly would be more ready to do this, than to relinquish a claim for the interest for four or five years, as we proposed last winter. Whilst we are obliged to pay 900*l.*, per year, interest on the above debt out of the tolls, we will not be able to divide to the stockholders more than two per cent, as a dividend. Perhaps some other way may occur to thee to propose, for them to afford us pecuniary aid.

The claims of the people at Still-Water are not yet satisfied. Suppose the directors were to lay a requisition, payable 1st May next, and the stockholders refuse to pay, the comptroller would pay for the shares held by the state, the claimants might then be paid; the corporation dissolved, and the whole stock of the Northern Company belong only to the state. I take the liberty of sending those hints, in hopes thou wilt be so good as to improve them, and if it meets thy approbation, to draw a petition to the legislature on behalf of the Western Company, containing something like what I have mentioned in the preceding part of this letter, and a copy for the consideration of the Board, with such further remarks as will occur, to be sent to the vice president as soon as possible. Thou wilt excuse my anxiety to have this communication early, as I expect to leave here for the north, and soon after the assembly meets.

The attorney general says, he had a good deal of conversation with thee, relative to the proposed law, to fix a punishment for small offences, and for regulating county prisons. I beg to remind thee of the plan I proposed, subject to thy improvement, viz. In each county prison, to have as many rooms (or cells) made as is convenient, six by eight feet. A single justice to sentence an offender to be confined therein, from twenty-four hours, to ten days. Three justices to sentence a criminal for thirty days, and the Court of Quarter Sessions, ninety days; all greater offences, to be sent to the state prison for one or more years. No intercourse to be allowed with untried prisoners, or debtors, and a total prohibition to their wives, chíl-dren, friends, or any person whatever. Inspectors to visit the prison, at least once every month, to examine into the conduct of the keeper, who should have rules made by the inspectors, for his government. The rooms should, by law, be directed to be white washed twice every year, and no other than a low diet be allow-ed, and strictly to prohibit any spirituous liquors. The inspectors might be appointed by the county court, or supervisors, or by council of appointment. Many of the jails at present are taverns; this should be by law prevented. An allowance to the keeper sufficient to procure a man of fair character should be paid out of the public treasury. As our laws now are, the keeper, as he must have charge of the debtors, must be appointed by the sheriff.

If what I have suggested meets thy approbation, I know thou wilt considerably improve my plan; if so, and thou hast leisure to draw a bill, it will much oblige me to be favoured with a copy.

Be pleased to accept my best wishes for thy health, and believe me respectfully, and very truly,

Thy affectionate Friend,

THOMAS EDDY.

Philadelphia, 2d month, 24th, 1815.

DEAR FRIEND.

During the inclemency of the weather this morn-ing, my mind has been turned towards several absent Friends, and I determined to let them know it; per-haps this may be the only sentiment worth commu-nicating to thee; if it so turn out, thou mayest credit me accordingly.

The peace which has been lately concluded between Great Britain and this country, whilst it is a subject of general greeting and rejoicing, will, I hope, impress our minds with thankfulness to him who is the author of every good and perfect gift; and dispose us in future to harmonize more with each other. That political trick and juggle, by which many have contrived to direct the minds of the innocent and unwary, brought us to a precipice, to which it is even now difficult to look back without shuddering. If honesty of intention, and integrity of conduct, were but the rule and practice of those appointed to direct the affairs of the nation, I think, with the warning we have had, we might long remain a separate and peaceful people; but whether we are or shall soon become fit to receive, and capable of enjoying, such blessings, is known only to him whose ways, though past finding out, must be infinitely great and good, and must have for their object the happiness of his creature, man.

Not only have I contemplated the subject, as to its general effect; but also as to its effect on some of my personal friends. I have anticipated the pleasure of hearing that it will effectually relieve those in New York, who have been threatened with pecuniary loss and embarrassment, by reason of the failure of Minturn and Champlin, and that they themselves will be restored to a state of as much ease and affluence as will do them good. I should be made glad by hearing from thee, to this effect.

Another anticipation I have indulged in. That thyself and wife will give us your company at the time of the next Yearly Meeting. Nor do I mean to confine it to you only, but such other of the family as may accompany you.

Present my Sally's love to Hannah and the children, and accept the assurance of my esteem.

SAMUEL W. FISHER.

To Thomas Eddy, and Thomas C. Butler, Esquires.
RESPECTED FRIENDS,

Having been informed that you can give us information relative to the penitentiary in New York. We have to address you in the name, and on behalf of "the Philadelphia Society for alleviating the miseries of public prisons," which, at. a late meeting, directed the secretaries " to correspond with such persons as are engaged in the conduct of penitentiaries, instituted in the different states of the union, wherein the humane and improved system of penal laws are enforced; and, especially, to ascertain the influence thereof, on the subjects of such treatment, as well as their effect on the general condition of society."

Since the establishment of this institution, many of its zealous and benevolent founders have gone down to the grave. Some few, however, continue actively interested in its concerns; who were early engaged in those humane exertions, which, regardless of the influence of prejudice, and the example of ages, aimed at the accomplishment of a reformation in the penal jurisprudence of Pennsylvania. With these are now united others, who, from a conviction of the importance and utility of those labours, as well as knowledge of the success of the experiments which flowed from them, have been induced to give their assistance to the same philanthropic cause.

To both these descriptions of our members it hath become an interesting inquiry, what have been the effects produced in your state by the adoption of a meliorated code of criminal laws? Whether, allowing for the increase of population, since their creation, crimes have diminished in their number, or degree of enormity? Whether individuals, who, by their errors, have unhappily been the subjects of your penitentiary system, are, since its wholesome correction, restored to usefulness in the community? and, generally, whether the moral condition of society has been improved, and the security of its members promoted, by the abolition of punishments, which were not less vindictive and cruel, than was the employ-

X

ment of them degrading to the character of our species?

It is not only for our own satisfaction, that we are desirous of obtaining whatever information you can furnish in relation to these interesting subjects, but because we believe the combined experience of all those who have been engaged in this great object of state polity, cannot fail to advance its value in the estimation of others, and thereby subserve, at once, the purposes of justice, and the cause of humanity.

We believe that, in our own country, the number of its friends is gradually multiplying; and it is with peculiar satisfaction, we have heard of the exertions which some benevolent individuals, in their private capacity, as well as enlightened statesmen, in their public character, are employing in Great Britain, to render the laws of that kingdom less sanguinary.— These advocates of reformation have had the candour to acknowledge, that they were encouraged to commence the laudable work, from the success which had followed our experiments; and hence we see the importance of embodying all the evidence which can be collected. to support, in England, this effort of mercy, and of diffusing these beneficent principles, through all those nations and states, by which they have not yet been adopted.   We are, very respectfully, &c.

CALEB CRESSON, junr., $\rbrace$ *Secretaries.*
ROBERT VAUX,

New York, 6th month, 5th, 1802.
RESPECTED FRIEND,

Thy sentiments on crimes and punishments communicated to the public, in two excellent works on the Police of London and the Thames, has induced me, without the pleasure of a personal acquaintance to inform thee of the progress of an experiment making in this state, by adopting a plan similar to the one formed, soon after the revolution, in Pennsylvania, for the amelioration of the penal laws.

Some years ago, I was led to reflect on the state of
the criminal code in this state, and warmly impressed
with the belief, that all laws not founded on the
principles of truth and justice, the common feelings
of humanity, and the rights of mankind, should be
repealed; I took a very decided and active part in endeavouring to obtain a repeal of our former system, and
establishing one more consistent with the pure principles of Christianity. In 1796, our laws were altered,
a state prison was directed to be built, and I was
appointed one of the board of inspectors. My zeal
for promoting a plan, which I conceived would tend
to soften the dispositions of those concerned in government, and thereby enlighten and prepare their minds
for still more improving the condition and state of
mankind, induced me to leave extensive mercantile
pursuits, and reside near the prison, about two miles
from the city, in order that I might strictly attend to
its concerns. To reduce such a description of men
to a regular course of labour, decent behaviour, and
cleanliness, was a task that required unremitting
attention, and on the success of the scheme, depended
whether society should revive the former, or continue
the new system. I was exceedingly anxious that
our prison should furnish a model for other states,
and have therefore attended, when in health, almost
daily, to superintend its concerns, and every winter
for five years past, visited Albany, in order to promote
the passing of such laws or alterations of former
ones, as were deemed necessary, to perfect the present code. I have lately published an account
of the prison, for the information of the public;
and with a view to excite other states to follow our
example. I take the liberty now, to present thee
with one of those publications, which will give full
information of the management, economy, &c. of the
prison.

I understand there are some prisons in England,
where the convicts are employed at labour. I should

be very glad to obtain information of the kind of work carried on; if the product is sufficient to pay for their support, clothing, &c. I expect there are printed accounts of them; and also some late books, or pamphlets, on crimes and punishments, and on prisons. I therefore take the liberty to request of thee, to be so obliging as to give my good friend, Charles Wilkes, a memorandum of such as in thy opinion may be worth my procuring. I should be very glad to obtain the report of the Committee of the House of Commons, on Bentley's plan; also, any or all of his writings. I have Howard, and the first edition of Police of London and Thames. If thou hast published any thing lately, be pleased to insert it in the list. My friend Wilkes will take the trouble of procuring from the booksellers, and forwarding to me, such books as thou wilt be so obliging as to recommend.

I enclose the last report of the inspectors of the state prison to the legislature; they passed a law to build a prison, for solitary confinement, on the plan recommended in the Report. I have often thought that this would be an excellent plan in the city of London, for the punishment of petty offences, and for preventing greater ones.

I am clearly of opinion, that *all* prisons intended for the confinement of convicts for a term of years should be so constructed as that they should lodge in separate rooms; by being kept thus solitary and separate from each other, it would be more likely to produce reformation, and prevent escapes.

There are in the prison 145 of the convicts employed at shoemaking, and that business has hitherto been carried on, by purchasing leather, &c., and disposing of the shoes and boots when manufactured. As this required a considerable capital, and was always attended with inconvenience, we have lately dropped conducting the business in this mode, and have agreed with shoemakers in the city, to take in work at a fixed price, for making each pair of shoes and boots, according to the size and quality—in this manner of employing those 145 men, they now earn twelve hundred dollars per month, and it is now certain, that the labour performed by the prisoners will be more than sufficient to support and clothe them, pay for bringing them from the counties, and other incidental expenses.

I have hitherto acted as agent, but the system being now completed, equal to my most sanguine expectation, I intend this summer to resign that situation.

I am, with regard and esteem,
Very respectfully,
Thy assured friend,
THOMAS EDDY.
To P. COLQUHOUN, London

Eastbourne, in Sussex, 28th August, 1802.

SIR,

Your very acceptable letter of the 6th June, accompanied by your valuable and interesting publication, giving an account of the State Penitentiary House in the city of New York, was recently left at my house in Westminster, by Mr. Wilkes, and has since been transmitted to me to the country, to which I have retired for a short time, with a view to a little relaxation from the labours attached to an arduous public duty.

My temporary retirement has furnished me with an early opportunity of perusing with attention, and also with much interest, your very excellent statement of important and useful facts, and I consider myself under infinite obligations to you, not only for the knowledge of these facts, but for the acquaintance of the worthy and respectable author, who has devoted so much time, and made so many sacrifices, to promote the cause of humanity, and the good of his fellow creatures.

It is a peculiar gratification to me, to have thus
16

discovered that my literary productions have fallen under the cognizance of one who is able, and also so thoroughly disposed, to carry the principles they contain, on the subject of crimes and punishments, into practice ; and it is no small gratification to me to find, that upon a subject so interesting to virtue and humanity, our sentiments are completely in unison.

Your exertions, and those of your worthy colleagues, appears to have done much for the State of New York, and I entertain no doubt of the sentiments of all the worthy and reflecting part of the community being on your side in a short time; that the great and good work, your unexampled perseverance has so happily accomplished, will produce consequences which will not only bring conviction to the minds of the most prejudiced, but also that you will live to see and experience that reward, in the ultimate and complete success of the design, which, to a mind like yours, must go far beyond the praises and encomiums of the world.   Your details are so clear, so accurate and interesting, that they will be read with avidity all over Europe.

To me it has been no small gratification, although I have, on account of the war and other circumstances, made as yet small progress in the objects I have recommended to be adopted in this country, that my writings have been translated into most of the languages in Europe, with a prospect of general benefit to mankind, since, in all countries, the vices and crimes of individuals are similar, and only differ as to their extent.

I had read some years since, with the most heartfelt pleasure, two different accounts of that most excellent institution, the Penitentiary House in the city of Philadelphia, which is the more valuable as it furnishes an irrefragable proof to all Europe, as well as America, that the great desideratum has been accomplished, of rendering the labour of criminals productive, to a degree more than equal to their maintenance, and what is of more importance, of restoring them again to society with amended morals, and in a situation to become useful instead of noxious members of the community.

The criminal police is an object of the greatest importance in all countries, but particularly in America, not only as a new country, but as a Republic, exposed, from peculiar circumstances, to be contaminated by importations of the scum and outcasts of all Europe. This, and other considerations, have excited great doubts in my mind, whether the introduction of Europeans in the present state of the population of America, is not, upon the whole, injurious. This is exemplified in no inconsiderable degree in the comparative view you have given of the countries to which the different classes of convicts belong. It might be difficult and invidious to exclude the white people of Europe, and might be a reflection upon the national character ; but, surely, this policy does not apply to the negroes of the West Indies, who, I perceive, tend, in no inconsiderable degree, to increase the calendars of delinquency.

You have been rightly informed, that several very expensive Houses of Correction have been established in England, within the last twenty years, under the authority of acts of Parliament, the outlines of which I have laid before the public ; but, although the expense has been excessive, (in one instance 80,000*l.* sterling,) I am sorry to say, that, however excellent the theory, by a fatality which is not easy to be explained, no results that can be held out as an example, can be exhibited. In one or two, in particular, *Oxford and Gloster*, where, (like the Penitentiary House at New-York) some benevolent characters have devoted much time and attention to the economy of the establishments, the labour of the convicts has been rendered, in a certain degree, productive.--We have a superb establishment in Middlesex, to which I bestowed much attention at the outset, but, instead of being seconded, I found myself counteracted in all my anxious cares to introduce a system of useful and productive labour, and I lament to say, that, in addition to fourscore thousand pounds laid out in the buildings, it costs the county nearly 4000*l.* sterling a year, to maintain the prisoners.— Contemplating the difficulties and the consequent failure of most of the plans founded on Mr. Howard's ideas, and considering the obstructions which are opposed to evils, in their nature so gigantic, I have been induced to give a decided preference to Mr. Bentham's plan, as briefly explained in my treatise on the police, (6th edition) where he proposes to enter into a contract for the labour of convicts, and to become responsible for the reformation of their manners and vices.—When I return to London, I will procure from that gentleman a copy of the detail of his plan and will have great pleasure in transmitting it to you, with such other publications as apply to the subject of Penitentiary Houses. .I will also send, if I can possibly procure it, a copy of a report of the Committee of the House of Commons.—The whole of the reports have beerf reprinted in four volumes, among which twenty-eight treats of Police. They are all extremely interesting, and, I think, you will be desirous that they should have a place in your library ; when I have the pleasure of seeing Mr. Wilkes, I will consult with him how far I should go in this respect. The first edition of the police of London may be considered as only an *imperfect sketch.* It is in the sixth edition of that work that you will find those interesting topics discussed, to which your attention is at present so laudably directed.

The last report of your committee is extremely interesting, and you press upon the attention of the legislature, with great propriety, the evils arising from the excessive multiplication of *spirit houses*, and *public houses.* Nothing tends so much to the corrup-

tion of morals, or to promote habits of idleness, ultimately generating crimes: 1200 of these receptacles
of vice in so small a city as New York, are to be considered as an evil of the greatest magnitude.   In the
metropolis of the British Empire, which contains
twelve times the number of inhabitants, the magistrates do not grant licences to more than about 4000,
although, taking in the towns and villages in the
vicinity, we have upwards of 5000 in the whole.   I
have been at great pains, in forming and enforcing
rules and orders for the proper regulation of publicans, in different districts of the metropolis, where I
have acted as a magistrate—a copy of which I will
send you.   The indiscriminate mixture of young and
old offenders, in the same prison, I observe, is mentioned with great propriety in your last report.   I
have always considered this practice (which also
prevails here) as one of the greatest nurseries of
crimes; and I am glad to find you have brought it
under the review of your legislature.   The remedy
you propose, appears to me to be the wisest and most
effectual that can be devised.

Your proposition to authorize the police magistrates to try, in a summary way, all persons committing
minor offences, such as petty assaults, drunkenness,
and acts of vagrancy, &c., will prove a great relief to
juries, and will tend much to the diminution of
crimes.   In this country, the legislature finds it
necessary every session, to extend the summary
jurisdiction of magistrates; and experience has shown,
(as these magistrates are responsible,) that instead of
abridging, it extends the liberty of the innocent part
of the community; and I can safely affirm, that had
it not been for these summary jurisdictions, it would
have been impossible, in any degree, to have kept
the vices and crimes of the people within any moderate bounds.   The present state of society and morals,
in *what is called the civilized world*, render a species
of energy necessary, which can only be attained by
    Y   16*

summary proceedings. The great inlets to vice, idleness, and crimes, are, *ill regulated public houses, gaming, horse-racing, cock-fighting, profane swearing,* and *a contempt of religious duties on a Sunday:* to which may be added, generally, every species of dissipation, which has a tendency to congregate multitudes of people on the same spot. In a new country like America, where the general prosperity of the nation depends, in so eminent a degree, on the morals of the people, the legislature cannot promote the true welfare of the state, in a greater degree, than by authorizing magistrates to correct these evils, by inflicting mild punishments in a summary way, and by commuting, in various instances that will occur, the punishment of *imprisonment* by *pecuniary penalties*, to be applied to the expenses of the police. Female prostitution, particularly in the cities in America, also requires appropriate laws, which will apply to both sexes; and those should be administered in a summary way by the magistrates, by *imprisonment*, or *mild pecuniary fines.* In like manner, brothels ought not to be prosecuted by the tedious and circuitous process of indictment and trial by jury. The expense of such prosecutions in this country, tend much to the increase of the evils of prostitution, while, through the medium of the chicane of the law, many notorious delinquents escape justice.

I could not have conceived, until I perused your accurate reports, that such a number of larcenies could have been committed in the city of New York. It is impossible that depredations to such an extent should be committed, unless there were many *receivers of stolen goods;* such as *purchasers of old metals, old apparel, ships stores, rags, and hand stuff, &c.* These classes of dealers require the watchful eye of the legislature, and much advantage would be derived, from restraining them from dealing, unless under the authority of a licence, with power to the magistrates to withhold it on the succeeding year, in case of any information of improper conduct, and to forfeit it, in case of conviction—a power also to constables, to stop and examine the persons who convey parcels, &c. after dark, and to punish the offenders if they cannot give a satisfactory account to the magistrate, how they obtained the same, would tend much to the prevention of crimes. It is by these precautions, and by mild summary punishments, that the calendars of delinquency are to be diminished in every country, and a wise legislature will look to *prevention as a primary object*, that there may be occasion as seldom as possible, to resort to punishment.

As temperance operates powerfully in preventing diseases in the human body, so will preventives tend to diminish the evils in the body politic. In America, where old prejudices do not exist, and where the laws in their progress are verging towards maturity, this preventive system can be much easier accomplished than in Europe, and if the legislature is true to itself, it will see the vast importance of establishing, in the first instance, every safe-guard to the innocent part of the community, by shutting up, as far as circumstances will permit, *every avenue to crimes*. The true interests of the state requires it, and humanity to the unhappy individuals, who are tempted to perpetrate offences, from the temptations which assail them, plead strongly for the adoption of an appropriate preventive system, applicable to the local and peculiar state of the country.

Did I not know that I was addressing myself to a man of true philanthropy, who glories in his country's prosperity, and anxiously seeks for opportunities of doing good, I should make an apology for the length of this letter; but to you, sir, it is not necessary. That you may be long spared to society, and blessed with health and vigour of mind, to enable you to prosecute the good work, which you and your worthy colleagues have so successfully began, is the sincere and earnest wish of,

Sir, your most obedient, and humble servant,

P. COLQUHOUN.

To Mr. THOMAS EDDY, New York.

P. S. I refer you to the annexed copy of my letter written from Eastbourne in Sussex, on the 28th of August. I find since my return home, that Mr. Wilkes is still absent in the country, but I am nevertheless making progression, collecting various publications to be sent you; and as soon as I have the pleasure of seeing him, I will take measures for the purpose of conveying them to you.

London, 16th February, 1803.

SIR,

Your excellent work on the state prison of New York, has been considered of so much interest and importance, by several very elevated characters in this country, that a proposition has been made to reprint it. It is now in the hands of the members for the Home Department, through whose medium, I trust, and ardently hope, it may be rendered useful in this country. According to your desire, I have occasionally been employed, for some time past, in collecting every publication which appears to me to bear on subjects of this nature, as well as on other topics of political economy, which have appeared to me to be analogous. The whole are sent in a box addressed to you, by this opportunity, in conformity to a list now inclosed; and I have particularly to request that you will accept of them from me, as a mark of my esteem and regard.

You will trace in these various tracts a very great portion of zeal and genuine philanthropy, as well as strong marks of extensive reading and profound knowledge, on subjects calculated to promote the comfort and happiness of society, in every part of the civilized world.

The first object to be attended to, with a view to the comfort, happiness, and security of a nation, is a proper provision for the education of youth. " *That country is the happiest,* (says a great writer,) *where there is the most virtue.*" To suffer the youth of both sexes to be ill educated, and to be reared to maturity without a proper sense of religion and virtue, and an abhorrence of vice, is to establish a nursery for crimes.

In a new country like America, where the population increases so fast, it becomes an important desideratum, that the means and facilities to obtain a virtuous and proper education, should keep pace with the constant increase of the youth of both sexes. Where national institutions of this nature have been established in Scotland and in Switzerland, the happiest effects have been produced. On the contrary, where this great measure of state policy has been neglected, the manners of the people have exhibited strong instances of a deficiency, manifested by extreme ignorance and immoral conduct, as it respects a considerable proportion of the lower classes of society ; and hence it is that crimes multiply, and that the adult becomes often enervated and useless to society at that period of life, when labour ought to be most productive.

Upon the subject of education, the reports which I have transmitted, published by the society for bettering the condition of the poor, furnish many excellent hints and suggestions.

The next object, as it relates to criminal offences, and which is of the highest importance to civil society, is a proper attention to those, whose indigence or idleness render them burdens upon the other classes of society. This evil becomes a hydra in every nation, where appropriate regulations do not exist for educating the offspring of indigent and profligate parents, or orphans who are cast upon the public ; and also for propping up adults, reduced to a state of extreme poverty and wretchedness, so as to compel them, at least to the extent of their abilities, to assist themselves. The want of appropriate regulations, under an accurate and correct management, as it applies to this very difficult branch of political economy, is one of the chief causes of the numerous criminal offences which afflict society in Europe. It is one of the greatest nurseries of crimes, from which you are already not exempted in the larger societies in America, perhaps from this scene of turpitude; this *gangrene*, not having as yet sufficiently attracted the notice of your government.

Upon this important branch of political economy, much useful information will be found in the reports of the society of the poor, exhibiting a vast scope for the exertion both of public and private benevolence, particularly the latter; as it respects the former, the preliminary sketches on the poor, by Jeremy Bentham, Esq., furnish much curious and important matter, which will be read with great interest by the philosopher, the statesman, and the philanthropist.

Periods of scarcity are not so likely to happen in America as in Europe: yet as the food of man rises to an enormous price in the United States, as often as extraordinary demands are made upon you, the condition of your poor, in the large cities, must, in a certain degree, claim the occasional attention of the benevolent; and therefore, as it may be interesting to know what has been accomplished in this country, and particularly in this great metropolis, during the recent periods of scarcity, I have taken the liberty to send you several tracts, and other papers, upon this subject, which have been chiefly compiled by myself, for the use of the public, and the various societies with which I was connected, where I generally had the labouring oar. These papers are the more interesting, as they tend to prove how much may be gained by an economizing system, and at how small an expense, under proper management, it is possible to feed and to prop up families in distress. The attention and labour are indeed excessive; and the reward to the numerous benevolent individuals* who came forward on this occasion, was felt to be complete, since it produced the wished for effect.

On other effects immediately connected with objects of beneficence, I beg leave to refer you to Doctor Lettsom's recent work, which I also send you, *by his particular desire*, in which you will find much useful and interesting information, calculated to improve the state of civil society, as it relates to the poor, and to analogous distempers, &c. &c. On the last subject, namely, analogous fevers, and particularly the typhus or jail distemper, you will find some new and interesting information, in a tract detailing a variety of successful experiments, which has been published and circulated by the society for bettering the condition of the poor, by which it appears emersion in water, or the shower bath, is a certain cure.

Turning from this subject, to that which relates to the preservation of morals, and the prevention of criminal offences, I must refer you to my observations on public houses, (of which I send you two copies,) and also my treatise, recently published, on the duty of a constable. The first will furnish some useful hints relative to regulations which, ere long, will be found necessary in America, (particularly in the large towns,) with respect to dram shops, and the excessive and unrestrained use of spirituous liquors, than which, when indulged in to excess, nothing can be more pernicious, both to the health and morals of the labouring people. It is the chief source of the multiplication of crimes, which afflict society in the city of New-York;—to which I might add, those persons who are permitted, without control or inspection, to

---

* On this interesting occasion, the public were under infinite obligations to the Society of Friends resident in London; without their assistance and steady perseverance. we could not have accomplished the relief which was afforded.

deal in *old metals, old ships stores, and apparel and furniture bought at second hand.* The first, namely, dram shops, corrupt the morals; while the second, by holding out facilities to thieves, by purchasing whatever may be offered for sale, without asking questions, and that too at an under price, become the fosterers of crimes.

In the tract on constables, you will see, under various heads, what provisions our laws have made for the prevention of the corruption of morals, and the commission of crimes. By the adoption of the farther regulations recommended in my treatise on the police of the metropolis, and also by the select committee of the House of Commons, much might be done in this country to diminish the number of offenders of all descriptions. Not being able to procure a copy of this very interesting report in a separate volume, an opportunity is afforded me of requesting your acceptance of the whole of the interesting reports of the select committee on finance, from which the statesman, the politician, the financier, and the political economist, will be able to acquire much useful information, highly beneficial to America. The twenty-eighth report in the second volume, treats on the *general police*, where, on this subject, you will find details highly interesting, as they relate to the measures proposed for the prevention of crimes, and the punishment of offenders.

On the subject of penitentiary punishment, I send you Mr. Bentham's two volumes, explaining the construction and general currency of his Ponoplicon; also, a parcel containing the annual reports of the penitentiary house in Dorsetshire, with other papers delivered to me by that distinguished senator, William Morton Pitt, Esq., member of Parliament for the county of Dorset, to whose indefatigable attention this establishment owes its superiority over every similar institution in this country. Mr. Morton Pitt has been much fascinated by your work, and as I have already mentioned, is anxious it should be reprinted in England; but as this desideratum may not be attained, it would be very gratifying if I could have it in my power to present to the Speaker of the House of Commons, to him, and to some other distinguished characters in this country, a copy of the work. I have inquired at different booksellers, and also of Mr. Wilkes, but I do not find that it is to be purchased.

On the subject of prisons in this country, I have only farther to call your attention to a work just published by James Nield, Esq., who, following the example of the great, the benevolent Howard, employs an easy fortune, and much of his time, in visiting the different prisons in Great Britain. His chief attention, however, has been directed to the situation of poor persons confined for civil debts, to whom, as you will observe from his work, and also from his exertions as treasurer of the society, he has been *a friend indeed.*

On the subject of punishments, I send you inclosed the last statement of the delivery of the gaol at Newgate, which has been recently sent me by the Secretary of State, and contains a general view of the disposal of prisoners for the last year, for the more aggravated offences tried at the Court of Oyer and Terminer at the Old Bailey. In this statement, however, neither the numerous persons tried at the London, Westminster, and Middlesex Sessions, nor at the Assizes and Sessions in Southwark, which makes a part of the metropolis, are included. I have no means at present of ascertaining the amount of these; but I have reason to believe they are equal, or perhaps exceed, the number stated in the last (sixth edition) of the treatise on the police.

The only use which can be made of this melancholy catalogue of depravity, is to stimulate those in power, in every country, to the adoption of such measures, as shall forewarn the unwary, arrest the

Z 17

hands of evil doers, and thereby lessen the demand for punishment. To you, sir, and to many other benevolent characters, the United States are under great obligations; but your labours are not yet terminated. Since by punishment alone, we are not to look for that amelioration in the state of society, which is to arise from the diminution of crimes, the minds of your chief magistrates and active senators, ought ever to be alive to the means of prevention. To those who are likely to commit offences, there cannot be a greater act of humanity; while on society at large, a greater benefit cannot be conferred. It is not the mere loss of property that is to be deplored. In the ramifications of vice extended broad and wide, a nation bleeds at every pore in that general contamination, which poisons the mind, renders the corporeal functions useless, and abridges that industry and exertion in beneficial labour, which constitutes the support of every state and body politic.

It is not enough to frame excellent laws to punish delinquents. The history of all civilized countries, has proved how inefficacious they are in the improvement of morals. With every attention which human wisdom can bestow, where multitudes are congregated together in gaols, who have long been apostates from virtue, vice must in general be triumphant. As you advance in population, under the unavoidable hazard of contamination by frequent importations of depraved characters, who have fled, in many instances, from the punishment due to their crimes in Europe, a vigilant and active preventive police becomes necessary. Nor should a free country complain of such a system, since crimes and criminal people constantly abridge the privileges of innocence. Restraints which attach only to evil doers, can never disturb the proceedings of the peaceful citizen in the general intercourse of society. Let the American government, before it becomes too unwieldy, guard the morals of its people as its best prop. What may be found easy and practicable in the yet infant state of society, may become difficult, and perhaps impossible, when evil habits descend from generation to generation, until at length it becomes too gigantic for human exertion. Comparatively speaking, the country is yet virtuous. To permit it to retrograde, as it becomes more wealthy and more populous, by an inattention to the general progress of evil habits, would be to entail upon posterity an excessive calamity. The task is certainly not difficult at present, since in the country there is little to fear, and hence it would seem, that the energy of police would only be necessary in the great towns, checking and restraining those propensities, which lead to the corruption of morals.   Nor ought it to be forgotten, that an indulgence in many propensities, which half a century ago were divested of their evil consequences, from the then infant state of society, became noxious as population increases. It is then *drunkenness, gaming, lewdness,* and other offences, leading to the corruption of morals, acquire their sting.   They promote idleness; while want of employment, where labour is necessary for subsistence, is the never failing inroad to crimes.

I am induced to enlarge upon this subject, from the facts you have disclosed, relative to the criminal offences committed in the city of New York.   They appear to me to be of a magnitude to excite a considerable degree of alarm with respect to the increase of criminality in the American towns; inasmuch as it would appear that they greatly exceed the number of larcenics and misdemeanours, committed in towns in Great Britain, of an equal or even a greater population; and although I have not had an opportunity of ascertaining the fact, I have an impression on my mind, that the annual convictions in the whole of Scotland, where the population approaches two millions of people, are short of those which take place yearly in the state of New York; and yet that country, from the rapid influx of riches and luxury, and extensive manufactures, cannot be said to be improving in morals. I fear the reverse is the case; since I have been recently applied to by some of the first public characters in that country, to suggest means for the improvement of their police. Arrangements and checks upon evil propensities, must be accommodated gradually to the existing state of society. The intention of all governments is to render human nature as perfect as possible, since from this perfection results the security and the comfort of the whole; but errors and imperfections incident to human nature are unfavourable, and ever will be so, to such a state of things, which can only be maintained by good and appropriate laws, wisely and prudently administered.

If the information I have transmitted, or what I have communicated in this and my former letter, (which I hope you have received,) can be of use in promoting any of your benevolent objects for the benefit of your country, it will afford me the sincerest pleasure.

I am, with great respect and esteem, Sir,
Your most obedient and
Very faithful servant,
P. Colquhoun.

A List of Books and Pamphlets transmitted to Thomas Eddy.

Tracts on the Education of Youth, and the Poor.— Two volumes containing a series of reports, of the Society for Bettering the Condition of the Poor in London, &c. A series of numbers containing the remaining reports, down to the present period, thirteen in all.

Tracts on the means of supporting the Poor, and preventing Idleness and Vagrancy.—Preliminary sketches on the Poor, by Jeremy Bentham, Esq. sent by the desire of the author. Letters to P. Colquhoun, Esq., on the subject of the Jewish poor in the metropolis.

Tracts and papers written during the late scarcity in Great Britain and Ireland.—Suggestions for economizing human subsistence, during the scarcity, with various Tracts and Addresses written by P. Colquhoun, Esq., during that eventful period.

Hints on Beneficence, and Tracts on Analogous Fevers.—Hints on beneficence, in three volumes by Doctor Lettsom, sent by the author's desire.— Tracts on Analogous Fevers, and Fever Hospital in Dublin.

Tracts applicable to the Police, to the Corruption of Morals, and the prevention of Crimes.—Observations on public houses in the metropolis, (two copies,) by P. Colquhoun. A Treatise on the functions and duties of a Constable, explaining in what manner the police of England is at present conducted, by P. Colquhoun. This work, with a few alterations, will apply to every part of the United States. Nothing upon the same plan has ever been published.

Financial and Police Reports.—Two volumes containing a history of the finances of Great Britain, and the system of public offices, &c. The twenty-eighth report in the second volume relates to police.

Penitentiary Establishments.—Ponoplicon system for reforming criminals, by Jeremy Bentham, Esq. Two letters by the same author, drawing a comparison between his system and the present mode of transportation to New South Wales. Reports on the penitentiary establishment in the county of Dorset, sent by William Morton Pitt, Esq., member of Parliament. Rules and orders proposed for the better management of the House of Correction for the county of Middlesex, situated in Cold Bathfields, Clerkenwell.

Prisons in England.—A survey of the prisons in England, with a view to the relief of Poor Debtors, by James Nield, Esq.

17*

Commercial Police.—Regulations of the port of London, and instructions to Reve Constables, by P. Colquhoun.

A packet from Jeremy Bentham Esq. to Mr. Eddy. —Mr. Eddy will see that Mr. Bentham has read his work on the New York state prison.

List of papers inclosed—also pamphlets.—1. A statement or summary view of the prisoners committed to Newgate for trial in the year 1802, with the various results. 2. Introductory letter to the fourth volume of the reports of the Society for Bettering the Condition of the Poor. 3. Extracts from Doctor Williams' publication on the effects of dram-drinking, three copies. 4. Extracts of cases of the typhus fever, recovered by affusion in cold water. 5. Hints for making straw hats, &c.

The letter, to which the annexed is an answer, is missing. It related to the agency here spoken of, respecting the Constable estate.

New-York, 5th mo. 22d, 1803.

ESTEEMED FRIEND,

Almost immediately after receiving thy esteemed favour, of the 10th February last, business called me from the city, from which I have been absent several weeks. This must be my apology for not sooner replying to thy letter. During my absence, I have been to Philadelphia, and have made some inquiries concerning the matters to which thou hast requested my attention.

It would afford me very sincere pleasure to be of service to one, for whom, though personally unknown, I cherish the highest respect and esteem, and whose benevolent and active exertions, to diminish the evils of civil society, claims the gratitude of every citizen of the world.

In consenting to take upon me the agency of thy lands here, it is proper for me to state, that, having devoted the last seven years wholly to the promotion of a favourite object, the amelioration of the penal laws, and the establishment of a penitentiary house in this state, I have been prevented from bestowing the necessary attention to my private affairs.

This object, which I have had so much at heart, being now so far accomplished, and put into a train of successful experiment, as to permit me to withdraw from that close application which has been hitherto requisite, I shall have leisure to attend to other things.

Some property which I have in Vermont, and Pennsylvania, will demand my earliest regard. Not intending to return again to mercantile pursuits, I mean to give some portion of the remainder of my life (as Providence may spare it) to the service of the poorer classes of society.—It would not, therefore, be agreeable to have any considerable obstacle interposed, which may impede the course I wish to pursue.—But the scheme of action I have proposed to myself, will not prevent my using every exertion to promote thy interests, and to fulfil thy wishes.

In whatever I do for thee, I beg to be clearly understood, as disclaiming every pecuniary compensation, beyond the actual and necessary expense attending the transactions; but I may find it for thy interest, and my own satisfaction, to use the advice and assistance of my particular and valuable friend, William Johnson, Esquire, of this city, whose disposition will prompt him to feel an equal and lively interest in whatever concerns thee, as he has read thy works with singular avidity and pleasure, and has conceived the highest respect for thee; and if he can be induced to accept it, I should cheerfully relinquish to him every compensation which thee may feel disposed, in the result of the business to bestow.—I should prefer, if it meets thy approbation, to have his name inserted with mine, in thy power of attorney, as from my intimacy with him, founded on a clear knowledge of his integrity, his philanthropy, and excellent talents, that it would decidedly be to thy interest and advantage.

I intend to send this letter by the Juliana, Captain Brown, and shall deliver to his care a small box, (marked Patrick Colquhoun, Esquire, London,) containing twelve copies of the Account of New-York State Prison, and an equal number of the last report. A packet contains two, which thou wilt be so good as to send to William M. Pitt, Esquire, whose obliging letter and reports merit my warmest thanks.—To the politeness of Jeremy Bentham, I feel much indebted, and request his acceptance of two copies of the same book, the residue are intended for thyself, and other friends.

I have not yet time to read all the books which thou sent me; but intend to do so very soon, and shall write to William M. Pitt, and Jeremy Bentham. This is intended as a letter of business; in my next I shall speak to thee on the subjects mentioned in thy most valuable interesting letters, received in answer to mine, by Charles Wilkes.

Should an edition of the work, I have sent, be printed in London, it would add much to its value, if the last report (now sent) was printed with the appendix, as it contains results more flattering than those of any former; some preliminary remarks, by thyself, or Jeremy Bentham, would stamp a greater value on the work, and give it a wider circulation.

I am, with very great regard and esteem,
  Truly,
   Thy assured friend,
    Thomas Eddy.

New York, 7th mo. 15th, 1803.
Esteemed Friend,

I have the pleasure to acknowledge the receipt of thy very acceptable and instructive letter, of 16th February, and to request thee to accept my sincere

thanks for the information it contains; and, particularly, for the truly valuable and interesting collection
of books and pamphlets, with which it was accompanied. These productions display, in a most striking manner, the zeal of the English nation (distinguished above all others for its extensive practice of
Christian charity) in the great cause of benevolence
and humanity. The perusal of them will furnish
many valuable hints to myself and others, in this
country, and animate us to follow the illustrious
example which you have set before us. Happy for
us, many of the evils which afflict and deform the
more populous societies in Europe, either do not exist
among us, or only appear in a small degree. This
exemption is the result of the peculiar state of the
country, where the wants of men are easily supplied,
the incentives to industry and enterprise numerous
and powerful, and temptations to vice comparatively
few. Thy excellent remarks, however, on public
education, and the preventive system of police, are
applicable to America, as well as every other nation;
and I have thought them of so much importance,
and so likely to do good, that I have taken the liberty
to make thy letter public ; coming from one so distinguished for his knowledge on the subjects, and
whose character and station claims the highest respect, they will have much greater weight than any
thing that could be said by one of our own citizens.
I trust the motives which have actuated me, will be
a sufficient apology for the freedom I have taken in
giving thy letter to the world.

Your society for bettering the condition of the poor,
is a most excellent institution, and cannot fail to produce the most happy effect. This, and similar associations, reflect the highest honour on your country.
The immense sums bestowed in charity, and the
active exertions of so many enlightened and dignified characters, in works of benevolence, is indeed
without example. If the good produced be, in any

2 A

degree, proportionate to the extent of the means employed, much misery must be prevented, and many evils be exterminated. Your efforts in establishing a preventive system, and in diffusing a knowledge of the means of self-correction to the lower classes of society, are the wisest that can be imagined; you strike at once at the root of the tree of evil, instead of lopping a branch here and there, which, sooner or later, shoots out again in new vigour.

The United States, particularly those states in which slavery is unknown, or almost eradicated, possess signal advantages for securing themselves from the dreadful evils which oppress society in Europe; happy will they be, if they have foresight and wisdom enough rightly to estimate, and use, the means that Providence has been pleased thus to put into their hands.

A law passed our state legislature, authorizing the corporation of this city to erect a prison for solitary confinement, to be *solely* for the punishment of petty offenders, to be kept on low diet, and in solitary apartments, for a term not exceeding ninety days; some accounts of this plan may be seen in the account of the State Prison, page 62. From observing the effects of this mode of punishment, in the State Prison, where it is used to correct those who violate the rules of the prison, by profane swearing, quarrelling, want of cleanliness, or neglect of their alloted task of labour, &c., I have been led to believe it is the most efficacious that can possibly be adopted. The average number of convicts is nearly 400, most of whom observe a uniform, regular, and peaceable course of conduct; the hardened and refractory are kept in good order, by occasional punishment in the cells, which strikes such a terror on their minds, that it often happens, that not a single person has been punished for eight or ten days. Certain I am, that a punishment of this kind will be far more beneficial than that of the Bridewell, or even the State Prison, for a short term; nothing so effectually subdues the intemperate and ungovernable passions of men, and checks the growth of depraved habits.   I am apprehensive the prison will not be erected the present year, but I retain a strong hope that the plan will be carried into effect.

By the Juliana, Captain Brown, I sent a small box, containing a number of copies of the account of the State Prison, and reports for 1802, for thyself and friends.   The flattering result of this institution, to be found in this report, constitutes one of the most pleasing circumstances of my life, since it not only exhibits the practicability of a system calculated to produce the greatest good to society, but has entirely removed those strong prejudices against it, in the minds of many good men, who often treated me as an enthusiast, and visionary, but who now are admirers of the establishment, and the warmest advocates for the present penal code.

I have the farther pleasure to state, that there is abundant reason to conclude, that the profits on the labour of the convicts, for the current year, will be considerably greater than at the time of the last report.   I inclose an abstract of the accounts for six months, ending the 1st of the present month.   Should it be thought expedient to reprint the " Account of the Prison" in London, it would add very much to the value of the new edition, if the report last printed was subjoined; and it would give it additional credit and circulation, if some remarks were prefixed by thee, such as would naturally occur to thy mind, and which thy leisure might permit thee to make. If this is undertaken, I should be glad if the bookseller might be directed to send me one or two hundred copies, to be distributed in this country, and I will remit to him the cost.

On a late visit which I made to the Penitentiary house in New Jersey, I was disappointed to find that the plan of the building was bad, and little adapted to answer the design of such an establishment; the Keeper appears to be a decent and respectable man, and well qualified for his station; the apartments are not so cleanly as I expected to find them. There are fifty-nine convicts confined, fifty-seven men, and two women, who appeared decent, orderly, and industrious; they were employed in the manufacture of nails, shoes, and cloth. The Inspectors are very worthy citizens, who reside in the neighbourhood of Trenton. They informed me, that the profit on the labour of the convicts, was sufficient to defray the expenses of the prison. It is about four years since its estabishment.

I also visited several times the prison of Philadelphia. This building was erected *before* the alterations were made in their penal code, and is, therefore, not well calculated for the purpose of a penitentiary. Prisoners *before* conviction, vagabonds, and disorderly persons, are also kept there, and the system of order, &c. does not appear equal to that of New York prison. This difference is not to be imputed to any inability, or want of attention, of the Inspectors of the former, but to circumstances not in their power to control. Unfortunately for Pennsylvania, the vast number of emigrants, from every country, who have settled there, and the violence of party spirit, tend much to distract the government, and destroy the influence of its best citizens. The political changes in the administration, caused by this spirit, have also been extended to the penitentiary, and those who have most contributed to its establishment and support, are displaced to make way for new men, wholly unfit to manage its concerns. The friends of the institution feel apprehensive of the effects of this change on its future prosperity. It is, indeed, to be lamented, that the spirit of political parties should be so violent, as to check the progress of improvement, in what so essentially concerns the safety and happiness of all. But I must

apologize for touching on subjects of a political nature, so foreign to the design of this letter, and the
habits and pursuits of my life.

The penitentiary house in Virginia has been established about three years. The Inspectors are respectable, good men, and are appointed by the Governor and
Council, who also appoint the principal Keeper. I
am informed, political reasons influenced the Governor
and Council, in the appointment of a principal Keeper,
who disagreed with the Inspectors, and refused to
submit to their directions, and is said to be a very improper person for his place. This proves the propriety
of vesting in the Inspectors the power of appointing
the Keeper, and making *them* responsible for his conduct. On the 5th January last, there were sixty-eight
convicts, who were employed mostly at making nails
and shoes. They are allowed meat only two days
in the week; other days, mush, with a small portion
of molasses and potatoes. The laws of Virginia
direct, " that the male convicts shall have their *heads*
and beards close shaven, at least once in every week."

The foundation of a similar prison, has been laid,
this year, at Boston. The state of society in Massachusetts, is so very favourable to good order and
improvement, the opinions and habits of the people,
so consonant to the *true* principles of liberty and good
government, that there is every reason to expect that
this establishment will be equal, in every respect, to
any in America, and, I have no doubt, will reflect
great honor on the state which formed it, and on the
Inspectors who may have the management of its
internal government.

The comparison made by thee, between the number of convicts in Scotland, and this state, is extremely unfavourable to the latter, and I am unwilling to
admit the inference that might be made from it. As
to the state of society here, I am certain, that a much
less number of criminals escape conviction here, than
in Great Britain, an effect that may be ascribed to
18

the smallness of population, the facility of detection, great vigilance in the police, and the mildness of our punishments. If this be true, the calendar of our convicts may appear comparatively larger here, while the number of crimes may be, in part, much less than in Scotland. But, on this point, I do not possess sufficient information concerning that country, to draw any satisfactory conclusion. Both there and here, spirituous liquors are, undoubtedly, the great corrupters of morals. Alcohol, in all its modifications, is the insidious enemy of virtue and happiness; it saps the foundation of all the useful qualities that belong to man, and is the great cause of the increase of vice and criminality. How is this wide spreading mischief to be destroyed? By an entire prohibition of home distillation, and a heavy impost and excise on foreign spirits. But this is impracticable here; no legislature would dare to pass such a law, and no administration could carry it into execution. A partial application of impost and excise has produced some effect, yet no great, in diminishing the consumption in the country. It is painful to reflect, that it is only in our power to attempt partial remedies, and to endeavour to regulate what we cannot prevent. I hope, with the assistance of others, to procure the adoption of a plan to prevent the increase of taverns and dram shops in this city, and to lessen the number of those which already exist.

I regret that it is not in my power to make an adequate return for the large fund of valuable information which thou hast been so kind as to send me. I can only reiterate my grateful thanks to thee for thy liberal communications, and to assure thee, that I am, with sentiments of great respect and esteem, thy very obliged friend,   THOMAS EDDY.

New York, 6th month, 20th, 1804.

ESTEEMED FRIEND,

I have to thank thee for thy kind favour, of inclosing me Lancaster's pamphlet on education, which has afforded me a considerable degree of satisfaction, and I have been so much pleased with the outlines of it, that I have had one thousand copies printed in this city and Philadelphia. I flatter myself his plan will be adopted in our schools, when it becomes more generally known; and I hope to introduce it in a very large school, which I expect soon to get established under the protection of our city corporation, for the benefit of poor children, who are at present under the care of our alms house. I should be much gratified to obtain such printed accounts as have been published of your schools, established on the plan *of promoting industry,* as well as useful learning.

In the course of last year, some persons were appointed inspectors of our state prison, who, in my opinion, were no way qualified to promote the design of the institution, and whose opinions respecting the general management and economy were widely different from mine, in consequence of which, my situation there became so unpleasant, that I was induced, in January last, to resign my place as an inspector. I devoted seven years in endeavouring to establish this excellent institution, and am not a little mortified, that there is some reason to apprehend all my labours are like to be lost. I have, however, the consolation of having the most satisfactory and pleasing proofs of the marked approbation of every officer in our government, and of all my friends. Some of the convicts, about three weeks since, set fire to the prison, and destroyed the whole of the roof of the north wing; it is now repairing, and will soon be under cover. This circumstance happened, in consequence of neglect in the assistant keepers, who have all been appointed lately, as all the old ones resigned immediately after myself and the old inspectors.

I have delivered to Captain Matlock, of the ship

Hardware, a small packet, containing reports of the inspectors for last year, and also an account of the New York Hospital, which has been lately published under my direction.

I am, with the greatest regard and esteem,

Thy assured friend,

THOMAS EDDY.

To P. COLQUHOUN, London.

London, 8th August, 1804.

MY DEAR SIR,

I am quite ashamed to discover, on recurring to my correspondence on the affairs of philanthropy and humanity, that I have been so long your debtor for a reply to your favour of the fifteenth of July last year, which reached me on the twenty-first of September following; since which period, even until this hour, my time has been so constantly occupied, by a necessary attention to a great variety of public business as a magistrate, a deputy lieutenant, &c., that I have had scarce any time for those pursuits, to which I am so much inclined to direct my attention. This circumstance, however, has not prevented me from establishing two schools in the city of Westminster, where I reside; the one for 200 boys, who, with the assistance of monitors, selected from the most acute of the pupils, act as ushers under *one master;* and I have also establised since, a school for 200 girls, who are taught agreeably to the same system, by *one mistress.*

Inclosed I send you one of the proof sheets containing an account of our proceedings, by which you will perceive the vast disparity on the score of expense, between the new and old method of communicating appropriate instruction to the lower classes of the people. I likewise send you one of my reports, which were circulated early in the present year, which procured us, as you will observe, the countenance and support of the first characters residing in this quarter of the metropolis.

Mr. Lancaster has received from me every countenance and protection in his laudable exertions, which I could afford, either by advice or recommendation; and the result has been, that many of our philanthropists, as well as some of our first nobility, have visited him, and now afford him both their countenance and protection; and you will perceive from the inclosed advertisement, that he has attempted the gigantic task of teaching by his own efforts, no less than *one thousand boys,* with the assistance of monitors. I consider his system as a great and important discovery, favourable to the improvement of the rising generation, in habits of religion and morality; and I trust and hope, it will become universal all over Great Britain, Ireland, and the United States; as a means of ameliorating the state of society in future times, and of diminishing the mass of crimes, and the demand for punishment, among those who are to succeed the adults of the present age, whose irregularities and turpitude cannot easily be kept within due bounds. And it is a matter of no little regret, that where efforts are used upon proper and correct principles, for checking crimes and penal offences, that we find in America, as well as here, cabals, and individuals disposed to place obstructions in the way of the due and proper execution of every good measure.

I am very much concerned, (from your letter of the 20th of June recently received,) that you have been compelled to abandon the superintendence of your excellent institution of the New York state prison. I have no doubt, however, but the *abuses, irregularities,* and *want of economy,* which will result from this new and erroneous principle of management, will become so prominent and glaring in the view of the community, as to produce that species of paramount interference, which will bring back to the aid of this

2 B 18*

excellent institution, those individuals who have acquired so much credit by its original formation, and whose success and perseverance have procured them the approbation of all the valuable and right-thinking part of America, and also those of the same spirit of benevolent research in Great Britain, who have had access to know and to admire what has been achieved.

I am much obliged to you for the reports sent me by Captain Matlack, which I hope to receive in a few days. I have in readiness to be sent you, a series of reports, published by our Society for bettering the condition of the Poor, since the last that I forwarded; and it is my intention to send you the succeeding numbers, as they are published; also the reports of a very active society for the suppression of vice, which was instituted in this metropolis about three years ago, and which has been productive of a great deal of good, in disclosing and bringing to punishment the perpetrators of acts of debauchery and wickedness, which, from the degree of turpitude annexed to it, almost exceeds credibility. Such are the evils which affect large societies, that it requires the constant and watchful eye of the *moralist* and the *philanthropist*, to keep them in check. You are happily free as yet from many of these evils; and an attention to the education of youth will be the only means of prevention; since, in the course of time, large cities will arise in America, and a population equal to all Europe will cover its forests in less than a century.

I am much gratified to find that my remarks on public education and preventive police met your approbation. Notwithstanding the unexampled benevolence and munificence which pervades this country, the interruptions we experience in obtaining wise and salutary laws, in consequence of the wars in which we are unhappily involved, is very great. This excessive calamity obstructs the adoption of many wise and salutary regulations, which the state of society imperiously calls for. I have circulated your excellent work on prisons among the very first and most elevated characters in this country and in Ireland, and I yet indulge a hope, that in the course of Providence we may enjoy the blessings of peace, when an opportunity will be offered, ere long, to follow the good example that is set before us. Your mode of correction by solitary confinement, under certain regulations, is excellent; and the result of the various experiments which have been made, prove it to be wise and salutary, and that the measure did not proceed from visionary or enthusiastic ideas. Where punishment produces amendment, and restores offenders again to society, renovated and reformed; and where this great desideratum can be obtained, without expense to a nation or to individuals, it may be truly affirmed, that this great and important branch of criminal police has arrived at the greatest height of perfection of which human institutions arc susceptible: but the misfortune is, that in the affairs of society, every thing depends on the *purity*, the *discretion, abilities*, and *zeal*, of those who conduct public institutions. In good hands they flourish; while under a less careful, zealous, and intelligent management, they retrograde and decay. It is to a diversity of opinion, often among well intentioned men, who do not well consider the subject, or whose judgments are deficient, or their passions predominant, that many excellent institutions are imperfect in their first concoction, and under these disadvantages, coupled with want of intelligence and zeal in the management, do not succeed. I am happy to hear so good an account of the penitentiary house in New Jersey. That of Philadelphia is well known from the various accounts which have been given of this excellent institution, and it is indeed much to be lamented, that the spirit of party should extend its influence, so as to disturb the economy of those establishments, which have been instituted for the general benefit

of the community at large.   Where any public concern in the minor regulations of the state is going on
well, changes constantly produce evil; and although
men of equal talents and integrity supplant those
that have been heretofore in the management of
gratuitous undertakings, the deficiency of knowledge
and experience never fail to generate evils, and to
check the progress of improvement.

It is a pleasing circumstance to hear, that penitentiary houses have been established in Virginia
and in Boston.   Various circumstances lead me to
expect that the latter will be well managed.   Whenever . political influence is interposed in the appointment of officers or managers, it rarely happens that
the best selection is made.

It is certainly true, that many actual criminals
escape punishment in Great Britain, and many reign
for a number of years, and continue in the pursuit
of crimes by which they support themselves, before
the public justice of the country can be made to
attach to them; and it is also true, that in America,
from the peculiar state of society, crimes by being
easier detected and proved, allow very few culprits
to escape.   But this apparent difficulty of conviction
is chiefly confined to this metropolis, and to the populous towns in different parts of the kingdom.   In
Scotland, however, which does not contain one third
of the population of America, it is somewhat similar
to your country, and I am inclined to believe, excepting in its capital, and two or three large towns, that
very few who are guilty escape detection and punishment.   The limited number of crimes in that
country, is to be attributed chiefly to the attention
heretofore paid to the religious and moral education
of the inferior orders of society.   I am sorry, however,
to learn from persons of intelligence in that country,
that the progress of wealth, arising from productive
industry, and the extension of manufactures, has
produced changes not favourable to the morals of the

people, which, of course, will have the effect to generate crimes. Such is the evil consequences of natural wealth suddenly acquired, that it is always counter-balanced by evils in the opposite scale.

What you have most of all to dread in America, as a general corrupter of morals, is the want of a due control on public houses and liquor shops, in your bung-hole towns. Until publicans of all descriptions are licensed, and put under strict regulations, the abuses through this medium will increase, and produce excessive evils, which will be almost without a remedy, if not prevented in due time.

The prohibition of distillation can never be expected in any country, and therefore all we can hope for, *is a strong control over those who deal it out to the profligate and the idle*, and to those who are influenced by their example.

At the commencement of the last year, I published a tract on the duty of a constable, which I first meant for the instruction of those in Westminster; but in the progress of the composition, while the press was going, I was induced to snatch an occasional hour from public business, and to extend it so as to apply to all England. In the appendix to this tract, I have introduced *rules* and *orders* for publicans. I shall send you this work, with others. You will find in it a tolerable epitome of the manner in which the general police of England is conducted. I wish I could say it was conducted according to the true and genuine spirit of the laws, upon which the system is founded.

I conclude with my best thanks for the obliging communications you have made to me, and the valuable books and papers you have had the goodness to send me on the interesting subject of Police.

And I am, with the greatest respect and esteem,

My dear sir, your very obliged friend,

P. COLQUHOUN.

Mr. THOMAS EDDY, New York.

P. S.   I am extremely gratified to hear such
favourable accounts of Francis Kerr.   To your friendship and humanity, he owes his being saved from
misery and *destruction*, and I trust his gratitude will
be commensurate to the extensive obligations he
owes you; although, at the same time, I well know
you consider yourself as amply repaid, in the satisfaction of witnessing his reform, as the result of
your kind interference in his behalf.

Bloomingdale, 9th month, 27th, 1805.

ESTEEMED FRIEND,

Since I had the pleasure of receiving thy much
esteemed favour of 8th of August in the last year, I
have been several times absent on distant journeys,
and have not enjoyed my health equal to former
years, but this is not sufficient to excuse my very
great neglect, and particularly in not acknowledging
the receipt of thy very acceptable parcel of books by
the Alexander, for which be pleased accept my sincere thanks.   I repeatedly intended writing by different ships that sailed from New York, but unac-
countably put it off from one opportunity to another,
and now not being able to justify my neglect, I have
only to crave thy indulgence in excusing it.

The pamphlet on guineas, &c., by Henry Boner,
Esq., afforded me much entertainment and useful
information.   The subject of paper credit is highly
interesting, and particularly so to us on this side the
Atlantic, where paper currency is largely emited by
a great number of banks, spread over almost every
state in the union.   The solidity of these establishments are rendered exceedingly hazardous, by discounting mostly what is termed accommodation
notes, which are renewed and continued at the end
of sixty days, and go on year after year.   The bank
notes issued of course must be very considerable,
without any thing solid to represent them, except
the credit of the names of the drawer and endorser.

In my apprehension, the business of banks should be confined to discounting what is termed business notes, except only under some peculiar circumstances, otherways the credit of the banks is liable to be materially injured.

I am not well acquainted with the affairs of our Prison, since myself and colleagues resigned our places. The present inspectors, in my opinion, are not so suitable characters for the government of that institution, as might have been selected amongst our citizens; the mode of treating the prisoners is in some respects more severe than was thought necessary by the former board of inspectors, and the profits on the labour of the convicts are considerably short of what was produced the year ending 1st July 1803. Cleanliness and good order throughout the prison, is perhaps as well observed as formerly, and notwithstanding the increased expense for supporting the prison, the legislature remains firmly attached to our present criminal code, and I trust it will continue an ornament to our country, and serve as an example to other governments.

The excellent sentiments contained in thy several letters and the pamphlets thou so kindly sent me, has so interested me in the subject of affording a suitable education to the children of the poor, that I have been much engaged in a new establishment for schooling poor children, who are not provided for by any religious society. Our state legislature have passed an act incorporating this society; the mayor of the city is president, and the public appear much interested in its support. I trust the poor will derive great benefit by means of it, and we expect next winter our legislature will provide sufficient funds for supporting it. It must afford great pleasure to every feeling mind, that the plan of affording religious and moral instruction to the poor of your country, has so much engaged the attention of so great a number of highly respectable characters, and

I sincerely hope the time is not very far distant, when you will have the countenance and assistance of your government in improving your poor laws, which undoubtedly have hitherto tended to increase the number, and indeed the misery of the poor.

I beg thou wilt accept of my most hearty thanks, for the reports of the Society for Bettering the Condition of the Poor, which I expect to receive the next time of my going to the environs of the city.

I should be much gratified, if thou wouldst be so good as to inform me of the present state of the school under the care of Lancaster. I wrote him about two years ago, but possibly my letter did not reach him, as I had not the satisfaction of hearing from him.

With great regard and esteem,

I am, very sincerely,

Thy affectionate friend,

THOMAS EDDY.

London, 10th October, 1806.

DEAR SIR,

I have postponed acknowledging the receipt of your acceptable favour, of the 9th September, last year, from month to month, in hopes of being able to make such communications on the subject of political economy, as I conceived ought to be acceptable ; but my public duties have become so multifarious, as to afford me less time than I could wish, although I can conscientiously say, that I do not waste a moment in any pursuit that has not public or private utility for its object. The banking system, if conducted on a proper principle, has certainly a great tendency to give efficacy and extension to human labour, which, you well know, is the only source of wealth in every country ; and, perhaps, no nation upon earth has been more indebted to the powerful effect of credit and confidence than this, in giving a spring to the industry and enterprise of the people, and thereby rendering every species of human labour extremely productive. I have been turning my thoughts a good deal of late to this interesting branch of political economy, as it relates to the effect produced in Great Britain, through this medium, and the result of my researches have perfectly astonished me. Seeing that the rapid increase of our taxes, and the enormous public expense, occasioned by the war, did not appear to diminish, in the smallest degree, the splendour of living, or the general comfort of the people, I was induced to search for the causes which produced what appeared to me to be a very extraordinary phenomenon, namely, the *sources from whence have sprung those forty millions*, for the purposes of the state, and *five millions* and upwards, for the support of the poor, and other purposes, and to leave behind a surplus sufficient to enable so considerable a proportion of our population to live in ease and affluence. I was apprehensive all was not sound, because, in order to support this expense, a new property from *labour* must be created yearly; and, the question to be solved was this, in what manner, and by what means is it exacted?—I found after much research, that it arose *solely from six branches of industry*, and that these, upon a full investigation of the subject, upon which I recently occupied myself without intermission, for four weeks, secluded in the country, amounted to the enormous sum of 222,000,000 *pounds sterling yearly !*—The produce of the land, in vegetable and animal productions, has arisen to a height beyond all belief, while the bowels of the earth yield a very large sum annually, from mines and minerals. Our manufactures, of every kind, produced from labour and machinery, invigorated by skill, enterprise, and capital, in working up raw materials, have so exceedingly augmented, that our exports alone are ascertained to exceed forty millions sterling a year. Our foreign commerce exhibits an export and import, which, together, exceed one hundred millions annually, and all these sources have

2 C 19

been progressively increasing, while our colonial East India possessions add considerably to the great mass of property which centres in the country.

1st. The value of what is created by the produce of the land, including corn, cattle, horses, sheep, butter, cheese, hay, wood, &c. &c. turns out, upon close examination, to exceed in value - - - - 95,000,000*l*.

2d. The produce of mines and minerals 7,000,000

3d. The net produce of manufactures, after deducting the cost of the raw materials, at least - - - 90,000,000

4th. The value of food, obtained by the coast, for horses, from labour 1,000,000

5th. The profit arising from foreign commerce, and for horses - 25,000,000

6th. The money remitted from colonial and East India possessions, to individuals residing in this country, and thereby making a part of the national income, - - - 4,000,000

Total, - - - 222,000,000*l*.

Such are the resources of the country, by which it is enabled (exclusively of the resources of Scotland and Ireland) to oppose itself to one of the most powerful tyrants that ever assailed the liberties of mankind, or afflicted the nations of Europe.—And, after all, this income is confined to nine millions of people, in England and Wales; and, high as the taxes are, even including 10 per cent. upon income, they do not exceed 18 per cent. upon the new property annually created; while the national debt in sterling money is not yet much above two years value of the national income, while the sinking fund, applicable to its reduction, now amounts to *twelve millions* a year, and from the accumulating operation which it possesses, is daily increasing.

Such, my good sir, is the effect of well directed labour, aided by skill, enterprise, and capital; and such are the means by which England continues to enjoy that elevated height to which she has attained. Yet, these advantages are not without their evils, and disadvantages. In the year 1688, (118 years ago,) Mr. Gregory King, an eminent political economist of the 17th century, estimated the national income at 48 millions, on a population of 5,500,000 persons; now, it is estimated at 222,000,000*l.* in a population of somewhat less than nine millions, in England and Wales. The incoevenience we feel, is, that dissoluteness of manners, and moral and criminal offences, increase with the opulence of the country.

Our poor, either wholly or partially, maintained at the public expense, have been found, upon an accurate investigation, to exceed 1,040,000 persons, and the whole annual expense, applicable to them alone, is somewhat more than 4,700,000*l.* a year, which exceeds the whole revenue of most of the nations of Europe, and is more than that of Denmark and Sweden put together.

In order, as far as possible, to counteract this gangrene in the body politic, and to give energy and effect to the industry of the country, and to contribute to its happiness and prosperity, I have published, this last Summer, a tract on the education of the poor, which I send you, under cover. I know you will read it with avidity, because it is not only a subject in which you have, on all occasions, very much interested yourself, but because it is treated in a manner somewhat new, while it contains many strong points, calculated not only to excite attention, but, I trust, to be useful in America, and in every civilized country. I am, at present, engaged in compiling another work on the subject of the poor, which is also treated in a manner different from other authors who have written on the subject. I hope, in a couple of months, to present it to the public, when I shall not fail to send you a copy; and, I trust, it may be found to contain matter applicable to America, where the morals in vulgar life are so assimilated to those of England, that the same remedies will apply in both countries. You will see, however, in the treatise on education, that I have given some details, relative to the criminality of the country, which I have enlarged upon in the treatise on indigence, which now occupies my attention. The war eases us of many idle and dissolute characters, who find employment in the army and navy; yet, the calendar of delinquency greatly exceeds what could be wished, and much remains to be done to counteract the evils which opulence produces in society, joined to a want of proper attention to the religious and moral instruction of the poor. You will see, from the subject of this letter, that it is only meant for your own eye, or that of your private friends. I shall soon write you again, and send you the report, published last year, by our society for bettering the condition of the poor. I fear nothing but legislative measures, adapted to the present state of society, will produce that general amelioration, which is so much wanted.

I remain, with the greatest regard and esteem,
Dear Sir, your sincere and affectionate friend,
P. COLQUHOUN.

Mr. THOMAS EDDY, New York.

London, 26th July, 1808.

MY DEAR SIR,

I send you a series of the reports which have been published for Bettering the Condition of the Poor, since I last had the pleasure of transmitting the former ones. I shall, in a short time, have the pleasure of addressing you on our economical system here. I lament to say, that the dreadful state of Europe, *I mean the continent,* tormented by the decrees of its extraordinary ruler, *excluding all commercial intercourse; tearing from the peaceful citizens their best hopes, their youth, by an anticipated conscription extending to the year 1810, to fight the battles of ambition to aggrandize his family; the violence done to the great body of the catholics on the continent, by the degradation of the Pope of Rome; and, above all, the treachery by which the Spanish Government is attempted to be wrested from its ancient sovereigns, with whom, as it now appears, the mass of the people were well satisfied,* are features of a nature so atrocious, as when taken together, and working, all at once, on the minds of so many millions of people, can scarcely fail to produce results which must bring this lamentable contest, so productive of the effusion of human blood, to some important crisis. We have indeed lived in an extraordinary age, which certainly has no parallel in the history of the whole world. The affairs of Spain now become extremely interesting, but time alone can develop the result of this extraordinary struggle. The Spaniards have now passed the Rubicon, and can scarcely recede. The eyes of all Europe are turned towards them, and I verily believe there is only one wish prevails, if they durst (like this country) avow it, and that wish is, that they may be successful.

Adieu, my dear sir; believe me always,

Yours, sincerely,

P. COLQUHOUN.

To Mr. THOMAS EDDY, New York.

Lymington, Hampshire, 12th Sept., 1808.

MY DEAR SIR,

I have been waiting from month to month, in consequence of the constant revolving of things in Europe, in the expectation that the gloom which had overcast the political hemisphere would have been dispelled, and that I should be able to resume my too long protracted correspondence, by the contemplation of subjects more congenial to your feelings and my own, than those which the present times have gene-

19*

rated.   My constant occupations too, as a magistrate,
presiding in a court of justice every day of my life,
(Sundays only excepted,) while I am in London, joined
to other important occupations, I am sure will plead
my apology for delaying for so long a period, to
notice your two obliging letters of the nineteenth of
March and fifth June, last year, which I am ashamed
to say, that I now find among my unanswered letters.   For a good many years past, I have been able
to arrange matters, so as to be able to retire with
my family for a few weeks during the summer season to some part of the country near the sea; and in
this seclusion, I generally devote my time to that
species of business which my numerous public duties
in the metropolis oblige me to postpone. I have,
therefore, brought to this retired picturesque country
all my unavoidably postponed letters; and among
the rest, your two favours above mentioned.

It cannot fail to afford me the most heartfelt satisfaction to learn, that the works I send you on *Indigence*, and on the *Education of the Poor*, are likely,
under the sanction of your patriotic exertions, to
prove useful in ameliorating the state of society in
America, and of diffusing comfort and happiness
among the *inferior orders* in the United States, who
constitute the mass of the people in all nations.   A
disposition certainly exists in this country, to adopt
many of the public measures I have recommended;
but I have written at an era, when in the rapid
succession of the most extraordinary events, *fears*
have been generated, even for the security of the
liberties and independence of our own country,
arising from the growing power of the ruler of
France, and the wreck of nations, and ancient kingdoms and states, which have, in rapid succession, been
brought under his sway; and hence, from an attention to the primary object of guarding against dangers, which appeared to become more and more
imminent, all considerations connected with internal

economy, are either neglected or postponed—and my chief, and only consolation, under such circumstances, is this, "*that having put my statements and proofs upon record, and finding that they meet the approbation of all good men, that the time will come,* (perhaps when I cease to exist in this world,) *when these writings will be legislated upon:* and that essential benefit will be derived from them to millions of people yet unborn, not only in my own country, but in many parts of the civilized world."

You and I, my dear sir, have indeed lived in wonderful times: since the wildest efforts of the most romantic fancy could not have imaged the extraordinary events, which for the last fifteen years, have been passing under our review; and it should seem that Europe is now upon the eve of tracing back the steps, which have already so much convulsed it. The events which have recently taken place in Spain, indicate a *complete revolution in the government and character of the people of that country,* who, according to all human appearance, are likely to succeed in their arduous struggle; the result of which will be, that they will secure to themselves a greater portion of civil liberty, and may become a great and a powerful people: while other nations on the continent, emulating their example, and stimulated by their success, may also be able greatly to improve their existing hard and miserable condition. Towards the completion of these great events, under Providence, England is likely, by her prowess and opulence, greatly to contribute, and thereby to re-establish her influence and preponderance in the scale of Europe. This state of things cannot escape the penetrating minds of the rulers of America; and I trust will incline them to cling closer to the parent country, and be less disposed to indulge partialities to foreign countries, where councils are more insidious, and where political views and maxims have never, in one instance, been directed towards the real interest of

the United States; who, if they concede, or appear
to concede any thing, it is only with a view to make
America an instrument in the hands of France, to
assist her in the ruin and the subjugation of Great
Britain, that she may aftewards, in the plenitude of
her power, also subjugate America.

When all hopes of commercial intercourse seemed
to be at an end, with respect to the continent—when
all the powers submitted to the mandates of a
formerly obscure individual—Three short months
have produced most extraordinary events—*The great
peninsula of Spain and Portugal have thrown off the
yoke.* Their ports are not only open, but they are
actually now become the allies of Great Britain!—
What a change!—how vain the hopes of men!—
how uncertain the issue of the schemes of the most
powerful and the most fortunate dealer in war. An
all wise Providence frustrates at once the arrogant
pretensions of the boldest, and for a while, the most
successful adventurer.

Lamentable to say, it should seem, that the struggle for dominion, and the din and clangour of war
is only commencing. Formerly, it was between an
usurper and ancient sovereigns: now, it is between
the people at large, struggling for liberty, and the
different usurpers of ancient thrones. *The shutting
up the ports of Europe—depriving the Pope of his territories—the treacherous conduct of the ruler of France
towards Portugal and Spain, and their respective sovereigns—and the forced anticipated conscriptions to the
year* 1810, tearing *three*, instead of *one son*, from the
bosom of their families, to gratify the ambition of
one individual:—all these measures taking effect
within a few months of each other, and all of them,
either producing immediate distress, or working upon
the religious prejudices of the mass of the people,
could scarcely fail to produce convulsion;—and hence,
already symptoms of the spirit of resistance manifested by Spain, begin to manifest themselves in

Italy, and other parts of Europe, indicating disposition towards new revolutions, and new scenes of rapine and bloodshed. It must be so, in order to improve the state of society, since the result of the measures and policy of Buonaparte, has been only to bind the people faster in chains, and to make his vassal kings the contemptible instruments whereby these chains were to be rivetted upon themselves and their people. It is only, I fear, by new revolutions, therefore, that the ameliorated state of things, which you conceive likely to arise out of the troubles in Europe, are to be effected. In the meantime, England has gained a great point with respect to her commerce; since, not only *all Spain and Portugal*, but their vast possessions in the west and east, will be opened to this country; since these countries and their future independence have only been saved, *under Providence*, by her paramount naval power, and her prompt assistance by *armies, military stores, clothing, arms, and money*.

Let us hope that these evils will determine America to enter into a close alliance with this country—she has nothing to fear from France. Her embargo has rather been of service than otherwise to England. It will probably throw into the hands of the British the French colonies of Guadaloupe and Martinique. It will compel this country to call forth all the energies of the British American colonies, by large bounties and other encouragements, to cultivate, in a greater degree, those articles which the United States were accustomed to send to the British West Indies, in order to be secured against the recurrence of a similar measure—*another embargo*. The privations suffered by a temporary suspension of trade between Britain and America, will be useful to both countries. It will enable the people to pay their old debts, without, at the same time, commencing new ones, and will cause a great capital to enter with the British creditor. I declare to you, I never could view the embar-

2 D

go in the light of a misfortune to this country—I rather consider it as an advantage. My treatise on indigence will show you how small a proportion of the national wealth is derived from commerce, great and unexampled in point of extent as it unquestionably is—perhaps equal to all the nations of Europe put together.

In another point of view, it may be considered, under Providence, to be the only bar that existed to the *total subjugation of all Europe and America to the yoke of France.* If her maritime power had not existed, and she had abstained from, or waved what she calls her maritime rights, upon which her power chiefly depends, what would have become of the world at this era? The United States, but for this powerful barrier, must have ultimately fallen under the power of the tyrant of Europe; whose ambition has no bounds, and who may justly be considered as a scourge in the hands of the Almighty, to punish the offences of the nations of Europe, and permitted to reign for a time. Let us hope that his career is nearly at a close; and that the nations of Europe, convinced of the folly and the great calamities of war, will resolve to cling to the olive branch, and cultivate the arts of peace. America, above all countries in the world, ought to avoid war—she is every way vulnerable, without the means of defence. England is not what she was during the war of the revolution. Her unexampled naval power has banished the belligerent flag every where from the ocean; and powerful as the French are on land, yet when they come in contact with British troops on that element, they are compelled (as has been seen almost in every instance) to yield the palm to *British valour and discipline.* Let us, therefore, hope that England and America will form a permanent union, as the best means of preserving the peace of the world, and promoting the best interests of the human species.

The attainment of this great object now that

men's minds are becoming more enlightened, would open an extensive field among the higher ranks of society, for diffusing those blessings which would be conferred upon mankind by *good laws*, and useful regulations in civil polity. Much as has been done, it is yet but little in comparison to what is still required to complete this great work. I would willingly flatter myself, when the happy period of peace arrives, that the improvements will not be confined to the British dominions, but will extend over all Europe, and the civilized world.

The lower orders of the people, from whose labour we derive all that we possess, have never been proper objects of attention in any country. Much might be done to render them better subjects and citizens—to extend to them greater comforts, by a stronger sense of religious and moral duties; and to add much to the means of subsisting themselves and families in a better manner. The wise and benevolent rulers and statesmen in every country, have much in their power in this respect; whereby a nation may be rendered happy and contented with its government, indisposed to changes and revolutions, and prone by industry and sober habits to add to the state of national happiness. Perhaps, at no period in the history of this country, has there existed so great a disposition among the well educated ranks to promote these benevolent views. But *war—fatal war*—checks the progress of every thing that is good. Let me hope so great a calamity will never afflict the United States. The efforts of individuals are useful in promoting all benevolent purposes: but the aid and countenance of the State is necessary, to give permanency and consistency to all measures tending to ameliorate the condition of the labouring people; and to check, where it is necessary, the zeal of individuals, when not accompanied by good judgment. Hence the immense sums bequeathed in England for benevolent purposes, under circumstances often so *crude, indigested,* and *whimsical,* as to be productive of more injury than benefit. Hence, the injuries arising from these excellent institutions, the Friendly Societies, as now constituted in this country. We have resources within our grasp, capable of compassing *any thing,* and *every thing,* that is good, praiseworthy, *and benevolent,* if we could be made to see how we should avail ourselves of our powers. I trust that period is fast approaching, and that new and better prospects will enliven our declining years.

I rejoice exceedingly, to find that the schools you have benevolently established through the medium of a society in New York, assisted by my publication on the education of the poor, according to Doctor Bell's excellent plan, has succeeded to an extent equal to your most sanguine expectations. I will be very thankful to you for a copy of the report, which the trustees proposed to publish, as soon as it is printed. It occurs to me that an account of the *origin, use,* and *progress of these schools,* with the advantages which have resulted from them, accompanied by some useful reflections, would form an excellent article in the periodical reports of our society for bettering the condition of the poor : and if you will have the goodness to draw up a paper on the subject, with that particular view, I will take care to get it inserted. It may induce many in this country to follow your laudable example.

The bill brought in to the Commons' House of Parliament, for the establishment of parochial schools in England and Wales, was lost in the house of lords. The system proposed had by no means the approbation of many respectable persons, who had bestowed much time in considering the subject; but when peace is restored, the question will no doubt be again agitated—or perhaps sooner.

On the twenty-sixth July, I wrote you a short letter, with the reports of the society for bettering the condition of the poor which have been published since the former series of reports were sent you. I shall be glad to hear that they have reached you in safety. Soon after, I retired with my family for a couple of months for the benefit of sea-bathing, several of them having enjoyed bad health for a considerable length of time, and I found a little relaxation necessary for myself, in consequence of the fatigues of business. I brought as usual with me, your letters, with many others, which the pressure of public business in town would not permit me to attend to; and these, with my daily correspondents on official and other business, joined to some important state papers, which required to be drawn up by me with that degree of attention which could be best done in solitude, has kept me constantly employed. I am happy to say, that my family are considerably improved in health, and I feel myself better of the country air, necessary at my time of life, being now in my sixty-fourth year, and not enjoying very good health.

Mrs. Eddy has not called on me as I expected she would do, and the truth is, that having received your letter when at Brighton last year, and endorsing it with other letters which did not require an immediate reply, and having a great deal of business on my hands after my return home, I was prevented from referring to it, and under the pressure of other affairs it totally escaped me; but I have now taken down Mrs. Eddy's direction in my common place book, and the moment I return to town, and can find a vacant hour (of which I have very few) I will make a point of calling upon her, and shall rejoice to have it in my power to render her any acceptable services, either by my advice or otherwise.

On the subject of the Brantingham Tract, I have addressed a separate letter to you and Mr. Johnson jointly, to which I beg leave to refer you.

I remain, with great regard and esteem,

My dear sir, your very affectionate friend,

P. COLQUHOUN.

20

New York, 5th month, 19th, 1815.

MY DEAR FRIEND,

A number of benevolent persons of the city of Hartford, in Connecticut, have formed an association, with a view to establish an institution for the instruction of the deaf and dumb; and being desirous of availing themselves of the information gained by those who have conducted similar establishments in Europe, they have deputed the bearer, Thomas H. Gallaudet, to make a visit to England and France. I beg leave to introduce him to thy kind notice, and shall esteem it as a peculiar favour, if thou wilt afford him such advice and assistance, as may aid him in prosecuting the great and good work in which he has embarked.

I send by my friend Gallaudet, a packet containing a few pamphlets.

1. A view of New York state prison, published the present year.

2. Hints for introducing an improved mode of treating the insane, by T. Eddy.

3. Report of the Philadelphia Association of Friends for the instruction of poor children.

4. Report of the governors of the New York Hospital.

5. Report of the Free School Society of New York.

6. A solemn review of the custom of war, showing that war is the effect of popular delusion, &c.

I do not know who wrote the view of our state prison; it appears to me the information it contains is very correct. The institution is now conducted by persons who are very capable of managing its concerns. The great benefits derived to the public, by the alterations of our present system, is acknowledged by all our citizens, and similar establishments of prisons have taken place in almost every state.

I am, with much respect and esteem,

Thy affectionate friend,

THOMAS EDDY.

To P. COLQUHOUN, London.

Holdgate, near York, 20th of 7th month, 1815.

DEAR FRIEND,

It was pleasing to me to receive a letter from thee, with the testimony of thy continued remembrance and regard; and it afforded me additional satisfaction to believe, that as life advances, and its close approaches, thy solicitude for the welfare of thy fellow creatures, and a preparation for thy own final well being, is more and more ardent and impressive. A little longer period will manifest to us both, the infinite importance of this solicitude and preparation.

I am pleased to perceive by thy letter, that many of you at New York, are deeply interested in promoting the recovery and relief of insane persons; and I hope you will be encouraged in the pursuit of this benevolent and good work.

I did not know how I could better answer thy views and wishes, respecting your proposed asylum, than by putting thy pamphlet and letter into the hands of my benevolent and zealous friend, Samuel Tuke, who has paid great attention to this subject; and I am gratified with introducing you to the acquaintance of each other.

Thy request to me respecting the plan for an asylum, came very seasonably. The magistrates for the West Riding of Yorkshire, intending to erect an institution for pauper lunatics, advertised for plans, and gave out correspondent instructions. The result was, the production of a great number and variety of plans. That one which obtained the preference and the highest premium, thou will find delineated in the "Practical Hints" of Samuel Tuke, which I send to thee with this letter. This pamphlet was very lately published, and was composed by him, to satisfy the justices on several important points; and I believe it received their warm approbation. The work will, I doubt not, be very gratifying to thee. Thou will perceive that, in order to adapt the plan to your views at New York, he has introduced into it some modifications. On the whole, I venture to presume, that the "Practical Hints," the letter of my friend Samuel Tuke to thee, and the modified plan of the intended Wakefield Asylum, will very materially assist you in adopting such a building and establishment, as will answer the end you have in view.

I have pleasure in being the instrument of conveying to thee these subjects of information; and remain

Thy sincere and affectionate friend,

LINDLEY MURRAY.

To Mr. THOMAS EDDY, New York.

P. S.—My wife joins me in kind remembrance to thy dear wife. Remember me also kindly to thy ingenious son, who obligingly sent me copies of his very neatly executed maps.

New York, 11th month, 28th, 1815.

MY DEAR FRIEND,

Inclosed is the copy of a letter, addressed by me to Barent Bleecker, of Albany. I beg to claim thy attention to the subject of this letter, and if, in thy opinion, it would be advisable for the Board of Directors of our Canal Company to offer a memorial to the legislature, embracing the several matters contained in the letter, it is probable it will be adopted by the Board; if any thing further occurs to thy mind on the subject, please inform me.

Thou wilt recollect that, when I had the pleasure of seeing thee at Albany, we agreed, that it would be highly proper for the people in the western part of the State, to send to the legislature, this winter, a memorial, urging in strong terms the necessity of adopting some plan, for improving the internal navigation of this State, by means of Canals, &c., and proposing one to be made from Rome to Salina. Benjamin Wright engaged to correspond with thee on the subject of such a memorial; he is very active in endeavouring to promote the plan of beginning at Rome. I am perfectly satisfied, that unless you in the western country will come forward, and by a memorial press the subject on the legislature, we shall not be likely to get any thing done.   Please write me as soon as convenient; and believe me, very respectfully and truly, thy affectionate friend,

THOMAS EDDY.

To ROBERT TROUP, ESQ.

New York, 11th month, 11th, 1815.

RESPECTED FRIEND,

My friend, Judah Colt, Esq. of Erie, proposed for me to send the inclosed letter for Samuel Huntington, Esq. to thy care, as he could not inform me to what place to direct it; thou wilt please forward it to our friend, Samuel Huntington, as soon as in thy power. I have left the letter open for thy perusal, and should be glad if thou wouldst take a copy of it, which may serve to show to thy friends, as you are all equally interested in the subject alluded to in the letter—and if it meets thy approbation, I should be glad if thou would act in the same manner, as if it was addressed immediately to thyself.   This important subject, I trust, will claim thy most serious and close attention, and that with our friend Huntington, you will jointly adopt some plan, to excite an interest in the minds of your most intelligent and influential characters, in different parts of the State.   I am, however, well satisfied, that nothing would so effectually hasten the business, as a communication being made on the subject from your legislature to ours.   Very few of the members of our legislature are acquainted with the geography of your country, and the close connexion of your waters with Lake Erie, by which a communication may be easily opened extending to the Hudson, binding together the interests of both States, by means of a close friendship, and extended trade and commerce.   I shall be much pleased to hear from thee by mail, and am, &c.

THOMAS EDDY.

To E. AUSTIN, Ohio.

2 E   20*

New York, 11*th mo.,* 11*th,* 1815.

RESPECTED FRIEND,

I have had considerable conversation with our mutual friend, Judah Colt, Esq. of the town of Erie, on the subject of the proposed Canal from Erie to the Hudson, and being extremely desirous of knowing the sentiments of the citizens of your State relating to a plan, that appears to me, so interesting to you as well as to us, I take the liberty, in conformity to the recommendation of my friend Colt, to crave of thee, to give me such information as may be in thy power. I have been, for twenty years, a Director in the West Inland Canal Company of this State, and have frequently visited our western country; and as one of the Commissioners appointed by our legislature, for the consideration of all matters relating to the improvement of the internal navigation of the State, I explored in company with the said Commissioners all our western waters, as far as Lake Erie. I mention these circumstances, merely to account for the zeal I may discover, in wishing to promote an object of the highest importance, and incalculable value, as it regards the state of New York, and most of the other States in the Union. No person who has sufficiently reflected on the subject, would hesitate one moment on account of the cost, as it is a well known fact, that the resources of this State alone, are fully equal to the undertaking. During the late war, the subject of course did not command much public attention, but since we have enjoyed the blessings of peace, the minds of most of our citizens appear to be anxious to have it accomplished. Still we shall have many difficulties to encounter—with the timid, who are afraid of the expense —and the ignorant, who are incapable of appreciating its importance and advantages. I have lately received a letter from a gentleman, who resides on the Allegany River in this State, who states he has lately been in the State of Ohio, as far as the falls of the

Ohio, and that your citizens appear to take a very decided part in favour of promoting the contemplated connexion of the waters of Lake Erie with the Hudson River; and he adds, that many persons expressed an anxious desire, that your legislature should make a communication to our legislature on the subject, stating the great advantages that would be afforded to the State of New York, if this grand project was once accommplished. On this I crave to remark, and beg thy particular attention. If your legislature could be induced to make such a communication, there is not the least doubt to be entertained, but that it would have so much weight with our legislature, as to induce them immediately to commence the work. It is true, the commissioners, as well as others, have endeavoured to make the legislature understand, that the Canal of course would draw your trade to New York, but owing to a want of knowledge of the geography of the country, they are, many of them, incapable of forming a correct judgment on the subject. It will then be readily conceived, how much it might enlighten their minds, and influence their judgments, if a suitable communication was made in the manner before mentioned. I beg leave to refer this part of the subject to thy serious attention, and possibly it may correspond with thy views, to use thy influence, and unite it with other influential characters in your State, to introduce it before your legislature. Our sessions commence at Albany in January. Congress have large tracts of land in your State—suppose your legislature should apply for a grant of a portion of land, expressly for the purpose of promoting the completion of the Canal, and then you were to offer it to the legislature of New York, on condition that the citizens and produce of the State of Ohio, should pass through the Canal and Locks without paying toll. This is offered as a hint for your examination; you are more capable of judging as to the mode and manner of making the communication. I will add, that if it should be concluded, that such a communication ought to be made, it would have an incalculable good effect, if it could be presented to our legislature about the time that the Commissioners offer their annual report. This may be done, if your legislature meets in January, as I am informed it will.

I send by the mail, two copies of our reports to the legislature, and a letter from Robert Fulton to G. Morris, on the advantage of Canal navigation. I shall be very glad to hear from thee soon by mail,

And am, &c.,

THOMAS EDDY.

To SAMUEL HUNTINGTON, Ohio.

Geneva, Ontario County, 29th December, 1815.

MY DEAR SIR,

I was favoured, about ten days ago, with your letter of the 28th ultimo, enclosing the copy of one from you, of a prior date, to Mr. Barent Bleecker.

The shortness of the days, and the pressure of my agency business, with some other circumstances, not necessary to be mentioned, have prevented me from returning you an earlier answer.

As yet, I have received no communication from Mr. Wright, on the subject of the memorial, which he was to set on foot, at Rome, and other places.

Last week there was a meeting of the Directors of the Seneca Canal Company, in this village ; and I embraced the opportunity, which the meeting afforded, of consulting the Directors on the expediency of the proposed Canal, from Rome to Salina. I found them unanimously of opinion, that the measure was well calculated to improve the navigation—that it ought to be zealously pursued—and that they would individually contribute their best endeavours to promote its success.

The work of canalling the Seneca Falls, is progressing with every prospect of being completed by next October, if sufficient additional funds can be procured for the purpose. The contractor for the work is a Mr. Marshal Lewis this gentleman seems to unite rare talents, with uncommon application, and exemplary integrity ; and he has thus far brought forward the work in a style supposed to surpass, as well in durability as in appearance, any canal work in the United States. This fortunate result, however, is in great part to be ascribed to a species of stone, discovered by Mr. Lewis, at the head of the Seneca Lake ; which is taken from the quarry in large masses, is of a blueish colour, and though of solid texture, yet it is sufficiently soft to yield, with ease, to the stroke of the hammer. Mr. Lewis has gone so far beyond his contract, in the good quality of his work, that the sum he is to receive will fall near ten thousand dollars short of what is requisite to finish it ; to supply which deficiency the Directors intend to apply to the liberality of the legislature.

All our accounts from the settlers in the neighbourhood of Lake Ontario, and from the traders residing within our territory, but doing more or less business in Montreal, agree that the British have their eyes wide open, to the importance of the trade of this country, and are adopting measures to secure it. Among other means, they have put in train the building of steam boats on the Lake, to carry freight to and from Fort Wellington, late Prescott ; and they are, moreover, contemplating the improvement of the navigation of the St. Lawrence, by canalling the rapids ; which, it is said, will not be a very difficult undertaking.

Such being the policy of the British, it behooves our state to wake from its slumber—to be active, and to strain every sinew of its ability, to counteract it. I need not observe, on the almost wonderful increase of wealth, which the state would derive from a constant and uninterrupted flow of the products of this large and fertile district, into the cities of Albany and New-York. The very idea of parting with this wealth, by suffering the products to be carried to Montreal, there to nourish and fatten the commerce of a rival nation, cannot fail to excite painful reflections in the minds of every man whose heart is warmed with the love of country. I say, that the state ought to strain every nerve of its ability, to counteract the policy of the British, because the magnitude of the object utterly forbids all hope of accomplishing it by the money contributions of individuals

What renders it more imperiously the duty of the state to interpose with its ability, is the absolute necessity of regulating the rates of toll by a scale so moderate, as to make the expense of transportation to Albany palpably less than the expense of transportation to Montreal. This is the grand desideratum to be aimed at in every scheme for improving the Lake navigation between the Lakes and Hudson's River. If the expense of carriage to Albany exceeds the expense of carriage to Montreal, the trader will be sure to send his produce to the latter only ; and, if the expense be equal, he will be apt to do the same, in as much as the Lake, and its outlet, form the natural highway for conveying the products of this country to an Atlantic market, and the use of this highway is attended with less trouble and risk, and with greater despatch. At all times, and under all circumstances, it is difficult to change the course of nature, with success ; and, in the present case, it can only be done by giving the trader a deep interest in preferring the Eastern to the Northern route.

The expense of transporting a barrel of flour from this village to Montreal, is one dollar and seventy-five cents ; whereas the expense of transportation to Albany is two dollars and fifty cents ; and, as long as this difference continues, Montreal will be likely to maintain a successful competition with Albany and New York.

You will readily perceive, my dear sir, from what has been said, that I place no confidence whatever, in the power of any company, incorporated on the basis of private credit, to rescue us from the criminal act of permitting the British to sever from the body of our commerce what may be truly called its right arm. I conceive that the stream of our western trade can only be forced into the Hudson by the mighty power of our legislature. It is, therefore, my clear opinion, that it will be the true policy of our company to lay the axe to the root of the evil, by going to the legislature with a frank and manly memorial, representing the immense value of our western trade—the measures which the British appear to be contemplating to monopolize it—the high importance of defeating those measures—the utter impracticability of effecting this great object, by the efforts of any incorporated companies, relying on the funds and credit of individuals—and praying the legislature to put in requisition its vast resources, and by exerting them, to save the state from the dishonour and the mischiefs it will incur, by sitting with folded arms, and seeing the dismemberment of its commerce.

I have it in purpose immediately to begin drawing a memorial to the legislature, corresponding with the sentiments herein expressed, and to put it into general circulation for signatures.

With the most unfeigned regard,
I am, my dear sir,
Your humble servant,
ROBERT TROUP.

To THOMAS EDDY.

P. S. I have read this letter to a number of respectable gentlemen in this village, as well merchants as others, and they highly approve of its sentiments.

R. T.

Geneva, Ontario county, 11*th January,* 1816.

MY DEAR SIR,

I have been absent a few days, at Canandaigua, which has prevented my attention to the important business of improving our canal navigation. Last night we had a meeting of the citizens of this village, and we agreed on a petition to the legislature, and appointed a committee of correspondence, to communicate with the other towns in this county, and with the towns in the other counties more immediately interested in the navigation. I think we shall, by our proceedings, put this county in motion.

We have just learnt the proceedings in New-York, on the subject of the canal, and are much gratified to find they are alive to the importance of another application to the legislature.

Now is the accepted time—now is the day for adopting, and carrying into effect, a policy which is likely to be productive of incalculable advantages to the commerce of our state.

I hope our friends in Albany will also be awakened to see their interest, and that our applications to the legislature will also be sanctioned with one from the great body of its citizens.

Our proceedings are in the hands of the printer ; and as soon as they are published, I will send you a copy of them. It may be pleasing to our fellow citizens in New York to see that, in this country, we are not unmindful of our duty to them, or to ourselves.

In great haste, very sincerely your's,

ROBERT TROUP.

To THOMAS EDDY.

Geneva, Ontario county, 10*th February,* 1816.

DEAR FRIEND,

I have been favoured with your letter of the 3d instant, and I am not a little pleased at learning, that our Western Lock Navigation Company, has lately so much improved in strength, as, not only to walk, but even to run, nearly as fast as any of the bank companies; in proof of which, I readily admit a declared dividend of eight per cent, for the last year, to be very good evidence.

We sent our circular letters, with copies of our proceedings, to Mr. Wright, Mr. Geddes, Mr. Forman, and to various persons in other quarters. On the 6th instant, I received a letter from Mr. Wright, dated at Rome, on the 3d instant, in which he says, " When I had the pleasure of seeing you in Albany, in November, I promised to write upon the subject of the canal from Erie. I have delayed until now, because we, in this part of the country, have delayed acting; and the memorial from New York, and the doings of the meeting at Geneva, has aroused to exertions ; and, yesterday, Mr. G. Huntington, and myself, made a visit to Utica, for the purpose of meeting the gentlemen there, and conferring on this very important subject. Those gentlemen met us, and a rough draft of a memorial was drawn up, and will be circulated rapidly, and soon be laid before the legislature."

From this extract it appears that Mr. Wright, and his friends, were in a profound sleep, until awakened by the proceedings in New York, and in this village.

I fear there is too much apathy every where, in regard to this great state object ; and that I shall be disappointed in my expectations of the quantity of public opinion that will be carried into the legislature. We are collecting the petitions, circulated for signature in this neighbourhood, and, in a day or two, they will be forwarded to Albany.

The expense that would attend the appointment of a committee to go to Albany, and there act as lobby members, in favour of the canal, utterly forbids the adoption of such a measure in this county.

I think I shall be able to procure the information

2 F 21

you wish,' relative to the canal work at the Seneca Falls ; and I shall, accordingly, apply for it, and, when obtained, no time shall be lost in transmitting it to you.

I cannot express to you, in terms sufficiently strong, my grateful feelings for the New-York memorial. Being now in the number of old men, it is almost a matter of course that my opinion should have little or no weight ; but I assure you, it is my solemn belief, that if the legislature should not be able to rise so far above the paltry considerations of party spirit, and local interests, as to come to a level with the magnanimous policy of undertaking the canal, as a state work, we may bid adieu to the object, and most probably forever !

With the most perfect regard,

I remain, dear sir,

Your humble servant,

ROBERT TROUP.

To THOMAS EDDY.

New York, 2d mo. 14th, 1816.

DEAR FRIEND,

By direction of the Governors of the New-York Hospital, I now send the petition, annual report, and annual account of patients admitted and discharged, for the year 1815. The House (as customary) will, on a motion being made for that purpose, order these documents to be printed. The printed account of patients will be tedious, and take much time ; I would, therefore, take the liberty to suggest to thee, to direct the printer to serve each member with the *Petition* and *Report,* immediately as they are printed. I mention this, as it is important to bring the business before the legislature, before other business crowd on them.

Our cause is a noble one, and I cannot but entertain full confidence, that our application will be favourably received, and acted on with promptness, and a spirit of liberality. I believe thou wilt agree with me, that we ought not to expect a sum sufficient to erect all the necessary buildings (say $70,000) would readily be granted us, but I am of opinion they would cheerfully allow us $10,000 a year, to be paid out of the fund arising out of the sales of goods sold at vendue ; and, they may more readily do this, as the amount from this source, for 1815, will be *very* considerable. A part of this fund is to be paid to our corporation for the support of foreign poor, some *of this part* might possibly be diverted for our use, *if we cannot otherwise succeed.*

If we could complete this establishment, *all* the insane in the *state* might be accommodated ; and the number at this moment in the several counties must be very considerable. If this city contains one tenth of the inhabitants of the whole state, and has one hundred and twenty lunatics, the number in the country must be very great ; but, it is very possible, it may not be in the same proportion, owing to the use of spirituous liquors being more prevalent in the city than in the country.

If we could obtain 10,000 dollars a year, I would propose, that the Governors should open a loan, to borrow 70,000 dollars, at six per cent ; this would require 4,200 dollars to pay the interest, and the remainder, 5,800, might be appropriated towards the expense of supporting the establishment. If we can obtain this annuity, it will be highly important that we should have it for as *long* a period as possible. Suppose (in order to keep the *time* out of sight) thee should move to fill up the blank that will be left in the draft of the bill, thus : " Ten thousand dollars, annually, in quarter yearly payments, the first quarter to be paid the 1st of May next, and the same to be paid every year hereafter, during the period mentioned in the first section of the act, passed 14th March, 1806, entitled, ' an act for the better and more permanent support of the Hospital in the city of New York,' limiting the period for the payment of an annuity therein expressed."

The crowded situation of our state prison makes it necessary, either to enlarge the present building or to erect a new one at Albany, Utica, or some other place.

The plan of the present prison was entirely my own, and, although I visited Philadelphia, and examined many of Howard's plans, and was furnished with several by my friend William M. Pitt, a member of Parliament for Dorchester, of prisons in England, yet a most striking error was committed in our plan;—it should have contained 500 rooms, 7 feet by 9 feet, in order to keep the prisoners separate at *night*—in the *day* they are at work, and have keepers constantly with them, so that they have no opportunity to corrupt each other;—this entirely destroys the designs of a penitentiary establishment, intended to amend and improve the habits of the convicts. A few years since, one of the commissioners appointed to build a penitentiary at Boston, came to New-York, with a view to get information as to the plan for them to adopt; I urged them to have a separate room for each prisoner, and had such a plan drawn under my direction; this was adopted, and it is the only prison in this country calculated to answer the design of forming such establishments. Having so many rooms, does not increase the expense, as the prison need not be built so strong, because there is less danger of escape. If another prison should be erected, I sincerely hope it may be on the plan of having a separate room for each convict.

The number of convicts are considerably increased (at least in this city) on account of the sum which makes grand larceny—this is twelve dollars and a half; it was fixed at fifty dollars, it would considerably lessen the number of prisoners in the state prison. I respectfully offer these hints, as some subject relating to the state prison, or the existing penal laws, may be presented to the legislature. I, also send thee a work published some years ago, containing an account of the prisons.

D. A. Ogden, and others, have purchased of the Holland Company, the presumptive rights to all the Indian reservations in this state, and they are contriving to get the Indians to sell to them for a small sum; the poor Indians have been always cheated, except by William Penn, who uniformly done them justice, and thus preserved the high esteem and regard of the natives, by which means peace was preserved in his province, and no war or bloodshed for seventy years; and this would have continued, if his grand children, in 1756, had not attempted to cheat the Indians, in purchasing their land. In short, I am perfectly satisfied, that in every war that has occurred between the whites (Christians!) and Indians, the former has been aggressors. The condition of these poor people is shamefully neglected, and is truly deserving our sympathy and commiseration. We enjoy, in a full extent, every blessing of Heaven, on the very land they formerly occupied, in security, peace, and plenty, as to game, fish, &c.; we have abundance, whilst they often suffer for want of food, clothing, &c. Under these considerations, it appears to me, we ought to do all in our power to meliorate their condition, to protect them from the violence and imposition of the white people, and generally to contribute to their comfort and happiness, as far as circumstances will permit. I will take the liberty to state hints of a plan, that, in my opinion, might be productive of lasting benefit to the Indians.

A board of seven or eight commissioners, to be selected from the different religious societies, and appointed to take into consideration all matters and things relative to the Indians within the state, without salary.

1st. To meet annually during the sitting of the Legislature.

21*

2nd. To appoint a committee of two, who should visit, yearly, every nation of Indians in the state—inquire into their situation and wants, improvement in religion and morals, school learning, and agriculture; and use their best endeavours to prevail on them to consent to divide their lands into farms of 100 acres each, not to be alienated or leased, but to descend to nearest relations, &c.; hear their complaints of whites attempting to defraud them, as to their lands, &c.; and report to the Board at their annual meeting.

3d. The Board to employ suitable *religious* characters, to reside among the Indians, to instruct them in agriculture, the useful arts, and school learning.

4th. The Board to report annually to the Legislature, and recommend the enacting such laws as they might deem necessary.

5th. The Commissioners to be allowed the same pay (*when on duty*) as members of the Legislature.

6th. To be allowed 3000 dollars yearly, to be appropriated as they might judge proper for the benefit of the several tribes, in order to carry into effect the design of this plan.

As to the sublime project of uniting the Western Lakes with the Hudson River—but am fearful thou will think me already tiresome—I shall, therefore, leave this subject for a separate letter.

I am, &c.

THOMAS EDDY.

To P. A. JAY, Albany.

3d mo. 2d, 1816.

ESTEEMED FRIEND,

We have lately been informed by some of our friends who reside near the Stockbridge Indians, that near one hundred white persons have settled on the lands belonging to the said Indians—" that, although they have been proceeded against, as the law directs, yet, by their influence with the chiefs, the matter has been so represented to the Governor, that he and the Attorney General have directed that further proceedings against them be stopped for the present, and the probability is, that the chiefs may address the Legislature, requĕsting a law to permit them to remain."

We are part of a committee of our society, appointed for the purpose of promoting, among the Indians, a disposition of improvement in agriculture, and generally to meliorate their condition; and we have always found, that they have been exceedingly injured in their morals, &c. by the whites getting on their lands, and mixing with them.

From the conferences which some of us have had with thee, relative to the Indians, we have been induced to believe thou feel an interest in the welfare of that people, and disposed to exert, not only thy private influence, as an individual, but thy official powers, as chief magistrate of the state, in promoting a redress of any grievances they may labour under—as well as co-operating with the well meant endeavours of others, so that every proper step may be taken which justice and humanity may dictate in the premises.

We have a confidence that every thing on thy part has, and will be done, for the welfare of the Indians; but, as an application may be made by the white people to the Legislature, for some law to be passed, by which they may unjustly get an advantage over the Indians, and as thou art, likely, very much occupied at this time, it is possible the subject may escape thy memory; and we, therefore, take the liberty to make the present communication, and respectfully to solicit a continuation of thy friendly regard, to a description of our fellow men, who seem incapable of taking care of their own interest, and whose peculiar situation and circumstances seem to demand our sympathy, and require our assistance.

THOMAS EDDY.

To Governor TOMPKINS.

London, 19*th April,* 1816.

MY DEAR FRIEND,

I much fear that I have hitherto omitted to thank you (which I now do most cordially) for the very interesting pamphlets, which you had the goodness to send me by Mr. Gallaudet, who I had not the pleasure of seeing, until after he had received all the information he required, respecting the institution established here, for instructing the *Deaf* and *Dumb.* I only saw that gentleman for a few moments, while I was engaged in my magisterial duties on the bench ; and I regretted much that I had not the pleasure of seeing him afterwards, as I fully expected, since it was my wish to have shown him all those civilities which are justly due to any friend recommended by you.

I had, also, the pleasure of receiving your letter by Doctor Francis, who did me the favour of dining with me, and which afforded me the opportunity of introducing him to a very intelligent physician, my son in law, Doctor Yates, from whom he received much of that species of information, of which his very active and intelligent mind was so eagerly in pursuit. Doctor Francis has gone to Paris, but will soon return, when I shall be happy to show him every attention in my power.

Among other philanthropic establishments which are yearly rising in the great metropolis, we are now anxiously engaged in forming *a Provident Institution,* or *Saving Bank,* in the western district of the city, upon the principle suggested and explained in my Treatise on Indigence, published in 1806, but on a far more limited scale. The practical effect of these establishments, was first manifested in Scotland, since which they have been extended to several towns in England, and are likely to become *very general.* Their utility scarcely requires explanation. The object is, to assist the labouring poor to preserve a portion of their earnings for old age, and to give them provident habits. I send you, under cover, the plan of our institution, which has just commenced, and which has been the result of much discussion and deliberation. When Doctor Francis returns, I shall trouble him with a few of such publications as you may wish to possess. My various occupations, joined to an advanced period of life, render me less able than I could wish, to take an active share in the management of many institutions of a charitable nature, to which I must be satisfied only to be a contributor. Many of them are excellent, while not a few have been established without the aid of that caution and good judgment which is calculated to produce utility, which tends to reduce the funds of others, whose beneficial efforts are obvious and certain; and hence it is, that much money is expended where little practical benefit results. Our Free Schools, for the education of the poor, are now become very general all over the country, which, I trust, will give a new and improved character to the rising generation among the poor, which is so much wanted in England. Referring you to my next, I remain always,

My dear friend,
Your's affectionately,
P. Colquhoun.

Mr. Thomas Eddy, New York

New York, 5th mo. 2nd, 1816.

Esteemed Friend,

Thy very kind favour of 9th mo. 17th, was received some time since—its interesting details have afforded considerable satisfaction, and, with the work on the constitution of Lunatic Asylums, will be highly useful to us. I should have replied to thy letter sooner than this date, but the Governors having applied to our Legislature for aid towards completing the proposed establishment, I waited to know the result, in order that I might inform thee. I have now the

2 G

pleasure of stating, that a law was passed, 17th ult. to pay the Governors of the New-York Hospital, ten thousand dollars a year, in quarter yearly payments, for and during the term of forty-one years. This generous and liberal grant, is fully equal to our expectations, and will be amply sufficient to enable us to erect extensive buildings, and every other improvement. We purchased thirty-eight acres of land, six miles from the city—it is on high ground, and commands a most delightful and very extensive view of the village of Haerlem, Long Island, and the surrounding country. As to health, and good water, it is equal to any in the state of New-York. Some have fears, that it is too far from the city; but on that account, it appears to me, there is no cause to be afraid that it will not be duly inspected—it is true, the Governors all reside in the city, but in the vicinity of the premises there are a number of very respectable suitable persons, (members of the Corporation of the Hospital) who would very cheerfully undertake the charge of visiting, &c. so humane an institution.

Several of the Governors have seats in the neighbourhood, and are out one half the year. It is proposed, the intended building shall accommodate two hundred patients, calculated for all ranks of life—as well those of affluent as indigent circumstances, and, also, paupers, who are supported by the city, and the respective counties throughout the state—the latter to be paid for at the rate of two dollars per week, and others from three to ten dollars, according to their circumstances, and the accommodations they may require.

In my opinion, if it is well conducted, and managed with prudence, it will, not only essentially serve, and be a great blessing to the state at large, but may be very profitable, and produce a considerable revenue to our hospital. I have no doubt, we shall have it full in two years after it is ready to receive patients. On one part of the premises there is abundance of valuable good stone, but it may not be of a suitable or handsome quality, to make a good face for the front or outside walls; if so, I was thinking we may put on a coat of rough cast, or plaster—this has been done on some of our public buildings, but, in some instances, it is apt to peel, or fall off, owing (likely) to severe frosts, or the want of knowing how to make a strong and good cement. In the north of Europe, and, I believe, in England, they make a plaster that would stand our climate, and would answer the purpose effectually. I have been told they mix tarras, (which we have imported from Amsterdam,) or Welsh lime, that is considerably exported from Bristol. If thou could procure for me a receipt, from some distinguished mechanic, to make a suitable plaster that would answer the purpose, it might very much serve us, and I should esteem it as a particular favour. It is not probable we shall do more this year, than lay the foundation of the building. The remarks in thy letter to me, and thy work, entitled, Hints on the construction of Lunatic Asylums, will very much assist us in forming our plan, and when this is drawn, and concluded on, I propose sending thee a copy, in hopes thou wilt furnish us with thy observations for our government in improving of it.

If any thing farther occurs to thee, that would probably improve our plan, or aid us in executing it, I should be much obliged by thy communications. Do be pleased to present my wife's love, in the most affectionate manner, in which I most heartily unite, to Ann Alexander, and very particularly to our beloved friends, Lindley Murray and wife. I send thee the last Report of our Hospital.—Lindley Murray would be pleased to peruse it.

I am, thy affectionate friend,

THOMAS EDDY.

SAMUEL TUKE.

New York, 5th mo. 4th, 1816.

My good Friend,

I scarce know how to begin this letter, as I feel ashamed and mortified that I have so long neglected replying to thy last very acceptable communication.

I rejoice to find such a number of your good people in England are engaged so devotedly in improving the condition of the lower classes in society ; your Bible Society, and the immense sums raised for the poor, who have suffered by the calamity of war on the continent, is truly astonishing, and I sincerely trust and believe, will procure the blessing of Divine Providence on your nation. The communications of the British and Foreign Bible Society, show that genuine religion is held in veneration, in many parts of the continent, to a much greater extent than many heretofore believed. I trust it will yet appear more fully in France, notwithstanding that deluded nation seemed to have been dead as to any sense of it. As the spirit of our most holy religion spreads over the world, the condition of mankind will be meliorated— the minds of men will be softened, instead of being filled with bitterness, revenge, and hatred—they will learn of Christ to love each other, and thus, in God's own time, an end be put to war and bloodshed. Owing to the late war, the morals of the people of this country have been (as was reasonably to be expected) much injured. Notwithstanding this, there is a general religious improvement evidently increasing amongst all denominations of Christians—so that I entertain a hope, which, I trust, is well grounded, that, on the whole, we are growing better. Bible Societies are established in all directions of the United States, except Virginia, and other slave states,* and great attention is paid to schools, and otherwise to improve the state of the common people.

* In most of these states, Auxiliary Bible Societies have since been established.

Prisons, on the plan of our state prison, are established nearly in every state. The affairs of our
prisons have been, of late years, sadly mismanaged,
otherwise the avails of the labour of the convicts
would be sufficient to defray the annual expenses.

I have been, for some time, much engaged in improving a plan of an establishment for the accommodation of insane persons; the mode of treatment that
ought to be pursued, (and which was recommended
by me to the Governors of the New-York Hospital,
in April last year, of which communication I now
send a copy) is the one adopted at the Retreat, by the
Society of Friends, near New York.

The Governors have purchased thirty-eight acres
of land, about six miles from the city, and propose
to erect a building to accommodate two hundred
lunatic patients—the thirty-eight acres to be divided,
and laid out in walks, gardens, &c. for the amusement and exercise of the patients who are fit to partake of useful employment and recreation. Our
Legislature has acted very liberally, and generously
granted us 10,000 dollars a year, payable quarterly;
one half of this sum will enable us to make a loan
of 80,000 dollars, so that we shall have very ample
funds for erecting suitable buildings, and making
every necessary improvement. I send thee the last
Report of the Governors, which contains a memorial to
the Legislature on the subject, and fully explains the
plan we propose to pursue. About a month ago, I
attended the Legislature, at Albany, for the purpose
of aiding our application, and obtained the loan
alluded to, granting us the above-mentioned annuity,
for and during the term of forty-one years.

It is a considerable time since, that I met with, in
the Quarterly Review, an account of thy very important publication on the wealth, power, resources, &c.
of the British nation, and I have been extremely
anxious to procure a copy; it is highly spoken of by
those who have met with it in England, and it is

22

wonderfully strange, that I cannot meet with a single copy in this city, or Philadelphia.

Our Free School Society, under the patronage of the state, is in a flourishing situation ; we have two schools under our care in this city, containing about one thousand scholars; we have ample funds, and propose to erect two other school houses next year.

There are now a school in every town in each of the counties throughout the state, all under the patronage of the state; the sum of 60,000 dollars is now divided among them, according to the number of scholars in each school, and this fund, in a few years, will reach 200,000 dollars; besides this, they are obliged, each town, to raise, by tax, a sum equal to what they respectively receive from the state.

I shall esteem it as a very particular favour, if thou will be so good as to continue thy correspondence on the general state and improvements of the numerous benevolent establishments in England.

It is owing to thy very valuable correspondence with me, that our New-York Free School is in so flourishing a situation as it is at present, and that the condition of the poor, in many respects, have been considerably improved.

I am, with the warmest sentiments of esteem and regard, thy affectionate friend,

THOMAS EDDY.

To P. COLQUHOUN.

P. S. Inclosed in a packet, per Jeremiah Thompson, to be sent by him from Liverpool, per coach :

1. Memorial on Canal, from Erie to the Hudson.
2. Report of Female Association.
3. An act concerning Common Schools.
4. Report of Free School Society, for 1814.
5. Hints respecting improving the treatment of the Insane.
6. Report of New York Hospital, for 1815.
7. Account of New York Free School Society.

London, 14th June, 1816.

My dear Sir,

On the 3d instant, I had the pleasure of receiving your esteemed and acceptable letter of the 5th ultimo.—No doubt can be entertained of the benevolence and good disposition of our nation, where the charity of all ranks, who have any thing to spare, ramifies in all directions. Besides the relief afforded at home, nearly half a million of money has been sent to *Spain, Portugal, Germany, and Russia,* during and since the war, for the relief of the sufferers. In the course of the last and the present year, nearly a million more has been raised from individuals for the relief of the wives, and families, and relations, of the soldiers who fell at the great battle of Waterloo; besides a reward to those who survived this great struggle, which terminated a war of unexampled length, and which desolated the greatest part of Europe. But this benevolence is not confined to one object. It has ramified in all directions. The sums subscribed to the Bible Society, has been immense; and no doubt is entertained of its being supported in preference to charities of every kind.

I trust that you and I shall never, in our days, see the sword of war unsheathed. There appears now a strong disposition on the part of the sovereigns and rulers of all the great powers in Europe, to cultivate the arts of peace. The still perturbed and unhappy state of France is now the only circumstance that is likely to disturb our tranquillity.

Our legislature, now freed from the distresses of war, is sedulously devoting itself to the state of our police and internal policy. *Mendicity, mad houses, saving banks, the pauper system,* &c. &c., at present engage their attention : and the leading object is to promote humanity, and to improve the state of society by education, provident habits, and good laws, for the prevention of moral and criminal offences.

A penitentiary house, on a very large scale, is partly finished, in fields within the liberty of Westminster, at the public expense, with all the improvements which experience has suggested, and a bill is now in the house, for regulating insane establishments, and appointing periodical visitants for the purpose of promoting humanity and preventing abuses. But, after all, much remains to be done. A continuance of peace may do much. The legislature, however, is perhaps very properly slow in adopting new measures and in abolishing old customs. These feelings do not operate with the same force in a new country.

I am surprised to find that my last work on the *Population, Power, and Revenue of the British Empire*, had not been on sale in America; as the first edition went off in eight months, although a very expensive book on account of the number of tables. I have no doubt of its being reprinted in America. Already there are two translations of the work in German, and I believe also in French. I believe Mr. Clay, when here, carried out a copy of it. He told me he intended to do so. I send you under cover an epitome of this work. It has been purchased by the ministers of all the nations of Europe, as well as many other foreigners. Through the medium of this work, much has been disclosed on subjects tending to promote the happiness of nations, and to prevent many of those errors by which their decline has been effected.

It is a pleasing circumstance, to find your country is following our example, with respect to free schools. We, at last, discover here, that the general education of youth is not only the best prop to the state, but to the happiness and prosperity of the people. I trust your schools are established on a stable basis, which can undergo no unfavourable change by the death or removal of the first benevolent founders. For want of this, many excellent institutions have fallen into decay, when their original founders were no more. As yet, our legislature has afforded no pecuniary aid to the numerous schools established in this country;

they are entirely supported by the benevolence of the public. I trust, ere long, their permanence will be secured by a national institution, embracing the whole population.

I feel much gratified by the opportunity you afforded me, of making the acquaintance of Dr. Francis. A mind more ardent in the pursuit of useful knowledge, perhaps, never existed ; and, I have no doubt he will, in a few years, stand at the head of his profession. I introduced him to my son-in-law, Dr. Yeats, who is an able and learned physician, ; he entertains a high opinion of your friend's talents, and, I am sure, will, at all times, be happy in the opportunity of being useful to him.

My health declines, as may naturally be expected, as old age approaches ; but, upon the whole, I have no reason to complain. Regularity and temperance are my chief and best medicine for all complaints.

I shall always be happy to hear from you, and to make such communications as I conceive may be useful to mankind in general ; but let me entreat of you, my good friend, *not to make my letters public.* Engaged, as I constantly am, in a great variety of pursuits, I can only snatch a moment occasionally for private correspondence, which can never be sufficiently correct for the public eye.

I send by Dr. Francis, a parcel, containing such publications as are likely to prove interesting to you. A list of them you will find hereunto annexed.

With every sentiment of esteem and respect,

I remain always, dear Sir,

Yours, truly and affectionately,

P. COLQUHOUN.

To Mr. THOMAS EDDY, New York.

1. An Account of the different Saving Banks recently established.

2. Hand and Posting Bills, relative to the Bank in Westminster.

2 H 22*

3. The 35th and 36th Report of the Society for Bettering the Condition of the Poor.

4. The New School for Education.

5. The Barrington School.

6. Report—Indigent Blind.

7. Report—Refuge for the Destitute.

8. Report—Relief of the Working Manufacturers.

9. Report—Relief of the Poor in the City of London.

10. House of Recovery in Typhus Fever.

11. Society for the Encouragement of Sunday Schools.

13. Scheme of Finance.

Geneva, Ontario County, 9th December, 1816.

SIR,

The letters, dated on the 18th July last, and which, as Secretary of the Board of Commissioners, constituted by the act, entitled, " an act to provide for the improvement of the internal navigation of this state," you addressed to us, respectively, came to hand, with their enclosures, in due season.

We have forborne advertising our appointment, or taking any step to procure and receive subscriptions in lands, or money, to be applied to the construction of the contemplated canals, from a conviction that an appeal to our fellow citizens for voluntary aid, under existing circumstances, would be premature. Until the Legislature has passed an act, whereby the public faith is pledged for beginning and completing the canal, we apprehend no discreet citizen will be disposed to deprive himself of the use of his land, or money, for a considerable period of time. The sole object of the act appointing the Commissioners, is to obtain, from their report, a mass of useful information, for the purpose of guiding the judgment of the Legislature, in deciding on the expediency of undertaking, or rejecting, the proposed enterprise. Although we are well persuaded that the trusts reposed in the Commissioners will appear to have been executed with great ability, and the utmost fidelity, yet, their report, from the novelty and magnitude of its subject, may induce the Legislature to seek further information, before it finally decides on the course to be pursued. Thus, a final decision may be delayed longer than the ensuing session of the Legislature; and, when every proper source of information has been exhausted, that decision may be against the enterprise. There is nothing in the present act to preclude such decision ; and hence we are of opinion, that the act furnishes no adequate motives for private subscriptions, either in lands or money.

We submit these sentiments to the Commissioners, with all deference, and we remain, with respect,

ROBERT TROUP.
JOHN NICHOLS.

S. YOUNG, Esq.

New York, 12th mo. 10th, 1816.

ESTEEMED FRIENDS,

Your favour of 28th ult. was last evening laid before our Committee on Indian Affairs, and we were directed to communicate to you such remarks as we might judge suitable, relating to the subject alluded to in your letter.

Many of our Committee have been, for some time, attentive to the situation of the Seneca nation, and have had great fears lest they might be sadly imposed on, by the person who has purchased the pre-emption right of the Holland Company. It may be useful to state, that all the land on the west side of the River Genesee, belonged originally to the state of Massachusetts—that is, the right of soil, or the exclusive right of purchasing the same of the Indians; the right of jurisdiction has always been considered to be in the state of New York. The state of Massachusetts sold their pre-emption right to the whole country, to Gorham & Phelps, and they sold to Robert Morris, and he to the Holland Company; the latter (several years ago) purchased all the said land of the Indians, except certain tracts which they reserved, one situated at the Cattaraugus, one at Buffaloe, one on Allegany, and one on Genesee ; possibly there may be more. The Holland Company sold their pre-emption right, for the whole of these reservations, (we are told at 50 cents per acre,) to a person who is now a member of Congress, and resides at Hamilton, on the St. Lawrence. About three years ago, he employed Joseph Richardson (formerly of Perkcoming, Philadelphia county,) to hold a treaty at Buffaloe, for the purpose of trying to persuade the Indians to exchange their reservations for lands (which he *said* he owned) on White River, in Illinois Territory; you know the result of that treaty, and are, likely, acquainted with the remarkable speech of Red Jacket. This treaty was unlawful, as the laws of the United States prohibit any treaty being held with the Indians, for the purpose of purchasing their lands, *unless a Commissioner appointed by the President should be present.* All the reservations are said to be lands of the very first quality, and particularly the one at Buffaloe, which is very valuable; a part of it, adjoining the village, is said to be worth from 100 to 200 dollars per acre, if the Indian title was extinguished. It has been said, that on an average, that reservation would sell for more than thirty dollars per acre— possibly this may be estimating it too high. The present holder of the pre-emption right is esteemed a respectable man, and, perhaps, would be more scrupulous in the means he might use, in effecting his purchase of the Indians, than some others might; yet, as the temptation is powerful, and as in the general practice of men, (who are commonly *called* honest,) it is really considered not to be criminal to impose on *Indians*, advantage has been taken of their ignorance and credulity;—a man's character seems not to be lessened in the esteem of his acquaintance, if he should endeavour to get the chiefs in a state of intoxication, in order to gain their influence over the nation, with a view that he may make a profitable bargain. It is, we believe, true, that the consent, or act of the chiefs, binds the whole nation, in sales of their lands; but, generally, the whole are consulted, yet often (mostly) the chiefs are bribed to consent, in order to influence the others. Although no treaty can be held for purchasing without a Commissioner, appointed by the President, be present, to prevent the Indians being imposed on, yet it would probably not be difficult for him to get such a man appointed as would answer his purposes. Many persons, (high in office in this state,) who profess, and, indeed, seem to be well disposed and friendly to the Indians, have openly and decidedly given their opinions, that it would be better for them to sell their reservations, and remove to some remote situation to the Westward; they say that now they are exposed to a constant intercourse with bad whites, who supply them with rum, and in every way try to cheat them, and corrupt their principles, and, if they remain, the consequence will be, that they will be soon extinct. They add, that the Christian party, at Oneida, owing to their having more intercourse with the whites, are more depraved than the Pagan party. It is, perhaps, not in our power to say, whether such removal would, eventually, be better for the Indians or not; but it appears to us, that if they should go far West, they will still be exposed to the same evil, and would suffer still worse, from a kind of white people, who are not so much under the restraints of law as the same description of whites who now surround them. At present, the influence of many respectable persons, who reside near them, serves much to protect them from frequent injury and imposition, and the assistance they would, from time to time, receive from Friends, might, at least, preserve them from going backwards, and possibly tend to advance them in agriculture, &c.   Taking a view of the whole subject, in all its various ramifications, we cannot but believe it would be most for the advantage of the Indians, to remain on their respective reservations.

It may be useful to examine, 1st. Suppose the Indians should conclude to sell their present possessions, is it expedient for Friends to offer them assistance and advice?   2nd. If it is deemed proper for Friends to interfere, then what course would be most advisable?   3rd. What advice should be given to them, in case the Indians should ask for it?

In reply to the first proposition, we are of opinion, that if they should conclude to sell, it would not be expedient to offer assistance, or advice, unsolicited, as it would irritate the person who holds the pre-emption right, and the conduct of Friends might be wrongly represented to both Indians and whites, and in many ways it might prove injurious to the cause in which we are engaged.

In reply to the second proposition, we think Friends cannot be indifferent spectators, if the Indians should agree to dispose of their lands, as our minds are impressed with a belief, that great unfairness would most probably be shown towards them.   It might be right to interfere, so far as that a sub-committee, from your general committee, might wåit on the President, and confidentially communicate to him the propriety of his being on his guard in selecting a person as Commissioner, urging to him the necessity of appointing a person of established good reputation, of undoubted integrity, and purity of character.   If the Indians are induced to make application, and *solicit* the advice of Friends, it appears to us Friends might (and perhaps ought to) afford every assistance and advice they might require ; but, even then, it would be necessary to exercise great prudence and circumspection in every movement.

In reply to the third proposition—If the Indians *ask* for advice, after they may have determined on a sale, the advice proper to be given them must depend upon circumstances that may then be unfolded. If they ask for advice, whether they had best remove to the westward, or, if it would be best for them to remain on their reservations, the sentiments of Friends might then be communicated to them, and, if they should be fixed in their intention to make sale, perhaps it might be well to propose to them to sell one of their reservations, or, if each reservation belongs to a particular tribe, then each tribe to sell a portion of their respective reservation; for the remainder, (not sold,) they might, perhaps, be persuaded to employ a surveyor, and have it divided into lots of 100 acres each—a lot to be the separate property of each Indian family—to go by descent to nearest kin, in the same manner as estates with us.

We have thus far, in freedom, endeavoured to exhibit to your view, our sentiments, as they have occurred; and have been more particular, as the lands are in this state, and, therefore, thought, perhaps, you might not be acquainted with all the circumstances connected with the subject; but as you have been longer conversant with Indian affairs than ourselves, we leave the subject to your farther investigation, and, if at any time we can be useful, we will very readily attend to any farther communications you may think proper to make to us.

As to the situation of the Brothertown Indians, we may inform you, that many years ago, (perhaps thirty,) the Oneidas, taking into consideration the situation of the remains of several tribes of Indians on the east end of Long Island, Narraganset, and other parts near the sea shore, concluded to make them a present of a piece of land, (now called Brothertown,) six miles square, without the power of alienation. Some families of those Indians moved on to this tract, and the white people soon got in among them, persuaded the Indians, when in a state of intoxication, to sell them their improvement, with several lots of 100 and 200 acres. About the year 1794, a deputation of Indians, from Brothertown, came to some Friends of this city, and stated their situation to be very deplorable, owing to the imposition and very bad conduct of the white people, whom they had admitted into their settlement. Two Friends went with these deputies to the Governor, and the situation of the Indians were represented to him. Agreeably to the orders of the Governor, the sheriff took a number of civil officers, and turned off the intruders. In two years after this, the Indians came again to New York, and represented that the white people had returned with additional numbers. and that their situation was now much more deplorable. The subject was referred to the Legislature, then in session. An act passed, appointing three Commissioners to proceed to Brothertown, and adjust the business, with the concurrence of the Indians, in any way they might be of opinion would be most to their advantage. It was agreed by the Commissioners, with the consent of the Indians, to set off in one corner of the tract, about 6000 acres, and settle the same in lots of 50 to 100 acres to each of the intruders, who were to pay the state for the same five or six dollars per acre, the state to pay the interest (seven per cent.) on the proceeds of the sale (amounting to 2169 dollars a year) to three persons, to be appointed superintendents of the affairs of the Brothertown Indians, to be laid out by them, for supporting a school, and other purposes, for the benefit of the Indians. The remainder of the land was divided into 100 and 50 acre lots, and allotted, 100 to a family, and 50 to a young man. By an act confirming the acts of the Commissioners, five Indians were to be annually appointed, called peace makers, who were to act the same as justices of the peace, to hold a court monthly, to settle differences, and issue execution to an Indian constable, for debts under ten dollars, &c. This act you may find in the revised laws of New-York, passed 1813. (See 2d vol. page 160.) You may, likely, meet with it at the Mayor's office, or with some lawyer in your city.

We are your affectionate friends,
THOMAS EDDY.
And for SAMUEL PARSONS, by his request,
R. R. LAWRENCE.

New York, 4th mo. 9th, 1817.

MY DEAR FRIEND,

I return thee my most sincere and warmest thanks for thy kind letter and valuable pamphlets, sent me by Dr. Francis, and should, before this time, have made my acknowledgments for these favours, had I met with a suitable opportunity of a person by whom I could have sent some tracts.

I have the pleasure to state, that at Hartford, in Connecticut, they have formed a valuable and extensive establishment for instructing the deaf and dumb, which has been aided by their legislature, and considerable subscriptions of private individuals of that State, and citizens of this and other adjoining States. The Institution is to be under the superintendance and management of my friend, Gallaudet, who will have, as an assistant, a Frenchman who is deaf and dumb, and who was a professor, several years, in the institution at Paris. Nothing of the kind exists in any other part of the United States; and, in my opinion, the Hartford establishment will be sufficient to serve all the states north of Pennsylvania.

Among the many philanthropic institutions with which your country abounds, there is none that appears to me more likely to be useful than saving banks. They are certainly most admirably calculated to be beneficial to the poor, by promoting amongst

2 I 23

them a spirit of independence, economy, and industry. Immediately on receiving from thee an account of the provident institution in your metropolis, I proposed to a number of my friends to establish a similar one in this city. A plan was formed, and a number of our most respectable citizens agreed to undertake the management of it; but we found that we could not go into operation without an act of incorporation, for which we made an application to the legislature, and the result is not yet known.

An act is now before our legislature, for completing a canal from Lake Erie to the Hudson. Our mutual friend, John Grieg, Esq., has with him a map and profile of the track of the canal, the inspection of which will be interesting to thee.

We have now, in this city, twenty-seven *Sunday* schools, at which 5000 scholars are instructed. I lately visited two of them, kept for black people, adults; at one of them, I noticed two black women, one of them seventy, and the other ninety years old. They both seemed to please themselves very much with the prospect of being soon able to read the Bible.

Our legislature passed a law about two weeks ago, declaring that every person now held in slavery, shall be free after 4th July, 1827. In the eastern States, and in the State of Ohio, slavery is prohibited.

Free schools and Sunday schools are spread, and are increasing throughout our State, and our government have made very liberal provision for their support; and Bible Societies receive great patronage, and are established in almost every part of the United States.

I have lately lost thy excellent and very valuable work on Indigence, published in 1806, and shall esteem it as a particular favour, if thou wilt be pleased to send me another copy.

The asylum for lunatics, mentioned in my letter of 4th May, is intended to be commenced building this season. The plan being adopted through my recommendation, I feel myself under an obligation to pay attention to it, and this occupies, at present, a great portion of my time. We propose to have separate buildings for men and women patients, about 300 feet distant from each other, besides one other building, remote from these, for violent *noisy patients ;* this will be a great improvement on the *old* system, of having them *all* under one roof.

There is no one evil prevalent in this country, we have so much reason to lament and deplore, as the intemperate use of ardent spirits. It is distilled mostly from grain, in every part of the United States, and sold at about seventy-five cents per gallon. The quantity of brandy, gin, and rum imported from Europe and the West Indies, and whiskey, &c., made in this country, is equal to twenty-four millions of gallons, so that, supposing the population of the United States to be eight millions, this gives to each man, woman, and child, three gallons a-year ! In the late war, it is supposed six thousand persons lost their lives, owing to that dreadful calamity, and that a greater number of persons were destroyed during that period by the use of spirituous liquors. This vice enervates the mind to such a degree, that of the individuals whose habits are fixed in the use of it, scarcely one in one thousand leave it off ; attention to wives, children, friends, their own interest, health, character, rank in life, and reputation, are all sacrificed to gratify their inclination for this most dreadful poison. There appears no remedy sufficient to cure this disease of the mind, but the operation of the power of religion.

I am, with sentiments of great regard and esteem,
Thy affectionate friend,
Thomas Eddy.

To Patrick Colquhoun, Esq.

1. Report, &c. of Committee on Subject of Spirituous Liquors.

2. Seven numbers of Friend of Peace.

3. Annual Account of Hospital.

4. Account of Massachusetts State Prison.

5. Constitution of American Bible Society.

5th mo. 16*th,* 1817.

RESPECTED FRIEND,

The Commissioners to connect the navigable
waters of Lake Erie and the Hudson River, have not
yet appointed an engineer, and it is difficult to select
a person for so important and responsible a situation. The appointment will be a very honourable
one, and it is very desirable it should be conferred
on a man fully competent, and deserving entire confidence ; to direct the manner in which the various
parts of the work should be executed—to make contracts with the workmen, &c. &c. requires a combination of talents, industry, and intelligence, that is rarely to be found in an individual. I have been long
acquainted with the general character of Thomas
Moore, of Maryland, and it occurred to me, that he
would answer the views of the Commissioners, but
having no personal acquaintance with him, and not
being possessed of a knowledge of his abilities, sufficient to justify one to recommend him to the Commissioners, I am induced, by the recommendation of
my friend J. B., who has just been appointed to the
mathematical department, as surveyor, to take the
liberty of making application to thee for information.

Not having the pleasure of an acquaintance, I must
confide in thy well known public character, and disposition to aid every improvement interesting to our
common country, to excuse the liberty of addressing
thee on the above subject, and beg thee to believe me,
with great respect and esteem, Thy assured friend,

THOMAS EDDY.

THOMAS JEFFERSON.

New-York, 5th month, 15th, 1817.

MY DEAR FRIEND,

I arrived here the day before yesterday, and I have this day received the appointment of surveyor for the contemplated grand canal. My friend, Thomas Eddy, of this city, has generally been in the first rank amongst his fellow citizens, as an active and efficient promoter of useful and benevolent works, has long been one of the Commissioners for this particular object, and though he is not now one, still retains all his wishes for its success, and the energies of his mind are still in full activity for its accomplishment. He has mentioned, in conversation with me, his views, that the task of the ascertainment of lines, and the superintendence of the work of making the canal, would be too burdensome for *one man*— that the magnitude of the object, would not only render expedient, but necessary, the employment of two Superintendents, an Engineer, and a Mathematician, each in his appropriate department. I perfectly accord with him in these views. I mentioned to him Thomas Moore, a man whom I know to be eminently qualified for the undertaking—of a sound and discriminating mind—a judicious and practical engineer, and one with whom I shall be glad to act. I remarked, that thou wast well acquainted with his qualifications and talents, and suggested the propriety of his addressing thee on the subject, and requesting thy opinion. He alleged he had no acquaintance with thee, but if I would write, he would enclose my letter in a few lines from himself.

I know not whether Thomas Moore would accept such an appointment, but I am induced to believe the Commissioners would be liberal in their offer; and I also believe his correctness and economy to be such in the application of public money, that more would be saved by giving *him* a salary of 10,000 dollars a year, than employing one less qualified for nothing.

23*

Accept, dear friend, my love and affectionate salutations.

ISAAC BRIGGS.

THOMAS JEFFERSON.

New York, 9th mo. 24th, 1817.

RESPECTED FRIEND,

I return thee my most sincere thanks for thy very polite and friendly letter, by Captain Brown, dated 17th May. I have been prevented from sooner acknowledging the favour, by absence from the city for some months past. I now send some books, which, I trust, will be interesting, and of which I request thy acceptance. Amongst them thou wilt find the last Annual Report of our American Bible Society, which be pleased to present to your Bible Society. If that Society would address the American Bible Society, announcing their formation, and forward a copy of their constitution, with a sketch of the prospect before them, it would be the means of opening a correspondence between the two Societies, that might prove mutually useful.

The American Society have printed a number of French stereotype bibles, containing the Old and New Testaments, and would cheerfully supply yours, at the cost of printing and binding.

A highly respectable society has been formed at Washington, for the purpose of colonizing the free people of colour in the United States. I send thee a pamphlet, stating the views of this society; but they have not yet concluded to what part of the world it would be most advisable to recommend their emigration. This society is about sending an agent to Africa, to endeavour to procure an asylum for them at Sherbro, near Sierra Leone, or some other part of the continent. I am of opinion it would not answer for them to go to your island, unless a permanent peace was established. When that happy event shall have taken place, it will certainly be more for their interest to remove there, than any other part of the world. Many of them are sober and industrious, are well acquainted with agriculture, and are good mechanics.

A young man left here a few months ago for Port au Prince, who was sent from England by the British and Foreign School Society, for the purpose of introducing schools in your island, on an extensive and improved plan. I am anxious to know if he is likely to succeed, and should be much gratified in learning that you have a number of schools, established in different parts of thy government. To thy enlightened mind it is unnecessary for me to enlarge on the importance of this object, to advance which your government cannot appropriate too much money.

I have also sent thee a volume of the Transactions of the New York Literary and Philosophical Society. If you have any pamphlets or other objects, relating to the natural history of your island, they would be very acceptable.

It would afford me singular pleasure to render thee any services; and if, in any way, it is in my power to be useful to thee in this city, I beg thou wilt freely command me. I am, with sentiments of the greatest respect and esteem,

Thy assured friend,

THOMAS EDDY.

To President PETION.

London, 20th February, 1818.

MY DEAR SIR,

I have to acknowledge the receipt of your obliging favour of the 9th of April last, with the accompanying books and pamphlets, which were safely delivered by Mr. Greig, and for which I beg you will accept of my best thanks. I should have done this at an earlier period, had I not waited for Mr. Greig's return, which has been protracted far beyond the time either he or I had calculated upon. He has been so obliging as to take charge of a parcel for you, in which, according to your desire, you will find a copy of my Treatise on Indigence, and the three last reports of our Society for bettering the Condition of the Poor, with several other tracts, which I trust you will find interesting.

It is pleasing to observe the rapid progress you make in originating, and carrying into effect, useful institutions for improving the state of society in your country, in all which you appear to act a prominent part ; and well may it be said, *that you deserve well of your country*, since your whole time and attention are bestowed in promoting measures tending to the *prevention of criminal offences, to the religious and moral instruction of infants and adults, to the relief of mental and bodily infirmity,* and *to the general improvement of the morals of the people.*

You will observe, that so far back as the year 1806, I recommended Provident Banks, in my Treatise on Indigence, upon a national plan. The idea of such institutions originated with me ; but the public mind was not then prepared for such institutions, and I much fear they will not be rendered permanent under the present system, on account of the labour attending the gratuitous management, although our legislature has afforded them some facilities, with respect to the deposits. Had my plan been adopted in 1806, I am certain that not less than seven millions sterling of the property of the labouring classes would have now been yielding interest. The institutions, however, as now constituted, have become popular, and they are spreading fast all over the country ; but the demand for labour, in consequence of the happy return of peace, is unfortunately much less than the supply, and the poor, out of work, or being only half employed, and wages being generally reduced, they have little to spare ; but, upon the whole, more money is deposited than could reasonably have been expected. In 1816, and part of last year, there was much distress in the country, in consequence of the general stagnation of trade and manufactures, and the low price of agricultural produce; but of late a favourable change has taken place : the manufacturers are generally well employed, and the agricultural produce makes a fair return to the farmers.

This country has made great efforts, as well as very considerable pecuniary sacrifices, to induce the nations of Europe to abandon the odious slave trade, and they are likely to be successful at last ; and, after the lapse of two years, I trust, it will no longer exist. We continue to go on here in promoting philanthropic institutions; but it requires much good judgment, and a perfect knowledge of the world, to select those which, in their practical effect, shall produce that good to the community, which will compensate the expense and gratuitous labour which is required. Theories are often fallacious, although of much promise, and it is only in their practical effect that their real utility is discovered.

Our London hospitals have undergone much improvement of late, especially since they have attracted the notice of the legislature ; and, I trust, they will be farther ameliorated.

We find here the same corruption of morals, arising from the immoderate use of ardent spirits in vulgar life, which you experience at New York. It is a malady in the moral world which is difficult to cure, and our only hope is, that the rising generation, from being better taught, in consequence of the general dissemination of free schools, will conduct themselves with more propriety. The quantity of gin drank by the lower orders of society in this great and overgrown metropolis, in which so many loose and dissolute characters are congregated, exceeds all calculation, and there is no doubt of many thousands being sent prematurely to the grave, by indulging in this odious vice. I have for twenty-five years, as a

2 K

magistrate, exerted myself to the utmost to check the progress of this crying evil, by suppressing liquor shops; but, as those licensed to sell ale and beer, or porter, are also entitled to retail spirits, the task became extremely difficult. In this country it is a productive source of revenue. Referring you to our mutual good friend for further particulars, I remain always, with the most genuine regard,

My dear sir,

Yours, very affectionately and sincerely,

P. COLQUHOUN.

To Mr. THOMAS EDDY, New York.

New York, 6th mo. 7th, 1818.

DEAR FRIEND,

I have to acknowledge the receipt of thy acceptable favour of 3d mo. 5th, which has been communicated to the Board of Trustees of our Free School Society. They were highly pleased with the care and attention of the British and Foreign Society, in procuring a person, by thy account, so suitably qualified to take charge of the schools under their care, as Charles Picton. We hope he is now on his passage to this country, and that he will soon be with us. Our annual report is now printing, and I hope to get a copy in time to send thee by this opportunity. We have just established a third school near this city, of about two hundred scholars, and we are about erecting a school house, (No. 4,) to accommodate six hundred, so that at the close of this year the Society will have under their charge about two thousand children. The system is spreading in a most remarkable manner in every part of this state, and indeed very generally through the United States. The slave states are much behind all others in every thing that relates to religious or moral improvements. The Sunday School Society in this city have succeeded in a most wonderful manner. They have thirty-six schools open every first day, and in the whole about three thousand five hundred children are regularly instructed in school learning, and much pains taken in their religious and moral instruction. The best school in this city is the African Free School, under the care of our Abolition Society. They have in this school from two hundred and fifty to three hundred children; besides this, some young women (Friends) have a first day school for black women. I lately visited it, and noticed one woman seventy-two years of age, and another ninety-one!—Including these schools, and Sunday schools, there are about six hundred people of colour who receive the benefits of education in this city.

I should esteem it a particular favour if thou wouldst send me a number of your last Annual Report, of the British and Foreign School Society, and also some of the former years. If you have published a historical account of that society, it would also be very acceptable.

Inclosed is a letter from Mary Knight, handed me by a valuable friend, left open for thy perusal; he requests thy kind attention to have it safely delivered as directed.

During the last sitting of our Legislature, I sent to a member the following resolution, and proposed to his consideration to offer it to the House of Assembly:

" Resolved, If the Hon. the Senate concur therein, that the Governor be empowered, and he is hereby empowered, to appoint three discreet and competent persons, citizens of the state, as Commissioners, for the purpose of considering what amendments, if any, are necessary in the existing penal laws, and to devise the best plan for the management of the State Prisons; and that the Commissioners, so appointed, after due consideration of all matters and things relative to the present penal code, report to the next Legislature, such alterations and amendments of the existing laws relative to crimes and their punishments, as in their opinion may best conduce to the welfare of the state, by the prevention of crimes, with such reasons and observations as they may deem requisite to explain and elucidate the alterations or improvements they may recommend; and to inquire into and examine the first and present administration of the State Prison, and to point out the defects, if any exist, in the management and government thereof, and what alterations and improvements in their opinion may be necessary; and also to devise and propose a plan of prisons to be erected in different parts of the state, for the confinement of persons convicted of minor offences; and generally to suggest all such other matters, as in their opinion may conduce to the improvement and perfection of the penal code. And that the Commissioners so appointed, be authorized and empowered, and are hereby authorized and empowered, to send for persons and papers, and to reduce all examinations and evidences taken by them to writing, and annex the same to their report."

The foregoing resolution was presented to the Assembly, passed that House, and was sent to the Senate. I believe it also passed that branch of the Legislature, but am not informed if Commissioners have been appointed; if they should be, their report, I think, might afford interesting matter for your Society, on the melioration of the penal system. It has been a favourite object with me for some years past, to have prisons built in districts throughout the state, two or three counties to form a district, for solitary confinement, and divided into rooms six feet by nine, and to be appropriated solely for the punishment of minor offences—*to be kept perfectly clean and neat,* and the term of confinement not to exceed sixty or ninety days; their friends not to be permitted to visit them, except by special permission in writing, directed to the keeper of the prison. They should not be employed at any kind of work, and no book allowed them except the Bible, or some suitable religious tract.

The plan mentioned by thee of a Reformatory for six hundred boys, is the wisest and best ever proposed, provided it be so built as that each boy be lodged in a separate room; in the day, when at work, they will have keepers constantly with them, and *then* it will be very easy to prevent them talking or having any improper communication with each other;—if more than one is in a room at night, they would assuredly corrupt each other, and thus your design, or reformation, must be defeated.

The administration of the New York State Prison has been very badly managed for many years; the amount of expenditures are from twenty to thirty thousand dollars yearly more than the amount produced by the labour of the convicts. When Friends had the management, it was entirely different, as will be seen by my book, published in 1804, a copy of which was sent thee some time ago. In Philadelphia, the affairs of their State Prison are managed with much care and prudence, and the profit on the labour of the convicts is several thousand dollars more than the cost of support and maintenance. The friends to the penitentiary system have been in some degree disappointed as it regards reformation of the convicts, and this, in my opinion, is entirely owing to the improper construction of our prisons. The rooms are calculated too large, and in consequence of this, twelve to fifteen are put in each room at night, and of course they corrupt each other, and it is not unreasonable to believe that many become more wicked and incorrigible from their imprisonment. The only wise plan then is, for keepers to be constantly with them during the day whilst at labour, and at night, let each one be lodged in separate cells.

I have many numbers of the Philanthropist, and would be thankful if thou wouldst direct them to be regularly sent me.

The pamphlets, and Montague on Punishments, &c.,
24

came safe, and am much obliged by thy kind care and attention.

15*th.*—We have just been informed of the safe arrival of John Griscom; it is pleasing that he may reach London in time to attend the yearly meeting, and the annual meeting of the British and Foreign Bible Society. I wrote him a few weeks ago, but it is out of my power, by this conveyance, as I am just warned that the vessel is about sailing; please to remember me in the most affectionate manner to him. I beg him to write me very frequently, respecting his movements, prospects, &c. I am, very truly, thy affectionate friend,   THOMAS EDDY.
     To WILLIAM ALLEN.

List of pamphlets directed for William Allen.—Christian Herald; Monthly Magazine; Annual Report of the Philadelphia School Society; Memorial from the Virginia yearly meeting to the Legislature; Two Annual Reports of New York Free School Society, 1818; Evening Post, containing the Report of the Society for the Deaf and Dumb, in Connecticut; Gleaner, containing an Indian Speech; Annual Report of the Female Association in the city of New York, 1818; Description and Historical Sketch of the State Prison of Massachusetts, 1816.

                              London, 20th June, 1818.
DEAR SIR,
     I had the pleasure of writing you on the 20th of February, by my friend Mr. Greig, and I have recently had the satisfaction of learning from him, that the papers he was so good as to take charge of, were safely delivered into your hands, and that you were in good health. You will see by referring to my Treatise on Indigence, which I sent you, that I was the first to suggest the establishment of saving banks, so far back as the year 1806. Happy would it have been for this country, if this, and my various other suggestions for the amelioration of society, had been

attended to at the time they were brought forward; but the public mind in this country, and particularly the Parliament, do not see good objects quickly. The proposition was made, when a leading member brought in a bill for amending the Poor Laws in 1806, which did not pass the Lower House. Three years ago, the establishment of local banks for savings originated in Scotland, and their utility being (as I had predicted) rendered manifest, they got a footing in this country. They have recently been recognized by government, and there are now about two hundred establishments in different parts of Great Britain and Ireland: but as the superintendence is gratuitous, and the organization of a nature not to ensure permanency, (which was the main feature in my plan,) I doubt their success on the present footing.

A gentleman of the name of Woodson, has proposed an improvement. He sent me his pamphlet, (a copy of which I inclose you,) requesting at the same time, that my assistance and influence might be exerted in his behalf. He thought he had made a new discovery, but was surprised when I showed him that I had brought forward a similar plan twelve years ago. I assured him, however, of my co-operation, and he is now attempting to carry his plan into effect. If it succeeds, it will be one of the best establishments which was ever made, for the purpose of giving provident habits to the poor, and of rendering them independent of parish relief, which adds greatly in other respects to their comfort.

Having now reached the seventy-fourth year of my age, and having resolved, as soon as I can, in consequence of declining health, to resign all my public laborious situations, and to devote my remaining life to charitable objects only; in the contemplation of this retirement, a friend of mine wished to possess my papers, that he might give a brief view of my public life. This he has done, and I hasten to send you a copy of it, from which you will see that I have not devoted any time to what is called *the pleasurable amusements of life*. In my progress I have encountered many difficulties, and have subjected myself to the most excessive labour, stimulated thereto by a conviction, that success would generate pleasing reflections. You too, my good sir, have pursued the same track, perhaps in a greater degree, although you had not so wide a field: but you exceed me by far, since to charitable objects you have devoted your whole time, while mine has been occupied by a great variety of objects. I trust, however, most of them have been useful to my fellow citizens.

I had resisted the solicitations of the editor of the European Magazine, to set forth my portrait, and to permit him to introduce my biography into his work for more than twenty years, promising at the same time, that at a future period (meaning at the close of life) I would comply with his request. I have now redeemed the pledge, and the biography now sent you, will be found in the Magazine for *March*, *April*, *May*, and *June*, in the present year. Probably the three first numbers may have found their way to the United States before this reaches you, the fourth is not yet published.

Nothing, in my opinion, will cure the excessive evils arising from the immoderate use of ardent spirits in your country, (which is even worse than here,) than the universal diffusion of properly organized *Savings Banks* in each of the states, sanctioned by *legislative regulations*. They are calculated beyond all other institutions, to give *provident habits* to the labouring people. Provident habits never fail to generate industry, and to promote moral and religious feelings. In my treatise on Indigence, you will perceive that I call it to be a *god-like work*. All the regulations and restraints of the legislature, and all the efforts of the clergy, will, without this great auxiliary, be of little avail.

Our free schools go on prosperously: but until they

are made *completely national,* and not made to depend on voluntary subscriptions, and voluntary superintendence, I have my fears as to their permanency. They should be placed on the footing of those in Scotland, established in every parish more than a century and a half ago, to which is to be attributed the superior moral habits of the labouring classes in that country beyond all others in Europe. We expended 4000*l.* raised by subscription, in erecting a new school in this quarter of Westminster, for the education of 1000 male and female children, which school I founded in 1803. I send you our last report.

We have in this great metropolis, many useful, and I am sorry to say, many useless charities, suggested by benevolent well-meaning persons, whose minds are not sufficiently enlarged to foresee that the expense produces little practical results; while others, such as the hospitals for the sick and diseased, (where the benefits are unquestionable) are overlooked. Many of the wards, in the different establishments, are occasionally empty for want of funds; and the admission of patients, from this circumstance, is precluded.

Inclosed I send you the under noted publications, which I hope may prove interesting.

With great regard and esteem,

I remain always, my dear Sir,

Yours very affectionately and sincerely,

P. COLQUHOUN.

To THOMAS EDDY.

List of Pamphlets enclosed.

1. Biography of P. Colquhoun.
2. Mr. Woodson on Savings Banks, by Mr. Woodson.
3. Minutes of a public meeting to promote his plan.
4. Dialogue to promote Savings Banks.
5. Report on the Fever Institution.
6. Report of the Westminster National School.

2 L 24*

London, 24th June, 1818.

SIR,

I have the pleasure to acquaint you, that the committee for the improvement of prison discipline, &c., have unanimously elected you an honorary member of the society.

I request your acceptance of a few copies of their report, recently published, containing an account of their past proceedings, and explanatory of their future objects; and I shall be happy to forward to you, from time to time, the future publications of the society.

I am, Sir, your obedient servant,

SAMUEL HOARE, junr.,

Chairman of the Committee.

To Mr. THOMAS EDDY, New York.

New York, 7th month, 8th, 1818.

MY DEAR FRIEND,

I wrote thee soon after thy departure from this country, and once since, and about ten days ago received thy esteemed favour, dated, Liverpool, 5th month, 7th, which gave the pleasing intelligence of thy safe arrival. How highly gratified I should be, by being with thee for a few months, and mixing with that kind of society, that thou wilt be constantly meeting in thy tour through England. As this is not to be my lot, it would be the next most pleasing enjoyment, to hear frequently from thee, with very full details of thy observations on men and things, in the course of thy travels. I was much pleased with thy account of William Roscoe, and in consequence of thy recommendation, have put up a large bundle of pamphlets, amongst which are accounts of Philadelphia, New York, and Boston Prisons. Such a man, engaging with zeal in the cause of humanity, particularly as it relates to a melioration of the penal laws of Great Britain, might do wonders. To effect this, requires patience and perseverance;—the whole work may be ruined by men, who in England are called Oppositionists or Reformers, (in America, Democrats,) and who, actuated by an overstrained zeal, do not know how to take hold of things at the right time; like many religious zealots, they press on the people more than they are able to bear. The light with which Providence has been pleased to enlighten the minds of men, as it regards moral or religious truths, is gradual—as was the commencement of the abolition of slavery. If the good people in England, who are now engaged in endeavouring to effect an alteration in the penal system, act wisely, they will be exceedingly prudent and cautious not to press for too much in their first application— *eventually* they *must* succeed in so righteous a cause.

I expect thou wilt procure a fund of information, relating to public institutions, particularly Lunatic Asylums. I requested of thee, if thou shouldst visit York, to find out, if in thy power, on what account it is, that Samuel Tuke seems offended with me—It may be for my publishing one of his letters to me, in doing which I conceived it was promoting the public good by using his name. I am very sorry, if in any way, his feelings have been hurt, owing to any part of my conduct.

I hope thou arrived in London in time for the Annual Meeting of the Bible Society, and also for our yearly meeting—do they manage their matters better in London than with us? The last London printed epistle, was not printed by our yearly meeting as usual; this was opposed by E. Hicks, Willet, and others of his disciples, on account of it containing some pointed good remarks, on the observance of the First Day—it was advocated by G. Dillwyn, &c. &c., but they were obliged to yield, in order to preserve peace and harmony.

For some days past, we have had the company of J. Wistar, T. Stewardson, William Newbould, Samuel Bettle, and R. Hartshorn, appointed by the Indian committee of Philadelphia, on the subject of Indian affairs, but particularly respecting the purchase made by D. A. Ogden and others, of *all* the Indian reservations.

Our Pauper Society does not get forward with any spirit, and, in my opinion will cease, till thee return to revive it. I wish W. Allen would direct the Philanthropist to be regularly forwarded to me—I have had no numbers since those received from thee—I wrote him about two weeks ago, and sent him some pamphlets—please return to him my thanks for a parcel he sent me, which came safe to hand, and were very acceptable. R. Mott and wife propose to spend the summer mostly at his farm—S. Hopkins and D. Sands, deceased. Our friends generally are well as usual—R. Bowne's health unexpectedly improving.

Last First Day, Samuel Bettle preached for us at Pearl-street about an hour, equal to the best, if not the best sermon I ever heard delivered—truly orthodox on important doctrines—the language was excellent—his manner of delivery extremely agreeable,—and a most uncommon solemnity seemed to cover the whole meeting, equal to any thing of the kind I ever witnessed.

8th month, 5th.

Absence from the city, and other circumstances, prevented me sending this as soon as intended. I have now to mention the decease of our mutual valuable friend, R. Bowne, on First Day evening last, in the seventy-fourth year of his age—the funeral at 5 o'clock this day. Reuben and Jane got here last evening from Philadelphia—I intend writing again soon, and shall send the last report of the American Bible Society—I have been anxiously expecting a letter after thee reached London—pray do not omit writing me often—Eastburn & Co. are about publishing a third edition of Professor Silliman's Travels.

I am, very truly, thine, &c.

THOMAS EDDY.

J. GRISCOM.

New York, 8th month, 8th, 1818.

RESPECTED FRIEND,

In a late letter from my particular and valuable friend, John Griscom, he informed me of the peculiar gratification he enjoyed in thy company at Liverpool, and of thy being a warm advocate in favour of obtaining an alteration of your penal code, and requested me to forward thee some printed accounts of the Penitentiary system in this country. It is with much pleasure that I comply with my friends request, and now send to care of Cropper, Benson, & Co., a bundle containing several pamphlets relating to our prisons, and have added some others that I conceived would be interesting to thee. We have in this state two large prisons, one in this city that has about 750 convicts, and one at Auburn, (about 150 miles west of Albany,) built last year, that will accommodate about the same number. The affairs of the prison in this city have been badly managed for some years. That punishments *mild* and certain will more effectually prevent crimes, than those which are sanguinary and severe, there can be no doubt; and this would have been most completely verified, if the plan of our prisons had been adapted to the design and intention of our Penitentiary system; they should have been so built, that each convict might be confined at night in a *separate* room—say six by eight feet—but unfortunately the rooms, in all our prisons are calculated for eight to fourteen prisoners, so that when they are lodged together at night, they have full opportunity to corrupt each other, and most frequently come out of prison more hardened and depraved than when they entered it. During the day, whilst employed at work, and at their meals, as keepers are constantly with them, it is very easy to prevent them conversing with each other; and if, at night, each of them were confined in a separate room, there would be some good chance for reformation; indeed, in this way the punishment would be more severely felt, and the term of imprisonment might be shortened. I interested myself in vain with our government, to have the prison lately built at Auburn, divided throughout into rooms, to accommodate only one prisoner; they however agreed to have 140 such rooms, in order to keep separate the most abandoned characters. In a late conversation with our Governor, he regretted very much that the prison had not been built agreeably to the plan recommended by me. I am perfectly satisfied that until all our prisons are on this plan, the expectations of those who are desirous of a rational reform will not be answered. If you should succeed in obtaining an alteration of your penal laws, it would be a fortunate circumstance, if your prisons should be calculated throughout on the plan of rooms to lodge one person.

I inclose thee a printed copy of a paper read before the Governors of the New York Hospital, in which I recommended them to erect an extensive Asylum for Lunatics, and have now the satisfaction to state, that they have purchased thirty-four acres of land, near the city, and have commenced erecting a building for the accommodation of 300 insane patients, and intend to pursue the same mild plan of treatment as adopted at the retreat, near York, in England.

One section of the grand canal, intended to connect the waters of Lake Erie with the Hudson River, will be completed this year—this section commences at Utica, on the Mohawk River, and extends to Seneca River, about fifteen miles west of Onondaga Lake, a distance of seventy miles.

Thy affectionate friend,
THOMAS EDDY.

WILLIAM ROSCOE, Esq.

A List of Pamphlets sent William Roscoe, Esq.

A Memorial and Petition of the Society of Friends, by B. Bates.

A Discourse on the death of Captain Paul Cuffee.

The Report of the Committee on Pauperism.

Report of the Society of Philadelphia on Charity Schools.

Information of the progress of the Asylum near Philadelphia.

Governor Clinton's Discourse before the New York Historical Society.

Report of the New York Hospital Society—1817.

Report of the Female Association—1818.

Historical Sketch of Massachusetts State Prison.

Report of the Commissioners on Internal Naviga tion, state of New York—1811, 1812, 1817.

Account of the New York State Prison, by Thomas Eddy—1801.

View of New York State Prison—1815.

Account of Massachusetts State Prison.

Statistical view of the operation of the penal code of Pennsylvania.

Map of the Western part of the State of New York.

Map of Niagara River.

Map of the countries between the Great Lakes, and the Atlantic Ocean.

Hints for introducing an improved mode of treating the Insane.

American Bible Society Report—1818.

Liverpool, 30th September, 1818.

DEAR SIR,

I avail myself of this opportunity to express my grateful acknowledgments for your valuable communication of Reports and Documents respecting your state prisons and other institutions, which have arrived at a moment when they will be of important service to me, in a publication which I intend shortly to send to press, on the state of our criminal law, and the reformation of offenders.

I have observed with great concern, the unfavourable change which seems to have taken place in these establishments on your side the Atlantic, and am convinced, from the best consideration I can give the subject, that they are occasioned, in a great degree, by the causes mentioned in your letter—the inadequacy of the buildings, and the want of separate apartments at night for the convicts; but, independent of this, there are other circumstances which appear to me to be of great importance, and which I intend to state pretty much at large. I hope in the course of six or eight weeks to be enabled to send you a copy of my publication, in which I have the pleasure to think you will find a close conformity to your own opinions and recommendations, so clearly stated, and so strikingly enforced, in some of the works with which you have favoured me.

I shall only at present beg leave further to observe, that I am sorry to find some indications of an intention on the part of your managers, to abolish the power of pardoning criminals, and to render punishment *certain* as *to duration*—a measure which, as it appears to me, would put an end to Penitentiary establishments altogether. That this power may have been indiscreetly used, is possible, but it is not *the sending convicts out,* but the *receiving them in again,* that occasions the evil complained of, as I hope you will see stated in the sheets I shall send you.

Our good friend, Mr. Griscom, is travelling on the continent of Europe, with another friend of mine, and I believe intends to make a visit to Italy.

I think myself happy in being favoured with this friendly interchange of opinion, with one whose attention has been so long, and so successfully devoted to the subject. And with sincere esteem and attachment, remain, Dear Sir, your much obliged and faithful friend,

W. ROSCOE.

To Mr. THOMAS EDDY, New York.

New York, 12th month, 28th, 1818.
To THOMAS ELLICOTT & PHILIP E. THOMAS.

David A. Ogden holds the pre-emption right of purchasing all the Indian reservations in our state. He is very desirous the Indians should remove to the Westward, and sell to him their reservations. These Indians west of Genessee River, have been under the care of Friends in Philadelphia, and they have uniformly advised the Indians not to remove. Ogden prevailed on Calhoun to address to him a letter which he then communicated to the Indians.

One Jabez Hyde, a Presbyterian minister or schoolmaster, residing among them, published the letter. When we met our Friends in Philadelphia, we found their minds much soured and prejudiced against government, and particularly against the Secretary at War; they asked, why should any confidence be placed in men who would talk so smooth to us, and at the same time write a letter, with a view to have it shown to the Indians, stating that Friends "were their worst enemies." It did not serve to alter the opinion so strongly taken up by them, that we urged our own belief, and that of T. McKenney, that Calhoun did not intend any way to allude to Friends. We believed, we told them, that Ogden had stated to Calhoun, that a number of whites residing near the Indians, constantly urged them not to remove, and who, by trade and artifice, got from the Indians, every year, the amount of the annuities paid them by government; and thus it became the interest of this class of people, to use every means in their power to persuade the Indians not to remove. In making such a representation, Ogden induced Calhoun to write this letter. I am satisfied that he (Ogden) never mentioned to the Secretary that *Friends* had advised the Indians to remain on their lands—it would have been bad policy for him to have urged such sentiments. In short, I do not believe Calhoun thought of Friends when he wrote the letter. It is probably

2 M   25

true, that at that time, government supposed it would be for the interest of the Indians of New York to remove to the borders of the Mississippi; but I am well convinced they have changed their sentiments, and that now they agree most decidedly with us, that the Indians ought to remain on their reservations.

We found that Friends, at their last meeting for sufferings, held in Philadelphia, appointed a committee to draft a Memorial, which is prepared, and some Friends in a few days will be appointed to attend Congress with it. From the representation we made to them of our kind reception at Washington, and our urging that we had full confidence in the assurance given to us of the kind disposition of the President, Calhoun, McKenney, &c., their minds seemed to be in some degree softened—still they seemed as if they could not be reconciled to Calhoun's letter to Ogden. Owing to people coming in, and constantly interrupting me, it is with difficulty I write, but thought it was best to give you these hints—you may consider if it would be proper for you to address a confidential letter to McKenney, requesting an explanation of Calhoun's letter, and probably our Philadelphia Friends prejudices might be removed.

Not time to add, &c.

THOMAS EDDY.

P. S. We pressed very earnestly on our Friends in Philadelphia, to forward you such matter, as would enable you to furnish the committee of Congress the proofs they required—but we are fearful they will put it off till the committee goes to Washington. I hope you will, without delay, further to Southard your own materials, with what we left with you.

Liverpool, 20th February, 1819.

DEAR SIR,

With this you will, I hope, receive two copies of my promised Treatise on *Penal Jurisprudence, and the Reformation of Offenders,* which I submit with great diffidence to your judgment and experience; and should feel still more, if I had not, in almost every respect, conformed to your views, and availed myself of your excellent writings on this subject, which do the greatest credit both to yourself and your country ; on which account, you will find I have not only occasionally quoted you, but have given the Report of the State Prison of New York for 1815 (which contains so many of your excellent remarks) entire.

From the portion of my tract which relates to this country, you will perceive, that we are not insensible to the great importance of the penitentiary system, and that some idea of such a plan has been entertained, even from a remote period; but *that* which has always been wanting, has been to place it on a proper ground, and to substitute a system of benevolence and reformation for one of revenge and punishment.

If this can be fully effected, every thing else will naturally flow from it, as from a parent stream ; and from the united efforts that are making in almost every civilized part of the world, and the free communication of sentiments between those who are earnest in the cause, I trust that such a foundation will be laid for the moral improvement of mankind, as may allow us to indulge the warmest hopes of a speedy and happy result.

The publications you were so good as to send me, were of the highest value, as they show, by a variety of experiments, not only what ought to be done in establishing a penitentiary system, but what ought to be *avoided.* On this head, you will see I have expressed myself with great freedom, and will, perhaps, think I have been more ready to blame than to commend. If, however, I have written without reserve, I have also endeavoured to give reasons for my opinions; and it would give me the greatest pleasure, if any suggestions of mine should be thought worthy the attention of those in your country, who interest themselves in the promotion of these most important and benevolent plans.

Accept, once more, my sincere thanks for your kind attentions, and believe me, with the most grateful respect and attachment, Dear Sir,

Your faithful friend,

And humble fellow-labourer,

W. ROSCOE.

To Mr. THOMAS EDDY, New York.

New York, 8th mo. 9th, 1819.

ESTEEMED FRIEND,

I duly received thy kind favour, dated 20th February, accompanied with two copies of thy Treatise on Penal Jurisprudence, &c , which were truly acceptable; and, from a careful perusal of the work, am well satisfied it will be extensively useful in your country, and also in the United States. I had some expectation that an edition would have been printed here, but in this have I been disappointed. If a few copies could be sent by Robinson, bookseller, Liverpool, to James Eastburn & Co., booksellers in this city, they might be readily sold, and I am well satisfied would be of great use, as they would, no doubt, be generally read by the members of our legislature, at their next session in January. The subject relating to the affairs of our penitentiary system, &c., will then be before them. The success of the establishments in Boston, New Jersey, Pennsylvania, Baltimore, and, I believe, in Virginia, has been equal to the warmest expectations of our friends; but, in this state, every thing has been sadly mismanaged for some years past. In Pennsylvania, a prison is building, calculated to lodge each convict in a separate room, and I am in hopes we shall have one erected on this plan in this state. I am satisfied, that until our prisons are all *so* built, we shall never have the system perfect. My sentiments on this are fully mentioned in the first letter I had the pleasure of addressing to thee.   I expect shortly a communication from Cadwallader D. Colden, Esq., mayor of New York, on the effects of our present code of penal laws, as to the increase or diminution of crimes.   There is no person more capable of forming a correct judgment, and none whose opinions would have more extensive influence on the minds of our citizens.   He has been a warm friend to the system for many years.   As soon as I get this communication, a copy shall be sent thee, and also some other materials that I expect to procure.   I am, very truly,

Thy affectionate friend,

THOMAS EDDY.

To WILLIAM ROSCOE.

Weston, George Town, March 19*th,* 1819.

RESPECTED FRIEND,

I am gratified at the interest you take in our Indian concerns, and thank you for your letter of the 3d inst., and for the pamphlet which accompanied it.

I have not yet learned the views of the President, respecting the application of the 10,000 dollars, appropriated near the close of the late session of Congress, to aid in the business of Indian improvement. My own opinion is, (and it is only my opinion,) that it will be applied through the benevolent agencies which are, or may be, put in operation ; and at such points as it shall be likely to do the most good, according to the intentions of the act of Congress. Those establishments, so it strikes me, will be recognized as most in accordance with this view, that are, or may be, organized *in the Indian country ;* and which embrace the two branches of improvement, implied in *letters* and the *agricultural arts,* united also with a system of *moral improvement.* This particular application, it strikes me, will be, as the sum is, to the number of Indian children taken in by these liberal associations of men for education. Thus, if there be ten schools of instruction, for example, in

25*

the Indian country, averaging each one hundred children, there will be one thousand dollars for each establishment.

The amount appropriated is so small, when compared with the object of general or universal improvement, that, to make it useful, it can be used only as an auxiliary to the resources which individual bounty has provided. I will just name one school in the Cherokee country, in charge of the good Mr. Gambold. He is labouring, and has been for fourteen years, in this generous cause; and his plans have not been developed, nor his scale of usefulness extended to its limits, for lack of pecuniary resources. Five and six children are as many as his means have ever enabled him to instruct. I don't know what his resources are, but I will suppose them to be at the rate of fifty dollars per annum for each child; and, suppose he can educate and instruct out of his own means, in the various branches of improvement which his school embraces, only five children; and suppose it shall turn out, in the general estimate, that a hundred dollars can be applied, out of the 10,000 appropriated, for each child,—that would enable Mr. Gambold to take fifteen children, or ten more than the number to which, I suppose, he has been hitherto confined. I merely refer to this case, as being the first that has struck me; and to this mode of illustration, without knowing what plan the President may adopt. I incline to the opinion, however, that his contemplated tour may prevent him from doing more than acquire a collection of information applicable to the case, against his return.

It seems you have, in the state of New York, 4976 Indians, and that these Indians have 271,323 acres of land as reservations. I am glad they are so well off in the land way. How would it sort with your convenience to let me know, how many schools for improvement are organized in their settlements, exclusively for Indian education? and where located?—

and how many children are attached to each of them? and, as far as you may be able, what state of improvement they are in. In truth, my good friend, I look to the Indian *children* for the realization of Indian civilization. The main efforts should be made to apply to them. The old ones are like the mountain oaks, (here and there some exceptions,) and it were an almost hopeless task to attempt their conformity with civilized life. But they must soon die off—such is nature's decree; and if vigorous measures be adopted for *the children*, they will, when they arrive at maturity, appear like the vernal year, in contrast with the barrenness of a recent winter prospect. My wish is, that the principles of improvement be extended to as many Indian children as they can be made to reach. They are the virgin soil—the seeds sown in them will grow, be they bad or good.

I am sure the President would be gratified to recognize your recommendation of agents to go amongst the New York Indians, if it shall come within his scheme to make such appointments. It is certain you would name none, but such as would promote the great object of their civilization and improvement.

The Indians at Allegany and Onondago are in a fair way. They have banished the greatest evil, the small-pox not excepted, that ever desolated any people. It is literally *the Indians' curse*. In excluding ardent spirits, they have got the top upon Pandora's box, and may a kind Providence help them to keep it there!

It would be gratifying all round, no doubt, to promote the views embraced in your suggestions; and, if the principle of distribution shall be adopted, the New York Indians will get, through the benevolent channels, where I think it likely it will be all made to flow, some portion of this small sum. The appointment of an agent or two, as you suggest, is a good plan; especially as the New York Indians are in so many separate clans; for then the agent could superintend the improvement of them all more generally, by going amongst them, and counselling them according to your plan. But will it not cost an *over* proportion of the appropriation in *that* direction, if $1600 be necessary?—especially as these Indians are doing so much better than many others, in every way. Or would not $1600 for 4976 Indians, leave too small a sum to go to the four nations on our borders, whose numbers may be estimated at 100,000? This may go to show the propriety of using this appropriation as an *auxiliary* to existing organizations, where its effects may tell upon a congregation of children, and give means to increase their numbers, or power to confer additional improvements upon those already admitted. For I think (for myself) the children should be the subjects of our *special* care. This, however, is not intended to exclude the Indian children in New York from their proportion of benefits; and hence, I have suggested that you favour me with the information I have referred to. But all this is my own first thinking, very hastily thrown together, not one point of which may be adopted in the regulations which shall be finally made.

I will cheerfully lay any communication you may make on this subject before the Secretary of War, who will be the organ to the President in this matter.

I have sent after a copy of Heckwelder's book. No doubt I shall enjoy it, and derive benefit from it, in the way of information.

With regard,
I am, dear sir, your friend, &c.,
J. L. McKENNEY.

Mr. THOMAS EDDY, New York.

N. B. This letter is in the hand-writing of the Choctaw boy, whom you saw at my house, and for whom I am gratified to have it in my power to state, Mr. Calhoun has authorized an extension of benefits, in the way of scholastic acquirements. His promise is great.

Schenectady, November 8, 1819.

My Good Friend,

I have thought much on the great subjects talked over at our late interesting and very pleasant inter view at your house.   I have since conversed with many distinguished gentlemen in your city, on board the steam boat, and in the city of Albany, particularly with the Governor, Lieutenant Governor, and Mr. Van Rensselaer, (the Patroon)—all enter very heartily into our views.   The Governor, and Mr. Van Rensselaer, are both going in a few days to New York, on a visit of several weeks.   I expect to meet them there.   They will be pleased to have a conference with you on the subjects which interests us, and them also.   The Governor suggested the idea of having a meeting, after my return to your city, of a number of gentlemen, who are like minded with ourselves, and of intelligence and influence, to confer on the best measures to ripen our plans, and to carry them into effect.   Mr. Van Rensselaer will be present, and will probably be willing to go on to Washington this winter, and aid in effecting our purposes there, particularly in forming a new association which you suggested, of all denominations, to do every thing for the Indians, except introducing *particular* religious instruction.   This plan, I think, will take.   I think I shall make an effort to go myself to Washington, and hope, by all means, you, my friend, will calculate to go—and then we shall feel strong.   The object is a great and good one, and worthy a great effort.   It opens here very auspiciously, and I am full of hope.

I write after the fatigues of the day, in the bustle of a public house—but I will make no farther apology.

With kind regard to your good family, believe me, very sincerely,

Your friend,

JEDEDIAH MORSE.

Thomas Eddy.

2 N

New York, 11th mo. 15th, 1819.

RESPECTED FRIEND,

Thy very obliging favour of June 24th, 1818, was received some time since, and to which I should have replied before this, but delayed, because I wished to make some communication relating to the objects that particularly claim the attention of your respectable society. Some of the prisons established in America have not answered the expectation of the advocates for the penitentiary system, most of whom were led to believe, that the avails of the labour of the convicts would be sufficient to defray *all* the expenses of their maintenance, &c. This has certainly not been the fact as to the State Prison in New York, owing entirely to the appointment of persons, who have had the management of its concerns, not being rightly qualified for executing the duties required of them. The consequence of this has been, that the expense of supporting that prison has been very considerable. However, considering the great advantage contemplated to result from the penitentiary system, the mere expense is a matter of secondary consideration. Yet experience has proved in New Jersey, Philadelphia, Baltimore, and Virginia, that under prudent direction and good management, the profits on the labour of the convicts will produce sufficient to pay all the necessary expenses of their support, &c. I think the best conducted penitentiary we have in America is at Baltimore. I visited that prison a few months ago, and was highly gratified in observing the order, cleanliness, regularity, and industry of the prisoners. I never visited any institution that exhibited such a perfect degree of cleanliness, decency, and regularity, throughout its whole concerns, as the Baltimore prison, the effects of which were evidently marked in the countenance and general deportment of the convicts. The present very promising state of the Maryland penitentiary is owing to the excellent management of their Board of Inspectors, which is composed of gentlemen of the first character in the city of Baltimore. The institution is also much indebted to the judicious care and good conduct of the present keeper, who is an active and intelligent man. I requested him to send me a direct account of the expenditures, &c. of the prison for the last year, which I have received from him, forwarded me by one of the Inspectors a few days ago ; and believing that this document may be interesting to your Society, I have had it copied, and now inclose it.

There is one remark respecting the penitentiary system, which I beg leave to mention. *No* benefit, as it regards *reformation,* ever has been, *nor ever will be* produced, unless our prisons are calculated to have separate rooms, six feet by eight feet, so as that every man can be lodged *by himself.* If, as is common, twelve to twenty are lodged at night in one room, they surely will corrupt each other, and leave the prison far more depraved than when they entered it. I think there is good reason to believe that our legislature will direct the state prison in this city to be sold next year, and order a new one to be built, to be divided in rooms of six by eight feet each. I would further observe, that during the day, when the prisoners are employed at their work, they are, of course, constantly under the immediate eye of a keeper, and no improper intercourse or conversation can take place. At Pittsburg, (Pennsylvania,) a prison, on the plan of separate rooms for each convict, is now building, and I am told they intend erecting a similar one in Philadelphia. Several years ago, I mentioned to my friend, P. Colquhoun, of London, that no reformation could possibly be expected from the operation of the penitentiary system, unless the prisons were built on a plan for the convicts to be separately lodged at night, and I think he stated that some in England were on that construction, but in his late letters to me he is silent on the subject of prisons. I am told that there is a prison in the environs of London, built to accommodate seven hundred prisoners, and each lodged in a room seven by nine feet. If this is a fact, I should be much gratified by having some account of it. My friend William Allen, some time since, wrote me that it was proposed to build a prison solely for lads under eighteen years of age, to be called a Reformatory, but I have not heard if this has been completed.

Our Society for the Prevention of Pauperism, has appointed a committee to consider of the present state of our prisons, &c. The committee will probably report in a few weeks, when a copy shall be sent to your society.

I am very sensible of the favour conferred on me by your society, in electing me an honorary member, and beg leave to return them my sincere thanks for this mark of their respect. I shall, with much pleasure, forward any publications on the subject of prisons, &c. that may appear to me likely to be interesting to your society.

I am, with much esteem

Thy assured friend,

THOMAS EDDY.

To SAMUEL HOARE, junr. Chairman of the Committee
for the Improvement of Prison Discipline.

Albany, 21*st November,* 1820.

MY WORTHY OLD FRIEND,

As you assured me you would write our mutual friend, Robert Troup, Esq., of Geneva, as to your recollection about the old Canal affair, and his conformity to the letter I left for you in New York—and as Troup writes me of the 17th instant, he had not read it, and his pamphlet is suspended, waiting to receive it; he is anxious on the subject, and wished me to say to you, he apprehends you have wrote by some private person, and that the letter has miscarried. He will thank you to take the trouble to send him a duplicate, by mail, not doubting from your known habits of punctuality, and a scrupulous regard to your word, but you must have wrote him.

Be assured, in this matter, there is no tincture of party—we both gave our votes to Clinton in April last—and you will find by a perusal of the work, (which I hope you will do me the honour to admit in your library,) that I did Clinton the most ample justice.

Truth and justice is all our aim to establish—your just claims will also be speedily noticed—and posterity will not fail to hold your eminent services in grateful remembrance.

I am, my Dear Sir,
With great respect,
E. WATSON.

To Mr. THOMAS EDDY, New York.

Geneva, Ontario County, 29th Nov. 1820.

MY DEAR FRIEND,

I beg leave to return you a thousand thanks for your very obliging letter of the 14th instant.

I am writing an argument on the subject of the canal policy of this state, to vindicate myself against a scandalous charge I met with in the first number of Tacitus; which is understood to have been either written by Governor Clinton, or under his eye and direction.

Your letter speaks of a particular fact, in relation to the Canal Bill of 1792; and as it tallies with all my other evidence, I shall take the liberty of using your letter as far as the particular fact is concerned.

My argument will go to the press to-morrow or next day, but it will not be ready for forwarding to my friends in a pamphlet form, until the beginning of December. I shall beg the favour of your accepting one from,

My dear friend, yours most fervently,
ROBERT TROUP.

Mr. THOMAS EDDY, New York.

26

New York, 11th month, 3d, 1820.

RESPECTED FRIEND,

I am extremely desirous of obtaining some information of an establishment at Aversa, near Naples,
which, I am told, is solely for the accommodation of
Lunatics. As I have no acquaintance with any person residing at Naples, from whom I could procure
the information wanted, I applied to my friend,
Stephen Grellet, who immediately mentioned to me
thy name, and stated, from his personal acquaintance, he was well assured of thy benevolence and
kindness, and that I might take the liberty of addressing a letter to thee on the subject of my inquiry. This,
I hope, will be kindly received, as an apology for my
taking this freedom.

It is said, that the mode of treatment towards the
patients at Aversa, is replete with tender and affectionate care and attention, in place of the harsh, cruel,
and rigorous treatment, that has heretofore been
administered towards Lunatic patients. This mode,
called 'moral treatment,' has been pursued with great
success, at an Asylum called the Retreat, near York,
(England,) under the care of the society of Friends,
for the accommodation of the members of their own
society. Near this city we have just completed a
large handsome building, exclusively for Lunatics,
which will accommodate more than 200 patients;
attached to it is about eighty acres of land, ornamented with extensive gravel walks, shrubberies,
gardens, green-house, &c. Here it is intended to
employ the patients in Horticulture and Agriculture,
and other pursuits, as far as may be practicable, and
also to afford them every rational amusement. I
have been one of the governors of the New York
Hospital for many years; and about four years ago,
introduced to them, a proposition to establish an
Asylum about six miles from the city, solely for
Lunatic Patients, on the plan of "moral treatment,"
as pursued at the Retreat near York.

The governors adopted the proposed plan, and have expended on the building, land, &c., $150,000. It is very desirable, that the managers of this concern should be as perfect as possible, and I am therefore induced to crave thy kind aid, in procuring for me a general and ample account respecting the establishment at Aversa; as to the general mode of treating the patients, diet, employment, &c. I am very fearful of giving thee too much trouble, but perhaps much may be saved, if printed accounts could be procured. They might readily be translated in this city. I have made up a package containing accounts of some of our benevolent institutions of this city. Also reports relating to the grand canal, which is intended to open a communication between Lake Erie and the Hudson River, a distance of 325 miles.

It is three years since this great work was commenced, and already one hundred miles are completed; near one hundred more is this year in such a state of forwardness, that it will also be completed early next year. The whole extent, 325 miles, will probably be finished by the year 1824. The cost of this great undertaking, (from Erie to the Hudson) will be about five millions of dollars. I send thee a small map, which will serve to show the route of the canal.

There are three American young gentlemen who expect to visit Naples next spring; William Charning Woodbridge, Cornelius Tuthill, and Theodore Dwight, junr.; their connexions in this country are very respectable. These young men, on getting to Naples, will probably wait on thee, as I have requested their connexion to desire they would do so, as it will afford an opportunity for thee to send any dispatches thou mayest have for America. Any attention shown by thee to these young men, will be most gratefully acknowledged by their friends, and also confer on me a singular obligation.

Our mutual friend, S. Grellet, desires me particu

larly to say, that he wishes to be most kindly and affectionately remembered to thee and thy good lady.

I am, with great respect and esteem,

Thy assured friend,

THOMAS EDDY.

To Sir HENRY LUSHINGTON, H. B. M. Consul General, Naples.

New York, 11*th month*, 14*th*, 1820.

MY DEAR FRIEND,

Having been informed that it is thy intention to publish some account of the inland navigation of our state, and of the progress made in improving it since 1792; and being requested by our mutual friends ——, to communicate to thee, how far, in my opinion, the statements made by Elkanah Watson, contained in his book, entitled, the "History of the Rise and Progress of the Western Canals," are correct; I shall submit the following observations. I have no doubt of the fact, that it was in consequence of Elkanah Watson having communicated to General Schuyler the observations he had made during his tour to the western part of the state in 1791, and particularly as to the great benefits that would result by improving the Mohawk River, and opening a canal communication at Fort Stanwix, to Wood Creek, and from thence to improve the navigation to the Seneca Lake, that first turned the attention of General Schuyler to these important objects, and induced him to offer to the Senate, the act incorporating the Western and Northern Inland Lock Navigation Companies. Indeed, General Schuyler, about the year 1790, often mentioned this fact to me; and during the remainder of his life, I several times accompanied him, in examining the Mohawk River, and westward, as far as the Seneca Lake, with a view to ascertain the practicability of improvements by canal navigation, &c. The Western Canal Company expended a vast sum of money in improving the Mohawk, &c.; and being well satisfied that the stockholders would not consent to advance any further sums, for making improvements west of the Oneida Lake, I called on Judge Platt one evening at Albany, in 1810, and mentioned to him the propriety of proposing to the legislature, to appoint commissioners to explore the country as far west as the Seneca Lake, and to report their opinion, how far it was practicable to connect that lake by a canal with the Hudson River; and stated, that from my own knowledge of the face of the country, I was perfectly satisfied a favourable report would be made, and that, considering the immense advantage that would result to the state by such an undertaking, there could be no doubt the legislature would readily be induced to adopt the plan.

Judge Platt was at this time a member of the Senate, and being well acquainted with the geography of the state, readily agreed with me in sentiment, but he remarked, that if commissioners were appointed, they ought to be directed to explore and examine the country as far as Lake Erie, to ascertain if it was practicable, to connect that lake by canal navigation with Hudson River. I replied, that I was fearful the legislature would be deterred from making any appointment of commissioners, if so great an undertaking should be proposed, and that by proposing for them to examine the country only as far as the Seneca Lake, they might then be induced to adopt the measure. After some farther conversation, it was agreed to propose going as far as Lake Erie, and Judge Platt immediately drafted a joint resolution, to be offered to the Senate next morning. The next morning I was in the Senate chamber, and we called out De Witt Clinton, communicated to him the subject we had in view, and handed to him for his perusal the proposed draft of a joint resolution—he expressed himself highly pleased with the project, said it had his hearty concurrence, and should have his decided support. Judge Platt immediately returned to his seat, and presented the resolution to the

2 O   26*

Senate, which was seconded by De Witt Clinton, and passed unanimously; it was then immediately sent to the Assembly, and also passed there without opposition. These commissioners made several reports, all which are likely in thy possession; the joint resolution was dated 15th March, 1810. After the war, it seemed necessary to excite the attention of the legislature to the prosecution of the grand canal. Judge Platt being in the city in 1816, we conversed on the subject, and were of opinion, that it would likely produce a good effect, if a general meeting of our citizens could be had, and they be induced to present a memorial to the legislature, stating the advantages that would result, by connecting the waters of the Great Western and Northern Lakes with the Atlantic Ocean. On consulting with De Witt Clinton and John Swartwout, it was agreed to address circular letters to several of our most influential citizens, requesting them to attend a regular meeting at the City Hotel. This meeting was large and respectable, and Judge Platt introduced the object for which the meeting was convened, and was followed by Clinton, Swartwout, and others. A committee consisting of De Witt Clinton, J. Swartwout, and myself, were appointed to draft a memorial— this was drawn by De Witt Clinton, and was certainly one of the most able and best drawn papers, that has been written on the subject, of the advantages that would result by completing a canal the whole route from Erie to the Hudson. Copies of this memorial were sent to thyself, for the county of Ontario, and also to several others of the counties, and when they were presented to the legislature were signed by many thousands of our citizens throughout the state; and the prosecution of the canal is certainly owing to the circumstance of *this memorial* being at that time presented to the legislature.

The remarks made in Watson's book, page 73, as

tó the perseverance and efforts of Governor Clinton,
are certainly correct, but in speaking of Colles he is
in error.   I was well acquainted with Colles, since
the year 1773; about that time he arrived at Philadelphia, from Ireland; he was a very honest man,
but did not possess as much knowledge and experience as many ascribed to him; he was never in our
western country, and certainly never projected a plan
of canal from Erie to the Hudson; but possibly might,
merely by examining the map of the state, have
spoken of it as an event that would, at some future
period, take place.

I am, with regard and esteem,
Thy sincere friend,
THOMAS EDDY.

To ROBERT TROUP, ESQ.

New Orleans, May 15th, 1821.

RESPECTED FRIEND,

The reasons which prevented me from doing more
than merely acknowledging your kind letter of September last, and thanking you for the valuable collection of pamphlets which accompanied it, have
continued ever since I wrote; but being now (as you
will perceive by the enclosure) seriously at work in
the formation of a criminal code for this state, I am
extremely anxious to receive the report of your committee on the penitentiary system; from which I
have a right to expect so much important information, I hope you will not fail to forward a copy to
me as soon as it appears.

I regret very much, that for the reasons I formerly
stated, I could not contribute any thing to the work.

Unless I hear reasons much stronger than any
which have been presented to me, either by reading,
conversation, or reflection, I shall not give the punishment of death a place in the code which I shall
present; it appears to me to be a most inefficient punishment, to say nothing of its irremediable nature;

almost all writers on the subject, join in a degree to acknowledge this, and yet almost all recommend it for some offences; this I cannot understand, unless it be the effect of a vindictive sensation against atrocious crimes, which ought not to be indulged in legislation.

I am sorry to find, that an opinion of the inefficacy of the penitentiary system is gaining ground, and should be still more grieved if I thought it well founded; but I do not, and am inclined to think, that all the great defects in the system, arise from parsimony in preparing the establishments. If the buildings were sufficiently spacious, the prisoners might be classed, and reformation reasonably expected, instead of the corruption which indiscriminate confinement produces; and injudicious pardons of old offenders need not be given to make room for new convicts;—if they were sufficiently solid and strong, the hope of escape would never be indulged or realized—but to erect spacious and strong buildings requires large funds, and it is easier to condemn a whole system, than to lay taxes to execute it. I trust, however, that a fair experiment will be made in New York; there, if any where, we must look for enlarged views and useful institutions.

As it is not very probable that I shall ever return to my native city, my desire to live in the remembrance of my friends there has become more important to me; among them I have always counted you, and hope you will still allow me to do so.

EDWARD LIVINGSTON.

To THOMAS EDDY.

Naples, November 13th, 1821.

SIR,

On my return to Naples, after an absence of several months, I found your letter, dated New York, November 3d, 1820. I am not at present sufficiently acquainted with the system pursued at the Lunatic

Asylum, at Aversa, to give you the information you require, but I will make it my business to obtain every particular in my power, and transmit the result to you by the first opportunity.

I thank you for the package, and the maps which points out the route of the canal; it is a most magnificent undertaking, and I trust will answer the expectations of the promoters of it.

I am extremely sorry, that my absence from Naples, deprived me of seeing the young gentlemen you mention, and of showing them such little attentions as might have been in my power.

Pray remember me most kindly, to our mutual friend, Grellet; tell him I regret to say, that all the good he has so anxiously strove to do to this wretched country, has vanished into nothing. I hope Grellet received the books I sent him several months ago through Allen.

Believe me, yours truly,
H. LUSHINGTON.

To Mr. THOMAS EDDY, New York

Albany, 23d December, 1822.

DEAR SIR,

William S. Burling lately solicited me to recommend to our friend Colven, the introduction of a plan for laying an excise on spirituous liquors, and I partly promised him that I would; but on further reflection, I consider it most suitable that the overture should emanate from his constituents, and with this view I now write to you.

In some well written essays, published on this subject in Walsh's paper, it was estimated that fifty millions of gallons of spirituous liquors are annually consumed in the United States, at an expense of thirty millions of dollars, and with the sacrifice of thirty thousand lives. If this be only an approximation to the truth, what a field for reflection does it open to the moralist and the statesman.

After deducting foreign importations of spirits, say to the amount of six millions of gallons, and allowing for four millions produced from foreign molasses, there would still remain forty millions of gallons manufactured from our own materials. Does not this astound us with its enormity, and alarm us with its terrific aspect!

An excise of one shilling a gallon, would produce a revenue of five millions of dollars a year. Double the duty, and you will raise a fund that will pay off the national debt, and line and intersect the country in all directions with canals and roads.

Every considerable increase in the price of any article, tends to check its consumption. And hence, the revenue of the country would be an auxiliary to its morality—a noble union in the eye of a great statesman.

I am, Dear Sir, your friend,
DE WITT CLINTON.

To THOMAS EDDY.

New York, 4th mo. 24th, 1823.

RESPECTED FRIEND,

I am particularly obliged by thy kind attention, in sending me a copy of thy last work on penal jurisprudence. I have read it with peculiar satisfaction, and, considering that the circulation of it would be highly useful in this country, it is intended to have five hundred copies immediately printed, to be sent to persons of influence in the different states, who are known to be friendly to the *improvement* of the penitentiary system.

It is expected the prison in Philadelphia will probably be completed this year. I am well satisfied the plan they propose, of having the convicts *closely confined in the cells*, to work during the day, is wrong; and I have no doubt they will abandon it in a year or two. Let them sleep in their respective cells, and work during the day in the yard and shops, attended by a sufficient number of keepers, to prevent *all* conversation and improper intercourse. I *well* know, from having had four years' experience in our prison, from 1800 to 1804, that this can *effectually* be done. The cells should only be used as a punishment *day* and night.

I send thee a report to the legislature of Louisiana, on the plan of a penal code for that state, by my friend, Edward Livingston of New Orleans, who is, at present, a member of Congress. I am, very respectfully, and with much esteem,

Thy affectionate friend,

THOMAS EDDY.

To WILLIAM ROSCOE, ESQ.

New Haven, 24th May, 1824.

MY WORTHY AND DEAR FRIEND,

I received your kind letter by Mr. Dwight, who is just the man wanted to engage in the society. His appointment to the office you mention, can be made without a doubt, should the seat of the society be transferred, as it might, and will be, to New York. I will take care of the business at Washington, on my return from Boston, a fortnight from this, and will depend on you, my friend, Doctor Milnor, Doctor Milledoler, Mr. Dwight, and his father, with such others as will heartily engage in the business, to do whatever is necessary to be done, in a way of preparation in New York. I will correspond with you, if agreeable, on the subject. If Mr. Dwight spends a considerable part of his time in the business, the society must compensate him.

The first report of the society, which is in the press, and will be out the last of this week, and one hundred sent to Mr. Dwight and yourself, will be, I think, a good introduction to the business of the removal we contemplated. As we have no funds in our treasury, we are obliged to tax those who receive the books, and as I am pledged to pay the printer—

I have paid all the past expenses of the society to a considerable amount, I must ask the favour of your direction and influence, with the exertions of Mr. Dwight, who will do the business to dispose of these one hundred pamphlets, and more, if wanted, at the price mentioned (twenty-five cents,) and to remit me the amount for the printer. This report will give information of the nature, objects, and operations of the society, and should, therefore, be in the hands of men who have right feelings on the subject—particularly all the members (*ex-officio*) of the society—the clergy of all denominations—officers of Colleges, and of religious and benevolent institutions, &c. I must leave this distribution to you, my friend, to direct, and Mr. Dwight to execute. On this particular subject, I wish to meet a letter at my house, from you, on my return, say 4th June. The way we have done here, is to open a subscription—subscribers to put down the number of copies they will take; a number here take twenty, and down to four. Such a paper, headed by Governor Clinton, is in circulation through your city. As soon as the reading of this report shall have informed the influential men of your city, we will then, if thought advisable, by those of you who are on the ground, move in the business of the transfer of the seat of the society.

I have written in much haste, being on the wing for Boston.

I am, very truly and affectionately,

Your sincere friend,

J. MORSE.

To Mr. THOMAS EDDY, New York.

P. S. When all matters are ripe for action, I may make another short trip to your city.

Mr. Dwight can help us much in his paper, in the proposed transfer, and in the sale and circulation of the report. Will you confer with him on the subject; and with my son, Editor of the New York Observer? I have not time to write them.

Will you and Mr. Dwight bethink of a set of queries, embracing the objects of the society, for a circular from the Secretaries?

Philadelphia, January 10*th,* 1825.

I have the pleasure to inform you, that on the 3d inst. you were unanimously elected an honorary member of the Pennsylvania Society for promotion of Internal Improvements in the Commonwealth, of whose Constitution a copy is enclosed.

It will give great pleasure to our Society to cultivate a correspondence with you, on the important subjects in which you have taken so distinguished a part, and for the promotion of which we have associated ourselves.

We will always be happy to furnish any information in our power to advance internal improvements in our sister States.

I am, with the greatest respect,
Your obedient servant,
GERALD RALSTON,
Corresponding Secretary.

To THOMAS EDDY.

Toxteth Park, near Liverpool, 31*st March,* 1825.

DEAR SIR,

It is with sincere pleasure that I avail myself of the present opportunity, to transmit you a copy of the third and last part of my observations on penal jurisprudence, which is now ready for publication here, and in which I have endeavoured, to the best of my power, to recommend to my countrymen an improved system of reformatory discipline, similar to that adopted in the United States of America, and in the establishment of which you have had so important a share. I do this with the feelings of a disciple, who looks up to his master for the approbation of his labours—there being no person living, whose ideas on this subject I more implicitly adopt, than your own.

2 P 27

Within these few days, and after my work was printed and ready for publication, I have received from Mr. Hopkins, one of the commissioners appointed by the legislature last year, to examine and report on the state of the prisons at New York, their report on that subject, which has given me more surprise and concern than I can express, as it appears to me to recommend an entire abandonment of the reformatory system, and the introduction of a plan of compulsory labour, more severe than any that has ever yet been proposed. On the receipt of this document, I lost no time in drawing up a few remarks upon it, with the view certainly, but scarcely with the hope, that if they should arrive before the passing of the proposed act, they might have some effect in strengthening the opposition which will, I trust, be made, for preventing, or at least modifying, the measures proposed. Of these I send you a few copies, entreating you to put them into the hands of such of your friends, as you may think proper; as it is my decided opinion, that if the system now proposed should be adopted, the United States of America will forfeit their chief glory, and will be as remarkable for the cruelty of their penal code, as they have hitherto been for their enlightened humanity.

In the hope of hearing from you on this most interesting subject, and of learning that you continue to enjoy a good state of health, I remain, with the most sincere attachment and affectionate respect,

Most truly yours,
W. ROSCOE.

To Mr. THOMAS EDDY, New York.

The lines on solitary imprisonment, are by my youngest daughter.

New York, 4th month, 14th, 1825.

ESTEEMED FRIEND,

I send thee to the care of Cropper, Benson, & Co., a report of commissioners appointed by our state legislature, to make inquiry respecting our prisons, &c.; some part of this report I think thou wilt find interesting. The state penitentiary at Auburn, mentioned in the report, I believe is the best constructed of any in this country, and the superintendant most remarkably well qualified to conduct such an establishment; and under his management I think the penitentiary will succeed, and fully answer the expectations of those who are friendly to the system of reform. I sent thee some time ago, a report to the legislature of Louisiana, by Edward Livingston, on the plan of a penal code for said state. I have been informed this report has been printed in London. I now send thee, as above, a system of penal law, prepared by my friend Livingston, containing codes of offences and punishments, &c. &c.

I am, with great regard and respect,
Thy affectionate friend,
THOMAS EDDY.
To WILLIAM ROSCOE.

New York, 12th month, 15th, 1825.

MY DEAR FRIEND,

Thy very kind and acceptable favour of 31st March, came to hand some time ago, and I feel not a little mortified that it has remained so long without acknowledging its receipt; and also thy last publication on penal jurisprudence which accompanied it, together with remarks on the report of the commissioners, and the verses on solitary confinement, with which I was very much delighted.

Though the state of society of latter years has been greatly improved, yet daily experience teaches us, that we are very far from that degree of perfection on various subjects, we are capable of attaining; the work goes on slowly, and mostly imperceptibly to all human observation; we may, however, rest assured, that all principles and practices, no matter how long they have been continued and supported by deep rooted prejudices, founded on the blindness and wickedness of our species, that are clearly contrary to the laws of God and our own reason, will come to an end.   The slave trade, and the general abolition of slavery, is a striking proof in support of this sentiment.   It is now almost certain that the trade, and slavery itself, will not exist many years longer. Equally against the laws of God and right reason, are all laws relating to crimes and punishments, enacted on the principles of a vindictive spirit; such laws are calculated frequently to violate common justice, and all distinctions of morality, and, in many cases, tend to debase the mind, and by the undue severity they inflict, aim to make fear the motive of obedience:—in short, these laws are more calculated for slaves than freemen, and seem intended to punish delinquents, rather than to prevent crimes.   It is true, a course of improvement has been commenced of latter years, which claim the approbation of the just and the sanction of the wise, but no radical reform can take place, until the public mind is more fully convinced of the absurdity and wickedness of vindictive punishment.   In proportion as this evil governs our public laws, so the difficulty is increased in forming wholesome laws for the support of prison discipline, calculated for the government and reformation of convicts.   I am exceedingly mortified to find that my friend Captain Lindes, keeper of Auburn prison, advocates (and practices) inflicting corporeal punishment, for violating any part of the prison discipline. I the more regret that this man should entertain such sentiments, because, on the general subject of penal jurisprudence, and the government of a penitentiary, I esteem him superior to almost any other man that I ever conversed with :—he formerly was in the army, and had only had the advantage of a good common education, but possesses a good share of understanding, great integrity, an amiable disposition, and an extensive knowledge of human nature, as regards

the middle and lower classes of society. As a discipli-
narian, it would be difficult to find his equal; owing
to his superior management of the convicts, under
his charge. They love and fear him—they regard
him as their friend and protector—he furnishes them
with plenty of good wholesome provisions—keeps
them constantly employed, but never imposes immoderate tasks on them—he holds no conversation with
them except in directing their work, and this course
is strictly pursued by all his subordinate keepers—
he disdains the idle notion, that extreme severity is
the only appropriate mode for the government of a
penitentiary. I never conversed with a person,
whose sentiments as respects the management of
convicts, so cordially met my views, and in my opinion are so well calculated to promote their general
welfare, and produce reformation. It is my opinion,
that there is no prison in the world equal to Auburn
prison, as regards cleanliness, industry, and good
conduct. The rules and regulations of the prison
are made known to each convict, and the moment
any of them are violated, the offender is punished—
it is owing to the certainty of this, that it is very
rare any punishment is inflicted. I perfectly agree
with him in every particular he advances, except as
to the mode of punishment adopted by him. I have
in vain urged to him, that whipping is totally incon-
sistent with the principles of that mild system we
wish to establish. I cannot persuade him, that prompt
punishment, by confinement, in a solitary cell on
bread and water, will produce the same effects as
whipping. I allow he will not exercise this power
unless accompanied with a degree of justice, as to
the nature of the offence committed, but certainly
others may abuse it, and therefore it never ought to
be allowed in any prison. I have told him that
during several years, that the New York state prison
was subject to my direction as one of its inspectors,
there never was a single instance of inflicting corpo-

27*

real punishment, and yet perfect order was completely preserved. He, however, persists in his notion,
that it is impossible to preserve order without whipping. I am firm in the belief, that Captain Lindes
will, in time, alter his opinions. He is a complete
enthusiast in favour of the penitentiary system, and
has those peculiar qualifications, that will enable
him to carry it to a degree of perfection that it has
never yet attained. The quietness of the prisoners
subject to his care and management is much to be.
admired. Some months ago, in company with our
mutual friend, Professor Griscom, I visited Sing Sing,
situated on the Hudson River, about thirty miles from
New York. At this place is erecting a state prison,
within a hundred yards of the margin of the river —
the banks are about one hundred feet high, and contain large and extensive marble quarries, of excellent
quality, which is excavated, and hammered, and
formed for the building, which will contain eight
hundred cells;—the state has purchased about one
hundred and fifty acres of fine land adjoining the
building—the erecting the prison is committed solely
to the care and management of Captain Lindes—the
plan is his own, and, in my opinion, the best in the
world. The flooring, ceiling, and sides of each cell,
are entirely of marble, and the doors iron. He has
with him one hundred and thirty convicts, which he
brought from Auburn prison-—besides these, he has
one master carpenter, one mason, and one black-
smith—*no other persons except convicts are employed ;*—
he commenced last spring, and next year the work
will probably be completed. There is no wood used
in building this prison—it is all of stone. Convicts
are employed in quarrying, burning lime, (from marble,) forming the stone, mason work, and making
iron doors for the cells, &c. The whole cost of the
building will not exceed $75,000, about £16,500 ster-
ling. The decent order and conduct of the convicts
is wonderful; they are allowed plenty of beef and

pork, and excellent bread, but no other drink than good water; those employed as smiths never worked at the trade till they came to Sing Sing, and the neatness and excellence of their work in making the doors and locks for the cells, are really astonishing. The mason work appears to be done in the best manner—the men all have a chain about fifteen pounds. Their first work was to erect sheds with pine boards, to lodge in at night; they are not allowed to speak to each other, of course, the whole work is quietly conducted, without the least noise or confusion; they have enjoyed remarkable good health, and though the summer was uncommonly hot, and they had to work exposed to the sun, yet, I think, only two have been sick; they never missed working every day, and but one has escaped. Six men, each with a musket, are stationed at equal distances from each other—the river in the front, serves also to prevent an escape. When the prison is finished, all the convicts in the New York state prison in this city, about five to six hundred, are to be removed, and it is intended to employ them in making lime, and preparing marble in various ways to be transported to the city, to be used for purposes of ornament, building, &c. The work is admirably calculated to promote good health, and so simple, that every man can be employed; all the marble they can send to this city, and to Albany, and other places on the Hudson River, will meet with an immediate sale, and considerable will be exported to the Southern states. Order, and consequently the important work of reformation, will be far more certain, than if various trades were pursued. And here, permit me to observe, that I think thy remark, that each convict should learn some trade, does not apply to this country so much as it may to England. Some of our convicts have been brought up to trades, but most of them have been employed at farming and as labourers. If they are willing to work, they may readily get employment in the city as labourers, or in the country as farmers. I agree with thee in most of the sentiments contained in thy private remarks, and have handed a copy to the leading members of our legislature, who, I know, are heartily disposed to improve our penal code, and establish the mildest penitentiary system. I have the fullest confidence, that the most objectionable parts of the commissioners report will not be adopted; and, in time, I am satisfied, that confinement in cells, on bread and water, for breach of prison discipline, will be practised instead of corporeal punishment. The public feeling, and the principles of common sense, will prevail, and do away the deep rooted prejudices of our public legislation—the work is slow, but sure. My friend Hopkins, whose character is known to thee, is a good man, but the report of the commissioners serves to prove, that he has some very incorrect notions respecting the penitentiary system; however, I believe his mind is now got to be more enlightened on the subject. My particular and intimate friend, Cadwallader D. Colden, an eminent lawyer, and formerly mayor of this city, and now a member of the Senate of this state, has been closely united with me for many years, in endeavours for the improvement of our penal laws and penitentiary system. He has been uniformly most decided in his sentiments in favour of the great object we have in view; and I have full confidence in his judgment, zeal, and attention to any legislative business, that may be introduced in the course of the present winter.

The prison building in Philadelphia to accommodate six hundred convicts, will be finished next year, and will cost five times as much as ours at Sing Sing, which will have eight hundred cells. Their plan is, that a convict sentenced for three, four, or five years, shall, during the whole period of his sentence, be confined in his cell, at some kind of work; this, they say, will produce complete reformation, and they are so fixed in their opinions of the superior efficacy of this plan, that it is in vain to urge to them that it is cruel and impolitic. The projectors of this plan, are my particular friends, of the first rank and respectability in the city of Philadelphia. I have no doubt but the experience of one year will convince them of their error.

I cannot be reconciled to think myself deserving thy very handsome compliment, in attributing to me having an important share in the establishment of the reformatory system in this country; the chief credit is due that truly wise and good man, William Penn, whose example and hints relating to this great subject, was acted on and improved by a number of my valuable friends in Philadelphia, soon after Pennsylvania was declared an independent state.

I have been very much gratified with thy communications, and most particularly by the several publications on the subject of penal jurisprudence, and I do beg, thou wilt be so kind as to favour me, occasionally, with some account of the progress made in the reformatory system in England, and if any thing is doing relating to it, on the continent.

I remain, yours, &c.

THOMAS EDDY.

To WILLIAM ROSCOE, ESQ.

Albany, 31*st December,* 1825.

DEAR SIR,

I have received your letter of the 27th. Every time I visit Buffalo, I am fully convinced that the contiguity of our settlements is destructive to the fractional or remnant population of the red men, and that therefore their only salvation lies in removal to a distance. I have, however, never authorized any communication through Captain Parrish, or any other agent, on that point. My rule has been to leave them to their own volitions.

2 Q

All travellers agree, that in the ratio of their distance from the white, in that ratio is the prevalence of the good qualities of the red men. All experience confirms this remark; they acquire our vices without any of our virtues; and they melt away on our approach, like snow at the mouth of a furnace. My kind regards to your family.

I am, your friend,
DE WITT CLINTON.

MR. THOMAS EDDY, New York.

When Doctor Hosack contemplated writing the life of his friend, Thomas Eddy, he addressed a note to Mr. Roscoe, requesting him to furnish any information he might have in regard to the philanthropic labours of the Howard of America—to which the Doctor received the subjoined reply. It was dictated by the accomplished author of the LIVES of the Medici, and of the Sovereign Pontiff, Leo X., when the writer could no longer bear the fatigue of writing a single page with his own hand. It came from a mind about to depart to a better world, but which then reflected the images of virtue, sentiment, and affection, as purely as it did in the prime of his existence. In the soul of Roscoe there was no sediment; the last rays of the lamp of life were redolent of taste and poesy. There was no envy, no aversion, no repinings breathed from his lips, and his criticisms have the weight of truth and sincerity, which can only flow from a pure and exalted spirit. Praise from such a man, under such circumstances, can never be forgotten. I could not contract this letter. I had no right to do it.

MY DEAR SIR,

Some time previous to the receipt of the letter with which you honoured me, dated the 29th April, 1829, and accompanying the present of your valuable memoir of Governor Clinton, I had an attack of paralysis, which had interfered with my usual occupations, and for some time interrupted my correspondence; and, although by the blessing of God, and by the aid of repeated depletion, and powerful remedies, I have been restored to such a state of health as to be able to devote a prescribed portion of my time to the society of my friends and the perusal of my books, a result at my time of life (approaching my 78th year) scarcely to be expected ; yet it has not been till of late that I have been able to undertake the perusal of so large a work as yours, which I have now read, not only without any injurious consequences to my health, but with great information and amusement.   At the same, time I have imbibed a very distinct idea and favourable opinion of the truly great and good man, whose character you have so admirably depicted, and whose great and various merits you have so ably illustrated and explained. Writing, as I now do, under the immediate impressions derived from the perusal of your noble tribute to the memory of your friend, it would be unjust in me to suppress the feelings with which I have been actuated, or to deny that, highly as I estimate such a character in a nation abounding in great men, I consider your production as having shown you worthy to have been his biographer, and whilst you have raised an imperishable monument to his fame, to have given the surest earnest of your own.   In addition to the regret I feel, in not having been able to reply sooner to your letter, I am sorry not to have transmitted you the few documents requested by you, respecting my late highly esteemed friend, Thomas Eddy, of whom I have read several very interesting memorials in your work ; but the same calamity that prevented me from writing, also prevented me from performing this duty, having taken me when my papers were in such a state of derangement that they could not, for a long time, be looked into.   I am, however, in some degree, consoled by the consideration, that you will not have been delayed in your intended account of Mr. Eddy, by my apparent negligence; my correspondence with him being only occasional, and extending to little more than the interchange of new publications, although I always entertained a very high opinion both of his benevolence and his literary talents. As the indisposition to which I have referred, attacked me at a time when I was engaged in a debate with some of your countrymen, on the subject of prison discipline, my medical friends advised me, for a time, not to enter again upon that subject, and it is only of late that I have been able to have the satisfaction of hearing of the system of discipline recently established at Pennsylvania; whence, for many years, I have been led to expect the adoption of the horrid punishment of solitary confinement, without permitting the convicts to labour; with which view, the legislature has erected two large and expensive prisons, intending to confine the criminals in such a manner that they should be separated, not only by night but by day, and should be deprived of the liberty of working, lest it should be an alleviation of their suffering. Against this inhuman and unchristian-like system, my humble voice has been raised, amongst those of many others of more importance, for several years past; but it is only a few weeks since that I have learnt, by a communication of authentic documents from Philadelphia, that the legislature have at length given way to the feelings of humanity, and have determined that the convicts shall be allowed to labour in the day, and shall be instructed for that purpose, as well as in whatever else may be requisite for their reformation. The commissioners, whom the legislature had appointed to consider and report to them on this subject, had, indeed, recommended to them, in their report, that the convicts should be permitted to labour in companies, under proper restriction; but with this the legislature would not comply, which I cannot but greatly regret; although I cannot but rejoice, at the same time, that so much has been accomplished; considering the object of labour, or no labour, as being, in fact, the only question in debate, and being of opinion, for various reasons, that the legislature will be obliged to resort to the plan recommended by their commissioners. By this decision, I conceive the great question of prison discipline, as far as regards the United States, is finally settled; every other place, except Philadelphia, already adopted that plan, thereby making crime to counteract itself, and repair, as far as possible, the evils it has occasioned. In no country has this principle been so well understood, or carried so far, as in your own, and the relinquishment of it for the Bastile system of solitary confinement, would have grieved me more than I can express; but, thank God, my dread of that is over; and I shall now die in peace, convinced that the time will arrive when my own country will follow the example.

You will not be surprised to hear that our canal navigations, which have hitherto been very productive, are depreciated by the completion of our railway from Liverpool to Manchester; which is shortly expected to be succeeded by one from Liverpool to London, and by several others in different parts of the kingdom; but our small dykes bear no proportion to your magnificent aqueducts, which, I suppose, set all competition from railways at defiance.

I send you an account of the Liverpool and Manchester road, as just published, by my next neighbour, Mr. H. Booth, the Treasurer of the undertaking, which, I think, will interest you. I have also added a copy of my discourse on opening the Liverpool Institution, and of a work I published some years since, entitled, "Illustrations of the Life of Lorenzo de Medici," one or both of which you have probably before seen; but which I beg you will accept, as a mark of sincere respect and attachment, with which I am, my dear sir, your very faithful and obliged friend,   W. ROSCOE.

28

I have been obliged to avail myself of the pen of my youngest daughter, the only one of my family who at present resides with me, and who desires to be recorded with me as sincerely attached to a country where she has already many highly valuable friends.

W. R.

Toxteth Park, near Liverpool,
July 13*th*, 1830.

DAVID HOSACK, M. D., F. R. S., New York.

———

On the 23d December, 1817, Mr. Eddy lost his son, John Hartshorne Eddy. He died in the 34th year of his age. He was a remarkable young man. At the age of twelve years, he lost his hearing from the scarlet fever ; he had then only the common and ordinary instruction of a boy of that age. On his recovery, he discovered an ardent desire for knowledge, and commenced with zeal the process of self-instruction, and that so successfully, that, at eighteen, he was far advanced in polite literature, having acquired a good knowledge of the Latin and French languages. He was accomplished in drawing, botany painting, and poetry ; and, at the same time, pursued, with assiduity his mathematical studies. We have known more than one instance, in which the misfortune of deafness has given new acuteness and energy to the mind. The restlessness that generally attends this misfortune, drives the mind to examine its own resources, and to weigh its own powers ; and it is astonishing how much can be done, when we are obliged to do it, either by motives of advancement, ambition, or necessity ; and no necessity is stronger than that of preventing the mind from preying upon itself. The paintings of young Mr. Eddy showed taste and skill, but he did not choose to follow the art as a profession ; it had too much to do with others to satisfy him. He painted only for amusement. He loved poetry in early life, for it gave him an opportunity of pouring out his feelings without disguise; but he found, at a later period, how much excitement it costs to make images from nature and truth, to bathe them in the purest blood of the heart, and then to send them out to a cold, critical world. At length, he, in a good measure, gave up his muse, and devoted his time to the sciences. In the pursuit of mathematics, geometry, astronomy, and topography, there are no throes or agonies, and but few difficulties of any kind in the pathway. To these studies he gave almost undivided attention. In this almost pure abstraction, the memory is not busy, and the heart is still. He pursued his scientific course several years; and, for exercise and amusement, he made topographical surveys in every part of the state of New York, and drew several maps. His large map of the state, the best that had ever been drawn of it, was published the year after his death, but it was in the hands of the engraver before his decease. In his tour of topographical surveying, he improved his knowledge of botany, for there was nothing painful in this science; for, while the flower and herb give delight to the senses, they are subjects of soothing contemplation to the mind. The wonders of nature are as fully developed in the humble violet or daisy, as by the whole forest, and, to the mind of the philosopher, as distinctly prove the existence of a God, as the astounding cataract or terrific volcano. Mr. Eddy was ready, with his pen, to perform any service to science or the arts. Dr. John W. Francis, to whose literary taste and talents we are often much indebted, in a memoir of his friend, written soon after his decease, says,—"Mr. Eddy was the author of a number of essays which appeared in the newspapers, on botany and other branches of natural history; on geography, and the internal improvement of this state. An essay on geography, which he intended for publication in this magazine, will probably shortly appear. He was a member of the New York Historical Society, and, in 1816, was elected to a similar honour in the Literary and Philosophical Society of New York. To this latter association he communicated an interesting memoir on the geography of Africa. That unfortunate mariner, Captain James Riley, the narrative of whose sufferings has awakened so large a portion of public attention, had applied to Mr. Eddy to draw for him a map of part of Africa. This gave Mr. Eddy the occasion of examining the different accounts that had been published by different travellers, on African geography ; and, without passing sentence of condemnation on any writer for wilful misrepresentations, he gives due credit to the statement of Captain Riley. Captain Riley has, indeed, been pronounced a loose writer by an anonymous reviewer ; but the testimonies to his worth and veracity are most respectable, and, besides, he is subject to the evidence of living witnesses. It cannot be denied, that his work contains most important views of interior Africa ; and it is gratifying to observe, that a gentleman possessed of the talents and learning of Hugh Murray, Esq., should, in his enlarged edition of Leyden's Historical Account of Discoveries and Travels in Africa, pay the tribute of high regard to our American narrator.

Enough has been said to show, that the strongest principle of action in John H. Eddy, was the laudable desire to be useful ; that he was superior to making a trade of liberal pursuits, and generous in pecuniary matters, is admitted by those to whom he was best known. To conclude this hasty sketch, it is unfortunately too frequently our lot, to lament the seemingly untimely departure of aspiring genius and worth ; but it may confidently be said, seldom could our regret and lamentation be more feelingly bestowed, than on the subject of this brief memorial. Time and talents have rarely been more constantly or more undeviatingly directed to objects of substantial importance; and it is painful to reflect, that his fatal illness was prematurely induced, in consequence of such exertions. Let the qualities of his heart and his moral excellence command our regard; for the services he has rendered, let the debt of gratitude be paid to his memory. W.

The following specimens of Mr. Eddy's poetry are sufficient to convince any one who reads them, that he had a cultivated mind, a feeling heart, and a fine imagination. THE LAMENT on his misfortunes, written when the author was only eighteen years of age, is, beyond all question, an honourable proof of mind and taste.—

> In former days how blithe my moments past,
> Each New Year's day was happier than the last;
> Unknown to sorrow, and serenely gay,
> In mirth and frolic passed my harmless day;
> Unconscious of the ill by fate design'd
> Fond dreams of glory filled my youthful mind—
> Now, sad reverse! though scarce to manhood grown,
> Has dire misfortune mark'd me for her own.
> No social converse charms my listless ear,
> In death-like silence rolls my lonely year,
> Lonesome I sit, of every hope despoil'd,
> The sons of pleasure shun misfortune's child.
> Unfit for me are those whose hours employ
> The voice of gladness and the song of joy.
> In careless apathy I pass the day
> With some dull book to trifle time away,
> Or take a lonely walk, or pluck a flower,
> Or mark the presage of a coming shower,
> Or paint some landscape on the verdant plain,
> Or bounding vessel on the wat'ry main,
> Or muse in silence on an absent mind
> And dream of pleasure that I ne'er shall find,
> Or pore upon the news with serious face,
> And mark what slaughter Europe's realms deface.
> Thus pass my days—but when the evening ray
> Smiles in the west, with purple lustre gay,
> I mark the moon that skirts the fleecy cloud,
> Or veils her beauty in the misty shroud,
> While stars unnumbered deck the blue profound,
> Whose sparkling fires her silver throne surround,
> Light all the vast expanse, and move sublime
> Thro' Heaven's vast concave from the depths of time;
> Then shine the streams where silent vessels glide,
> And scarce a zephyr curls the glassy tide.
> O'er misty vales the mountains rise to sight,
> And shadowy grandeur fills the vault of night—
> This is reflection's hour—the shining scene
> Sheds o'er my pensive mind a soft serene,

2 R 28*

In bright succession fancy's visions roll,
And hope, sweet flatterer! soothes my troubled soul:
Perhaps e'en yet, the Almighty's boundless power
May crown my wishes in some happier hour,
May bid misfortune's iron hand forbear,
Or grant me fortitude, my doom to bear;
Perhaps e'en now his cruel seeming will,
By this, restrains me from the paths of ill.
Then cease this strain—these useless plaints give o'er,
What Heaven has done is right, repine no more.

The friendly poetical epistle addressed to his friend, William L. Fisher, after a pleasant visit in New Bedford, among those enlightened and excellent Friends, the Rodmons and Rotches of that place, is full of easy and courteous verse.

Health to my friend—may Heaven unceasing shed
Its choicest blessings on his youthful head;
Full two long months in one dull round have past,
From pleasing Bedford since I heard the last.
Whence this delay? but ah! I guess the cause,
'Tis love's soft chain, and powerful beauty draws
Thy thoughts away—and well at beauty's smile
Thou might'st forget an absent friend awhile.
This is the truth—I do not ask defence,
I know thy friendship, and forgive the offence.
I hope she smiles, for well I know the care
And painful hours rejected lovers share.
And can a nymph of Bedford's gentle train,
(The gentlest sure that ever trod the plain,)
The proffer'd hand of faithful love disdain?
In such soft bosoms can the spirit live,
That joys to triumph in the pains they give?
Sweet Bedford! Oft thy scenes I call to view,
And oft the moment when I bade adieu.
Tho' many a day on tedious wings have flown
Since thee I left, and sought the noisy town,
Where vice and folly hold alternate sway,
And care and langour wear my hours away;
Yet oft remembrance, kindly soothing power!
Recalls the scene of many a happier hour,
The evening walk along the dusky green,
The social circle and the smile serene,
The nymph's soft charms, the aged's various worth
All wake the sigh that pleases more than mirth.
May he, the chief, in length of years grown gray,
Still view with pleasure many a natal day;
His reverend head may dreams from Heaven compose,
And calm contentment and serene repose.
And he whose hospitality I prov'd,
Long may he live, respected and belov'd—
And she with every gentle virtue fraught,
Whose friendly kindness ne'er shall leave my thought,
May every gift, that generous fortune pours,
Gild the calm current of their peaceful hours,
May Heaven direct their steps remote from strife,
And smile serenely on their close of life,

And place, approving, in the realms of rest,
"Where virtue triumphs and her sons are blest."
  What pleasing visions charm the hours of youth,
When fancy cheats us in the guise of truth,
In life's gay morn, when hope's amusing ray
Shines on the opening mind serenely gay,
When all is rapture, and no cares control
The voice of nature in the youthful soul;
Hence joys long past in fancy oft we view,
A painful prospect, yet 'tis pleasing too;
Each magic charm of Laura's smile divine,
Each modest virtue in her thoughts that shine:
These wake the glow of sentiment sincere,
Oh! could my verse that sentiment declare;
But far unequal to the arduous strain
It drops a theme it never can sustain;
May she, sweet nymph, be Heaven's peculiar care,
And be she happy as her form is fair.
  Methinks I view each absent friend again,
Tho' wide the distance, yet 'tis wide in vain,
In vain the mountains rise, the billows roll,
They ne'er can change the feelings of my soul,
Those finer feelings to the world unknown,
Inspir'd by Bedford's calm delights alone;
Oh! were it mine those calm delights to share,
But fate vindictive disappoints my prayer.
By hard necessity's command I stay,
Nor tempt the dangers of the wat'ry way
While winter reigns around; but when the spring
Returns with fragrance on the zephyr's wing,
To thee and Bedford's calm delights I'll haste,
And leave the noisy town, true genuine joys to taste.
  With wishes for thy health, to thee, my friend,
From Hudson's bank this careless verse I send.
Accept the wishes of a rhyming swain,
The meanest vot'ry of the muses' train.
In artless numbers flow these careless lays,
Careless of censure, not unpleased with praise.
I write in verse, because in verse I find
I best can tell the feelings of my mind,
And oft the muse with kind assuasive power,
Can steal from sorrow many a pleasing hour.
For on my youthful days misfortune frowns,
And many a joy the stream of sorrow drowns;
And should my verse beguile one pensive sigh,
Or draw the approving glance from friendship's eye,
I'll thank the muse that gave the tuneful strain
To please my friend, and soothe my mental pain.

We have remarked, that Mr. Eddy gave up the sweet wanderings of literature, for the sciences of geography, topography, mineralogy, and statistics; but he never lost his love of botany. He had been taught this science by Doctor Hosack, and always felt grateful to his eminent instructor, for the pains he took in making him acquainted with herb, flower, and tree, *from the hyssop that springeth from the wall, to the cedar of Lebanon.* His mind had a most noble scope in the field of science, not confined to those we have named; for, before he was thirty years of age, he seemed determined to make himself acquainted with many things, then but partially known, as may be seen by the following extract from The American Monthly Magazine and Critical Review.

So long ago as the year 1814, the following queries were prepared by the late John H. Eddy, of this city. He had them printed in the form of a circular, and a number of copies were sent to various gentlemen in different parts of the country to which they relate. Few communications, however, were received in reply; and the multiplied avocations of Mr. Eddy compelled him to postpone the prosecution of his inquiries to a period of greater leisure. But an untimely death, arresting him in the midst of his labours, has torn him from science and his country, and left the task to other hands. With the view of reviving inquiry upon this subject, we publish the circular drawn up by Mr. Eddy, and solicit the attention of the scientific to the topics therein suggested. Any communications, addressed to the editors, will be gladly received, and immediately placed in the possession of one who will turn them to good account.

New York, March 14, 1814.

The unexampled progress of cultivation and improvement in that part of the state of New York, lying west of the meridian of the village of Utica, and the surprising increase of its population and produce, present a subject of inquiry highly interesting, not only as affording a basis for a correct calculation of the future advance of our interior settlements to the west, where lands, and the title to it, are good, and thus affording a glimpse of the scene our country is one day, we may hope, destined to present; but it has opened to the observation of the geographer and the geologist, a number of very curious particulars in its general topography, which do not, to my knowledge, exist, at least in so remarkable a degree, or to so great an extent, in any other part of the United States. To collect facts relative to these, and by comparing these facts with each other, and judging by the rules of analogy drawn from similar appearances in other parts of the globe, to endeavour to discover the probable cause of the singular features I have mentioned, has induced me to take the liberty of addressing you, and to beg the favour of you to answer the queries inclosed, as far as your knowledge extends, and as much in detail as you conveniently can. But before proceeding to the queries. I will add some conjectures of my own, drawn from the very limited means of information I at present possess.

It is well known that there are, at the Little Falls of the Mohawk river, evident marks of the rocks having been formerly washed by the waves, or by a current of water one hundred feet above the present surface at the head of the falls. Now it appears, by the levels taken by the surveyors employed by the commissioners of the Grand Canal, that the surface of the water at that place, is less than sixty feet lower than at Rome, therefore it seems to me there can be no doubt, that when the waters washed the top of the hill at the falls, the country above, along the valley of the river, as far as (and much, farther than) Rome, must once have been the bottom of a large lake, bounded on each side, at no great distance, by the uplands, and presenting, in shape, a long narrow arm, similar to the present lakes of Cayuga and Seneca; and as there is a gradual descent in the country west of Rome, as far as Three-River Point, and the elevation from that point to the falls of the Seneca river near Scawyace, is very inconsiderable, it seems to me equally undoubted, that the waters once reached so far, including the present Cayuga, Cross, Onondaga, and Oneida lakes, the last of which

I imagine was near the centre.   I suppose this great lake to have been bounded on the east by the hill at the falls; on the south by the uplands, giving rise to the head waters of the Susquehannah; on the north by the elevation of the great step from the lower falls on Gennesee to Oswego Falls; and on the east, by the uplands between the head waters of Mud Creek and Genesee River.   Its extent up the valley of Mud Creek I don't pretend to conjecture, but suppose its length from east to west may have been about a hundred and twenty miles, and its breadth in general about twenty.   All the country within these limits is a flat, surrounded by much higher land, and its soil, and likewise its small and almost imperceptible horizontal inclination is, I believe, precisely similar to the muddy bottoms of the lakes I have mentioned.   But the circumstance which seems to me most strongly to corroborate my opinion, is the known decrease in the waters of these lakes, and, of course, diminution in their extent, and the time probably is approaching when they will be entirely drained, and when the land left by the water is covered with timber, (which would soon be the case if left to nature,) it will present a country similar in appearance to that on the south side of Oneida Lake, the Cayuga marshes, &c., with creeks meandering through it like the Seneca River, Oneida, Cowaselon, and Wood Creeks, &c., &c.

Please favour me with your ideas on the subject, when convenient, and send me by mail, as far as may be in your power, answers to the following queries.

JOHN H. EDDY, *No.* 220 *William-street.*

1. Do you know of any additional circumstances confirming the above supposition, such as traces of water at other places much above its present level, and near the supposed boundary I have sketched out?

2. Are there any traditions among the Indians, that the country was formerly covered with water?

3. Do you know how far the ridge, on which the *ridge road* is constructed from Lewistown to the lower falls of Genesee, extends to the eastward of Genesee River, and do you know of any other remarkable ridge or steps, similar to that which occasions the falls of Niagara and Oswego? state its height, direction, extent and composition.

4. What is the composition of rocks in your neighbourhood, and how do they lie?—in strata or otherwise? inclined or horizontal?

5. What strata are observed in the earth in digging wells, &c.

6. What shells are found? on the surface or what depth? are they similar to the shell-fish at present existing in the adjoining waters, or are they of unknown species? are they found in the hills, or in the valleys, or in both?

7. Have any bones of animals been found?—of what kind?—in the hills, or in the valleys, or in both?

8. Do you know of any petrifactions in your neighbourhood?—of what kind? and do they resemble things now existing, or are they of unknown substances? are they found in the hills, or in the valleys, or in both?

9. What trees or plants are peculiar to the respective soils of the valley of the lake I have supposed, and the uplands? (Note, the botanical names of trees and plants should be mentioned, if in your power, the English names being applied to very different species in different parts of the country.)

10. Do you know of any means of ascertaining, or estimating, the age of the forest trees which grow on the old Indian fortifications?

11. Do you know at what rate per annum the lakes in your neighbourhood decrease? or how much have they decreased within your knowledge, or that of creditable people?

12. Are there any Indian hieroglyphics extant in

your neighbourhood? can you send me a copy, with the meaning, if it can be obtained—or drawings and plans of any Indian antiquities?

13. I have heard that the Indians on the Mississippi, whose language is totally different, can yet understand each other very correctly by means of signs; is it so with those in your neighbourhood, and can you describe their method?

14. What effect has the clearing and settling the country had on the climate—do the streams diminish, and in what degree?

15. What is the present variation of the magnetic needle with you, and what has it been formerly, and at what places observed?

16. It has been remarked in Europe that the variation was effected by an earthquake; can you recollect about the time of the late earthquakes, which extended (I believe) northeasterly from the Mississippi, about two years ago, that there was any change in the variation, and how much?

17. Have you ever observed the Aurora Borealis, or northern lights, in your neighbourhood? when and where? and describe the phenomena—can you recollect any change in the variation at the time? this has been observed in Europe.

18. What do you suppose may be the average elevation of the hills in your neighbourhood above their base?

19. Send me a description, and (if convenient) a drawing of any singular and unaccountable natural feature in the country, or of any extraordinary phenomena.

20. How far can the great step, which occasions the falls of Niagara, be traced into Canada, and in what direction—the same of the ledge which occasions the rapids at Black Rock?

21. Latitudes and longitudes of any part of the country will be very important in constructing a correct map of the state, and if you can furnish me

with any useful observations, they will be highly acceptable,—please to describe the observation, and the instruments used.

The mind that could pass from the inspirations of the Muse to such deep questions of philosophy, was one of no ordinary range ; and, by the very point of the questions, as well as from his own suggestions, we conceive a high idea of his powers, and feel distressed to think, that so laborious and sagacious a man should have died so young ; for much might have been expected from a scholar in the prime of life, pursuing such a course. There are but few in this country, who had, at the same time, leisure, inclination, and talents, to make such philosophical examinations.

The early education of Mr. Eddy was, as the fact is given by himself, miscellaneous and scanty. The most approved schools in his youthful days were very indifferent, compared with those of modern times, and but little more than the first elements of education could be had in them. He was in a good measure self-taught, and by observing a right course, he was constantly at school, while in the course of his business, and gained a knowledge of the world as he proceeded in the duties of life. Such knowledge, if not at first entirely correct, has a self correcting principle in it, which is experience.

His mind was so well disciplined, that every thing he gained he kept ; and in gathering up his treasures of knowledge, he always calculated on ulterior views, which were not then, even to his own mind, fully developed. He was ambitious of attainment, but never suffered his vanity to interfere with the means of gaining knowledge, for he was at great pains in getting the opinion of the wise and good on every subject ; but he never followed the opinions of any man, until he had studied the subject thoroughly,

2 S   29

and weighed every opinion offered. He compared all, and, as an optimist, selected for himself. He never seemed startled at any theory, however singular, but took the pains to examine it calmly, and if bound to refute it, did it mildly, but distinctly. In all his exertions, he always measured the means in regard to the ends, and was seldom deceived in his calculations; yet, at times, he was considered as a bold financier, full of expedients; but the results always justified his calculations, and there can be no doubt, but that the opinions which he offered on various subjects to the corporations to which he belonged, which were not adopted in the early part of his course, but which proved in the end to be the correct ones, gave him a greater influence afterwards, than if they had prevailed at the time they were given.

His mind was quick, shrewd, and logical. He caught a suggestion with great readiness, but was slow in making up his judgment. He looked on all sides of a question with immense care, for he was early taught precaution, the first ingredient in good sense. His combinations, comparisons, parallels, inferences, and arguments, were all familiar to him before his opinions were promulgated, but when his judgments were formed, they were not readily given up, upon any authority. If, in coming to a conclusion, he was slow and wary, in action he was rapid and indefatigable.

He never wrote until he had arranged his thoughts, and chosen his language to clothe them; of course, there is a neatness and fine connexion in his writing, which, if they do not exalt his style to classical beauty, make it a much better business vehicle. There are no extraordinary thoughts, no wonderfully brilliant sentences, in his productions, that could be quoted to show his strength of wing or boldness of flight, but in every work of his there are exhibited strong features, and as a whole, the production is always effective. A forcible thinker, with only a fair vocabulary, makes a clear and impressive writer. Mr. Eddy uses good words in their proper places, and that always makes a good style for any subject-matter. His logic has much of the Aristotelian clearness about it; but being exercised upon the practical affairs of life, instead of ingenious theories, it is not so apparent.

His time was all his own, for he had no days of gloom or hypochondriacism to weaken the energies of his mind, through the pulses of his heart. He indulged in no morbid views of life, nor suffered from over strained feelings at human misery, but he knew all the evils that existed, and had nerve enough to combat them. He depended for fame on no one brilliant deed, or no one fortunate occurrence, but on a life of active benevolence. A command over his passions, is the first lesson that he who intends to live for mankind, should learn. It is in this cool serenity that the mind gains its greatest strength and aptitude for action. When obtained, it gives to youth the habits and facilities that belong to riper years. This complacency increases every day by reflection, and keeps the mind from decrepitude and decay in more advanced years. In such a state, a man, like the mariner sailing before the refreshing trade winds, can calculate almost to a certainty what may be accomplished in a given time. When the imagination is under proper control, and man is guided by experience, he can correct yesterday's error, if one was made, by to-day's reasoning. In such a life, where every thing is accurately measured and surveyed, the world passes onward, not like the uncertain shadow upon the dial of life, flitting with every cloud, but like the heavenly bodies,

" Wheeling unshaken through the void immense."

The religious order to which Mr. Eddy was attached by birth and principle, have ever since their rise been remarkable for self-discipline. This characteristic gave Penn, and his successors, their influence over the Indians, which preserved peace for so many years in their borders. Such men suffer in turbulent times for not taking part in the bustle, but are amply repaid for this, in their prosperity in days of quiet. Mr. Eddy was a firm orthodox Friend, whose faith was unshaken in the midst of difficulties.

The recent separation which has taken place in the Society of Friends, is a matter of public notoriety, and it is also pretty generally known, that a difference of opinion, upon some of the leading doctrines, was the cause of this unhappy division. Although this separation did not take place in the society at New York, until after Mr. Eddy's death, yet as he, from the beginning, took such a deep interest in the controversy, which was carried on for many years previous to this event, it becomes the duty of his biographer to allude to it.

A late celebrated minister in the society, who, from his strong natural talents, purity of life, and patriarchal appearance, had obtained unbounded influence over a large portion of the members, for many years previous to Mr. Eddy's death, was very active and zealous in propagating his peculiar sentiments upon the doctrines of the atonement and divinity of our Saviour. Without meaning, in the least, to call in question his sincerity, or the purity of his motives, it must be admitted, that he held opinions on those important doctrines, and also respecting the holy scriptures, which differed materially from those held by Robert Barclay, and the early Quakers. They ever believed in the divinity of the Saviour, and in the efficacy of the outward atonement, in conjunction with spiritual regeneration; whilst *he* lowered the character of the Redeemer, to that of a *good man*, and holy pattern, and denied the efficacy of the atonement altogether, relying solely on the regeneration, as a means of Salvation. The founders of the society also, uniformly upheld the authenticity and inspiration of the scriptures, declaring them to be the only outward standard for determining the soundness of their doctrines, and the truth of their principles; whilst this modern preacher frequently called in question their divine authority.

Mr. Eddy, and other influential members of the society, took an active part in endeavouring to arrest the progress, of what they considered heterodox opinions, and they always openly declared, that the doctrines promulgated by the preacher before mentioned, were contrary to the fundamental principles of the society, and that therefore they could have no unity with him. Mr. Eddy was one of the warmest advocates in favour of orthodox opinions, and one of the earliest to detect the heterodoxy of the new principles. Regardless of worldly consequences, he had the courage openly and honestly to avow his sentiments, and thus became unpopular with those in the society, who took the opposite side; but this moved him not—and he continued, through evil report and good report, to show his marked disapprobation of those doctrines, until his death.

No cause was so dear to his heart, as the interests of the society in which he was born and educated, and for which he always manifested the most ardent attachment; he, therefore, most deeply deplored the division of sentiment, upon what he considered vital principles.

The yearly meeting of Friends in England, which may be aptly termed the *parent society*, has officially pronounced its condemnation of the novel doctrines which were promulgated here, and refuses to hold any intercourse with the Society in this country, which sanctions those doctrines.

So far, therefore, as human authority goes, Mr. Eddy's opinions have been completely sustained; and although he did not live to witness the division in the Society which now exists, yet he clearly foresaw, many years ago, that such must inevitably be the result of the controversy.

29*

The celebrated preacher alluded to, has since followed Mr. Eddy to the silent grave;—they are both removed beyond the sphere of human praise or censure, and we may safely leave them in the hands of Him who judgeth righteously, and who alone knoweth the secrets of all hearts.

When the mind is serene, there is nothing of the value of life lost in pungent regret for hasty conduct and irritable feelings, and nothing by the intoxicating influence of inordinate joy. To one prepared to be happy by religious philosophy and self-discipline, bent on pursuing " the even tenor of his way," curiosity, desire of knowledge, and love of fame, " the last infirmity of noble minds," are all subservient to happiness.

Mr. Eddy had fine powers of conversation. He was gently animated in speaking in public or private, and seemed to proceed with ease and fluency. If his eloquence had nothing in it of the force of the rapid stream, or the sweep of the tide, still it was more difficult to resist; it was like the gentle droppings whose continuance will wear away the stone. He had no equal in managing a matter before a deliberative body. He watched the "*mollia tempora fandi*," and said no more than just what was wanted for the occasion. He was unruffled when hardly listened to, and sometimes rudely treated; but at the next interview, it was seen that he had made an impression on him, who had, perhaps, in a moment of irritation, turned hastily away. Most minds are to be won, if the suitor only knows the means, and notices the proper seasons for his appliances.

He was conscious that he was acting for the public good, and was therefore always self-possessed.

As a neighbour, Mr. Eddy was kind and obliging, and attentive to all the little courtesies of life, and was loved and respected by those near him, which cannot always be said even of those who are striving to benefit mankind.

In the domestic circle he was pleasant and instructive, and seemed desirous of filling up every hour as of some value to himself and to others. He seemed desirous of examining the mind and habits of the young, in order to assist them in gathering up proper stores of knowledge, and of giving a right direction to their affections. This communion with young minds is as beneficial to those in years, as to the youth who listens to the lessons of age. The fresh and novel views of the world, coming all unsophisticated from the young, awaken the recollections of youth in the mind of one near the grave, and he seems to travel back again with pleasure to the days when every vision was bright, and hope had not known the companion of her later years—disappointment. The value of existence will unquestionably be increased, when we come to understand by the mental improvements which are going on, how much good we may do, and of how much happiness we are susceptible.

The person of Mr. Eddy bore no extraordinary marks to the casual observer. He was about five feet six inches in height, of a muscular, compact frame, capable of bearing great fatigue without inconvenience, and he delighted in corporeal activity as well as mental exertion. His head was large, and well shaped, the features of his face were strong and prominent, and his whole physiognomy bold and striking. The elevation of his eyebrows gave the whole countenance an air of profound meditation. He dressed with great uniformity and neatness. If his face bore deep traces of thought, there were none of grief. He commemorated the death of his friend with pious and affectionate propriety, but indulged in no feverish lamentations at their departure, bowing in humble resignation to the will of heaven. He had been failing for several months, but at last his death was as sudden as his life was serene. He died on the 16th of September, 1827, in the sixty-ninth year of his age, of paralysis. He, who had done so much to alleviate the sufferings of others, was not doomed to suffer much himself. For him death had no sting and the grave no victory. The sweet precepts and holy influence of Christianity had destroyed both.

More than four years previous to Mr. Eddy's death, he withdrew himself from the affairs of the New York Hospital, as appears by the following note, in order that the institution might have the benefit of the services of a younger man.

To the Governors of the New York Hospital.

GENTLEMEN,

As the annual election will take place in the course of this month, it appears to me my duty respectfully to inform you, that it is my wish not to be considered as a candidate to serve as one of the Governors for the ensuing year.

Having now been twenty-eight years engaged in the service of the Hospital, it is with extreme reluctance that I withdraw myself from any longer taking a part in the management of its concerns, but I consider it not consistent with the strict rules of propriety, to hold a station that might be filled with much more usefulness by some other person, not so advanced in life, and more active than myself.

I am, with sentiments of the greatest respect and esteem,   Your sincere friend,

THOMAS EDDY.

New York, 5th mo. 7th, 1823.

But notwithstanding the fact that he had retired from the labours of the Hospital, the Governors had not forgotten the services of their former President, and at the next meeting of the Board after his death, they entered the following resolution on their records:

The Secretary of the New York Hospital respectfully informs the family of Thomas Eddy, that at a meeting of the Governors of the New York Hospital, held 2d instant, the following resolution was passed.

Resolved, That this Board has heard with great regret the decease of their late President, Thomas Eddy, who, by devoting his time and talents during a long course of years, to the promotion of objects of philanthropy, and of public utility, has deservedly acquired the esteem of his fellow citizens in general ; and by his many and important services to this Institution, has merited particularly the gratitude of its Governors, and of all who are interested in its prosperity.

ROBERT J. MURRAY, *Secretary.*

The periodicals of the day, in their obituary notices, seemed to vie with each other in paying their tributes of respect to his memory. Two or three of these notices are before us, and demand from their intrinsic merits, an insertion among the matters contained in this life of this distinguished philanthropist.

New York Daily Advertiser, September, 1827.

In the death of Thomas Eddy, which was mentioned in our paper of yesterday, the community have lost a most worthy and benevolent individual, and the Society of Friends, to which he belonged, a most respectable and valuable member. A large portion of a long life has been spent in active usefulness, and in promoting, by his efficient aid, almost every public institution of charity and benevolence. For a long time he has been concerned in the government of the Hospital of this city ; and it is, in a great measure, owing to his exertions, that the Lunatic Asylum was established and endowed.

He was an early friend and supporter of the Penitentiary system of punishment ;—a zealous patron of the free schools, he encouraged, to the utmost of his power, every important project for the extension of general education ; he was a most cordial friend

2 T

of freedom, and a most determined opposer of slavery, wherever it prevailed.

Mr. Eddy was, from the establishment of the American Bible Society, a cordial and active friend and manager of the institution, where his conduct, in promoting its great objects, was always marked by the most liberal and orthodox temper and principles. An extensive correspondence with persons of distinction in Europe, and particularly in Great Britain, rendered his name and his character familiar to many of the great philanthropists of the age; and his death will be lamented by his friends in that country, as well as in this, as a public loss.

Freedom's Journal, September, 1827.

DIED, in this city, on the 16th instant, full of years, and full of honours, "rested from his labours," that "his works might follow him," the Christian, the patriot, and the Philanthropist, Thomas Eddy, Esq. His family and friends are not called upon to sorrow, as those who have no hope; but, with delight, may dwell upon the truths of the Gospel, as exemplified in the character of the husband, the father, and the friend. "Let me die the death of the righteous, and let my last end be like unto his."

The name of Thomas Eddy, and the deeds of worth which filled up his life, will be remembered and revered by the coloured population of our country, and their descendants, to the latest generations.

Commercial Advertiser, September, 1827.

DIED, yesterday morning, in the 70th year of his age, Thomas Eddy, for many years a highly respectable and useful citizen. He was an active member of most of our charitable institutions, in whose welfare and prosperity he was deeply interested, and in whose service most of the latter part of his life was spent. As a governor of the New York Hospital, he was eminently useful, and by his firmness of character, and close application to the interest of the establishment, filled the highest offices therein, to the entire approbation of his constituents. He was a firm and constant advocate of the Lancasterian system of education, and of the immense importance of public charity schools, in whose welfare he felt a deep and lively interest. His services as a director of the American Bible Society, were duly appreciated by his fellow members, and by them his loss will be deeply regretted. To the descendants of Africa he was a sincere and valuable friend, deeply sympathizing with them in their low and degraded state, and endeavouring by every means in his power, to break the shackles which bind them to the cruel yoke of their oppressors. He was an early advocate for internal improvements; and his name will be found among the first commissioners for the construction of the Erie canal.

In short, he was a charitable, a philanthropic, and a good citizen, a kind father, and a tender husband.

His funeral will take place on Tuesday afternoon, the 18th instant, at 4 o'clock, from his late residence, 424 Broome street. In the death of this gentleman, whose life has been long dedicated to deeds of charity and benevolence, our city sustains no common loss. His friends and connexions, and the members of the various societies with which he was associated, are respectfully invited to attend his funeral.

National Gazette, Philadelphia.

An obituary notice of Thomas Eddy of New York, was copied into our sheet yesterday, from the New York papers. It bears a just testimony, which we were glad to repeat, and to which we would add an humble tribute on our own part, arising from personal acquaintance, and a deep impression of the excellence of his character. Unaffected, inexhaustible goodness; sound sense; extensive information on the practical interests and objects of society; anxious, indefatigable benevolence—were the leading

traits which gained for him an extraordinary share
of fond esteem and confidence, wherever he was
known. He belonged to the religious denomination
of Friends, and in the modest simplicity of his tone
and habits, and the directness, equanimity, and toler-
ance of his spirit, as well as by the absolute usefulness of his pursuits and studies, he seemed to realize
the picture which William Penn himself sketched, as
that of a genuine disciple, and a true Christian, in
his interpretation of Christianity.

There are few, we believe, of the splendid internal
improvements, of the foundations of social charity,
or the plans for the amelioration of public morals
and education, that have signalized, during the present century, the judgment, benevolence, and enterprise of New York, with which the name of Thomas
Eddy is not connected, with more or less original
and acknowledged merit. He was among the first
projectors and promoters of the Grand Canal; he
took a principal part in the establishment and administration of hospitals, penitentiaries, high schools, and
houses of refuge; he entered into all their details
with equal zeal and intelligence; he read, he wrote,
he travelled, almost without intermission, for purposes of common good or special humanity :—he
united the bias and exertions of a Howard and a Bene-
zet, to those propensities and inquiries which immediately advance the trade, agriculture, and general comfort and beauty of a state. This is a rare
combination of tastes and endeavours, and in him it
was not in the least ostentatious or officious, but
wore a natural, easy, unobtrusive air, suitable to his
whole mien and style, and never failed to prove efficient, when it had scope and encouragement. So
beneficent a being is now enjoying a rest happier
than that of any of his race, who worshipped at
shrines of false glory, and wearied their powers in
seeking or achieving the triumphs of ambition, vanity,
or avarice. We have seen men of stout hearts, but

kindred dispositions, moved to tears, in first contemplating Thomas Eddy after a certain period of separation. We never approached him without experiencing a moral refreshment, analogous to the physical sensation produced by a pure, elastic, balmy atmosphere. The same delightful influence is always shed, in a measure, by veteran, unequivocal, active virtue; but the artlessness and serenity attending the source in this instance, the plain dress, the homely visage, the kindly eye, the chastened tone, and unsophisticated reason, caused it to be felt by more minds with superior force. It is merely justice to add, that the individuals and circles with whom this philanthropist communed and acted in New York, appreciated and honoured his peculiar worth, and will long praise and cherish his genial memory. All were alive to that spontaneous and invariable emanation of goodness which we have just noticed—all must be aware of its rarity, and regret its loss in any one example.

The following letter is from his friend, Governor Clinton.

Albany, 18th *Sept.* 1827.

Dear Madam,

Permit me to mingle my tears with you, and to offer to you and your family my heartfelt sympathies on the loss of your excellent husband and my invaluable friend : a man who was so much known, and so invariably engaged in doing good, has left a vacancy which it will be difficult to fill. His usefulness can be traced to our institutions of reform, education, and benevolence.

He has followed his excellent coadjutors in the same glorious cause, Robert Bowne and John Murray, Jun. to the grave, and I hope to heaven.

I am, truly,

Your friend,

De Witt Clinton.

To Mrs. Eddy.

30

Mr. Eddy left a widow, a son, and two daughters, to mourn his loss, and to cherish his memory.   Mrs. Eddy died the summer of 1832.   She fell a victim to that scourge of the human race—the cholera.   She was a virtuous woman, highly respected by all who knew her.   She was a helpmate to her spouse, as far as was proper for her sex, in all his labours of philanthropy.   The silent unobtrusive course of a good wife, has a wonderful influence on the character and fame of her husband.

APPENDIX.

MEMOIR OF WILLIAM ROSCOE, ESQ.

By Dr. Thomas Stewart Traile, F. R. S., E., &c.

"Clororum Virorum facta moresque posteris tradere antiquitus usitatum, ne nostris quidem temporibus, quanquam incuriosa suorum ætus omisit, quotiens magna aliqua ac nobilus virtus vicit ac supergressa est vitium parvis magnisque Civitatibus commune, ignorantiam recti et invidiam."—TACITI *Vita Agricolæ.*

In the sentence now quoted, Tacitus has justly indicated the true objects of biography; and, although in this humble notice of our late illustrious President, I do not profess the intention of handing down his character and virtue to posterity, (a task fortunately confided to abler hands,) yet I feel satisfied, that this attempt will not be displeasing to a society of which he was at once the ornament and the head. As our age cannot be justly accused of want of curiosity respecting our contemporaries, it does not deserve to be characterized as ignorant or envious of merit. If, in tracing the career of Mr. Roscoe, we find him rising, by his own exertions, from obscurity to eminence, that age and that country have some claims to commendation, in which the force of genius can overcome the obstacles of birth and fortune, and elevate its possessor to the society of the noblest and wisest of the land.

William Roscoe was born on the 8th of March, 1753, in the Old Bowling-green House, which still exists in Mount Pleasant, and is well known to many persons by the engraving from a drawing by Austin. His parents, in humble but comfortable circumstances, were little able to advance his education; yet anxious for his improvement, at the age of six they sent him to school, kept by a Mr. Martin, for the elementary instruction of children; whence in about two years, he was removed to the seminary of Mr. Sykes, at that time a considerable private school in Liverpool.

The instruction which young Roscoe here received was confined to English reading, writing, arithmetic, and the elements of geometry. At the age of twelve years he left school, from which period he may be said to have been, in a great measure, his own instructor, until about the age of sixteen, when he was articled as clerk to Mr. John Eyes, a respectable attorney in this town. During the four years that elapsed between his leaving school and entering Mr. Eyes' office, he occupied himself with desultory English reading, in cultivating some fields rented by his father, and in frequenting the painting-room of a porcelain manufactory in the neighbourhood, where he amused himself with painting on china.

At that period of his life, his English reading appears to have been rather confined. His favourite authors were Shakspeare, Shenstone, the poems of Mrs. Catharine Philips, and the Spectator. From the former he imbibed a decided predilection for poetry, and his taste for English composition was probably modelled on the elegant examples contained in the latter. It is curious to trace his attachment to botany and the fine arts to this early period. The phenomena of vegetation, and the cultivation of plants, appear to have made a deep impression on his youthful mind; and in the little cultivator of his father's fields, we can trace the embryo botanist, to whose ardent enthusiasm in after years, we owe our botanic garden, the world the new arrangement of Scitamineæ, and the superb botanical publication on the same beautiful order of plants. The early essays in painting china-ware seem also to have first inspired him with a love for the fine arts, and drew him on to cultivate his taste in the arts of design, in which he not only displayed the knowledge of an intelligent amateur, but such practical proficiency, which might have led to eminence, had his genius not been directed to other channels, as several slight but spirited etchings by his hand, yet in existence, amply testify.

The rudiments of Latin he acquired between the age of sixteen and twenty, by his own unassisted efforts, though at a later period he read several of the best Latin authors in company with his friends the late William Clarke, and Richard Lowndes, two young men of Liverpool, equally intent as himself on mental improvement.

I may here mention, it was not until a comparatively later period of his life, and, if I mistake not, after the publication of the Life of Lorenzo had given him celebrity, that he began to study Greek. In a copy of Homer, in possession of his family, we find the following note:—"Finished the Odyssey the day I came to Allerton, 18th March, 1799. W. R."

From his fifteenth to his twentieth year, he appears, from some memoranda which he has left, to have studied very assiduously during his leisure hours; and he luckily found some associates, with congenial tastes and habits, of whose friendship he always spoke, to his latest hour, with affectionate regard. Among those, the most conspicuous were Mr. Edward Rogers, Mr. William Clarke, Mr. Richard Lowndes, Mr. William Neilson, and Mr. Francis Holden. To the latter, whose various acquirements and extraordinary talents were, in after life, the frequent theme of Roscoe's enthusiastic encomiums, he was disposed to attribute his first inclination to the study of modern languages; and he had pleasure in acknowledging, that it was by the advice and encouragement of this young friend, that he devoted himself assiduously to the study of Italian. In his acquisition of the elements of French and Italian, he does not seem to have had any other assistance than the advice and encouragement of young Holden, who, seeing the aptitude and industry of his friend, strenuously urged him to pursue the path which his own genius had opened to his aspirations after literary distinction.

In fact, Roscoe owed very little of his acquirements to any instructors. What he drew from the conversation of his early associates, there is every reason to believe he amply repaid in kind; and, with the single exception of Burns, I do not know any of our distinguished writers who is less indebted to others for assistance in the road to literary eminence than William Roscoe—certainly few of them could with more truth exclaim, in the language of Phemius, when a suppliant to Ulysses,

'Αυτοδιδακτος δ'ειμι.

During the time of his apprenticeship, Mr. Roscoe formed an agreement with his friends Clarke, Lowndes, and Holden, to meet early in the morning, before the hours of business, for the purpose of reading together some Latin author, and discoursing on what they read. The example of these youthful students cannot be too earnestly inculcated on the rising generation of this place, while the success of one at least of them in the fields of literature is a striking proof of what may be obtained by such appropriation of hours too often lost to mental improvement. While classic authors thus engaged his morning leisure, Roscoe continued earnestly to cultivate Italian literature. It would seem that, before his twentieth year, he had read, in the original, several of the Italian historians, and, at that time even, had set his mind on becoming the biographer of Lorenzo d'Medici, the great patron of the early restorers of ancient learning.

He had, from an early period of his life, felt the force of poetic inspiration, and had undoubtedly cultivated the muses with high promise of brilliant success, ere he had attained his twentieth summer. A considerable number of his early verses remain, which breathe an ardent spirit of poetry. Some of these are addressed to a young lady of the same age, whose poetical genius had excited his warmest admiration, and who appears to have no less admired the talents of Roscoe. One of her MS. poems, written about 1772, contains the following lines, which at once prove the poetic powers of the author (destined afterwards to become the mother of an eminent poet,) and show her discernment in detecting, in the unknown attorney's clerk, the gem of future eminence:

> " But cease, my muse, unequal to the task,
> Forbear the effort! and to nobler hands
> Resign the lyre! Thee Roscoe! every muse
> Uncalled attends, and uninvoked inspires:
> In blooming shades and amaranthine bowers
> They weave the future garland for thy brow,

2 U   30*

And wait to crown thee with immortal fame;—
The Wisdom leads in all her lovely walks,
Thee Genius fires, and moral beauty charms.
Be it thy task to touch the feeling heart,
Correct its passions, and exalt its aims;
Teach pride to own, and owning to obey,
Fair Virtue's dictates, and her sacred laws;
To brighter worlds show thou the glorious road,
And be thy life as moral as thy song."

Congeniality of disposition and genius drew close the bands of friendship between this lady and Mr. Roscoe; and it is worthy of notice, that his first published production, the poem entitled *Mount Pleasant*, written at the age of nineteen, was originally inscribed to her, although, when printed, the address was omitted.

This poem, which exhibits, with considerable power of versification, a warm poetical feeling of the beauties of nature, is still more remarkable for the indignant apostrophe to Britons on the slave trade; an expression of generous sympathy with the suffering sons of Africa, which it required no inconsiderable share of moral courage to promulgate at that period, and in the chief seat of the odious traffic.

" Shame to mankind! But shame to Britons most,
Who all the sweets of Liberty can boast,
Yet deaf to ev'ry human claim, deny
That bliss to others, which themselves enjoy,
Life's bitter draughts with harsher bitter fill,
Blast ev'ry joy, and and to ev'ry ill:
The trembling limbs with galling iron bind,
Nor loose the heavier bondage of the mind."

These lines are here chiefly quoted to show how early Roscoe denounced the traffic in human flesh; and that the love of liberty, which marked his whole life, was in him not the creation of circumstances that brought him into public notice, but had grown up with his expanding faculties, and became confirmed by the reflections of his maturer years.

While Roscoe was thus improving his literary taste in the moments snatched from the fatigues of his profession, he devoted no inconsiderable portion of his attention to the study and promotion of the fine arts in his native town. He was the chief instigator, and most active member, of a small society formed here in 1772, "for the encouragement of designing, drawing, and painting;" and he read before the association, at one of its first meetings, an ode, addressed to the institution, which was afterwards published with the poem of *Mount Pleasant*, in 1777.

Soon after the termination of his articles of clerkship, Mr. Roscoe entered into partnership as an attorney with Mr. Aspinall, and in this profession he continues first with that gentleman, and afterwards with Mr. Joshua Lace, until the year 1796. It is proper to remark, that Mr. Roscoe, though eminent as a practitioner, never relished his profession, and had always expressed his deter-nation to retire from practice as an attorney, whenever the possession of a moderate competence should enable him to devote his attention to literary pursuits. He continued, however, for several years to attend sedulously to his business; but it was not until the year 1781 that the profits of his exertions enabled him to marry; when he was united to Jane, the second daughter of Mr. William Griffies, a respectable tradesman of Liverpool.

This union was productive of the utmost domestic happiness to the subject of this memoir, and made him the happy father of seven sons and three daughters; all of whom, except a son and a daughter, survive him.

For several years after his marriage, at intervals of leisure, he contrived to increase those rich treasures of literary information, and to cultivate that taste for the fine arts, which gave a peculiar charm to his conversation, and paved the way to his future celebrity.

In the year 1787, the agitation of the abolition of the slave-trade drew Mr. Roscoe into the field of political controversy, and he became the author of two anonymous pamphlets on that great question. The first was entitled, " Original View of the African Slave Trade, demonstrating its injustice and impolicy; with hints toward a bill for its abolition." The second was called forth by the publication of the Rev. Raymond Harris, entitled " Scriptural Researches on the License of the Slave Trade." That author had shewn much dexterity as a controversialist. The general scope of his argument is based on the practice of possessing bond-servants being mentioned in the Old Testament, without a condemnatory comment; and from the noted injunction of St. Paul to the Δουλοι of the New Testament, " Be obedient to them that are your masters, according to the flesh, with fear and trembling," it is inferred, that Christianity gives a warrant for holding our fellow men in slavery, The first proposition was supported by the fact, that Abraham and other very exemplary patriarchs purchased slaves or bond-servants, without any stigma being cast on their humanity or rectitude; and the second was defended by the repeated injunctions of the apostles to their converts to fear those in authority; a mode of reasoning which had been lately borrowed by two Presbyterian divines from this reverend Jesuit; whose work, it is said, was considered, by the Common Council of Liverpool of that day, as worthy of a donation of 200l. to the author.

Harris's pamphlet caused a considerable sensation; but was soon attacked by the Rev. Mr. Dannet, minister of St. John's, in Liverpool, who was evidently inferior as a controversialist to his Catholic opponent; but the doctrines of the latter were ably and warmly attacked in Mr. Roscoe's second essay, which bore the title of " Scriptural Refutation of a Pamphlet lately published by the Rev. Raymond Harris," &c., on the Christian principles that " all men are equal in the sight of God," and the benevolent injunction of the great Founder of our religion, " Therefore, all things whatsoever ye would that men should do to you, do ye even to them."

The question of the slave-trade, at that period, so engrossed the mind of Roscoe, that, in the same year, he published his well known poetic effusion, " The wrongs of Africa," in two parts: the profits from the sale of which he placed at the disposal of the committee then formed for promoting the abolition of the slave trade.

The Society for the encouragement of the Arts of Design had soon melted away; but Mr. Roscoe, about the time now alluded to, succeeded in forming a new association for a similar purpose; and to their exertions Liverpool is indebted for its first exhibitions of works of art, which were continued for several years with success. To this Society, which bore the name of "Liverpool Academy for the Encouragement of the Fine Arts," Mr. Roscoe delivered a series of lectures on the Progress and Vicissitudes of Taste, which remain in manuscript, and which he appears to have, at one time, contemplated to publish, as I find among them a title page, thus—" An Historical Inquiry into the Rise, Progress, and Vicissitudes of Tastes, as exemplified in Works of Literature and of Art. In two volumes. Vol. I." The manuscript, however, does not seem to have received his last corrections; though many of the observations are original and interesting.

He had also, for some years, a correspondence with Mr. Strutt, the engraver and antiquary, and author of the valuable Dictionary of Engravers. The letters of Strutt acknowledge the receipt of various important disquisitions on the history of engraving from Mr. Roscoe, of which, if I mistake not, Mr. Strutt availed himself, and incorporated them in the preliminary essays of his Dictionary.

About the same period, Mr. Roscoe commenced his fine collection of prints, which was particularly rich in painter's etchings, and engravings of the old masters. This collection was chiefly formed between the years 1780 and 1790; but continued for many years to receive valuable additions, by every journey to London, which his professional business often rendered necessary.

At a later period he began to collect drawings by great masters, and of these his collection was remarkably choice; his taste and judgment in that department being excellent.

From the time when his professional exertions put it in his power to indulge his elegant propensities, the formation of a library became a prominent article in his expenditure. Simple and refined in his habits, these were his chief expenses. He was not, however, a mere collector. His books, his prints, and other works of art, were diligently employed to store his mind, or to improve his taste, with the wisdom and art of former ages.

In the year 1789, after much previous study of Italian literature, he began to devote himself to the object of his early ambition, the Life of Lorenzo the Magnificent. In the course of that year, he communicated his intention to his valued friend William Clarke, (who, on account of his health, in the autumn of 1789, had fixed his residence at Fiesole, near Florence,) and requested his assistance in collecting manuscript documents relating to the subject. The fruits of the friendly exertions of that amiable man are best given in Roscoe's own words :

" An intimate friend, with whom I had been many years united in studies and affection, had paid a visit to Italy, and had fixed his winter residence at Florence. I well knew that I had only to request his assistance, in order to obtain whatever information he had an opportunity of procuring, from the very spot which was to be the scene of my intended history. My inquiries were particularly directed to the Laurentian and Ricardi Libraries, which I was convinced would afford much original and interesting information. It would be unjust merely to say that my friend afforded me the assistance I required; he went far beyond even the hopes I had formed, and his return to his native country was, if possible, rendered still more grateful to me, by the materials which he had collected for my use."

Of these documents, several are published entire in the appendix to Roscoe's work, especially the poems of Lorenzo; the existence of which had escaped the knowledge of the former biographers of the Princely Merchant.

From a very early period, Mr. Roscoe had taken a deep interest in political matters. In the year 1788, he took an active part at the meeting which, in Liverpool, as well as in other parts of England, assembled to commemorate the centenary of the revolution that expelled the family of Stuart from the throne of these kingdoms; and he composed an ode, which was recited on that occasion.

In the following year, the French revolution broke out; and, in common with many warm and generous spirits, he hailed its fair and auspicious dawn with all the devotion of a friend to the human race, the ardour of a patriot, and the enthusiasm of a poet. To those who recollect the flattering commencement of that extraordinary movement, it is unnecessary to observe, that it was viewed with unmixed satisfaction by a great majority of the people of this country, as affording the prospect of vast improvements in the social institutions of the European commonwealth. In various places meetings of the friends of liberty were held, similar to those of the preceding year, to celebrate another triumph of a great people over an unjust and tyrannical government; and at one of those assemblies, Roscoe produced his two admirable lyrics,

" O'er the vine-covered hills and gay valleys of France,"
and,

" Unfold, Father Time, thy long records unfold."

These brilliant and exulting strains were poured forth in the year 1789, while "the Genius of French freedom," in the nervous language of Currie, "appeared on our southern horizon with the countenance of an angel," and vanished ere she had yet "assumed the feature of a demon, and vanished in a shower of blood."

Mr. Roscoe had, on several occasions, made himself conspicuous by his attachment to the cause of civil and religious liberty, in such a degree as to attract the notice of several eminent statesmen, and particularly of the late Marquis of Lansdowne, with whom he maintained a close correspondence until the death of that nobleman. Literature, and especially politics, were the subjects of their correspondence; and the letters show how considerable were the parliamentary reforms advocated by the Whig statesmen of that period.

The violence of the second French National Assembly, in the two succeeding years, alienated a great many of their admirers in this country; but many good men still hoped that the ferment would subside into rational liberty, and deprecated the evident hostility which our government began in 1792 to exhibit. Among the latter was Mr. Roscoe. On the appearance of Mr. Pitt's famous proclamation against sedition, the minds of men were much agitated, and greatly divided. The friends of the minister in Liverpool convened a meeting to thank his majesty for the proclamation. Mr. Roscoe, seconded by the late William Rathbone, succeeded in carrying a counter-address; but, on the following day, a mob rose and destroyed the counter-address where it lay for signature. Party spirit, on that occasion, rose so high in Liverpool, that a small private literary society, of which Mr. Roscoe, Mr. Rathbone, and Dr. Currie were members, thought it expedient to discontinue their meetings, lest their objects should, by party malice, be represented as seditious or revolutionary.

On the breaking out of the war with France, Roscoe again appears as a political writer. He inveighed against the unjust and impolitic interference of this government with France; and, in a pamphlet entitled, "Thought on the late Failures," published in 1793, he attributes the mercantile distress of that period to the consequences of our meddling policy, a subject which he resumed in 1796, in "An Exposure of the Fallacies of Mr. Burke's celebrated invectives against the French Revolution."

We come now to the principal event in the history of our author, the publication of the "Life of Lorenzo de Medici," which appeared in the winter of 1795, in two volumes quarto. The work was printed by John McCreery in Liverpool, and is a fine specimen of provincial typography, both for accuracy and elegance of execution.

The sensation produced by this work was immense; the first edition was rapidly exhausted, and a second was demanded by the public within a few months. Letters of the most gratifying kind were showered on the author from high literary authorities in all quarters. Among others, the late Earl of Bristol, Bishop of Derry, then resident at Rome, hailed with the highest encomiums the appearance of an English work, which was the surprise and envy of the Italians themselves, and he immediately wrote to the publisher to know "what present of Italian books would be most acceptable to the accomplished author." Its success on the continent was no less gratifying. Besides a reprint of the original, the work was speedily translated into the Italian, French, and German languages; and it procured for Roscoe the esteem and correspondence of some of the most eminent literary men of Europe.

A work which has received such marked public approbation, which has gone through so many large editions in Britain, which has been translated into the most polished tongues of the continent, it is not my intention to criticise. I shall content myself with remarking, that the author's intimate acquaintance with the literature of Italy has excited the surprise even of Italians; and I well recollect the incredulous stare with which an Italian nobleman, of great literary taste and information, received my assertion that Mr. Roscoe had never been out of England.

The success of the Life of Lorenzo appears to have confirmed the author's intention of relinquishing his practice as an attorney; and some time after that event, he entered his name as a member of Gray's Inn, with a view of being called to the bar. This determination, however, he also relinquished, upon keeping a few terms.

In the year 1797, while his name remained on the books of Gray's Inn, he paid a visit of some length to London. In consequence of his literary reputation, and his intimacy with Lord Lansdowne, he was introduced into the first literary and various political circles: in particular, he used to state, that he then had the pleasure of becoming personally acquainted with Mr. Fox, and Mr., now Lord, Grey; and he formed besides many valued private friendships, which were dissolved only by death. Among those who then more particularly gained his esteem, he often mentioned Dr. Moore, author of Zelucco, of the spirited "View of Manners in Italy," and of a "Journal of a Residence in France," the father of the gallant and unfortunate Sir John Moore.

Mr. Roscoe's retirement from professional labours enabled him to devote himself with increased assiduity to Italian literature. To relieve his mind from the fatigue of more intense researches, he this year translated into English verse, the *Balia* of Tansillo, in which the long neglected beauties of the Italian poet are brought home to British ears and British feelings with admirable tact and spirit. His more arduous occupations were the vast stores of Italian history, about the period of the restoration of Letters, with a view to the life of Leo X.; a subject which had been recommended to him by Horace Walpole, (Lord Orford,) and some other literary friends, after his successful publication of the Life of Lorenzo the Magnificent.

In the year 1798, the want of a public reading-room, on a better footing than Liverpool then could boast, caused the foundation of our Athenæum. The plan suggested by Dr. Rutter was warmly supported by Mr. Roscoe, Dr. Currie, Mr. George Case, and some other gentlemen, who, exerting their influence among their friends, obtained so general a subscription in Liverpool, that the foundations of our magnificent Consultation Library and News-Room were speedily laid, and a considerable collection of books soon formed. In this institution, as creditable to his native town, Mr. Roscoe always took much delight.

The numerous strangers who were now attracted to Liverpool, chiefly by the reputation of our distinguished fellow-citizen caused such encroachments on his time, notwithstanding his retirement from business, that he resolved to retreat into the coun try; and with this view he purchased half of the estate of Aller ton from the representatives of Mrs. Hardman, and removed to that beautiful spot in 1799. In a playful letter to Fuseli the painter, Mr. Roscoe mentions his removal, and his intention of not again embarking in any kind of business, but of dedicating himself wholly to agricultural and literary pursuits. His tastes were simple, his views moderate, and his means fully competent to realize his plans; from which it is greatly to be lamented that any circumstances should ever have induced him to deviate. While employed as a professional man to arrange the involved concerns of the bank of Messrs. J. & W. Clarke, he was thus brought into contact with Sir Benjamin Hammet, a London banker, who held acceptances of the Liverpool Bank to an immense amount (I am informed for 200,000l.) Hammet was so struck with Roscoe's ability in arranging the affairs of his friends, that he wished him to become a partner in the concern. This he repeatedly refused; but Hammet threatening, in case of his refusal to join his concern, to make it bankrupt, Roscoe, satisfied that the assets were, in ordinary times, more than sufficient to cover the demands, finally consented, and for twenty years the principal part of his time was occupied in the management of that important establishment.

While thus employed, the hours which he was now enabled to devote to the history of Leo were abstracted from the period usually dedicated to repose or recreation. Yet, with all these demands on his application, the interest he always felt on great political questions did not suffer him to view in silence the crisis of 1802; but called forth his pamphlet, entitled, " Observations on the relative situation of Great Britain and France ;" a tract in which he has recorded his detestation of war, and his anxiety to see the two foremost nations of Europe engaged in the less guilty rivalry for pre-eminence in the arts of peace.

In 1802, the Botanic Garden of Liverpool was established, chiefly through the influence of Mr. Roscoe, and, at its opening, he delivered an address to the proprietors, which was printed.

In this establishment he always took the interest of a parent in a favourite child. Under his auspices, and the consummate skill of Mr. John Shepherd, the curator of the garden, it speedily became conspicuous among botanical establishments, and it still ranks among the first in Europe.

In 1805, he completed his history of "the Life and Pontificate of Leo X," which appeared that year in four volumes, quarto.

This elaborate work had been the fruit of much research, of intense previous study, and was always regarded by its author as superior to his Life of Lorenzo, yet it was not so favourably received by the British public; a circumstance with some truth attributed to the violent attacks on it in several of our periodical works.

The hostility of some of the reviews was evidently produced by political rancour towards Roscoe, as an opponent of the ministerial measures of that eventful period; in others, it sprung from anger at the manner in which he had treated the character of Luther, as the founder of a new church.

It appears to me, that Roscoe had sufficiently lauded the boldness and constancy of the man, to whom we owe the assertion of private judgment in religious and civil matters; that he had given the history of Luther with the impartiality of a searcher after truth, admitting his failings and his errors, while he applauded his courage and undoubted talents; that the early patrons of literature and the fine arts demanded our warm approbation and our gratitude, and that the historian of the Revival of Letters had wisely dwelt more on the unquestionable merits of Leo and his family, in promoting that great object, than in raking up, from the gross scurrility of a profligate age, imputed crimes of vices, which, after all, rest only on the doubtful authority of acrimonious and vindictive controversialists.

The merits of the Life of Leo were, however, differently estimated on the continent. It was speedily translated into the French, German, and Italian; and the extensive sale of several editions of it in Italy, where, it may be fairly presumed, the best judgment of its wants or its defects could be formed, sufficiently attests the character which foreign critics entertain of this great work of our author.

On the appearance of the British criticisms, Mr. Roscoe prepared a full answer to the objections of the reviewers, but this reply he never published; contenting himself with inserting a short abstract of it in the preface to the second edition, which appeared in 1806, within a year of the publication of the first. The chief objections, in addition to the criticisms above stated, were, that he was fond of paradoxical opinions, as instanced in the chivalrous defence of the character of Lucretia Borgia; and in his doubting whether Pope Alexander VI. was stained with every crime laid to his charge by his numerous enemies—that he was too fond of quotations from the poets; and that, by retaining the Italian orthography of proper names, he had made needless innovations on our language. These charges are not very important defects in such an elaborate work, even if we admit their justice. In my opinion, they are sufficiently answered by his few remarks; and the Life and Pontificate of Leo X. already ranks, by the beauty of its style, and the value of research, among our standard historical works.

While engaged in these occupations, on the dissolution of Parliament in October, 1806, Mr. Roscoe was, to himself, most unexpectedly called on to become a candidate for the representation of his native town. The requisition was signed only a few days previous to the election;—and, after a keen contest for eight days, during which there was a coalition against him, between the friends of the rival candidates, Generals Tarleton and Gascoyne, he was placed at the head of the poll by a large majority.

His parliamentary career was of short duration; but he had the satisfaction, in that short period, of declaring his sentiments on several subjects in which he felt a deep interest. He spoke and voted for Sir Samuel Romilly's bill, for rendering real estates subject to simple contract debts; he had the happiness to lift his voice in parliament for the abolition of the slave-trade, and to see that great act of national justice triumphantly carried; he had an opportunity of advocating the claims of our Roman Catholic brethren to an equality of political rights; and he delivered his sentiments with indignant energy on the dismissal of the Whig administration in 1807, on their attempt to redeem the pledge given by Pitt at the period of the Irish Union; a pledge, by themselves, always considered as just and expedient.

Mr. Roscoe's chief parliamentary friends at that time, were, Mr. Whitbread, Sir Samuel Romilly, and Mr. William Smith; but he never permanently attached himself to the ministry; and was by them regarded as a person who would rather act on his own views of what was right, than enter into the trammels of party.

On the dissolution of Parliament, he received another requisition to offer himself for Liverpool, and was escorted into town by a very numerous and respectable *cortége*. His opponents, however, had succeeded in prejudicing many of the populace against him, especially on the ground of his vote for the abolition of the Slave Trade—a traffick which they had been taught to consider as essential to the commercial greatness of the port; and the rage of zealots was kindled against him for his speech on the Catholic Question. The consequence was, that, on the arrival of the *cortége* in Castle-street, a serious riot took place, and Mr. Roscoe was induced, from the fear of hazarding the peace of the town, to decline allowing himself to be again put in nomination. I have reason to believe that this determination did not cause him much regret; a distaste for parliamentary duties was not unnatural to a man of his previous habits, entering on a new career at a rather advanced period of life. These considerations determined him to withdraw from the contest; but he was, without his concurrence, or that of his most intimate friends, proposed as a candidate on that occasion, as well as in 1812, when he was put in nomination in a similar manner at Leicester, without his consent, and polled a very considerable number of votes.

We have already noticed Mr. Roscoe as the earnest advocate of peace. In 1808, he published "Considerations on the Cause and Consequences of the War with France,"—a pamphlet which excited much attention, and speedily went through eight editions. It was followed in the same year by another pamphlet, entitled, "Remarks on the Proposals made to Great Britain for opening Negociations for Peace with France," in which he endeavoured to show that the advances of France had not been met with a sincere desire on the part of our Government to put an end to the miseries of a ruinous and bloody contest.

In 1810, Mr. Roscoe published a letter to the present Lord Chancellor, then Mr. Brougham, on the question of Parliamentary Reform. In that tract, he advocates a more extensive Reform than the partial measures then in contemplation by the Opposition; and the coincidence, in many respects, between his suggestions and a late measure, has, within the last few months, caused a republication of Mr. Roscoe's pamphlets.

This letter brought him into more immediate correspondence with Mr. Brougham; and when that gentleman was invited to become a candidate for the representation of Liverpool in 1812, Mr. Roscoe not only entered warmly into the contest to support Mr. Brougham, but on the return of Mr. Canning, the rival candidate, wrote a caustic review of the electioneering speeches of that statesman, which the enthusiasm of his admirers had collected into a bulky pamphlet. Such ephemeral specimens of oratory should, on all sides, be permitted to remain in the less ambitious pages of provincial newspapers.

At every period of his life, Mr. Roscoe was much attached to the study of botany. As we have stated, the establishment of our Botanic Garden was principally due to his suggestions. In 1809, he presented to the Linnean Society his valuable paper "On a new arrangement of the Scitaminean order of plants," which appeared in their Transactions, and established his claim to the character of an original thinker in this elegant department of natural history. His reputation, still more than the claims of private friendship, led Sir James Edward Smith, to institute the genus *Roscoea*, which now contains many species of that beautiful order.

A similarity of political principles, and congeniality of taste for agricultural improvements, had, for some time, made Roscoe acquainted with Mr. Coke of Norfolk. In 1814, he was invited to visit Holkham, the splendid seat of that eminent agriculturist. There he found ample employment in the magnificent library collected by the late Lord Leicester, uncle to the present posses-sor, a nobleman who, with vast wealth, possessed a highly cultivated mind, and a passion for collecting books and manuscripts. It was well known that the collection was immensely rich in classical manuscripts and unpublished works on Italian history. Mr. Roscoe readily undertook the examination of this superb collection, which had afforded to Drakenborck the manuscript copies of Livy, employed in his valuable edition of the Roman Historian, and which, among 600 manuscript volumes of ecclesiastical annals and Italian civil history, was discovered by Mr. Roscoe to contain one of the lost volumes of Leonardo da Vinci's *Treatises on Mechanics*, and the long deplored and precious volume in which Raffaello, at the desire of the Pontiff, had made *pen drawings* of the remains of ancient Roman magnificence, illustrated by short descriptions in his own hand-writing. Mr. Roscoe undertook to make a *catalogue raisonnée* of the manuscripts of the collection; a task which he some years afterwards, with the assistance of Mr. Madden, now one of the librarians of the British Museum, fully accomplished. This catalogue (of which a short account was given to this Society a few years ago) extends to four or five thick folio volumes, and is enriched with engraved *fac similies* and illuminated ornaments.

The manuscripts have been little attended to for many years. Many of them were in the original coarse paper covers, and some were injured by damp and time. The whole were some time afterwards consigned to Mr. Roscoe's care, who put them into the hands of our eminent binder, the late Mr. John Jones, who, by great industry and skill, succeeded in restoring crumpled vellum to its original smoothness, in pasting torn leaves with wonderful neatness, and who bound the whole collection in a durable and elegant manner. An ancient and admirable Hebrew manuscript of the Pentateuch,* written in a beautiful hand, on deer skins, forming a roll thirty-eight feet in length, was mounted, by the same ingenious artist, on rollers ornamented with silver bells, under the direction of a learned Rabbi, who believed the manuscript to be an eastern transcript of great antiquity.

Toward the close of 1814, by one of our too frequent commercial convulsions, and by the extent of their accommodations to persons engaged in business, the affairs of the bank in which Mr. Roscoe was a partner, became involved and the house found it necessary to suspend payments. For four years Mr. Roscoe devoted himself to the arrangement of their affairs ; entertaining throughout the most sanguine hopes of being able finally to discharge all their engagements, as the joint property of the partners was valued, at the time of the suspension of payments, at considerably more than the amount of their debts. The depreciation, however, of that property, combined with other circumstances over which Mr. Roscoe had no control, prevented the accomplishment of his most earnest wishes, and in 1820, he became a bankrupt. Previous to this, (in the year 1816,) his noble

* Believed to be more than one thousand years old.

library, his fine collection of prints and drawings, and his curious collections of paintings, were dispersed, and the proceeds of the sale were applied to the payment of the debts of the house. It will convey some idea of the collection, to state, that the books, consisting of about 2000 works, sold for no less a sum than 5150*l.*, the prints for 1886*l.*; the drawings for 740*l.*, and the pictures for 3239*l.*; making a total of 11,014*l.*

The beautiful sonnet* written by Mr. Roscoe on parting with his library, was given to a friend, and handed about in manuscript; but the Reverend William Beloc has since inserted it, without any acknowledgment, in autobiograph, as the motto to one of the chapters of that conceited work.

Several of Mr. Roscoe's friends, anxious to preserve to him various works, which they knew he highly prized, either for their intrinsic worth, or as the gift of esteemed friends, bought them up at the sale of his library, to the amount of 600*l.*, and presented them to Mr. Roscoe. The gift, however, was firmly but gratefully declined; and the subscribers resolved to present the collection to the Athenæum Library, to be kept together as a testimony of their esteem for their respected friend; and of that library the collection now forms a distinct part.

A selection from his pictures, comprising specimens of art highly illustrative of the progress of painting, was purchased by several of the same gentlemen, at a liberal price, fixed by Mr. Winstanly and myself, and presented to the Royal Institution by those admirers of Roscoe. This collection cost 50*l.* and forms an interesting part of the objects which attract strangers to our Institution.

I may here remark, that the original plan of the Liverpool Royal Institution originated, and was drawn up by me, in 1813: although it was carried into effect during my absence on the Continent, in 1814. Mr. Roscoe took an active part in this measure, was long the Chairman of the Committees while it was struggling into existence; and, as its first President, read an eloquent address on the opening of the Institution in the year 1817.

From an early period, Mr. Roscoe had been a warm advocate for a reformation of the sanguinary penal code of this country.

* SONNET.
" As one who destined from his friends to part,
  Regrets their loss, yet hopes again erewhile
  To share their converse, and enjoy their smile,
And temper as he may Affliction's dart,—
Thus, lov'd associates! chiefs of elder art!
  Teachers of wisdom, who could once beguile
  My tedious hours, and brighten ev'ry toil,
I now resign you—nor with fainting heart;
  For pass a few short years, or days, or hours,
And happier seasons may their dawn unfold
And all your sacred fellowships restore;
  When, freed from earth, unlimited its power,
Mind shall with mind direct communion hold,
And kindled spirits meet to part no more."
31*

His humanity and amiable mind revolted from the frequency of
executions; and he eagerly desired to see those statutes which
awarded death for trifling offences, and are too barbarous to be
enforced, in the present day, expunged from the code of British
jurisprudence. Shortly before the period of his misfortunes, his
attention had been turned to the subject of penal law and prison
discipline. In 1819, he published his tract, entitled, "*Observations
on Penal Jurisprudence, and the Reformation of Criminals ;*"
which was followed, between that period and 1825, by two other
dissertations on the same subject.

The principle of the system which he advocates is, that the
only legitimate object of punishment is the prevention of a repe-
tition of the crime, by a reformation of the offenders; which effect he proposed to accomplish by hard labour in penitentiaries,
and by moral instruction. He denies that we have any right to
punish for the mere benefit to society of the example. He inveighs
against the barbarous maxim, that revenge or expiation for the
injury committed, ought ever to be the principle of penal legislation; and cannot admit that retribution to the injured party can
be the proposed end of punishment. In the third part of his essay,
he seems to doubt the propriety of the punishment of death in any
case; (Part III. p. 166;) but, at all events, he considers that it
should be reserved for four or five crimes of the blackest dye.
These essays contain the outline of some principles which are
now generally acknowledged; and if the humanity and generous spirit of the author, have led him to form a too favourable estimate of human nature, and to overlook some difficulties in the practical application of his principles of legislation, we cannot but admire the benevolent enthusiasm and earnest appeal to the best
feelings of our nature which are stampt on every page of his
treatise.

In the second tract, he had pointed out the evil consequences
likely to result from too great severity in prison discipline, and
had entered a warm protest against the horrid punishment of long
continued solitary confinement, as a general measure for effecting
this reformation of offenders. He severely commented, in the
third part, on the atrocities which appeared to have been perpetrat-
ed in the Auburn Penitentiary, in the state of New York. This
drew him into a long controversy with several American writers
in the latter years of his life; and to the zeal with which he devoted himself to plead the cause of the outcasts of society, we have
to ascribe the first serious shock to his general health, as I shall,
by and by, have occasion to notice; but he had the happiness to
find, after much angry discussion in the newspapers of the western
world, that his arguments against solitary confinement, which he
stigmatized as the utmost refinement of cruelty, and utterly inef-
fectual as a punishment, were not lost on the Americans. The
infirm state of Mr. Roscoe's health at that time brought me much
into contact with my venerable friend; and when he learnt from

various quarters, that the change which was taking place in the prison discipline of America was in no small degree attributed to his expostulations, I heard him repeatedly declare, " that no literary distinction had ever afforded him half the gratification he received from the reflection on the part he had taken on this great question ; and he expressed his satisfaction that he now might be permitted to think that he had not lived altogether in vain."

I have, in noticing the conclusion of this controversy, anticipated some events of his life to which we must now return.

When released from the harassing cares of business, the mind of Mr. Roscoe, with the elasticity and application of youth, diligently entered on various literary projects. Since the first appearance of the Life of Lorenzo, he had obtained from Italy, and elsewhere, various documents illustrative of that work. This he prepared for publication, together with some strictures on the manner in which the character and biography of Lorenzo had been treated by Sismondi, and some other writers. This work appeared in an octavo volume in 1822, under the title of " Illustrations of the Lorenzo de' Medici." The strong terms in which Sismondi accused Mr. Roscoe of partiality to the Medici Family, and of palliating their crimes, drew forth an able and indignant answer; yet, it is pleasing to reflect, that when Sismondi, a few years afterwards, visited England, Mr. Roscoe formed with him a personal acquaintance in no way affected by their literary controversy.

About the same period, Mr. Roscoe published an amusing " Memoir of Richard Roberts," a self-taught linguist, well known in Liverpool, by the extraordinary number of languages which he can read, no less than by the filth of his person. The profits of this publication Mr. Roscoe humanely dedicated to the use of this singular person; whose intellect, defective in every thing but language, renders him as helpless as a child, and Roberts may now be seen in whole clothes, with his portable library stuffed, as in former times, between his shirt and his skin ; for he disdained a fixed abode.

An application having been made to Mr. Roscoe to become the editor of a new edition of Pope's works, and to furnish a fresh life of the author, Mr. Roscoe engaged in it with all the ardour of a poet, having ever been a warm admirer of Pope's genius. This was no trifling task—for he added notes on the poems with much care; and in the life, which forms the first volume of the edition, defended the talents and character of Pope from sundry imputations cast on him by Mr. Bowles and others. The date of publication was 1824.

About the same time, he superintended a new edition of the Lives of Lorenzo and Leo, to the latter of which he added many new notes.

In 1824, Mr. Roscoe was elected a " Royal Associate" of the Royal Society of Literature, founded by his late Majesty George IV. A pension of 100l. a year was awarded to each of ten associates, which Mr. Roscoe enjoyed for three or four years ; but which, from the neglect of providing a permanent fund for the purpose, would have ceased about the time of his decease. The great gold medal of the Society, value 50 guineas, was also awarded to him as an historian, two years before he died; and it remains with his family.

It would be unjust to omit, that the misfortunes of our distinguished fellow-citizen called forth the warm sympathy of his numerous friends, and prompted them to take steps for securing him against their immediate consequences. It is more necessary to state this, because many unjust imputations have been vented against the inhabitants of Liverpool, on account of their supposed neglect of Mr. Roscoe in his adversity. There was considerable delicacy necessary in the steps which were taken to testify their esteem and attachment. Mr. Roscoe had a noble and independent mind. He had steadily refused the proffered gift of a valuable selection from his library, even after it had been for that purpose bought by his friends at the sale ; and those who had the pleasure of being intimate with him, well know how necessary it would be to keep him in ignorance of what was intended, until it was accomplished. During a second visit which he made to Holkham, a private fund was quickly subscribed among his friends, for the purchase of an annuity on the lives of Mr. and Mrs. Roscoe. The delicate task of communicating what was done devolved on me; and the correspondence which ensued between us, though his pride of independence was at first alarmed, the example of his friend, Charles James Fox, under similar circumstances, was successfully urged, to reconcile his mind to receive this spontaneous homage to his talents and his worth from sincerely attached friends.

We have already noticed Mr. Roscoe's early attachment to botany, and his critical labours on the order *Scitamineæ*, to which he had long paid much attention, stimulated by the continual additions this order was receiving from the East and West Indies. The number of new species which the judicious care of Mr. Shepherd, the skilful curator of our Botanic Garden, had successfully cultivated together with the dried specimens which Mr. Roscoe received from various quarters, determined him to publish a work containing coloured figures of new or interesting species, with botanical descriptions. This gave rise to the most splendid botanical work that ever issued from the provincial press of any country; which occupied much of his time during the latter years of his life, and was only completed shortly before his death. Of this superb work, he printed too few copies ; and before the second number came out, there was a necessity of reprinting additional copies of the first. The work is highly prized by botanists; and it is particularly valued on the Continent, where, from the small number of impressions which Mr. Roscoe could be induced to throw off, it is extremely scarce. Many of the beautiful figures in his work are from his own spirited sketches; but the majority of them are the productions of the pencil of his daughter-in-law, Mrs. Edward Roscoe, or of Miss R. Miller, of this place.

My acquaintance with Mr. Roscoe commenced in 1806, and I soon had the felicity of being received as an intimate friend. From 1810 I was further honoured by being consulted as his physician, in which capacity I watched with much anxiety over his declining health. From the time of the first derangement of the affairs of the bank, the immense mental and bodily exertions which he made, produced great inroads on a constitution naturally good. He then began, on much application to any subject, to be seized with occasional faintness; and once, in 1816, he was attacked at the bank with a slight loss of memory, which speedily wore off. His habits of intense study, after this period, produced similar effects; and while engaged in the controversy on prison discipline, after writing for the greatest part of a night, to overtake a ship about to sail for America, he was affected, in the winter of 1827, with partial paralysis of the muscles of the mouth and tongue. I was immediately called; the patient was freely bled—on which he recovered his speech; and the introduction of a seton in his neck removed the paralytic affection of the mouth. Intense study was forbidden: and after a period of perfect relaxation from his literary occupations, he recovered sufficiently to be able to complete his botanical work, the catalogue of Mr. Cooke's library, and to correct for the press his latest tracts on prison discipline. It was a great satisfaction to find his intellect quite entire, and it remained so until within an hour or two of his death. His bodily feebleness, however, gradually increased; yet, by the affectionate care of his family, his infirmities were but little felt. His amusements were, various reading, the illustration of his son's translation of Lanzi's History of Italian Painting, by a small collection of engravings, together with putting the last hand to his botanical work. He was unable for the fatigue of receiving much company, or of seeing strangers, for some time before his death: yet he loved to converse with a few friends, and took a lively interest in the political events with which the last year (1830) was pregnant. On the French Revolution of July, he wrote a long and earnest letter to M. La Fayette, (with whom he had before occasionally corresponded,) urging him to use the influence of his name and popularity, to induce the French nation to spare the lives of the ministers then under arrest; pointing out how a sanguinary punishment would detract from the glory of the revolution, and what a noble opportunity the French people now had of setting an example of mitigation of the criminal code to all the nations of Europe. This letter, and another of gratulation to the present Lord Chancellor, on his attaining that high office, were the last public acts of his indefatigable and useful life.

In the month of June, 1831, he was attacked with influenza; and his exhausted frame being unable to struggle with the dis-

2 W

ease, effusion into the chest took place, and he expired on the 30th of that month, in the 78th year of his age.

Besides his published works, Mr. Roscoe has left behind him a large mass of papers, and an extensive and valuable correspondence.

Among the former, are various dissertations on the fine arts, some of which appear in a finished state. In the year 1814, Mr. Roscoe had proposed to the writer of this memoir to undertake the translation of Lanzi's Storia Pittorica della Italia, and he engaged to furnish notes, and a preliminary dissertation. I had made considerable progress in the translation, when Mr. Roscoe's misfortunes, and my own professional avocations, interrupted the work; which has since been well executed by his son, Mr. Thomas Roscoe. Among the papers of my venerable friend, I find a very interesting introductory dissertation, intended for our joint work, tracing the history of the art of painting and sculpture to a much later period than their supposed extinction in the west, indeed almost to within 200 years of their supposed revival by the Pisani and Cimabue. This treatise is in such a state that it might be published, and it would form an excellent introduction to Lanzi's work. It is entitled, " An historical Sketch on the State of the Fine Arts during the Middle Ages."

I find also a curious dissertation on *Painters' Drawings*, another *on the Origin of Engraving on Wood and on Copper*, a third, *on the Engravings of the Early German School*. There are large fragments also of a work on the Etchings of the Italian Painters, which contain much useful information; and a lecture " on the use of Prints," another on the " Practical Part of Painting," and two " on the Origin and Progress of Taste." There is also a poem on the origin of engraving, written in 1783, of which there are two copies in MS.

I have already mentioned, that the lectures on the Origin and Progress of Taste were extended into a Treatise, which is not finished. This is also the case with some dissertations on the state of letters and the arts anterior to the Greeks, and their progress among that people. The whole seem to have been parts of a great work on the fine arts, which he left imperfect.

Among his papers are some MS. essays on moral and political subjects; and a considerable one " *On the principle of Vegetation and the Food of Plants*."

His correspondence with various eminent characters is very extensive; and comprises a period of upwards of fifty years, during a succession of most interesting events. A selection of these letters will form an appendix to the Life of Mr. Roscoe, now in preparation.

The letters consist of,---

1. Correspondence on politicial subjects with the Duke of Gloucester, the late and the present Lord Lansdowne, Mr. Whitbread, Sir Samuel Romilly, Mr. Creevy, Mr. Coke, Lord Holland, the present Lord Chancellor, and President Jefferson.

2. On penal jurisprudence and prison discipline, with Mr. Basil Montague, M. de La Fayette, M. Van Praet, Mr. Fowell Buxton; with Dr. Mease, Mr. Roberts Vaux, Mr. Stephen Allen, Mr. Bradford, and other American gentlemen.

3. On literary subjects, with Lord Carlisle, Lord Orford, Dr. Parr, Dr. Symmons, Dr. Aikin, Mr. Samuel Rogers, Mr. Thomas Campbell, Mr. Montgomery, Miss Lucy Aiken, Mr. Dawson Turner, Mr. William Clarke, Professor William Smyth, Professor Wilson, Mr. Barnard Barton, Mr. Capel Lofft, Dr. Channing.

4. On matters relating to the fine arts, with Sir Joshua Reynolds, Sir Thomas Lawrence, Mr. Strutt, Mr. Fuseli, Mr. John Gibson, &c.

5. On botany and agriculture, with Sir Joseph Banks, Sir John Sinclair, Sir James E. Smith, Dr. Wallich, Dr. Carey, Dr. Hooker.

6. On his history of the Medici Family, with Fabbroni, Moreni, Mecherini, Professor Sprengel, Count Bossi, and Mr. Henke.

In person, Mr. Roscoe was tall, and rather slender. In early life he possessed much bodily activity : his hair was light auburn, almost inclining to red; his full gray eye was clear and mild, his face expressive and cheerful. As he advanced in life, the benevolent expression of his countenance remained, but the vivacity of the features was tempered into a noble dignity, which it was impossible to see without respect and admiration ; while the mouth bespoke taste and feeling, and the clustering hoary hair round his temples gave a venerable air to his manly features.

There are several representations of him ; but none of them appear to me so finely to express the characteristic traits of his head as John Gibson's medallion. The portrait in the Institution, and Spence's busts, give us Mr. Roscoe in his decline with great fidelity. Gibson's marble bust is said to recall his youthful appearance, but the Terra Cotta medallion is Mr. Roscoe, as I should wish to remember him. I may add, that it has been exceedingly well copied in the fine medal, published by Mr. Clements of this town, from a die by Clint.

Of Mr. Roscoe's genius and acquirements, his published works present a better memorial than any panegyric can confer ; but I may be permitted to state my conviction, after having examined a great mass of his unfinished manuscript dissertations, that had he been left to pursue his original plan of *literary retirement*, instead of again plunging into the cares and anxieties of *business*, he would have left behind a work on the History of the Fine Arts, far superior to any thing on that subject which British literature possesses.

In public life, Mr. Roscoe was a consistent and fearless champion of civil and religious liberty; the uncompromising enemy of oppression, and the humane advocate of a mitigation of the severity of penal enactments.

Of the qualities of his heart, as a private individual, it is impossible to speak too highly. In the relations of husband, father, and friend, his conduct was most exemplary; and it would be difficult to point out a man who possessed fascination of manner which attracts and rivets attachment, in a higher degree than William Roscoe. He had deep and solemn feelings of devotion, which it was not his practice to obtrude on his acquaintance; but which he occasionally expressed to his intimate friends in the language of heartfelt piety. The beautiful invocation to the Deity, which he substituted for the intended dedication of his great botanical work, breathes the deep fervour of his adoration of the Supreme Creator; and is also remarkable as the actual suggestion of a poet's dream at the advanced age of 76. An innate love of sincerity and truth; simplicity, combined with a playful vivacity, yet suavity of manners; a generous belief in the integrity of others, the consequence of his own rectitude of purpose; an anxiety to do justice to the merits of others; a liberal and judicious patronage of modest talent, struggling to escape from obscurity, joined to a natural cheerfulness of disposition; all united to convert into devoted and enthusiastic admirers, those who first sought his friendship from his literary reputation. The fame of Roscoe belongs to his country :---the memory of his inestimable qualities remain to his friends :

> " Multis ille bonis flebilis occidit—
> ———— cui Pudor, et Justitiæ soror
> Incorrupta Fides, nudaque Veritas,
> Quando ullum invenient parem ?"—HORAT.

MEMOIR OF GENERAL SCHUYLER.

PHILIP SCHUYLER, a major general in the American army, was born at Albany, in 1731. His family were respectable and opulent, and his education was liberal for the age in which he lived. In the war of 1755, he was an officer, and served with the provincial troops until 1759, when Wolfe fell in taking Quebec. After the repose given to the colonies by the treaty of 1763, he returned to the quiet of domestic life, with the high respect of the provincial and British officers. On the breaking out of the war in 1775, only two days after the battle of Bunker-hill, he was appointed a major general in the American army, and was directed to take charge of the northern forces, raised from New York and New England to secure the lakes and to penetrate into Canada. But sickness prevented him from discharging this great duty, and the command devolved upon the gallant General Montgomery. His prowess and his misfortunes are detailed elsewhere. After he had recovered, and the ill fortunes of the campaign were known, General Schuyler was assiduous on the frontier, and did all that a wise and brave man could do, to keep the Indians in order and to prevent predatory incursions. He was not the first general of whom the country expected more than he, or any one, could do. The New England people had so often bled and fought on the frontiers, and particularly at Ticonderoga, that they clamoured when they heard of St. Clair's defeat. The blame was put on Schuyler, but without the slightest foundation. He had done all that mortal could have done, with his means; but these murmurs had their effects on Congress, and Schuyler was superceded by General Gates. Schuyler met the crisis as a great man should. His conduct on this occasion was above all praise; it was not tainted by any mark of resentment nor indignation. With the utmost complacency, but with deep feeling, he delivered his papers and gave up his command to Gates, with these remarks: " Sir, I have done all that could be done, as far as the means were in my power, to injure the enemy, and to inspire confidence in the soldiers of our army; and, I flatter myself, with some success; but the palm of victory is denied me, and it is left to you, general, to reap the fruits of my labour. I will not fail, however, to second your views; and my devotion to my country, will cause me with alacrity to obey your orders" He had performed his duty to the utmost extent; for he had been in the forest and felled the tree, broken up the roads, and thrown a thousand obstacles in the way of the enemy. But these facts were then unknown to New England, who had not made particular inquiry, but who, like their mother country, placed all things on success. After the conquest of General Burgoyne, General Schuyler took the British officers and their friends to his hospitable mansion, and treated them as his friends, and tried to make them forget their situation. Lady Harriet Auckland, the Baroness of Riedesel, and the Lady Balcarras, spoke of General Schuyler, as one born to support the dignity of an officer of distinction. Burgoyne himself, the proud minion of his monarch, apologised to Schuyler, for burning his splendid house a few days before his capture, and intimated that he could not have any idea that it belonged to an officer of his rank and character. The reply was as piquant as gallant. " Make no excuse, my dear general, for this trifling incident; the loss is more than compensated by the honour of meeting you at my table." Burgoyne, always tasteful, said, afterwards, that my Lord Chesterfield could not have surpassed this; and, indeed, it had in it the essence of courtesy and keenness.

History shows us but few instances of patriotism that will compare with Schuyler's conduct. Epaminondas, deprived of the supreme command by the jealousy of the politicians of his city, marched to victory as a private soldier—he lived in an age of the greatest heroism; and Schryznecki of the Poles, removed by the folly of his countrymen, drew his sword in the ranks as a private soldier: but Schuyler was bred in British pride of rank, where no such examples had even existed; but he had the magnanimity to make a precedent for the good of his country If he had clamoured and raved as a little man would have done, he had so

32

many friends that confusion would have been produced in the army, and Burgoyne might have come on triumphantly to the city of Albany.

At the close of the war, as well as during the contest, General Schuyler was held in the highest reverence and admiration by all the officers and soldiers of the army, and by none more than by the New England troops. The Rhode Island brigade, then under the command of Major Allen, presented him a most affectionate address, which, if in existence as a document, is out of the reach of the writer of this short sketch, but the response of General Schuyler was found in his own hand writing, among the papers of Major Allen, in the possession of his son, and directed " To Captain Allen, and the other gentlemen of the Rhode Island corps, present." The original has this endorsement upon it. " Received at Saratoga, 16th of Dec. 1783."

SARATOGA, Dec. 16th, 1783.

Gentlemen: The great goodness of your hearts, has induced you to overrate the small services I have been able to render you ; most sincerely do I wish they had been in any degree proportionate to your merits, or to my inclinations. The polite and sentimental manner in which you have been pleased to convey your acknowledgments, is another instance of that urbanity which you have so constantly and invariably evinced to be happily possessed of, and which has afforded me a satisfaction, too sensibly felt by the heart, to be adequately conveyed by words.

To those sentiments of gratitude and esteem, which pervade me with regard to you, as a part of that gallant, persevering, and suffering band of Americans, to whom, under heaven, we are so immediately indebted for the inestimable blessings of peace, liberty, and independence—others of a private nature are superadded, arising from the contemplation of the attentions I have received, from the pleasures which have resulted from the social virtues which you cherish, and which have justly acquired you the esteem, and rendered you dear to all the vicinity.

Those wishes which you so warmly express for my prosperity, honour, and happiness, I implore the divine being to realize on each of you : may heaven impress the hearts of your fellow citizens with a proper and a generous sense of your sufferings and your services; may they never suffer a thorn to spring in your future path of life : and permit me to assure you, that I shall most readily and most cheerfully seek for, and improve, every occasion to serve you, and to evince the friendship, the esteem, and regard, with which my heart is penetrated.

I am, gentlemen, affectionately, and very

Sincerely, your obliged and obedient servant,

PH. SCHUYLER.

To Captain Allen, and the gentlemen of the Rhode Island regiment.

The war had closed, and the army was breaking up; the memory of the past was crowding on the souls of the brave, who had fought their country's battles, and the visions of the future were then so gloomy, that there was a solemnity and honesty in every thing that was said. The Rhode Island brigade was a highly respectable corps of men, and were in command of as gallant an officer as could be found in the service. This respect for the character of General Schuyler, had pervaded the whole army, from Washington to the humblest soldier. Never was there a man who had so entirely laid down all prejudice; and all were anxious to make amends for the early jealousies of a few. Brooks commended him as soldier, and Wigglesworth considered him as a scholar; and all knew him to be a patriot. This was enough for New England. The beauties of a social intercourse, in the American army, and the effort of mind upon mind during the awful struggle for freedom, will never be known; the day has gone for recording them. The great points of the drama of the revolution are and will be preserved; but the interesting under plots and by-play, if we may use such an expression, have passed away with the actors and the audience.

After the war had closed, General Schuyler was an active patriot, and laboured in the halls of congress, and every where, for the good of the country, without any narrow or selfish views. He was a member of congress under the old confederation, and was one of those who early saw that that form of government was not sufficiently energetic for the exigences of a great people. And he was a firm supporter of the constitution of the United States, and acted in concert with all the great spirits of the time, in obtaining something as a rule and guide for the nation, that would develop the character of the people, and the resources of the country. He was twice elected a senator of the United States, and served his country faithfully in that office. Into that august body he carried the principles of a patriot, the wisdom of a statesman, and the manners of a gentleman. He acted as a legislator in his own commonwealth, as well as in the United States government, and was a prominent man in making many good and wholesome laws.

He died November 18, 1804, near Albany, and in the seventy third year of his age, much lamented by all who knew him. The time must come, when we shall not complain of the scanty annals of one so deserving of his country's gratitude, for we understand that the papers of General Schuyler are now in the hands of one who is capable of doing justice to the subject, as he **has** done to the constitution and laws of his country.

MEMOIR OF JOHN MURRAY, JUN.

JOHN MURRAY, jun. was born in this city, on 3d of the 8th month, in the year 1758. He was the son of Robert Murray, the principal of the highly respectable commercial house of Murray, Sansom & Co., of London and New-York; and brother to Lindley Murray, of the city of York, in England, whose literary character is well known in Europe and America.

When about twelve years of age, he was a scholar with myself at Friends' Grammar School, in Philadelphia; the remainder of his education he received in England.

In his youthful days he was remarked as being of an uncommonly active and lively disposition.

Early in life he commenced business in this city with Moses Rogers, was very successful in his commercial pursuits, and after a few years, withdrew himself from this concern.

His mind for sometime had received deep religious impressions, and under the power of the mild and humanizing principles of the Gospel, his natural feelings were controlled, and, in a good degree, subjected to the benign influence of divine grace. From this time, he became zealously engaged to promote every measure, that would conduce to ameliorate the condition of mankind, without distinction of sect or colour. But that he might be rightly qualified, under the guidance of the divine spirit of his Lord and Master, he considered, that a sense of religious duty should precede his actions for promoting benevolent purposes, and thus secure the divine blessing on all his undertakings.

About this period, his father proposed to him, to admit him as a partner in the house of Murray, Sansom, & Co., which flattering offer he declined, from a sense of religious obligation.

Having acquired, as he conceived, a competent share of this world's goods, he apprehended it to be his duty, as a faithful steward, to show his gratitude to his Creator, in giving up a due portion of his time and substance, towards assisting the poor and indigent, by encouraging them in habits of industry, and in promoting the means of bestowing upon their children the benefits of education. In order to accomplish this purpose, he gradually relinquished all mercantile pursuits.

How rare it is to meet with a person, in the course of a prosperous business, to stop short, and say—I have enough—hereafter I will consider, what Providence has put into my hands, as a trust for the good of my fellow-creatures!

It would extend this memoir to an improper length, to attempt exhibiting his various pursuits in advancing the great cause of universal philanthropy, which, at different periods of his life, engaged his attention. I will therefore confine myself to some prominent features, that may serve to illustrate the general character of our late excellent and valuable friend.

The first public engagement of benevolence in which he embarked, was as a Governor of this Hospital, to which he was first elected in 1782, and successively afterwards to the present year, a period of 37 years. During this time, he rendered this institution many essential and important services, by his uniformly kind and affectionate attention to the sick, and in advancing the general interests of the Hospital. He was remarked for his punctual and regular attendance (when his health permitted) of the monthly and special meetings of this Board.

In the year 1785, he was sedulously engaged in the formation of the "Society for promoting the manumission of Slaves, and for protecting such of them as have been or may be liberated." At this period, the minds of most of our citizens were not enlightened on the great subject of African Emancipation, and their deep rooted prejudices were so violent, that the friends of humanity, in asserting the rights of the people of colour, had to encounter innumerable and serious difficulties; an enmity, accompanied with a bitter spirit, was excited in the minds of those, whose selfish interest induced them to consider the acts of the Society as an interference in their personal rights—the members therefore were constantly exposed to personal insult. But, knowing the integrity of their motives, and convinced of the justice of the cause, no difficulties could deter JOHN MURRAY from contributing largely, in a pecuniary way, and uniformly and zealously, by personal exertions, in support of a cause, that *he* conceived, was sanctioned by the principles and genuine spirit of Christianity. From the first formation of the Society, a great portion of his time was devoted, not merely to obtain the liberty of those who were by law entitled to their freedom, but to ameliorate their condition, by promoting their religious and moral improvement, and to afford to them the blessing of education. With these views, he proposed to the Society the establishing of a school exclusively for the education of coloured children, in the superintendence of which, much of his time was bestowed; for, although it was under the care of a board of trustees, yet for many years he was particularly occupied in advancing its interests as a trustee, and as a treasurer, in which latter capacity he served the Society from its first establishment in 1785, to the termination of his life.

The distressed situation of the aboriginal inhabitants of this country, excited much of his attention and sympathy. About the year 1795, he was instrumental, with several of his friends, in endeavouring to improve and ameliorate the condition of the Indians, residing within the limits of this State, by instructing them in agriculture and the useful arts, and in having their children taught the common branches of school learning, and thus to prepare their minds for the reception of a knowledge of the Christian religion. He performed several interesting visits to

2 X   32*

the tribes of Brothertown, Stockbridge, Oneida, and Onandago, and had to encounter, in the course of these journeys, considerable hardships and inconvenience, at a time when roads were extremely bad, and the accommodations for travelling very indifferent. Directed by an ardent zeal for promoting the best interests of humanity, he spared no effort to aid the religious and moral improvement of this afflicted and neglected portion of the human family.

The penal laws of this state, prior to 1796, were extremely imperfect, inflicting penalties very disproportionate to offences. In many instances the punishment of death was deemed indispensably necessary, to expiate certain crimes. Believing that these laws were alike opposed to humanity, to justice, and to policy, as well as to the mild spirit of the religion we profess, our worthy colleague united with some others of his friends, in an application to the leading members of our legislature, in proposing an entire repeal of the then existing penal code, for the purpose of introducing the present penitentiary system. In consequence of this application, and principally owing to the friendly aid and exertions of General Schuyler, and the present Chief Justice Spencer, then distinguished members of the senate, a bill was introduced by the latter gentleman, and passed into a law, by which the former penal laws were repealed, a more mild code established, and a state prison directed to be built in the vicinity of this city. To carry this law into effect, our deceased friend was appointed one of the commissioners, and he also voluntarily accepted the appointment of one of the inspectors of the prison. The first Board of Inspectors had an arduous task to perform, in organizing a plan for establishing cleanliness, order, and regularity amongst the convicts, and devising for them various modes of employment. During this period the affairs of the prison were greatly benefitted by the zeal of JOHN MURRAY, and the board derived considerable aid from his mild and conciliatory demeanour, which very much contributed to soften the minds of the prisoners, and to improve their moral habits.

There is perhaps no benevolent institution in the city, that has been more productive of real usefulness, than the New York Free School Society. It has now under its care four schools, that educate near two thousand poor children. Of this society, it may almost be said, John Murray was the founder. On its first establishment he was elected vice president, and continued as one of its most active trustees, as long as his health permitted.

In the year 1811, he was appointed by Governor Tompkins, one of the commissioners to report to the legislature a plan for the "better organization of common schools throughout the state of New York," intended to be supported by a fund, denominated "the Common School Fund," which is yearly increasing, and now yields about 80,000 dollars annually. The report of the commissioners was adopted, and a law passed, 1812, appointing a person as superintendant of common schools, and otherwise perfecting a system, which is likely to produce incalculable benefits to the present and future generations.

But in his career of usefulness, he was not confined to such institutions as may strictly be denominated benevolent; he felt an interest in whatever had a tendency to exalt the character of his native state. His name is recognized among the first members of the New York Historical Society, and on its formation, he made a handsome donation to its funds.

The yearly increase of paupers in our city, notwithstanding the great assistance afforded them by the numerous public and private institutions, induced John Murray to unite with several of our citizens, to establish "the Society for the prevention of Pauperism." Among many important public advantages produced by the efforts of this society, is the New York Savings Bank, incorporated by a law passed on an application by the board of managers. Perhaps no similar occasion served more to call forth the anxiety and energies of our deceased friend, than the success of this undertaking. In the act of incorporation, John Murray was named as the first vice president, and the directors also appointed him treasurer; a name that peculiarly served to render the institution popular amongst all ranks of our fellow citizens. He was prevented by his last sickness from rendering it any personal services, but the last inquiry, which it is believed he made, after any of the numerous public charities with which he was concerned, was, "how does the Savings Bank get on?" On being told of its unexampled success, he was too weak to say more, than that "it afforded him great satisfaction." Soon after his decease, the following entry was made in the minutes, and published by order of the directors of the Savings Bank:

"At a meeting of the Board, held in the Bank this day, Duncan P. Campbell, was unanimously elected to fill the office of Treasurer, vacated by the lamented death of John Murray, Jun. Esquire.

"The Board take this opportunity of expressing their deep regret, at the loss sustained by this institution, in the death of so distinguished a philanthropist as Mr. Murray. In doing it, they but join in the general sympathy of all who have witnessed his long and active course, in every thing which could meliorate the condition of suffering humanity, or promote moral improvement among every class of his fellow men. He now rests from his labour, and his works follow him.

"By order of the Directors,
JAMES EASTBURN, Secretary.
Bank of Savings, 11th August, 1819."

The society for promoting industry, established in this city in 1814, under the management of our most respectable and pious females, has been productive of incalculable benefit but for want of adequate funds, to carry into effect the views and wishes of the managers, they were often embarrassed and discouraged. At these periods, John Murray came forward, and by advancing money, and using his influence to prevail on others to make similar advances, the society was enabled to continue its extensive usefulness. The following extracts from the minutes of the managers, will serve to show how highly they esteemed the character of their late friend.

" While many able pens are engaged in deploring the loss, and commemorating the worth, of the late friend of humanity, John Murray, jun. the Society for the Promotion of Industry would raise their voice, however feeble, in the general regret; and gratify their feelings, by enumerating a few of the benefits they received from their late friend, who might justly be styled their best friend.

" The society was instituted in 1814, and at its commencement was honoured with his countenance, by expressed approbation, and a liberal donation to its funds, which was afterwards increased to double the amount." The minutes then detail the aid received from him, by his personal influence with the city corporation, in order to obtain from them pecuniary assistance, and also of his addressing a meeting of citizens, called for the purpose of supporting and extending the plan proposed to be pursued by the society. In the commencement of the present year, being informed that the society were again without funds, and had no other prospect but closing the House of Industry, John Murray addressed them by letter, in which he expressed his anxiety for the advancement of "the good work they are engaged in," and offered to advance them $100, to be taken out in work, and to loan them $500 for one year, without interest. This, with other assistance, enabled them further to prosecute the designs of the establishment. The minutes then close in the following words:—
" When the last enemy to be encountered, gained the victory over John Murray, jun. it is much to be feared that this institution received a mortal blow. The managers would still continue to raise their prayers to that God who seeth not as man seeth; and while the kind offices of their deceased friend, can never be effaced from their memories, they would humbly pray, that others may be induced to follow his example, and go and do likewise. Then may this institution still be a blessing to the public."

It would be unnecessary to detail more of the many public concerns, that engaged the attention of our late worthy colleague. During the last thirty years of his life, his time was mostly devoted to the service of the religious Society of Friends, (of which he was a member, and for many years a distinguished elder,) and to the various objects of public and private benevolence. The income of his estate was considerable, and he more than once mentioned to me, that he did not wish to reserve more than sufficient for his common expenses; the overplus was spent in promoting the benefit of his fellow creatures. His humility and self-denial were manifest in his plain manner of living, scrupulously avoiding any kind of extravagance, lest he might expend, in useless objects, what he conceived ought to be reserved for the use of the poor and needy. In his manners he was courteous, kind, and charitable; evincing a readiness on all occasions, to devote his time and talents to the best of all causes, the good of mankind. His private charity was great, and generally unknown to his most intimate friends. He was a member of a greater part of the charitable societies in the city; each of whom received from him a yearly anonymous letter, enclosing from fifty to one hundred dollars. His delight seemed to be, to clothe the naked, to feed the hungry, and to visit the sick and distressed; or, to adopt the language of an eloquent writer, "to survey the mansions of sorrow and pain; to take the gage and dimensions of misery, depression, and contempt; to remember the forgotten; to attend to the neglected, and to visit the forsaken."

In 1812, whilst attending, at Albany, a meeting of the commissioners appointed to consider the subject of improving the state of common schools, he left his lodgings one evening, to have an interview with a committee of the legislature, to whom was referred a communication made by the governor, proposing to substitute some mode of punishment for that of death. The streets of Albany were at this time covered with ice, which rendered walking extremely hazardous; our lamented friend had not proceeded far on his humane errand, when he fell, and was so seriously injured, that notwithstanding the care and solicitude of his friends, he was confined to his room some weeks, and never recovered from the injury he thus sustained. This accident subjected him to almost constant, and frequently excruciating pains; and, without doubt, hastened his death. But he endured all his sufferings with christian patience, and submission to the divine will; and when in company with his friends, generally exhibited a disposition remarkably cheerful. About the commencement of the present year, he became more seriously indisposed, and on the morning of the fourth of last month, he died, whilst in the act of supplication to that Lord whom he so faithfully served. His body was interred in Friends' burying-ground, after a solemn meeting in their meeting house, attended by a considerable number of his friends, who, it is believed, will long remember the solemnity of the occasion.

The religious character of John Murray, jun. was highly estimated by his fellow members of the Society of Friends, and also by those of other religious denominations, to whom he was personally known. He was by no means contracted in his opinions, but of a disposition liberal and enlarged. He often expressed his sincere desire, that Christians might more and more avoid unnecessary disputes about non-essentials, and unite in promoting the common cause, in which they all profess to be engaged; that, for his own part, he knew of no distinction of sect or party; but that the one true church is composed of individuals of all religious denominations, who, possessed of the spirit of divine love, are faithfully endeavouring to know and to perform the divine will concerning them. These, he would often say, are united in one head, even Christ, and in the fellowship of his gospel; they feel that they are all brethren. In his intercourse with mankind, he seemed to have adopted for his motto that saying of Luther, "Inquo aliquid Christi video illum diligo." " In whomsoever I see any thing of Christ, him I love." Possessed of these sentiments, it afforded him the most heartfelt satisfaction, to meet with a considerable number of highly respectable and pious men, of various religious denominations, who convened in this city, from almost every state in the union, for the purpose of forming a national Bible Society. He was a member of the convention, and frequently expressed his having enjoyed great satisfaction in witnessing its proceedings, conducted as they were in remarkable condescension and harmony, and in the spirit of gospel love. He was appointed a member of the first board of managers, and twice contributed to the general funds of the society. He often remarked, that one of the most evident designs of divine Providence, in establishing this highly important society, was, to bring together those of all denominations, by which means sectarian jealousies may be removed, and peace and love established between Christians. These considerations, so congenial with the mind of John Murray, and his solicitude to witness the diffusion of the holy scriptures amongst the poor and neglected, in every part of this widely extended continent, induced him, during the remainder of his life, to continue to be an ardent and active member of the American Bible Society. His sentiments of the importance and usefulness of that society, were fully evinced, in a speech he made, at its anniversary meeting, in the fifth month, 1818; an extract from which, as it serves farther to illustrate his general character, will, I presume, be considered as an acceptable and appropriate termination of the present very brief sketch of the life and labours of our deceased friend:

" In rising to speak on the present interesting occasion, I feel my mind solemnized, and it is with diffidence I attempt to offer a sentiment before this very respectable assembly. In making the motion which I have done, I have two considerations in view; the one is, to approve of the proceedings of the board of managers, the other to avail myself of the opportunity of communicating a few sentiments, in relation to the highly important nature of this society, formed for the express purpose of promoting a general diffusion of the holy scripture—a work of stupendous magnitude, contemplating incalculable good to the human family; more especially when we connect with it a practical observance of those moral and religious duties which they enjoin, and with which the scriptures of the old and new testament are replete. Hence it is, in a peculiar manner, obligatory on the members of a society, so noble and dignified as this, to be careful and solicitous to square their lives and conduct by the precepts contained in the book they are so assiduous and zealous to circulate; as it must be granted, 'that example speaks a louder language than precept.' I rejoice in the hope, that the efforts of Bible societies, and other associations and means for enlightening the human understanding, and improving the heart, will be blest in an eminent degree, not only in our own country, but in regions far more remote. I also indulge the consoling hope, that they will tend to dispel prejudice and bigotry, and to batter down that wall of partition which ignorance and illiberality of sentiment has raised up between the different religious denominations. I am glad in believing that I am no bigot, and that I can with great sincerity adopt the language of the apostle Peter, whose mind, like many others, had been biassed and warped by the prejudices of education, and the force of tradition; but, when his understanding became enlightened by the rays of Divine Light, he could then bear testimony to the universality of the love of God, uttering the following memorable expressions: 'Of a truth, I perceive that God is no respecter of persons, but that, in every nation, they that fear him, and work righteousness, will be accepted of him.' There is no doctrine more clearly and fully inculcated in the new testament, than that of charity, or, in other words, divine love. 'God is love, and they that dwell in him, dwell in love;' and by this, said our blessed Saviour, shall all men know 'ye are my disciples, if ye love one another.'

" The apostle Paul, in the 13th chapter of the first Espistle to the Corinthians, describes the excellency of this virtue in a peculiar and striking point of view. His illustrations go to prove that it is the prominent feature in the Christian character. Let us, therefore, my friends, cultivate this heavenly principle; let us, by the tenor of our lives and conduct, evince that we are the disciples and followers of Jesus Christ. I am thankful at feeling my heart glow with love to all my fellow-creatures, and that I meet with those of every Christian denomination, to whom I can give the right hand of fellowship.

" When I reflect, my friends, on the solemnity of the occasion. which has drawn together so large and respectable an assemblage of our fellow creatures, all of whom, I trust, are arraigned as candidates for an immortal and glorious inheritance, I hope we feel renewedly animated, in a cause which is calculated to promote the present and the future happiness of mankind.

" I do not wish to trespass either on the time or patience of this assembly; but, I do not know that I can close my communications with sentiments more appropriate, or with language better adapted, than was used by my late friend Henry Tuke,* at a

* An eminent Minister of the Society of Friends.

meeting of the Bible Society of York, in England, of which he was a distinguished member.

"'I feel,' said he, 'disposed to express the gratification which I experience, on seeing so large and respectable a meeting of my fellow citizens on the present occasion, and particularly with the union of christians of various denominations, in the support of this great cause. May we not compare the various sects of Christianity to the different tribes of ancient Israel? We, like them, may have some different views, and separate interests; but we acknowledge one God, and one Lord, even our Lord Jesus Christ. We profess to be governed by the same laws, which are contained in the Holy Scriptures, and though we may not unite in the construction of some of these laws, yet, when we consider in how large a proportion of them the professors of Christianity are agreed, and consequently how small is the part in which we differ, there is much cause for us to feel as brethren, and to unite, as has frequently been the case, in defence of our common faith; and I can truly say, it affords me no small pleasure to believe, that if it should ever be my happy lot to gain an admittance into that city whose walls are salvation, and its gates praise, I shall there, as well as here, have many fellow-citizens, and I trust, no small portion of those who now hear my voice; who, though I may differ from them on some points of Christian doctrine, or rather, perhaps, of Christian practice, I feel no difficulty in believing, will finally be added to that innumerable multitude, which the divinely eagle-eyed apostle saw standing before the throne, clothed in white robes, and having palms in their hands; but, who, though possessed of these emblems of righteousness and of victory, were far from claiming any merit to themselves, but ascribe their salvation wholly to the Lord God and the Lamb.'"

THE HON. AMBROSE SPENCER.

If it be true that high-minded men constitute a state,—and who will deny the axiom?—should we not make anxious inquiries to obtain just views of our own distinguished characters in the nation—men who should rank with the first in society now, as they certainly will leave an impress on the age in which they lived, when they shall have gone from the scene of action?

To wait until a man is dead, before we venture to speak of his merits, is as idle as not to count our treasures until we have lost them. It is aggravating to know what intellectual wealth we once possessed, when it is fled beyond recovery. It is fortunate that we are following the examples of Europe, in spreading before the public the deeds and characters of those who are still on the stage, acting their parts well. It is an historical truth, which but few will dare to controvert, that in the very best periods of every nation which has done any thing for mankind, that their great minds who were active in public affairs, were best known to each other, and enjoyed the fullest communion with the intelligent people at large. Some of the great men of Athens prided themselves in being acquainted with the character of almost every man in the country, and particularly in the city, in which they lived. They visited freely, and made it a point to converse on such subjects as would test each individual's claims to distinction. As the territory of Attica was small, this could easily be done; but not so with us—for some of our great men live a thousand miles apart; but, when personal interviews cannot be had, the press should make men acquainted with each other. We are beginning to grow wiser in this respect. The Memoirs of General Jackson, Mr. Adams, Webster, Calhoun, Clay, Story, and many others, have, with more or less fairness and ability, been given to us through the medium of the public journals. Poets, Divines, and Lawyers, have come in for their share of public notice; and any one, who has any claims to distinction, does not blush to see his name in works intended to instruct mankind. We now venture to add to these great names that of AMBROSE SPENCER, an eminent lawyer, and a profound judge, who has for many years filled a great space in his country's history, and who now, in a green old age, is able to take a part in all the affairs of the nation. It would be idle to tell the courts and bars of the United States any thing of the character of Ambrose Spencer; but as they make but a small part of the reading community, we will venture to give a slight, but, as far as it goes, a fair sketch of this great man,

Judge Spencer is the son of Philip Spencer, Esquire, who was a native of Saybrook, in Connecticut. Their ancestor was from England, and migrated to this country soon after the restoration of Charles II. Philip Spencer removed from Connecticut to Oblong, in the county of Dutchess, New York, in 1766. He was a respectable farmer, and filled with fidelity the office of Justice of the Peace for several years, and died at a good old age, in 1815. Judge Spencer was born in December, 1765, in the town of Salisbury, in Connecticut. He and an elder brother, after the necessary preparatory studies, entered, in 1779, the freshman class in Yale College, the Rev. Ezra Styles being then President of that college. The two brothers continued members of it, until the autumn of 1782, when they were honourably discharged, and, in the same autumn, were admitted members of the senior class in the University of Cambridge. They both graduated there in 1783. In the same year, Judge Spencer commenced the study of the law, under the direction of John Canfield, Esquire, of Sharon, in Connecticut; being, however, determined to pursue his profession in the state of New York, he completed his legal studies under the direction of John Bay, and

2 Y

Ezekiel Gilbert, Esquires, and was admitted to the bar of the Supreme Court of the state of New York, in 1788.

He commenced the practice of the law in the city of Hudson, and pursued his profession with great diligence; in 1793 he was elected a member of the assembly from the county of Columbia; in 1795 he was elected a Senator of the Senate of New York for three years; in 1798 he was re-elected to the Senate for four years; in 1796 he introduced a bill for meliorating the criminal code, and for the erection of a state prison in the vicinity of the city of New York. This bill he had the satisfaction of seeing become a law; it abolished the punishment of death in all cases but those of treason and murder, and substituted imprisonment in the state prison and hard labour. This law produced a great change in the penal code of New York; the then existing laws denounced the punishment of death on many offences, which the humanity of the executive, and the enlightened wisdom of the age, interposed to prevent the execution of, and experience has demonstrated that crimes have not increased in consequence of the mitigation of punishment. In 1796, Judge Spencer was appointed, under the administration of Governor Jay, District Attorney for the counties of Columbia and Rensselaer, which office he continued to fill until 1801. In 1802, he was appointed, under the administration of Governor George Clinton, Attorney General of the state, on the resignation of that office by Josiah Ogden Hoffman, Esquire. He continued in this office until February, 1804, when he was appointed, also under the administration of Governor George Clinton, a Judge of the Supreme Court of New York. In 1819, he was appointed Chief Justice of the state, under the administration of Governor Dewitt Clinton; he remained in that office until January, 1823, when, under a provision in the amended Constitution, all civil offices were vacated. After his retirement from the Bench, he resumed his profession as counsellor of law with great success, and continued therein until 1827, when he retired to a farm in the vicinity of the city of Albany, and since then has appeared very rarely at the Bar, though he has not declined entirely acting as chamber counsel.

In 1828, he was elected a member of the 21st Congress, from the county of Albany, and punctually attended to the duties of his appointment, during the two sessions; never having been absent from the House but two days. He was one of the managers on the part of the House of Representatives, on the impeachment of Judge Peck. He believed Judge Peck to have transcended his judicial duties, and to have violated the law from bad motives, in the imprisonment of one of his fellow-citizens; and, thus believing, he put forth all his energies to produce his conviction. He never questioned the purity of the motives of those senators, who pronounced his acquittal, on the ground that, although the law had been violated, the motives of the Judge were not impure.

At the first session of that Congress, he opposed, in a speech which has been published, a bill introduced by the Judiciary Committee, for increasing the number of the Judges of the Supreme Court of the United States.

Judge Spencer, although then a very young man, was decidedly in favour of adopting the Constitution of the United States, as it came from the hands of the Convention, and was so far a Federalist. He soon, however, became convinced that the Federal party held doctrines too high-toned for the interests of the people of the United States, and became an active member of the great Republican party.

It has been objected to him, that, whilst a Judge of the Supreme Court, he indulged too much in politics; those who now make the objection do not consider either the temper of the times, or the examples he had before him, or the change which public opinion has undergone in that respect. There was then no such thing known as neutrality of opinion in politics; and all his associates on the Bench were open and decided in their political opinions. It would, indeed, be a severe and lasting reflection, if it could be affirmed with truth, that these political feelings influenced his conduct as a Judge, and in the decision of causes.

He was a warm and decided friend to the declaration of war against Great Britain in 1812, and gave the war all the support and countenance which he consistently could. In the case of Vander Heyden *vs.* Young, 11 Johnson, 157, he delivered an opinion, in which the majority of the court concurred, in entire opposition to the doctrines advanced by Chief Justice Parsons, and Judges Sewall and Parker, (8 Mass. Rep. 549,) that the President of the United States, alone, is made the judge of the happening of an event, authorizing him to call forth the militia under the act of February, 1795; and this opinion was subsequently approved by the Supreme Court of the United States, in Martin and Mott, 12 Wheaton, 28.

The fact that Chief Justice Spencer was not re-appointed Chief Justice under the amended constitution, has never, it is presumed, occasioned him any mortification. It is well understood that the convention in New York, of 1821, was a party measure; it was a political tornado, which swept through the state, prostrating every institution, standing in the way of the dominant faction; and it is not too much to say, that, instead of improving the constitution of 1777, it actually introduced injurious innovations. It reduced the number of the Judges of the Supreme Court from five to three, and thus injuriously derogated from the authoritative form of decisions. Senators, elected immediately after the adoption of the amended constitution, partook of the feelings of the convention; not to be re-appointed under such circumstances can never detract from the private or public character of any of those officers, whose offices have been vacated to subserve party purposes.

Every one, who is acquainted with the professional character of Judge Spencer, or who has read his admirable opinions in the reports, or any of his speeches, will freely award to him a strong, discriminating, well-balanced mind. He sees the points of a cause with great sagacity, and goes directly to discuss them, without any painful circumlocutions, or unnecessary preliminaries about candour, disinterestedness, or any apologies for his honest decision. He keeps constantly armed for every field; and if it sometimes appears that his armour is too strong and weighty for the ordinary contests, still he does not, in the slightest degree, seem incumbered with it, but marches onward with dignity and ease.

His arguments are extensive, particularly in his profession. He has kept up, which requires no ordinary effort, with the science and literature of the age, out of the pale of his professional studies, and, on most subjects, converses as one who had thought much upon the very topics under consideration.

Disciplined in the halls of legislation and of justice, he is not only powerful in argument, but prompt in debate, and never cowers at the presence of any antagonist, however powerful. He never indulges in any flights of the imagination, nor ever labours for any ornaments, although he is frequently as felicitous in illustration, as profound in argument. The style of his eloquence is, moreover, manly and clear. If he ever thought of a model, which I very much doubt, it was that of Pericles, not of Cicero. His sentences are carefully turned and well arranged, but have no mellifluous flow, or extraordinary harmony in them; but the reader never mistakes his meaning, nor is ever offended by involution, harshness, or obscurity; for he goes on, step by step, never striving to charm, but always sure of "binding his audience in chains." In every sentence he utters, there is a combination of intelligence, a sense of duty, and an impression of responsibility, with "the lion-heart of independence," that never fails to interest all, and to secure the impartial. The weight of his arguments was always enhanced by the weight of his character; this even envy owns, since he is no longer on the bench, and, in a measure, out of political life.

The legal opinions of Judge Spencer are of the first authority, not only in the courts in New York, but also in every state in the Union. Many years ago, Parsons spoke of Spencer as an excellent judge, and perhaps he is as often quoted as an authority, as any one in the United States, at the present time. He put himself in the reports as willing to trust his reputation on what may be found there, and he need not fear the result.

It is said that, in his retirement, he has not forgotten his laborious habits, and that his pen or his book is constantly in his hand. A full life of De Witt Clinton may be expected from him at no distant day. No man knew Clinton better than Spencer. They lived in a bustling world together, and, after the lot of humanity, were sometimes intimate, and sometimes estranged; but Time, that softens asperities, and digs the grave of enmities, which arise out of the irritations of party, has preserved their friendships entire; and a correct biography of Clinton may be expected, from one who will be as free from adulation as from narrow views.

The person of Judge Spencer is tall and commanding, and his manners are dignified. His countenance is just such an one as an observer of human nature would mark in the greatest crowd; it has composure with strength, and solemnity without gloom or rigidity; at times, it is lighted up with the sunshine of friendly sympathies, and bears evidence of well-trained affections.

Although past the constitutional age, in the state of New York, for holding a seat on the bench, he is still as capable of sustaining the duties of a judicial station as at any period of his life.

The calm and peaceful days of the autumn of life, especially when the heat and burden of it has been spent in mental labour, and public usefulness, "are sweet as summer." If there be no second spring, in the life of man, to produce flowers anew; if there be no forming again the enchanting wanderings of youth, no fresh rhapsodies of sentiment to enjoy, and no dreams of ambition to indulge, yet, the mellow fruit from early culture, the gathering of industry, the odour of fame from past honour, the thousand fond recollections of the by-gone days, the increasing hopes and confidence for the future, throw a charm over this portion of human existence that no other season can know. It is the cool of the evening, when man converses with his Maker.

We sincerely hope that this autumnal sunshine may last long, that the world may be benefited by his ripe scholarship, and mature understanding.

MEMOIR OF JOHN HOWARD.

John Howard, was born at Hackney, in Middlesex, in the year 1726, and put apprentice to Mr. Nathaniel Newnham, a wholesale grocer, in Watling street. His constitution was thought very weak, and his health appeared to have been injured by the necessary duties of his apprenticeship; at the expiration of it, therefore, he took an apartment in a lodging house, in Stoke, Newington, kept by a Mrs. Sarah Lardeau, a widow, by whom he was nursed with the utmost care and attention. At length he became so fond of his landlady, that they were privately married, about the year 1752. She was possessed of a small fortune, which he presented to her sister. This wife, however. died in 1755, and he was a sincere and affectionate mourner for her death. About this time, it is believed, he was elected F. R. S., and, with an intention of visiting Lisbon after the earthquake, he at midsummer, 1756, set sail on board the Hanover packet, which was taken by a French privateer; and he behaved with so much hauteur, so much a l'Anglois, to the captain of the privateer, as might probably be the cause of his suffering so severely as it appears he did, and perhaps what he suffered on this occasion, increased (if it did not first call forth) his sympathy with the unhappy people. He afterwards, it is believed, made the tour of Italy; and at his return, settled at Brokenhurst, a retired and pleasant villa in the New Forest, near Lymington, in Hampshire; having, April 25, 1758, married Harriet, only daughter of Edward Leeds, Esq. of Croxton, in Cambridgeshire. Mrs. Howard died in 1765, in childbed. After the death of his second wife, he left Lymington, and'purchased an estate at Cardington, near Bedford, where he very much conciliated the esteem of the poor, by employing them, building cottages for them, &c. In 1773, he served the office of sheriff of the county of Bedford. This office, as he observes, brought "the distress of prisoners more immediately under his notice;" and with a view to its alleviation, he began his labours by visiting most of the county jails in England, and afterwards the bridewells, houses of correction, city and town jails, where he found multitudes, both of felons and debtors, dying of the jail fever and the small pox. Upon this subject he was examined in the house of commons, in March, 1774, when he had the honour of their thanks. This encouraged him to proceed in his design; he travelled again and again through Great Britain and Ireland, and also into France, Flanders, Holland, Germany, and Switzerland; and published "The state of the Prisons in England and Wales, with preliminary observations, and an account of some foreign prisons, 1777." In 1780, he published an appendix to this account, in which he extended the narrative of his travels to Italy, and gave some observations on the management of prisoners of war, and the hulks on the Thames. This Appendix he republished, in 1784; which publication included also an account of his visit to Denmark, Sweden, Russia, Poland, Portugal, and Spain. By this time his character for active benevolence had engaged the public attention, and it was proposed that a subscription should be set on foot, to erect a statue to his honour. This idea was so well received, that in fifteen or sixteen months, six hundred and fifteen persons subscribed 1533l. 13s. 6d.; but some of those who knew Mr. Howard best never concurred in the scheme, being well assured that he would never countenance nor accede to it: and the event justified their conduct; for the language that he held upon the subject, when first advised of it, was, "have not I one friend in England that would put a stop to such proceedings?" In consequence of two letters from Mr. Howard himself to the subscribers, the design was laid aside. In 1789, Mr. Howard published "An account of the principal Lazarettos in Europe, with various papers relative to the plague, together with farther Observations on some Foreign Prisons and Hospitals, and additional remarks on the present state of those in Great Britain and Ireland," with a great number of curious plates. Not satisfied, however, with what he had already done, he concludes his " Account of Lazarettos" with announcing his intention again to quit his country, for the purpose of revisiting Russia, Turkey, and some other countries, and extending his tour in the East. On this tour, however, he fell a victim to his humanity; for, having visited a young lady at Cherson, sick of an epidemic fever, for the purpose of administering some medical assistance, he caught the distemper himself, and was carried off in 12 days, Jan. 1790. The name of Howard will live in the remembrance of those who have been rescued, by his exertions, from the gloomy horrors of confinement, which might otherwise have been unlimited; alleviated in the pangs of disease, which might have been irremediable; and comforted in the still more agonizing reproaches of conscious guilt, which would inevitably have terminated in destruction. A statue to Mr. Howard's memory has been erected in St. Paul's cathedral.

I have been induced to insert the following interesting letter from the Hon. CADWALLADER D. COLDEN, addressed to Professor J. W. FRANCIS, on account of the very singular and important facts which it discloses concerning the case of insanity of the late distinguished Count REGNAUD DE ST. JEAN D'ANGELY; and because I find upon enquiry, that Mr. Eddy was one of the committee before whom the case was brought, when an examination *de lunatico inquirendo*, was instituted. Mr. Eddy's extensive practical knowledge enabled him to prove of essential service on this contested case, and the whole matter presents one of the most remarkable examples on record to show the intricate nature of mental aberration; juridical medicine is perhaps never more severely taxed for the exercise of its nicest principles, than in cases of feigned and real insanity. It need scarcely be added, that the disordered state of Count Regnaud terminated only with his life; which event took place, I believe, the very day of his arrival at Paris, upon his permission to return to his native country.

New York, July 1, 1833.

MY DEAR SIR,

I do not see how any thing relative to St. Jean D'Angely can be brought into the biography of Mr. Eddy, because I do not recollect that he had any connexion with the proceedings to which, in our late momentary interview, you referred, than that at the time they took place Mr. Eddy was a governor of the hospital where the Count was confined, and where the commission of lunacy was executed. I recollect, however, some circumstances connected with that affair, the relation of which may be amusing, and perhaps, interesting to you, whose attention has been directed to the derangements of the human mind. Posssibly you may be able to find a place for this subject, in the communication relative to Mr. Eddy, which I understood from you, you was about to make to Colonel Knapp.

I presided at the execution of the commission, which authorized me, and two other commissioners, (who they were, I cannot recollect,) to hold an inquest, as to the mental condition of the Count. When the commission was opened, the Count appeared in person. There was nothing in his manner that indicated in the least an aberration of mind, but there was a fierceness and restlessness in his eye which might not have been noticed, had it not been known that he was the subject of the inquiry we were authorized to make. As soon as the nature of the proceeding was explained to him, he, in a very formal and professional manner, objected to the form of the inquiry, and attempted to prove that it was illegal. As soon as he was informed that the commission had issued, he had possessed himself of a number of what the lawyers call books of practice, and seemed to have devoted his attention· particularly to Harrison's Chancery Practice, from which he undertook to prove, that the proceeding should be done by bill, which he should have had an opportunity of answering. He gave us the history of our chancery practice as derived from England, where it had been taken from the civil law. His address to the commissioners, showed that in the space of a few days, he must have read a great part of the books he had had in his possession; and that, however the other faculties of his mind might be affected, he retained his memory in great vigour. He did not confine himself, in what he said, to the ordinary bounds of law argument, but gave expression to his feelings in a speech of very considerable length, which, both as to manner and language, was highly oratorical; and though, from his ignorance of the laws of this country, he had assumed false premises, there was nothing illogical or irrational in his argument; on the contrary, if he were mad, there was certainly method in his madness. Finding that his objections to the form of the proceedings could not prevail, he submitted to the decision of the commissioners with great complacency. His course was, when a witness testified to some act of his, calculated to show an alienation of mind, to comment on the testimony, and give explanations, immediately. In some instances, he showed great art and ingenuity. It was proved, that he happened to be passing the Park at a time when they were cutting the grass. He bargained for the whole crop, which amounted to several cart loads, had it transported to his house, and stowed away in one of his bed rooms; when the testimony of this witness was concluded, he said, Gentlemen, I will give you a very satisfactory explanation of this fact: goat's milk had been prescribed for me. Just previously to my passing through the Park, I had purchased two of these animals from a ship, that had then terminated a long voyage. Seeing the grass in the Park, it occurred to me, how agreeable some of it would be to my poor goats. I made the purchase of so many tons, not knowing exactly what a ton was, but supposing it might be something like the bundles in which the same article is sold in France. I had directed my servant to let it be put away in a vacant room in my house, and when I saw it there, I was as much surprised at the quantity as you can be, and still more, to receive an apology from the man ·of whom I made the purchase, when he came for payment of his bill, for not delivering as much as he had bargained with me for, as he said the produce of the Park was not as many tons as he had calculated it would be. So you see my kindness to my poor goats, and my imperfect acquaintance with your language, are now to be tortured into evidence of my insanity.

It was proved by several witnessess, that he had disclosed to them a plan in which he was engaged, to rescue Bonaparte from his captivity at St. Helena. That he had stated to them, that he had a number of steam boats prepared for the expedition. To this he gave the following explanation : It is true that some of my friends in Europe, said he, had conceived such a project, and wrote to me, to ascertain whether I could procure the steam boats in this country. I applied to Mr. Livingston, who recommended me to a person, who I engaged to construct several models, and these are the steam boats of which I spoke to the witnesses. I endeavoured to engage them to join in the expedition, as I intended to do myself, when the plan should be matured. So that you see it is but a slight misunderstanding that has led the witnesses to testify that I had represented to them, that I had steam boats in readiness for such an undertaking. Count Real was one of the witnesses who were examined on this point. Immediately after he had concluded his testimony, St. Jean D'Angely took Count Real to one side, and said to him, as he afterwards testified, never mind all this, I have the steam boats all prepared, I have a competent force at Brooklines, awaiting my orders. But you do not believe me to be so mad, or such a fool, as not to be able to keep my course secret.

When Count Real was called to the book as a witness, his name, more than that of the Count St. Jean D'Angely, was in the mind of the person who administered the oath, and instead of saying, as he ought to have done, "the evidence you shall give in this matter, touching the lunacy of Count St. Jean D'Angely, shall be the truth," &c., he said, "the evidence you shall give, touching the lunacy of Count Real," &c. St. Jean D'Angely burst into a loud laugh, and said to Count Real, "ah, my friend, you see what is coming. It is my turn now, but it will be yours the next. The gentleman could not have made such a mistake, if he had not in his pocket a commission to inquire

2 Y

whether you are in your right senses; and no doubt, these witnesses intend to prove, that every friend of Bonaparte that comes to this country is mad, and to shut them up, as they have done me." I dare say, I could recollect several other anecdotes of the same character, but I find they cannot be told in writing in a few words. These may be sufficient to show that the case of St. Jean D'Angely, was one of those, where certain mental faculties may be exercised, as if the understanding was unimpaired, when the person is, as the jury found the Count to be, a lunatic.

Most respectfully yours,

CADWALLADER D. COLDEN.

SOCIAL PROBLEMS
AND
SOCIAL POLICY:
The American Experience

An Arno Press Collection

Bachman, George W. and Lewis Meriam. **The Issue of Compulsory Health Insurance.** 1948

Bishop, Ernest S., **The Narcotic Drug Problem.** 1920

Bosworth, Louise Marion. **The Living Wage of Women Workers.** 1911

[Brace, Emma, editor]. **The Life of Charles Loring Brace.** 1894

Brown, Esther Lucile. **Social Work as a Profession.** 4th Edition. 1942

Brown, Roy M. **Public Poor Relief in North Carolina.** 1928

Browning, Grace. **Rural Public Welfare.** 1941

Bruce, Isabel Campbell and Edith Eickhoff. **The Michigan Poor Law.** 1936

Burns, Eveline M. **Social Security and Public Policy.** 1956

Cahn, Frances and Valeska Bary. **Welfare Activities of Federal, State, and Local Governments in California, 1850-1934.** 1936

Campbell, Persia. **The Consumer Interest.** 1949

Davies, Stanley Powell. **Social Control of the Mentally Deficient.** 1930

Devine, Edward T. **The Spirit of Social Work.** 1911

Douglas, Paul H. and Aaron Director. **The Problem of Unemployment.** 1931

Eaton, Allen in Collaboration with Shelby M. Harrison. **A Bibliography of Social Surveys.** 1930

Epstein, Abraham. **The Challenge of the Aged.** 1928

Falk, I[sidore] S., Margaret C. Klem, and Nathan Sinai. **The Incidence of Illness and the Receipt and Costs of Medical Care Among Representative Families.** 1933

Fisher, Irving. **National Vitality, its Wastes and Conservation.** 1909

Freund, Ernst. **The Police Power:** Public Policy and Constitutional Rights. 1904

Gladden, Washington. **Applied Christianity:** Moral Aspects of Social Questions. 1886

Hartley, Isaac Smithson, editor. **Memorial of Robert Milham Hartley.** 1882

Hollander, Jacob H. **The Abolition of Poverty.** 1914

Kane, H[arry] H[ubbell]. **Opium-Smoking in America and China.** 1882

Klebaner, Benjamin Joseph. **Public Poor Relief in America, 1790-1860.** 1951

Knapp, Samuel L. **The Life of Thomas Eddy.** 1834

Lawrence, Charles. **History of the Philadelphia Almshouses and Hospitals from the Beginning of the Eighteenth to the Ending of the Nineteenth Centuries.** 1905

[Massachusetts Commission on the Cost of Living]. **Report of the Commission on the Cost of Living.** 1910

[Massachusetts Commission on Old Age Pensions, Annuities and Insurance]. **Report of the Commission on Old Age Pensions, Annuities and Insurance.** 1910

[New York State Commission to Investigate Provision for the Mentally Deficient]. **Report of the State Commission to Investigate Provision for the Mentally Deficient.** 1915

[Parker, Florence E., Estelle M. Stewart, and Mary Conymgton, compilers]. **Care of Aged Persons in the United States.** 1929

Pollock, Horatio M., editor. **Family Care of Mental Patients.** 1936

Pollock, Horatio M. **Mental Disease and Social Welfare.** 1941

Powell, Aaron M., editor. **The National Purity Congress;** Its Papers, Addresses, Portraits. 1896

The President's Commission on the Health Needs of the Nation. **Building America's Health.** [1952]. Five vols. in two

Prostitution in America: Three Investigations, 1902-1914. 1975

Rubinow, I[saac] M. **The Quest for Security.** 1934

Shaffer, Alice, Mary Wysor Keefer, and Sophonisba P. Breckinridge. **The Indiana Poor Law.** 1936

Shattuck, Lemuel. **Report to the Committee of the City Council Appointed to Obtain the Census of Boston for the Year 1845.** 1846

The State and Public Welfare in Nineteenth-Century America: Five Investigations, 1833-1877. 1975

Stewart, Estelle M. **The Cost of American Almshouses.** 1925

Taylor, Graham. **Pioneering on Social Frontiers.** 1930

[United States Senate Committee on Education and Labor]. **Report of the Committee of the Senate Upon the Relations Between Labor and Capital.** 1885. Four vols.

Walton, Robert P. **Marihuana, America's New Drug Problem.** 1938

Williams, Edward Huntington. **Opiate Addiction.** 1922

Williams, Pierce assisted by Isabel C. Chamberlain. **The Purchase of Medical Care Through Fixed Periodic Payment.** 1932

Willoughby, W[estal] W[oodbury]. **Opium as an International Problem.** 1925

Wisner, Elizabeth. **Public Welfare Administration in Louisiana.** 1930